S0-ABQ-243

Quantitative Economic Theory

Quantitative
Economic Theory
A Synthetic Approach

Hans Brems

Professor of Economics
University of Illinois

John Wiley & Sons, Inc.   New York · London · Sydney

RIDER COLLEGE LIBRARY

330.182
B 836

180051

Copyright © 1968 by John Wiley & Sons, Inc.

All Rights Reserved. This book or any part
thereof must not be reproduced in any form
without the written permission of the publisher.

Library of Congress Catalog Card Number: 67-27828
Printed in the United States of America

RIDER COLLEGE LIBRARY

To LISA
   MARIANNE
   KAREN

For in relation to economics, to politics and to all the arts, no single branch of educational science possesses so great an influence as the study of numbers: its chief advantage is that it wakes up the man who is by nature drowsy and slow of wit, and makes him quick to learn, mindful and sharp-witted, progressing beyond his natural capacity by art divine.

Plato, *Laws*, by R. G. Bury
(Cambridge, Mass., and London, 1926) Book V, 387 and 389.

PREFACE

This book is a system of simple mathematical models of the economy, and my emphasis in it is twofold.

As far as method is concerned, my emphasis is on solvability: All models presented are solvable—and solved. It follows that all my assumptions had to be made simple and explicit. The reader will need no mathematical equipment other than elementary algebra and calculus.

As far as scope is concerned, my emphasis is on synthesis: From models of household, firm, and industry equilibria I have tried very explicitly to build up simple models of general economic equilibrium. Once built up, these models may then collapse into models of aggregate equilibrium, static as well as dynamic. In this way I hope to have shown explicitly the connection between parts of economic theory often left unconnected. It follows that I could not have confined myself to either microeconomics or macroeconomics.

From the size-to-scope ratio of this book, it is obvious that it cannot be a survey of modern economic theory. I have not tried to cover all major contributions, old and new, not even by reference. The models I used were selected to serve the purposes just described; other models might often have served equally well.

If in certain places originality has crept in, and early readers insist it has, I thought of it neither as a purpose nor as a pitfall. As a result, such chapters as 14, 16, 17, 22, 28, 38, 44, 47, and 48[1] may serve the purposes of the book and yet not represent any consensus of professional opinion.

This book has evolved from graduate courses given at the University of Illinois and in summer terms at Berkeley, Harvard, and Michigan as well as at Göttingen and Kiel. I owe a considerable debt to the more inquisitive students in those courses. In and out of class, Charles E. Richter (economics) and David C. Heath (mathematics) untiringly checked all mathematical operations and proofs and have contributed to clarifying the argument

---

[1] After the manuscript went to press I became aware of R. M. Solow, J. Tobin, C. C. von Weizsäcker, and M. Yaari, "Neoclassical Growth with Fixed Factor Proportions," *Rev. Econ. Stud.*, April 1966, **33**(2), 79–115, offering within the framework of a one-sector model a determination of an equilibrium rate of interest very similar to that of my own two-sector model in Chapter 48.

throughout the book. Tables 17.1 through 17.4 are the results of a computer program written by Robert A. Meyer.

My colleagues and friends, Morris Adelman (M.I.T.), Dennis J. Aigner (Illinois), John Black (Oxford), Sven Danø (Copenhagen), Robert Ferber (Illinois), Donald R. Hodgman (Illinois), Wilhelm Krelle (Bonn), Jens Luebbert (Hamburg), Donald Roberts (Illinois), Procter Thomson (Claremont), and the late Poul Winding (Copenhagen), read individual chapters. Both Kenneth E. Boulding and Charles E. Ferguson read the entire manuscript. To all I am deeply thankful.

HANS BREMS

Urbana, Illinois
March 1967

ACKNOWLEDGMENTS

This book was written from scratch and utilizes, always in revised form and sometimes in revised substance, a small fraction of my earlier work. Permission to reproduce it was always given generously.

Chapter 10 is reprinted by permission of the publisher from Hans Brems, "Cost and Indivisibility," *The Journal of Industrial Economics* (March 1964), Basil Blackwell, Oxford, England.

Chapters 13, 34, and 35 are reprinted by permission of the publisher from Hans Brems, *Output, Employment, Capital, and Growth*, Harper & Row, New York, 1959.

Chapters 4, 22, and 35 are reprinted by permission of the publishers from Hans Brems, *Product Equilibrium under Monopolistic Competition* and "A Solution of the Keynes-Hicks-Hansen Non-Linear Employment Model," *The Quarterly Journal of Economics*, Cambridge, Mass., Harvard University Press, Copyright 1951 and 1956, respectively, by the President and Fellows of Harvard College.

Chapter 38 is reprinted by permission of the publisher from parts of Hans Brems, "Wage, Price, and Tax Elasticities of Output and Distributive Shares," *Journal of the American Statistical Association* (September 1962).

Chapter 45 is reprinted by permission of the publisher from Hans Brems, "Growth, Distribution, Productivities, and Thrift in Cobb-Douglas Models," *The Southern Economic Journal* (January 1963).

Chapter 44 is reprinted by permission of the Swedish Journal of Economics from Hans Brems, "Trade, Growth, and the Exchange Rate," *Ekonomisk Tidskrift* (September 1963).

Permission to quote from others was also given generously.

The Ricardo quotations in Chapters 36 and 37 are reprinted by permission of the publisher from *The Works and Correspondence of David Ricardo*, Vol. I, edited by Piero Sraffa, with the collaboration of Maurice H. Dobb, 1951, published for The Royal Economic Society by Cambridge University Press.

The Keynes quotation in Chapter 48 is reprinted by permission of the publisher from J. M. Keynes, *The General Theory of Employment, Interest and Money*, Harcourt, Brace & World, Inc., 1936.

Figures 5.1, 10.4, and 16.2 are reprinted by permission of the publishers from C. G. Winston, "An International Comparison of Income and Hours of Work," *The Review of Economics and Statistics* (February 1966), R. G. Bressler, *City Milk Distribution* (1952), and H. B. Chenery, "Engineering Production Functions," *The Quarterly Journal of Economics* (November 1949), Cambridge, Mass., Harvard University Press, Copyright 1966, 1952, and 1949 by the President and Fellows of Harvard College. The Harvard University Press also permitted me to reproduce the Plato quote on Page v.

The Bertrand quotes in Chapter 20 are reprinted by permission of the publisher from Bertrand's book review of Cournot's and Walras' works in the September 1883 issue of *Journal des Savants*, Librairie C. Klincksieck, Paris.

The Samuelson quote in Chapter 35 is reprinted by permission of the publisher from P. A. Samuelson, "Reflections on Central Banking," *The National Banking Review* (September 1963), published by the Comptroller of the Currency, United States Treasury.

The Leontief quotes at the opening of Chapters 29 and 31 are reprinted by permission of the publisher from W. Leontief, *Input-Output Economics*, Oxford University Press, New York, 1966, and W. Leontief, *Studies in the Structure of the American Economy*, Oxford University Press, New York, 1953.

Table 40.1 and numerous data in the Appendix to Chapter 48 are reproduced by permission of the publisher from A. Maddison, *Economic Growth in the West*, The Twentieth Century Fund, New York, 1964.

Numerous data in the Appendices to Chapters 42, 45, and 48 are reproduced by permission of the publisher from S. Kuznets, *Modern Economic Growth: Rate, Structure, and Spread*, Yale University Press, New Haven, 1966, and by permission of Professor Kuznets from *Economic Development and Cultural Change* (July 1961).

For all permissions I express my sincere thanks.

CONTENTS

xiii

PART 3 INDUSTRY EQUILIBRIUM

PART 4 GENERAL EQUILIBRIUM

PART 5 AGGREGATE EQUILIBRIUM LEVELS

PART 6 AGGREGATE EQUILIBRIUM TIME PATHS

Quantitative
Economic Theory

Introduction on Method and Scope

Mathematics is a great deal more than just a language.

L. Hurwicz [2]

1 THREE LANGUAGES

Economic theorists communicate with one another in three different languages; verbal logic, mathematics, and graphs. For an initial exercise let us try to present the same example from economic theory in these three alternative forms. As our example we shall choose the simplest one we can think of, that is, the celebrated Keynesian theory of output determination, and begin by trying to express this theory as rigorously as possible in simple English.

2 ENGLISH

Assume a country's consumption to rise if its output rises, but assume the amount of increase in consumption to be always less than that in output. Consumption may be partly autonomous.

Define the country's net investment as the part of its output not intended for immediate consumption. Let all investment be autonomous and assume the sum of net investment and autonomous consumption to be positive.

Call the sum of consumption and net investment aggregate demand. Now if output is to be in equilibrium, inventory must neither accumulate nor be depleted. This will be the situation only if aggregate demand equals output. Under our assumptions this condition will be satisfied by a positive level of output, for we have assumed consumption to increase by less than the increase in output. Consequently, consumption will fall short of output by an increasing amount, and there must exist an equilibrium level of output at which consumption falls short of output by an amount exactly equal to

1

net investment. Obviously, the greater the net investment, the larger the equilibrium output will be.

3 MATHEMATICS

In our Keynesian model we will use the following notation.

Variables

C = country's output consumed
X = net national output

Parameters

A = autonomous consumption
c = marginal propensity to consume
I = autonomous net investment

Use an aggregate short-run consumption function of the form

(1) $C = A + cX$

Equilibrium requires that the sum of consumption and investment demand for output equal output, otherwise inventory would accumulate or be depleted; thus

(2) $X = C + I$

Combine (1) and (2) and solve for output.

(3) $$X = \frac{A + I}{1 - c}$$

Thus equilibrium net national output is equal to the sum of autonomous consumption and net investment divided by the marginal propensity to save.

Now assume that $A + I > 0$ and $c < 1$. In this event, output is positive and unique.

4 PARAMETERS AND VARIABLES

Let us first consider the sharp distinction made between our variables C and X, on the one hand, and our parameters A, c, and I, on the other. We shall begin by examining the parameters.

In one sense, parameters are constants. For example, the econometricians may have told us that our consumption-function parameters are $A = 30$ and

$c = 0.75$. However, in another sense parameters are not constants. Our model works for $A = 30$ and $c = 0.75$, but it would also have worked for the values 31 and 0.76, respectively, for 31 and 0.74, respectively, etc. Worked in what sense? In the sense that equilibrium output as determined by (3) would still have been positive and unique. This observation may be trivial, but it says something very fundamental about the mathematical method. The very variability of its parameters bestows upon our mathematical model that priceless gift of generality which no numerical example and no graph can possess. For each new set of values of A and c, within the constraints that $A + I > 0$ and $c < 1$, we would have a new consumption function, but that function would still be a member of the family of consumption functions summarized by (1), and the resulting output would still be a member of the family of positive and unique equilibrium outputs determined by (3). Obviously, no finite number of numerical examples or graphs could match this generality; untried numerical values of $A + I$ and c would always remain.

However, if our parameters A, c, and I are constants in one sense but variables in another, how can we distinguish them so sharply from our variables C and X? The answer lies in the definition of a parameter as a magnitude to be fixed and manipulated at will by the investigator, using information originating *outside* the model. For example, the econometricians may tell him that $A = 30$ and $c = 0.75$, and surveys of businessmen's planned expenditures on equipment and plant may tell him that $I = 21$. Next year they may tell him something else. In contrast, variables such as C and X are solved for *within* the model.

5 SOLUTIONS AND MULTIPLIERS

A solution for a variable is an equation that has only that variable on one side and nothing but parameters on the other. Once such a solution has been found, we may study the effect upon it of manipulating any parameter by taking the partial derivative of the variable with respect to the parameter (such a derivative is often called a multiplier). That this can be legitimately done follows from the definition of a parameter given in Section 4. In contrast, variables cannot be manipulated at will; they are solved for within the model, and the solution must be respected. From this arises the importance of knowing which magnitudes are variables and which are parameters in a model.

Solution (3) permits the following multiplier, among others, to be found:

(4)
$$\frac{\partial X}{\partial I} = \frac{1}{1 - c}$$

Under the realistic assumptions that $A + I > 0$ and $c < 1$, this multiplier is positive. Therefore equilibrium output will rise if autonomous net investment rises.

6 COMPARISON BETWEEN ENGLISH AND MATHEMATICS

The French used to be fond of contrasting Gallic clarity with Teutonic obscurity, yet we find no evidence that any particular verbal language is a better vehicle for stringent thought than others. What about verbal logic as compared with mathematics?

Comparing our two presentations of the Keynesian model with each other, we notice, first, that English has an advantage as far as compactness is concerned; second, that the same conclusion emerges from both, that is, that equilibrium output will rise if autonomous net investment rises.

Can mathematics do anything that cannot be done verbally? In one sense, No, for mathematics is taught verbally, defining each word as we go along. Once we know what addition is we can define multiplication, and once we know what multiplication is we can define powers, etc. This was what Irving Fisher [1] had in mind when he said:

The deduction used in every physical truth could be reasoned out without diagrams or formulae. A railway will best convey a man from New York to San Francisco though it is perfectly possible to walk.

Bulldozers can do nothing that cannot be done by teaspoons. The Romans could multiply their numerals, and the British manage to do sums with their nondecimal currency. American plumbers and carpenters still use inches and feet. However, astronomers and physicists universally prefer the metric system, and above all they prefer mathematics. So here it is, a powerful analytical tool available to all of us, proofs already worked out. To this day no one has characterized it better than Plato, in the passage quoted on the title page of this book: "It wakes up the man who is by nature drowsy and slow of wit, and makes him quick to learn, mindful and sharp-witted, progressing beyond his natural capacity."

It is no more possible to demonstrate convincingly the superiority of mathematics as an analytical tool by applying it to the Keynesian model than the superiority of the bulldozer by applying it to laying out a flower bed. Our three magnitudes C, I, and X are so few and the relationships between them so simple that verbal English is both safe and economical. However, in problems closer to reality, such as solving an interindustry model, mathematics is unrivaled. Indeed, such problems came within reach of numerical solution only after World War II when large digital electronic computers became available.

In addition to being unrivaled in solving complicated problems, mathematics contributes to the clarity and safety with which any problem is solved, complicated or not, in two distinct ways.

First, mathematics forces its user to formulate his assumptions more explicitly. To him as well as to his readers, mathematics may well uncover assumptions otherwise unnoticed. At the very least this contributes to the honesty of his presentation, but it may do more than that. A striking example was pointed out by Fisher [1]:

Utility was first thought of as proportional to commodity. (That this was never *explicitly* assumed is a splendid illustration of how without a careful mathematical analysis in which every magnitude has definite meaning, tacit assumptions creep in and confuse the mind.) It was next pointed out that utility could not explain price since water was useful. So "utility" and "scarcity" were jointly privileged to determine price. It was Jevons' clear and mathematical exposition of utility which showed the shallowness of the former discussion and brought to light the preposterous tacit assumption, unchallenged because unseen, that each glass of water has an inherent utility independent of the number of glasses already drunk.

Second, mathematics helps its user to see what he is really doing. The blindness of the nonusers is well illustrated by the example of Menger, Wieser, and Böhm-Bawerk who, as Schumpeter [4] points out, held their own system to be superior to that of Walras on the grounds that the latter was merely "functional," whereas their own system offered "causal explanations." Not long after, other nonusers started the game of accusing one another of circular reasoning. When J. B. Clark said that the wage rate was determined by the marginal productivity of labor, did he not have to admit that the location of the margin itself was also determined by the wage rate? Or when Keynesians say that consumption is determined by income, do they not have to admit that income itself is also determined by consumption?

Menger, Wieser, Böhm-Bawerk, Clark, and Keynes alike were dealing with simple static equilibrium models. In such models, the use of mathematics teaches us the lesson that one variable is neither the "cause" nor the "effect" of any other. All variables are determined on an equal footing and simultaneously, and all are the effects of the only causes found in a model, that is, its parameters. The lesson is brought home particularly vividly in the definition in Section 5 of an explicit solution for a variable.

Wisely used, mathematics does wonderful things for us, but as Morgenstern [3] has reminded us, "The appearance of a formula in a paper or book does not automatically clarify a difficult problem or raise that piece to a higher level of value. On the contrary, the formula may obfuscate."

7 GRAPHS

Most textbooks and much original work in economic theory still rely heavily on graphs. What does our Keynesian model look like when represented as a graph? In Fig. 1, measure output X on the horizontal axis, aggregate demand $C + I$ on the vertical one. The equilibrium condition that the two be equal will then appear as the familiar 45° line, shown as the broken line in Fig. 1. The following set of numerical values for the parameters is used:

$$A = 30$$
$$c = 0.75$$
$$I = 21$$

For these values our consumption function becomes

(1a) $$C = 30 + 0.75X$$

We add $I = 21$ to both sides of (1a) and obtain a second relationship between $C + I$ and X, that is, $C + I = 51 + 0.75X$. This relationship is shown as the solid line in Fig. 1. In equilibrium, net national output must

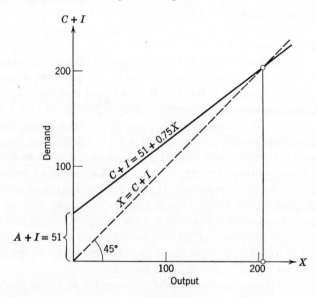

Figure 1

satisfy both relationships. Consequently, output must be the abscissa of the point of intersection between the broken and the solid lines, that is, $X = 204$. What would be the effect of a higher autonomous net investment? If I is raised above 21, the solid line in Fig. 1 shifts upward, and the abscissa of its intersection with the broken line rises—and as the lines are drawn the abscissa rises considerably more than I does, hence indicating a multiplier greater than One. So for the third time, we arrive at the conclusion that equilibrium output will rise if autonomous net investment rises.

8   COMPARISON BETWEEN MATHEMATICS AND GRAPHS

As we have already stated, the very variability of its parameters bestows upon the mathematical model that priceless gift of generality which no numerical example and no graph can possess. Why no graph? Because as it stands, Fig. 1 holds for no other instances than that in which the sum of autonomous consumption and net investment is 51, and the marginal propensity to consume is 0.75. In that sense no graph can be anything other than a numerical example visually illustrated. Yet graphs are widely felt to be not merely visual aids but somehow more general than numerical examples or even algebra.

The belief that graphs are more general than numerical examples rests upon a tacit, or even subconscious, assumption that a curve drawn represents a much larger family of curves. In our particular case, for example, a positive, unique, and stable output equilibrium similar to that shown in Fig. 1 will, in fact, emerge whenever aggregate demand is a straight line whose intercept with the vertical axis is positive and whose slope is less than one. If it is clearly stated that the line actually drawn stands for all such lines, then indeed the graphical method is more general than a numerical example.

However, this is rarely said. Ever since Marshall, economic theory abounds with curves in the first quadrant, each presumably a representative member of a much larger family of curves. It is usually left to the reader to guess which is represented. The family of straight lines? Of monotone functions? Of increasing monotone functions? Of decreasing ones? Of convex ones? Of concave ones? And why in the first quadrant only? Even if these questions are answered, they are sometimes answered without proof.

The belief that graphs are more general than even algebra rests upon the fact that it is just as easy to draw a curvilinear function as it is to draw a linear one. It is then triumphantly concluded that unlike so much algebraic economics, graphical economics is not restricted to linearity, hence is more general. Such an illusion will be exposed for what it is once we realize that without specification of the family of curves giving rise to similar equilibria, and proof that they do so, a graph remains a numerical example visually illustrated. Surely the mere drawing of the curvilinear function is easy. However, neither the specification of the family of curves giving rise to similar equilibria nor the proof that they do so are easy in the nonlinear case. Indeed it will sometimes be necessary and often practical to make excursions into analytical geometry, algebra, quadratic programming, etc., in order to supply such proof.

Much more obvious is a very practical limitation of graphs. Two dimensions can be represented well but graphs already lose much of their worth as visual aids whenever attempts are made to represent three dimensions.

9 METHOD OF THIS BOOK

This book is a series of solvable, and solved, simple mathematical models. In each we try to answer some important economic questions, that is, to determine the equilibrium values of important economic variables. (To help the reader see at a glance which particular economic variables we are trying to determine, each model is always preceded by a complete list of variables as well as parameters used.)

There is, of course, a price to be paid for finding explicit solutions to economic problems. We must commit ourselves to specific forms, preferably simple ones, of our behavior equations. Particularly simple forms are the linear equation with constant coefficients, $y = ax + b$, widely used in Keynesian models, or the linear homogeneous one with constant elasticities, $y = ax_1^\alpha x_2^\beta$, where $\alpha + \beta = 1$, widely used in production functions. We, too, shall use such forms, as well as the constant-elasticity-of-substitution form, in our production and utility functions, and without apology. If the solutions obtained seem "too special," they are actually less so than many verbal or graphical models in common use. The verbal or graphical models often seem general solely because their premises are invisible. Premises hide extraordinarily well in verbal or graphical argument. At least, an uncompromising mathematical approach rules out much playing hide-and-seek. However, even if the solutions are actually less special than many verbal or graphical ones, they may still be "too special." If so, maybe it is beneficial to the student. If upon solving his system the student feels a sense of accomplishment, he should also feel a sense of humility after pondering the dependence of his solution upon his choice of particular behavior equations formulated so explicitly. This sense of humility is a prerequisite for progress. The student will feel the urge to relax some of the assumptions and see what happens.

10 SCOPE OF THIS BOOK

A household spends, works, and saves. In Part 1 we try to determine its spending, working, and saving as responses to a price structure, given the household's utility function.

A firm absorbs inputs, produces output, and invests. In Part 2 we try to determine the absorption, production, and investment as responses to a price and demand structure, given the firm's production function.

Firms interact with other firms within the industry. In Part 3 we try to characterize the resulting equilibrium under pure competition as well as under noncollusive and collusive oligopoly. Firms also interact with labor unions in setting the wage rate, therefore in Part 3 we also briefly raise the bargaining problem.

Households, firms, and industries interact within the national economy, and national economies interact within the world economy. To provide the building blocks for a general-equilibrium model of such interactions is the purpose of much of Parts 1-3. Their use in Part 4 is their ultimate justification—and the ultimate excuse for their simplicity.

Aggregate equilibrium, whether static as in Part 5 or dynamic as in Part 6, is best seen as a collapse of the general-equilibrium model into a few large categories. Collapsing the model should be done explicitly, and will be, but some of the building blocks produced in Parts 1 through 3 survive the collapse and can still be used in Parts 5 and 6.

Thus while maintaining an equilibrium approach, we try to go beyond Marshallian "price theory" and to go behind Keynesian "income theory." We go beyond Marshallian theory and proceed to general-equilibrium theory. We go behind Keynesian theory and see it as a collapse of general-equilibrium theory. Apart from our search for synthesis, we shall pay more attention to oligopoly than Marshall did and more attention to capital and to international trade than Keynes did.

REFERENCES

[1] Fisher, I., "Mathematical Investigations in the Theory of Value and Prices," *Transactions of the Connecticut Academy* 9 (July 1892). See photoengraved reprint by the Yale University Press, 1925, pp. 111 and 117.

[2] Hurwicz, L., "Mathematics in Economics: Language and Instrument," in *Mathematics and the Social Sciences*, edited by J. C. Charlesworth, Philadelphia, 1963, p. 11.

[3] Morgenstern, O., "Limits to the Uses of Mathematics in Economics," in *Mathematics and the Social Sciences*, edited by J. C. Charlesworth, Philadelphia, 1963, pp. 25–26.

[4] Schumpeter, J. A., *History of Economic Analysis* (New York, 1954), p. 957 n.

Part One

Household Equilibrium

CHAPTER 1

The Utility Function

1.1 INTRODUCTION

Edgeworth [2] was the first to define the indifference map, and Fisher [3] was the first to see that the indifference map enables us to explain consumer behavior without using a numerical utility valuation. Yet such a valuation would be convenient, and von Neumann and Morgenstern [4] gave us one—at a price, of course. Let us examine this valuation and see how it can be used to construct a numerical utility function.

1.2 NOTATION

The following notation will be assigned.

Variables

$a, b, c, \ldots$ = events of consumption faced by the consumer
$\quad C_i$ = quantity consumed of ith output
$\quad q$ = a probability
$U, V, \ldots$ = alternative numerical valuations of utility

Parameters

A, B = parameters of a constant-elasticity-of-substitution utility function
α, β = parameters of a Cobb-Douglas utility function
$\quad L$ = constant term in the utility functions
$\quad M$ = multiplicative factor in the utility functions
$\quad \rho$ = an exponent in a constant-elasticity-of-substitution utility function

13

1.3 THE VON NEUMANN-MORGENSTERN NUMERICAL
VALUATION OF UTILITY

Von Neumann and Morgenstern [4, pp. 15–31] have determined a numerical valuation of utilities up to a linear transformation. Suppose that a consumer facing two events of consumption, a and b, prefers b to a; and let us assign the arbitrary numbers $V(a)$ and $V(b)$ to the events a and b, respectively, provided that the number assigned to b is higher than that assigned to a. Thus

(1) $V(b) > V(a)$

Now introduce a third event c which is preferred to both a and b. Offer the consumer the choice between the sure prospect of getting b, and the uncertain prospect of getting either a or c. Whether, in fact, he gets a or c depends upon the outcome of a random draw in which the probability for a is q and the probability for c is $1 - q$, where $0 < q < 1$. Let the consumer reveal that value of q which leaves him indifferent between the two prospects.

Indifference can only mean equality between the two prospects, each multiplied by its probability. Hence a number $V(c)$ may be assigned to the event c such that

$$V(b) = qV(a) + (1 - q)V(c)$$

or, after rearranging,

(2) $$V(c) = \frac{V(b) - qV(a)}{1 - q}$$

For example, if we had assigned the numbers, say, 1 and 2 to a and b, respectively, and if the consumer had revealed his q to be equal to 0.6, then Eq. (2) would have given us $V(c) = 3.5$. Why would we specify such simple numbers as 1 and 2 for a and b, respectively? Why not? The numbers were purely arbitrary except for the requirement (1). We are doing what Anders Celsius, the Uppsala professor, did when he assigned the number zero to the event of water boiling at 760 mm air pressure, and the number 100 to the event of water freezing at 760 mm air pressure. His assignments were no less arbitrary than those of another Uppsala professor, Carl von Linné, who turned Celsius' scale upside down and originated the centigrade scale now used. Neither was less arbitrary than the assignments made by their predecessor Gabriel Fahrenheit.

Centigrade and Fahrenheit measurements are numerical valuations of heat up to a linear transformation. This expression simply means that the temperature as expressed in Centigrade is a linear function of the same temperature as expressed in Fahrenheit, and vice versa. Let C stand for Centigrade and

F for Fahrenheit measurements of heat in the same place at the same time, then

$$C = -\frac{160}{9} + \frac{5}{9} F \qquad F = 32 + \frac{9}{5} C$$

1.4 THE VALUATION OF UTILITY IS DETERMINED UP TO A LINEAR TRANSFORMATION

Just as Centigrade and Fahrenheit measurements represent numerical valuations of heat up to a linear transformation, so von Neumann-Morgenstern measurements represent numerical valuations of utility up to a linear transformation. We show this as follows.

Initially, the arbitrary numbers $V(a)$ and $V(b)$ were assigned to the events a and b, respectively, subject to (1). Now, we assign instead the arbitrary numbers $U(a)$ and $U(b)$ to the same two events subject to the constraint

(3) $$U(b) > U(a)$$

First we must show that, subject to (3), no matter which pair of numbers $U(a)$ and $U(b)$ we choose, we may always express them as

(4) $$U(a) = L + MV(a)$$
(5) $$U(b) = L + MV(b)$$

To see this, simply think of (4) and (5) as two equations in the two unknowns L and M, having the parameters $U(a)$, $U(b)$, $V(a)$, and $V(b)$. Solving the system (4) and (5) for L and M, we obtain

(6) $$L = \frac{U(a)V(b) - U(b)V(a)}{V(b) - V(a)}$$

(7) $$M = \frac{U(b) - U(a)}{V(b) - V(a)}$$

From the constraints (1) and (3) it follows that L and M are both meaningful and unique. In addition, it follows that M is always positive. Hence no matter which numbers $U(a)$ and $U(b)$ we choose, the pair $U(a)$ and $U(b)$ would be a linear transformation of the pair $V(a)$ and $V(b)$.

Second, with the new arbitrary numbers $U(a)$ and $U(b)$ defined in (4) and (5), let us repeat the interrogation of our consumer. We assume that he has remained in exactly the same state. Since the events a, b, and c have not changed, and since he has not changed, his q has not changed either. Hence a new number $U(c)$ may be assigned to the event c such that

$$U(b) = qU(a) + (1 - q)U(c)$$

or, after rearranging,

(8) $$U(c) = \frac{U(b) - qU(a)}{1 - q}$$

Now how does the new measurement (8) compare with the old one (2)? By inserting (4) and (5) into (8) and using (2) upon the result,

(9) $U(c) = L + MV(c)$

Thus for the event c, according to (9), a U-scale measurement is the same linear transformation of a V-scale measurement as it was for the events a and b according to (4) and (5), respectively.

The procedure applied to event c may now be applied to further events $d, e, \ldots$. Then for each new event a U-scale measurement will be the same linear transformation of a V-scale measurement as it was for the events a and b according to (4) and (5):

(10) $U(d) = L + MV(d)$
(11) $U(e) = L + MV(e)$

$$\cdot$$
$$\cdot$$
$$\cdot$$

The axioms underlying the von Neumann-Morgenstern numerical valuation of utilities, set out at length in [4, pp. 26–29], rule out any positive or negative utility of the act of gambling itself. This is the price we must pay for such a valuation.

1.5   HOW TO CONSTRUCT A UTILITY FUNCTION

Let the consumer consume two goods only, outputs 1 and 2. Let their quantities consumed be C_1 and C_2, respectively. Let events $a, b, \ldots$ consist of consumption of alternative combinations of C_1 and C_2, for example:

Event	C_1	C_2
a	0	0
b	0	1
c	1	0
d	0	2
e	1	1
	.	
	.	
	.	

For each event we could determine its utility expressed, for example, on the V-scale. Consequently, we could express utility V as a function of the quantities consumed, C_1 and C_2:

(12) $$V = f(C_1, C_2)$$

1.6 FIXING AN ABSOLUTE ZERO

Anders Celsius and Gabriel Fahrenheit assigned the number zero to two different events, and modern physics assigns it to a third event, that is, the event of all molecular motion ceasing to exist. This is called the absolute zero.

Von Neumann and Morgenstern [4, p. 25 note 3] refused to fix an absolute zero, hence could determine a numerical valuation of utilities up to a linear transformation only. Convenience rather than necessity tempts us to go one step beyond von Neumann and Morgenstern and define an economist's counterpart to the physicist's absolute zero: Let us always assign the number zero to the event of the consumer consuming nothing of anything, for example, in our two-output case to the event a, where $C_1 = C_2 = 0$. We shall do this regardless of our choice of utility scale:

(13) $$V(a) = U(a) = 0$$

The constants L and M performing the linear transformation of the V-scale into the U-scale were defined by Eqs. (6) and (7). In our present case (6) and (7) collapse into:

(6a) $$L = 0$$

(7a) $$M = \frac{U(b)}{V(b)}$$

What would have been accomplished by thus fixing an absolute zero? We would have determined a numerical valuation of utilities up to multiplication by the constant factor M as defined by (7a), just as we are accustomed to a numerical valuation of, say, distances up to multiplication by a constant factor: Distances measured in kilometers can be converted into miles by multiplying by the constant factor 0.62137. Only a constant factor is needed, because the kilometer scale and the mile scale have a common zero. (Because they do and the Centigrade and Fahrenheit scales do not, United States tourists become accustomed to kilometers long before they get accustomed to degrees Centigrade when traveling in Continental Europe.)

Returning to our two-output example, then, if (12) is the utility function in the V-scale, fixing an absolute zero enables us to write it in the U-scale as

(14) $$U = Mf(C_1, C_2)$$

Let us now take a closer look at two specific forms of (14).

1.7 THE PARTICULAR CASE OF A COBB-DOUGLAS UTILITY FUNCTION

Let the utility function be of Cobb-Douglas form

(14a) $$U = MC_1{}^\alpha C_2{}^\beta$$

where $0 < \alpha < 1$, $0 < \beta < 1$, and $M > 0$. The utility function (14a) is adopted with three restrictions: $C_1 \geq 0$, $C_2 \geq 0$, and $U \geq 0$, thus ruling out negative or complex values of U. To study the properties of the utility function (14a), we shall take all first and second partial derivatives.

(15) $$\frac{\partial U}{\partial C_1} = \alpha \frac{U}{C_1}$$

(16) $$\frac{\partial U}{\partial C_2} = \beta \frac{U}{C_2}$$

(17) $$\frac{\partial^2 U}{\partial C_1{}^2} = \alpha(\alpha - 1)\frac{U}{C_1{}^2}$$

(18) $$\frac{\partial^2 U}{\partial C_2{}^2} = \beta(\beta - 1)\frac{U}{C_2{}^2}$$

(19) $$\frac{\partial^2 U}{\partial C_1 \partial C_2} = \frac{\partial^2 U}{\partial C_2 \partial C_1}$$

(20) $$= \alpha\beta \frac{U}{C_1 C_2}$$

What do all these partial derivatives show? Derivatives (15) and (16) will be positive if and only if α and β are positive, and for positive α and β, (17) and (18) will be negative if and only if α and β are both less than one—as we have indeed assumed them to be. Thus, for the utility function (14a), the marginal utility of any output has been shown to be positive and diminishing with that output.

Furthermore, (19) and (20) will be positive; hence the marginal utility of any one output has been shown to increase with the other.

1.8 THE FORM OF THE INDIFFERENCE CURVES

Some readers may be more comfortable looking at indifference maps than at utility functions. So let us examine the indifference map corresponding to the utility function (14a). Suppose the consumer changes infinitesimally his

C_1 by dC_1 and his C_2 by dC_2. The indifference curve is defined by the requirement that the total differential approximating the resulting change in utility be zero.

$$(21) \qquad dU = \frac{\partial U}{\partial C_1} dC_1 + \frac{\partial U}{\partial C_2} dC_2 = 0$$

By inserting (15) and (16) into (21), we obtain the marginal rate of substitution and the elasticity of the indifference curve, respectively:

$$(22) \qquad \frac{dC_1}{dC_2} = -\frac{\beta}{\alpha} \frac{C_1}{C_2}$$

$$(23) \qquad \frac{dC_1}{dC_2} \frac{C_2}{C_1} = -\frac{\beta}{\alpha}$$

Equation (23) defines the elasticity of the indifference curve[1] and shows it to be the constant $-\beta/\alpha$. As seen from the origin, is the indifference curve convex or concave? Inspect Eq. (22) and assume $C_1 > 0$ and $C_2 > 0$. Under the assumptions made about α and β, (22) is negative, therefore C_1 falls with rising C_2. The negative slope (22) will rise with rising C_2, hence the indifference curve is a negatively sloped convex curve of constant elasticity.

1.9 A CONSTANT-ELASTICITY-OF-SUBSTITUTION UTILITY FUNCTION

Let the utility function be the linearly homogeneous one whose elasticity of substitution σ is a constant.

$$(14b) \qquad U = M(AC_1^{-\rho} + BC_2^{-\rho})^{-(1/\rho)}$$

where $A > 0$, $B > 0$, $M > 0$, $-1 < \rho < 0$ or $0 < \rho$. The function (14b) is adopted with these three restrictions: $C_1 \geq 0$, $C_2 \geq 0$, and $U \geq 0$. The parameter ρ is related to the elasticity of substitution σ as

$$\sigma = \frac{1}{1 + \rho}$$

This relation will suffice at present. We shall define the elasticity of substitution and discuss it at length in Chapter 8.

To study the properties of the constant-elasticity-of-substitution utility

---

[1] Not to be confused with the elasticity of substitution to be discussed in Chapter 8.

function (14b) we again take all first and second partial derivatives.

$$(24) \qquad \frac{\partial U}{\partial C_1} = AM^{-\rho}\left(\frac{U}{C_1}\right)^{1+\rho}$$

$$(25) \qquad \frac{\partial U}{\partial C_2} = BM^{-\rho}\left(\frac{U}{C_2}\right)^{1+\rho}$$

$$(26) \qquad \frac{\partial^2 U}{\partial C_1^2} = AM^{-\rho}(1 + \rho)\left(\frac{U}{C_1}\right)^{\rho}\frac{(\partial U/\partial C_1)C_1 - U}{C_1^2}$$

$$(27) \qquad \frac{\partial^2 U}{\partial C_2^2} = BM^{-\rho}(1 + \rho)\left(\frac{U}{C_2}\right)^{\rho}\frac{(\partial U/\partial C_2)C_2 - U}{C_2^2}$$

$$(28) \qquad \frac{\partial^2 U}{\partial C_1\,\partial C_2} = \frac{\partial^2 U}{\partial C_2\,\partial C_1}$$

$$(29) \qquad = AB(1 + \rho)M^{-2\rho}U^{1+2\rho}(C_1C_2)^{-(1+\rho)}$$

For positive M, C_1, and C_2, the derivatives (24) and (25) will be positive if and only if A and B are positive. For positive A and B what signs will (26) and (27) have? To see this we need Euler's theorem[2], which holds for all linearly homogeneous functions:

$$(30) \qquad U = \frac{\partial U}{\partial C_1} C_1 + \frac{\partial U}{\partial C_2} C_2$$

The derivatives (24), (25), and Euler's theorem (30) help us to see that the numerators on the right-hand sides of (26) and (27) are negative. Consequently, (26) and (27) are opposite in sign to $1 + \rho$. They will be negative, then, if and only if $\rho > -1$, which we assumed to be true. Consequently, for positive A and B, the marginal utility of any output is positive and diminishes with that output. Derivatives (28) and (29) are both positive, hence the marginal utility of any output increases with the other.

1.10   THE FORM OF THE INDIFFERENCE CURVES

Again we examine an indifference map, this time one corresponding to the utility function (14b). Since the indifference curve is still defined by (21), insert (24) and (25) into (21) and obtain the following marginal rate of substitution and elasticity of the indifference curve, respectively:

$$(31) \qquad \frac{dC_1}{dC_2} = -\frac{B}{A}\left(\frac{C_1}{C_2}\right)^{1+\rho}$$

$$(32) \qquad \frac{dC_1}{dC_2}\frac{C_2}{C_1} = -\frac{B}{A}\left(\frac{C_1}{C_2}\right)^{\rho}$$

[2] For proof see, for example, [1].

Equation (32) shows that the elasticity of the indifference curve is no longer a constant; it now varies with the ratio C_1/C_2. As seen from the origin, is the indifference curve convex or concave? Look at Eq. (31) and assume $C_1 > 0$ and $C_2 > 0$. Under the assumptions made about A and B, (31) is negative, so C_1 falls with rising C_2. Since we assume that $1 + \rho$ is positive, the negative slope (31) will rise with rising C_2; hence the indifference curve is a negatively sloped convex curve of variable elasticity.

REFERENCES

[1] Allen, R. G. D., *Mathematical Analysis for Economists*, London, 1938, p. 317.
[2] Edgeworth, F. Y., *Mathematical Psychics*, London, 1881.
[3] Fisher, I., "Mathematical Investigations in the Theory of Value and Prices," *Transactions of the Connecticut Academy*, 9 (July, 1892). See photoengraved reprint by the Yale University Press, 1925, pp. 68–70.
[4] von Neumann, J. and O. Morgenstern, *Theory of Games and Economic Behavior*, Princeton, 1944.

CHAPTER 2

How to Derive a Demand Function from a Utility Function

2.1 INTRODUCTION

We use utility functions to explain household behavior: Households respond to a given price structure by maximizing their utility. Three such responses are of special interest to us. Households consume, work, and save, so we shall derive consumption demand, supply of labor, and supply of saving from the household's utility function. We begin with consumption demand.

2.2 NOTATION

In a microeconomic theory of the household the following notation will be assigned,

Variables

C_i = quantity consumed of ith output per annum
U = utility to the household resulting from its consumption

Parameters

A, B = parameters of a constant-elasticity-of-substitution utility function
α, β = parameters of a Cobb-Douglas utility function
M = multiplicative factor in the utility functions
P_i = price of ith output
ρ = an exponent in a constant-elasticity-of-substitution utility function
Y = budget per annum

2.3   A COBB-DOUGLAS UTILITY FUNCTION

Let the household have a utility function of the Cobb-Douglas type

(1) $$U = MC_1^{\alpha}C_2^{\beta}$$

where $0 < \alpha < 1, 0 < \beta < 1$, and $M > 0$. The utility function (1) is adopted with three restrictions: $C_1 \geq 0$, $C_2 \geq 0$, and $U \geq 0$, thus ruling out negative or complex values of U. M is a positive multiplicative factor dependent upon the units of measurement. It is unnecessary to assume that $\alpha + \beta = 1$.

The two outputs are substitutes in consumption but not perfect ones. If any of the two quantities C_1 or C_2 were zero, utility would be zero.

2.4   THE BUDGET CONSTRAINT

If we assume that the household always spends the sum Y on consumption,

(2) $$Y = P_1C_1 + P_2C_2$$

2.5   MAXIMIZATION OF UTILITY AT THE GIVEN BUDGET, FIRST-ORDER CONDITION

Use (2) to express C_2 as a function of C_1, insert the result into (1), and obtain

(3) $$U = MC_1^{\alpha}\left(\frac{Y - P_1C_1}{P_2}\right)^{\beta}$$

Equation (3) expresses utility U as a function of a single variable, the quantity consumed C_1. Take the first derivative of U with respect to C_1. The first-order condition for a utility maximum is that the derivative equal zero. Thus

(4) $$\frac{dU}{dC_1} = MC_1^{\alpha-1}\left(\frac{Y - P_1C_1}{P_2}\right)^{\beta-1}\left(\alpha\frac{Y - P_1C_1}{P_2} - \beta\frac{P_1}{P_2}C_1\right) = 0$$

Since the exponents $\alpha - 1$ and $\beta - 1$ are both negative, (4) can be zero only if the expression in the second pair of parentheses equals zero. Set that expression equal to zero and solve for C_1, then

(5) $$C_1 = \frac{\alpha}{\alpha + \beta}\frac{Y}{P_1}$$

Now insert (5) into (2) and solve for C_2:

(6)
$$C_2 = \frac{\beta}{\alpha + \beta} \frac{Y}{P_2}$$

Let us find the budget elasticities, the price elasticities, and the cross elasticities of (5) and (6):

(7)
$$\frac{\partial C_1}{\partial Y} \frac{Y}{C_1} = 1$$

(8)
$$\frac{\partial C_2}{\partial Y} \frac{Y}{C_2} = 1$$

(9)
$$\frac{\partial C_1}{\partial P_1} \frac{P_1}{C_1} = -1$$

(10)
$$\frac{\partial C_2}{\partial P_2} \frac{P_2}{C_2} = -1$$

(11)
$$\frac{\partial C_1}{\partial P_2} \frac{P_2}{C_1} = 0$$

(12)
$$\frac{\partial C_2}{\partial P_1} \frac{P_1}{C_2} = 0$$

Thus the first-order conditions permitted us to derive the two household demand functions (5) and (6), whose budget elasticities are *plus* one, whose price elasticities are *minus* one, and whose cross elasticities are zero.

2.6 SECOND-ORDER CONDITION

The second-order condition for a utility maximum is that the second derivative of utility U with respect to the quantity consumed C_1 be negative. Take that second derivative, simplify it by using (4), and write it:

(13)
$$\frac{d^2U}{dC_1^2} = -(\alpha + \beta)M \frac{P_1}{P_2} C_1^{\alpha-1} \left(\frac{Y - P_1 C_1}{P_2} \right)^{\beta-1} < 0$$

Since α, β, P_1, and P_2 are assumed to be positive, (13) is obviously satisfied for positive C_1, C_2, and Y. Thus the utility materializing when C_1 and C_2 assume the values (5) and (6) is a maximum one.

We should now like to try a slightly more general utility function, in which the two outputs may be either close or poor substitutes.

2.7   A CONSTANT-ELASTICITY-OF-SUBSTITUTION
UTILITY   FUNCTION

Less tidy household demand functions will result from a utility function of the constant-elasticity-of-substitution type such as

(1a) $$U = M(AC_1^{-\rho} + BC_2^{-\rho})^{-(1/\rho)}$$

where $A > 0$, $B > 0$, $M > 0$, $-1 < \rho < 0$, or $0 < \rho$. The utility function (1a) is adopted with the same three restrictions: $C_1 \geq 0$, $C_2 \geq 0$, and $U \geq 0$, as were used previously.

Unlike a Cobb-Douglas utility function, the constant-elasticity-of-substitution utility function may or may not permit the household to consume one output alone. If $-1 < \rho < 0$ and one of the outputs C_1 or C_2 were zero, utility U would be in direct proportion to the other output. This is the case of close substitutes and a high elasticity of substitution σ. We know that if $-1 < \rho < 0$, then $\sigma > 1$. If, on the other hand, $\rho > 0$ and one of the outputs C_1 or C_2 were zero, that zero would be raised to a negative power, and (1a) would become meaningless. Here (1a) does not permit the household to consume only one output. This is the case of poor substitutes and a low elasticity of substitution: If $\rho > 0$, then $0 < \sigma < 1$.

2.8   MAXIMIZATION   OF   UTILITY   AT   THE   GIVEN   BUDGET,
FIRST-ORDER   CONDITION

The budget constraint (2) is the same as before; therefore we use it to express C_2 as a function of C_1, insert the result into the new utility function, and obtain

(3a) $$U = M\left[AC_1^{-\rho} + B\left(\frac{Y - P_1 C_1}{P_2}\right)^{-\rho} \right]^{-(1/\rho)}$$

Again (3a) expresses utility U as a function of a single variable C_1. Take the first derivative of U with respect to C_1. The first-order condition for a utility maximum is that the derivative equal zero. If C_2 stands for

$$(Y - P_1 C_1)/P_2,$$

we obtain

(4a) $$\frac{dU}{dC_1} = M(AC_1^{-\rho} + BC_2^{-\rho})^{-(1+\rho)/\rho}\left(AC_1^{-\rho-1} - B\frac{P_1}{P_2}C_2^{-\rho-1}\right) = 0$$

Would setting the expression in the first pair of parentheses of (4a) equal to zero make the derivative (4a) zero? We distinguish two cases. First, if

$\rho > 0$, the expression in the first pair of parentheses would be raised to a negative power, and setting it equal to zero would result in a meaningless operation. Second, if $\rho < 0$, the expression would now be raised to a positive power, but we couldn't set it equal to zero without making utility itself, as expressed by (1a), zero.

Therefore set the expression in the second pair of parentheses of (4a) equal to zero, solve for C_1 and C_2 and find:

(5a) $$C_1 = H_1 Y$$

(6a) $$C_2 = H_2 Y$$

where H_1 and H_2 represent, respectively

$$H_1 = \frac{\left(\frac{A}{P_1}\right)^{1/(1+\rho)}}{(AP_1{}^\rho)^{1/(1+\rho)} + (BP_2{}^\rho)^{1/(1+\rho)}}$$

$$H_2 = \frac{\left(\frac{B}{P_2}\right)^{1/(1+\rho)}}{(AP_1{}^\rho)^{1/(1+\rho)} + (BP_2{}^\rho)^{1/(1+\rho)}}$$

Find the budget elasticities, the price elasticities, and the cross elasticities of (5a) and (6a):

(7a) $$\frac{\partial C_1}{\partial Y}\frac{Y}{C_1} = 1$$

(8a) $$\frac{\partial C_2}{\partial Y}\frac{Y}{C_2} = 1$$

(9a) $$\frac{\partial C_1}{\partial P_1}\frac{P_1}{C_1} = -\frac{1 + \rho H_1 P_1}{1 + \rho}$$

(10a) $$\frac{\partial C_2}{\partial P_2}\frac{P_2}{C_2} = -\frac{1 + \rho H_2 P_2}{1 + \rho}$$

(11a) $$\frac{\partial C_1}{\partial P_2}\frac{P_2}{C_1} = -\frac{\rho}{1 + \rho} H_2 P_2$$

(12a) $$\frac{\partial C_2}{\partial P_1}\frac{P_1}{C_2} = -\frac{\rho}{1 + \rho} H_1 P_1$$

Thus, from the constant-elasticity-of-substitution utility function (1a) and the budget constraint (2) we have derived the demand functions (5a) and (6a) whose budget elasticities are *plus* one.

The price elasticities (9a) and (10a) will be easier to interpret if we multiply the definitions of H_1 and H_2 by P_1 and P_2, respectively:

$$H_1 P_1 = \cfrac{1}{1 + \left[\cfrac{B}{A}\left(\cfrac{P_2}{P_1}\right)^\rho\right]^{1/(1+\rho)}}$$

$$H_2 P_2 = \cfrac{1}{1 + \left[\cfrac{A}{B}\left(\cfrac{P_1}{P_2}\right)^\rho\right]^{1/(1+\rho)}}$$

Thus $0 < H_1 P_1 < 1$ and $0 < H_2 P_2 < 1$. Consequently, (9a) and (10a) will be negative but may lie on either side of *minus* one. Thus, if $-1 < \rho < 0$, (9a) and (10a) are less than *minus* one. If this is true, demand is elastic. If $\rho > 0$, (9a) and (10a) are greater than *minus* one and demand is inelastic.

Next we discuss the cross elasticities (11a) and (12a). For positive prices P_1 and P_2 and under the assumptions made about A and B, (11a) and (12a) will be opposite in sign to ρ, for $1 + \rho$ was assumed to be positive, hence $\rho/(1 + \rho)$ has the same sign as ρ. Thus if $-1 < \rho < 0$, (11a) and (12a) are positive. This is true of close substitutes and here the Hicksian substitution effect overwhelms the income effect, so that a price increase of one output increases the demand for the other. However, if $\rho > 0$, (11a) and (12a) are negative. This is true of poor substitutes; here the Hicksian income effect overwhelms the substitution effect, and a price increase of one output reduces the demand for the other.

2.9 SECOND-ORDER CONDITION

The second-order condition for a utility maximum is that the second derivative of utility U with respect to the quantity consumed C_1 be negative. If we take that second derivative, simplify it by using (4a), and again let C_2 stand for $(Y - P_1 C_1)/P_2$, we write

$$(13a) \quad \frac{d^2 U}{dC_1^2} = -(1 + \rho)M(AC_1^{-\rho} + BC_2^{-\rho})^{-(1+\rho)/\rho}$$

$$\times \left[AC_1^{-\rho-2} + B\left(\frac{P_1}{P_2}\right)^2 C_2^{-\rho-2}\right] < 0$$

Under the assumptions made, (13a) is obviously satisfied for positive values of C_1, C_2, and Y. Thus the utility materializing when C_1 and C_2 assume the values in (5a) and (6a) is a maximum one.

CHAPTER 3

Generalization: Optimum Consumption

3.1 INTRODUCTION

Until now the household was assumed to consume two outputs only. This permitted us to see the essence of household equilibrium without applying anything more complicated than the maximization of a function of one variable. We shall now allow for the facts that, first, households consume more than two outputs and, second, households hold stocks of durable consumers' goods. Such generalization is not only aesthetically appealing, we shall need it in our duopoly models in Chapters 20 and 21.

3.2 THE GENERAL CASE

In a theory of the household the following notation will be assigned.

Variables

C_j = quantity consumed of jth output per annum
S_i = physical capital stock of ith durable consumers' good held by household
s = household surplus defined as household budget *minus* the money value of all output consumed and rental
U = utility to the household resulting from its consumption of outputs and holding of capital stocks of durable consumers' goods

Parameters

A_j = coefficient of C_j in constant-elasticity-of-substitution utility function
B_i = coefficient of S_i in constant-elasticity-of-substitution utility function
α_j = elasticity with respect to C_j in Cobb-Douglas utility function

β_i = elasticity with respect to S_i in Cobb-Douglas utility function
M = multiplicative factor in the utility functions
P_j = price of jth output
r_i = rental per annum of a unit of the ith durable consumers' good
ρ = an exponent in the constant-elasticity-of-substitution utility function
Y = household budget per annum

Let the household have a utility function

$$(1) \qquad U = U(C_1, \ldots, C_m, S_1, \ldots, S_n)$$

Thus the household consumes m different outputs and holds n different physical capital stocks. Let the household own all capital stocks held, the price of the jth output consumed be P_j, and the rental per annum of a unit of the ith durable consumers' good be r_i. Rental includes first, interest representing the cost of money capital to the household, second, depreciation, and third, repair cost. Define surplus per annum as household budget *minus* the money value of all output consumed and rental; then require that the surplus be zero. Thus

$$(2) \qquad s = Y - \left[\sum_{j=1}^{m}(P_j C_j) + \sum_{i=1}^{n}(r_i S_i) \right] = 0$$

We now maximize utility (1) subject to the budget constraint (2) or, using the Lagrange multiplier λ, maximize a new function

$$(3) \qquad V = U + \lambda s$$

Next, we vary the hth output consumed and the holding of the gth capital stock and we take first partial derivatives of V with respect to C_h and S_g. The first-order conditions for a constrained utility maximum are that these first derivatives be zero.

$$(4) \qquad \frac{\partial V}{\partial C_h} = \frac{\partial U}{\partial C_h} - \lambda P_h = 0 \qquad (h = 1, \ldots, m)$$

$$(5) \qquad \frac{\partial V}{\partial S_g} = \frac{\partial U}{\partial S_g} - \lambda r_g = 0 \qquad (g = 1, \ldots, n)$$

$$(6) \qquad \frac{\partial V}{\partial \lambda} = s = 0$$

By rearranging (4) and (5) we obtain a familiar result

$$(7,8) \qquad \frac{\partial U/\partial C_h}{P_h} = \frac{\partial U/\partial S_g}{r_g} = \lambda \qquad (h = 1, \ldots, m; \quad g = 1, \ldots, n)$$

That is, output consumed and the holding of capital stock should be carried up to some point at which the ratio between marginal utility and price (rental) is the same for all output and capital stock. But which point?

Table 3.1. The Hessian Determinant of the Bordered Second Partial Derivatives

$$H = \begin{vmatrix} \dfrac{\partial^2 V}{\partial C_1^2} & \cdots & \dfrac{\partial^2 V}{\partial C_1\, \partial C_m} & \dfrac{\partial^2 V}{\partial C_1\, \partial S_1} & \cdots & \dfrac{\partial^2 V}{\partial C_1\, \partial S_n} & \dfrac{\partial s}{\partial C_1} \\[2ex] \dfrac{\partial^2 V}{\partial C_m\, \partial C_1} & \cdots & \dfrac{\partial^2 V}{\partial C_m^2} & \dfrac{\partial^2 V}{\partial C_m\, \partial S_1} & \cdots & \dfrac{\partial^2 V}{\partial C_m\, \partial S_n} & \dfrac{\partial s}{\partial C_m} \\[2ex] \dfrac{\partial^2 V}{\partial S_1\, \partial C_1} & \cdots & \dfrac{\partial^2 V}{\partial S_1\, \partial C_m} & \dfrac{\partial^2 V}{\partial S_1^2} & \cdots & \dfrac{\partial^2 V}{\partial S_1\, \partial S_n} & \dfrac{\partial s}{\partial S_1} \\[2ex] \dfrac{\partial^2 V}{\partial S_n\, \partial C_1} & \cdots & \dfrac{\partial^2 V}{\partial S_n\, \partial C_m} & \dfrac{\partial^2 V}{\partial S_n\, \partial S_1} & \cdots & \dfrac{\partial^2 V}{\partial S_n^2} & \dfrac{\partial s}{\partial S_n} \\[2ex] \dfrac{\partial s}{\partial C_1} & \cdots & \dfrac{\partial s}{\partial C_m} & \dfrac{\partial s}{\partial S_1} & \cdots & \dfrac{\partial s}{\partial S_n} & 0 \end{vmatrix}$$

Consisting of $m + n + 1$ simultaneous equations, one for each output and capital stock and one expressing the budget constraint, the system of Eqs. (4) through (6) answers the question: How far should each particular output be consumed and each particular capital stock be held?

The second-order conditions are as follows. First form the Hessian $(m + n + 1)$-order determinant of the bordered second derivatives, shown in Table 3.1. Then form the principal minors of H. The principal minor formed by deleting the second through the $(m + n)$th rows and columns of H must be negative. The principal minor formed by deleting the third through the $(m + n)$th rows and columns of H must be positive, etc., the principal minors alternating in sign. Notice that the $(m + n + 1)$th row and column of H are never deleted, the minors are also bordered. When finally we delete no rows and columns, H itself must be positive if $m + n$ is even, negative if $m + n$ is odd.

The time has now come to make more specific assumptions.

3.3 FIRST PARTICULAR CASE: COBB-DOUGLAS UTILITY FUNCTION

Specify the generalized Cobb-Douglas utility function

$$(9) \qquad U = MC_1^{\alpha_1} \cdots C_m^{\alpha_m} S_1^{\beta_1} \cdots S_n^{\beta_n}$$

where $0 < \alpha_h < 1$, $0 < \beta_g < 1$, and $M > 0$. The utility function (9) is adopted with the $m + n + 1$ restrictions. $C_h \geq 0$, $S_g \geq 0$, and $U \geq 0$, where $h = 1, \ldots, m$ and $g = 1, \ldots, n$. The assumptions about the elasticities

α_h and β_g guarantee positive and diminishing marginal utility of any output or capital stock. The sum of the elasticities is not assumed to equal one hence increasing, constant, or diminishing utility to scale may exist.

By using (9) to find the derivatives in (4) and (5), we write eqs. (4) and (5) as

$$(10) \qquad C_h = \frac{\alpha_h}{P_h} \frac{U}{\lambda} \qquad (h = 1, \ldots, m)$$

$$(11) \qquad S_g = \frac{\beta_g}{r_g} \frac{U}{\lambda} \qquad (g = 1, \ldots, n)$$

By inserting (10) and (11) into (2), we obtain the solutions for optimum consumption of output and holding of capital stock:

$$(12) \qquad C_h = \frac{\alpha_h}{\alpha_1 + \cdots + \alpha_m + \beta_1 + \cdots + \beta_n} \frac{Y}{P_h} \qquad (h = 1, \ldots, m)$$

$$(13) \qquad S_g = \frac{\beta_g}{\alpha_1 + \cdots + \alpha_m + \beta_1 + \cdots + \beta_n} \frac{Y}{r_g} \qquad (g = 1, \ldots, n)$$

which are generalizations of solutions (5) and (6) in Chapter 2. Again we find that budget elasticities are *plus* one, price elasticities are *minus* one, and cross elasticities zero.

Are the second-order conditions for a utility maximum satisfied by (12) and (13)? By using (9), we obtain the second partial derivatives in the Hessian determinant in Table 3.1. Insert (10) and (11) into these second partial derivatives and express them as shown in Table 3.2. By using (2) we

Table 3.2 Second Partial Derivatives of Cobb-Douglas Utility Function

$\dfrac{\partial^2 V}{\partial C_f \, \partial C_h} =$		$\dfrac{\lambda^2}{U} P_f P_h$
$\dfrac{\partial^2 V}{\partial S_g \, \partial C_h} =$		$\dfrac{\lambda^2}{U} P_h r_g$
$\dfrac{\partial^2 V}{\partial C_h^2} =$	$\dfrac{\alpha_h - 1}{\alpha_h}$	$\dfrac{\lambda^2}{U} P_h^2$
$\dfrac{\partial^2 V}{\partial S_e \, \partial S_g} =$		$\dfrac{\lambda^2}{U} r_e r_g$
$\dfrac{\partial^2 V}{\partial C_h \, \partial S_g} =$		$\dfrac{\lambda^2}{U} P_h r_g$
$\dfrac{\partial^2 V}{\partial S_g^2} =$	$\dfrac{\beta_g - 1}{\beta_g}$	$\dfrac{\lambda^2}{U} r_g^2$

determine the first partial derivatives bordering the second partial ones in H. Appendix I proves that the signs of the principal minors formed from the Hessian determinant will indeed alternate as required.

3.4 SECOND PARTICULAR CASE: CONSTANT-ELASTICITY-OF-SUBSTITUTION UTILITY FUNCTION

Specify the linearly homogeneous constant-elasticity-of-substitution utility function:

(14) $\quad U = M(A_1 C_1^{-\rho} + \cdots + A_m C_m^{-\rho} + B_1 S_1^{-\rho} + \cdots + B_n S_n^{-\rho})^{-(1/\rho)}$

where $A_h > 0$, $B_g > 0$, $M > 0$, $-1 < \rho < 0$ or $0 < \rho$. Equation (14) is adopted with $m + n + 1$ restrictions: $C_h \geq 0$, $S_g \geq 0$, and $U \geq 0$, where $h = 1, \ldots, m$ and $g = 1, \ldots, n$. The assumptions about the coefficients A_h and B_g and the exponent ρ guarantee positive and diminishing marginal utility of any output or capital stock. Since for simplicity we are using a linearly homogeneous constant-elasticity-of-substitution utility function, we have committed ourselves to the assumption of constant utility to scale.

Use (14) to find the derivatives in (4) and (5) and express (4) and (5) as

(15) $\qquad C_h = U\left(\dfrac{A_h}{P_h} \dfrac{M^{-\rho}}{\lambda}\right)^{1/(1+\rho)} \qquad (h = 1, \ldots, m)$

(16) $\qquad S_g = U\left(\dfrac{B_g}{r_g} \dfrac{M^{-\rho}}{\lambda}\right)^{1/(1+\rho)} \qquad (g = 1, \ldots, n)$

By inserting (15) and (16) into (6) and using the result to find the solutions for optimum consumption of output and holding of capital stock,

(17) $\qquad\qquad C_h = H_h Y \qquad (h = 1, \ldots, m)$

(18) $\qquad\qquad S_g = G_g Y \qquad (g = 1, \ldots, n)$

where H_h and G_g represent, respectively:

$$H_h = \frac{\left(\dfrac{A_h}{P_h}\right)^{1/(1+\rho)}}{(A_1 P_1^{\rho})^{1/(1+\rho)} + \cdots + (A_m P_m^{\rho})^{1/(1+\rho)} + (B_1 r_1^{\rho})^{1/(1+\rho)} + \cdots + (B_n r_n^{\rho})^{1/(1+\rho)}}$$

$$G_g = \frac{\left(\dfrac{B_g}{r_g}\right)^{1/(1+\rho)}}{(A_1 P_1^{\rho})^{1/(1+\rho)} + \cdots + (A_m P_m^{\rho})^{1/(1+\rho)} + (B_1 r_1^{\rho})^{1/(1+\rho)} + \cdots + (B_n r_n^{\rho})^{1/(1+\rho)}}$$

Equations (17) and (18) are generalizations of (5a) and (6a) in Chapter 2. Again, budget elasticities are *plus* one. After taking derivatives of (17) and (18) with respect to P_h and r_g, respectively, we rearrange and find the price (rental) elasticities of demand.

(19)
$$\frac{\partial C_h}{\partial P_h} \frac{P_h}{C_h} = - \frac{1 + \rho H_h P_h}{1 + \rho}$$

and

(20)
$$\frac{\partial S_g}{\partial r_g} \frac{r_g}{S_g} = - \frac{1 + \rho G_g r_g}{1 + \rho}$$

where H_h and G_g are defined as before. The price (rental) elasticities (19) and (20) are generalizations of (9a) and (10a) in Chapter 2.

After taking the derivatives of (17) and (18) with respect to P_f and r_e respectively, we rearrange and obtain the following cross elasticities.

(21)
$$\frac{\partial C_h}{\partial P_f} \frac{P_f}{C_h} = - \frac{\rho}{1 + \rho} H_f P_f$$

and

(22)
$$\frac{\partial S_g}{\partial r_e} \frac{r_e}{S_g} = - \frac{\rho}{1 + \rho} G_e r_e$$

where H_f and G_e are analogous to H_h and G_g, respectively. The cross elasticities (21) and (22) are generalizations of (11a) and (12a) in Chapter 2.

Table 3.3 Second Partial Derivatives of Constant-Elasticity-of-Substitution Utility Function

$$\frac{\partial^2 V}{\partial C_f \, \partial C_h} = (1 + \rho)\frac{\lambda^2}{U} P_f P_h$$

$$\frac{\partial^2 V}{\partial S_g \, \partial C_h} = (1 + \rho)\frac{\lambda^2}{U} P_h r_g$$

$$\frac{\partial^2 V}{\partial C_h^2} = (1 + \rho)\lambda\frac{P_h}{C_h}\left(\frac{\partial U}{\partial C_h}\frac{C_h}{U} - 1\right)$$

$$\frac{\partial^2 V}{\partial S_e \, \partial S_g} = (1 + \rho)\frac{\lambda^2}{U} r_e r_g$$

$$\frac{\partial^2 V}{\partial C_h \, \partial S_g} = (1 + \rho)\frac{\lambda^2}{U} P_h r_g$$

$$\frac{\partial^2 V}{\partial S_g^2} = (1 + \rho)\lambda\frac{r_g}{S_g}\left(\frac{\partial U}{\partial S_g}\frac{S_g}{U} - 1\right)$$

Are the second-order conditions for a utility maximum satisfied by (17) and (18)? By using (14), we find the second partial derivatives in the Hessian determinant in Table 3.1. By inserting (15) and (16) into those second partial derivatives, we express them as shown in Table 3.3. By using (2) we obtain the first partial derivatives bordering the second partial ones in H. Appendix II proves that the signs of the principal minors formed from the Hessian determinant will indeed alternate as required.

APPENDIX I   PROOF THAT SIGNS OF PRINCIPAL MINORS DO ALTERNATE IN THE FIRST PARTICULAR CASE

Between C, α, and P on the one hand, and S, β, and r on the other, there is no mathematical difference; hence let us suppress S, β, and r, thus reducing the order of the Hessian determinant to $m + 1$. By using Table 3.2 we may write it as

$$H = \begin{vmatrix} \dfrac{\alpha_1 - 1}{\alpha_1} \dfrac{\lambda^2}{U} P_1{}^2 & \cdots & \dfrac{\lambda^2}{U} P_1 P_m & -P_1 \\ \cdots\cdots\cdots\cdots\cdots\cdots\cdots \\ \dfrac{\lambda^2}{U} P_m P_1 & \cdots & \dfrac{\alpha_m - 1}{\alpha_m} \dfrac{\lambda^2}{U} P_m{}^2 & -P_m \\ -P_1 & \cdots & -P_m & 0 \end{vmatrix}$$

Multiply $(m + 1)$st row by λ^2/U. Divide ith column by λ^2/U, $i = 1, \ldots,$ m. Divide ith column by P_i, $i = 1, \ldots, m$. Divide ith row by P_i, $i = 1,$ $\ldots, m$. Add $m + 1$st column to ith column, $i = 1, \ldots, m$ and formulate the Hessian as

$$H = \left(\dfrac{\lambda^2}{U}\right)^{m-1} (P_1 \cdots P_m)^2 \begin{vmatrix} Q_1 & \cdots & 0 & -1 \\ \cdots\cdots\cdots\cdots\cdots \\ 0 & \cdots & Q_m & -1 \\ -1 & \cdots & -1 & 0 \end{vmatrix}$$

where

$$Q_i = -\dfrac{1}{\alpha_i} \quad (i = 1, \ldots, m)$$

which is negative, because $\alpha_i > 0$.

Finally add $1/Q_i$ times each element of ith column to corresponding element of $(m + 1)$st column, $i = 1, \ldots, m$, and write the Hessian:

$$H = \left(\frac{\lambda^2}{U}\right)^{m-1} (P_1 \cdots P_m)^2 \begin{vmatrix} Q_1 & \cdots & 0 & 0 \\ \cdots & \cdots & \cdots & \cdots \\ 0 & \cdots & Q_m & 0 \\ -1 & \cdots & -1 & -\dfrac{1}{Q_1} - \cdots - \dfrac{1}{Q_m} \end{vmatrix}$$

$$= \left(\frac{\lambda^2}{U}\right)^{m-1} (P_1 \cdots P_m)^2 Q_1 \cdots Q_m \left(-\frac{1}{Q_1} - \cdots - \frac{1}{Q_m}\right)$$

Since $Q_i < 0$, $i = 1, \ldots, m$, the Hessian determinant H will be positive if m is even and negative if m is odd, and the signs of the principal minors will alternate as required.

APPENDIX II PROOF THAT SIGNS OF PRINCIPAL MINORS DO ALTERNATE IN THE SECOND PARTICULAR CASE

Between C, A, and P on the one hand, and S, B, and r on the other, there is no mathematical difference; hence we suppress S, B, and r, thus reducing the order of the Hessian determinant to $m + 1$. Using Table 3.3, we write it as

$$H = \begin{vmatrix} (1 + \rho)\lambda \dfrac{P_1}{C_1}\left(\dfrac{\partial U}{\partial C_1} \dfrac{C_1}{U} - 1\right) & \cdots & (1 + \rho) \dfrac{\lambda^2}{U} P_1 P_m & -P_1 \\ \cdots & \cdots & \cdots & \cdots \\ (1 + \rho) \dfrac{\lambda^2}{U} P_m P_1 & \cdots & (1 + \rho)\lambda \dfrac{P_m}{C_m}\left(\dfrac{\partial U}{\partial C_m} \dfrac{C_m}{U} - 1\right) & -P_m \\ -P_1 & \cdots & -P_m & 0 \end{vmatrix}$$

Multiply $(m + 1)$st row by $(1 + \rho)\lambda^2/U$. Divide ith column by $(1 + \rho)\lambda^2/U$, $i = 1, \ldots, m$. Divide ith column by P_i, $i = 1, \ldots, m$. Divide ith row by P_i, $i = 1, \ldots, m$. Add $(m + 1)$st column to ith column, $i = 1, \ldots, m$ and express the Hessian as

$$H = \left[(1 + \rho)\frac{\lambda^2}{U}\right]^{m-1} (P_1 \cdots P_m)^2 \begin{vmatrix} Q_1 & \cdots & 0 & -1 \\ \cdots & \cdots & \cdots & \cdots \\ 0 & \cdots & Q_m & -1 \\ -1 & \cdots & -1 & 0 \end{vmatrix}$$

where

$$Q_i = \frac{\dfrac{\partial U}{\partial C_i}\dfrac{C_i}{U} - 1}{\lambda P_i C_i} U - 1 \qquad (i = 1, \ldots, m)$$

which is negative. We see this by using Euler's theorem, which holds for all linearly homogeneous functions, and thus realize that the elasticity of utility with respect to any single output consumed C_i must be less than one.

Finally, by adding $1/Q_i$ times each element of the ith column to the corresponding element of $(m + 1)$st column, $i = 1, \ldots, m$, we get the determinant already found and evaluated for the Cobb-Doublas case of Appendix I. Consequently,

$$H = \left[(1 + \rho)\frac{\lambda^2}{U}\right]^{m-1}(P_1 \cdots P_m)^2 Q_1 \cdots Q_m\left(-\frac{1}{Q_1} - \cdots - \frac{1}{Q_m}\right)$$

Since $Q_i < 0$, $i = 1, \ldots, m$, the Hessian determinant H will be positive if m is even and negative if m is odd, and the signs of the principal minors will alternate as required.

CHAPTER 4

Optimum Replacement of Consumer Durables

4.1 INTRODUCTION

In Chapter 3 we determined, among other things, the optimum stocks of consumer durables to be held by the household. Clearly, the determination of optimum stock is one thing, the determination of the optimum flow of consumer durables required to maintain such a stock is quite another. To proceed from the stock to the flow of durables we need a model of optimum replacement of consumer durables. To provide such a model is the purpose of this chapter.

As a first approximation, we ignore interest rate, technological progress, style changes, and scrap or trade-in value. What is left as an inducement to replacement, then, is the phenomenon that as it grows older, the consumer durable needs repair more frequently. This phenomenon is important because of the low maintenance standards applied by the average consumer. Unlike firms he does not believe much in preventive maintenance and postpones action until his durable fails to operate.

Exactly which useful life is optimal under these circumstances? Consumer durables should not be replaced too soon, or the cost of acquiring them occurs too frequently. They should not be replaced too late either, or their repair costs become too high.

4.2 NOTATION

The following notation will be assigned.

Variables

n = total number of repairs over useful life of the durable consumers' good

R = replacement per annum per unit of durable consumers' good held by household

r = annual rental of a unit of durable consumers' good

u = useful life of consumers' good

Parameters

a = durability factor

α = elasticity of total number of repairs over useful life with respect to useful life

P = price of a new unit of consumers' good

p = average price of repair, including parts and labor

4.3 THE MODEL

A consumer durable gradually deteriorates with advancing age, and the older it is the more frequently it needs repair. Assuming that the number of repairs over the entire useful life of the durable is more than proportional to its useful life, we obtain

$$(1) \qquad n = \frac{u^{\alpha}}{a}$$

where $a > 0$ and $\alpha > 1$. The durability function (1) is adopted with the

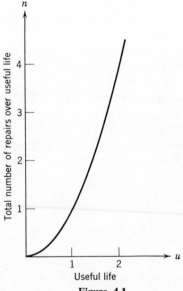

Figure 4.1

restriction that $u \geq 0$. Figure 4.1 shows (1) plotted for the special case where $a = 1$, $\alpha = 2$.

By definition, replacement per annum per unit of durable consumers' good is the reciprocal of useful life:

$$(2) \qquad\qquad R = \frac{1}{u}$$

4.4 RENTAL MINIMIZATION. FIRST-ORDER CONDITION

Assuming the possible need for fuel or power to be independent of the age of the consumer durable, we need only to consider rental per annum. Rental was defined as including, first, interest representing the cost of money capital to the household, second, depreciation, and third, repair cost. For simplicity we will ignore interest. We may equate depreciation with replacement cost per annum PR. As for repair cost, n is the total number of repairs over useful life; hence the number of repairs per annum is n/u. The average price of repair is p; hence cost of repairs per annum is np/u. Thus rental per annum is

$$(3) \qquad\qquad r = PR + \frac{np}{u}$$

By inserting (1) and (2) into (3),

$$(3a) \qquad\qquad r = \frac{P}{u} + \frac{u^{\alpha-1}}{a}\, p$$

Figure 4.2 shows the function (3a) and its two terms for $a = P = p = 1$, and $\alpha = 2$.

The consumer must necessarily compromise between reducing replacement cost per annum by lengthening useful life and reducing repair cost per annum by shortening it. Suppose he minimizes annual rental by adjusting useful life. The first-order condition for a rental minimum is that the first derivative of r with respect to u equal zero; then

$$(4) \qquad\qquad \frac{dr}{du} = -\frac{P}{u^2} + \frac{p(\alpha-1)}{a}\, u^{\alpha-2} = 0$$

4.5 SOLUTION FOR USEFUL LIFE

Solving (4) for u, we find

$$(4a) \qquad\qquad u = \left[\frac{Pa}{p(\alpha-1)} \right]^{1/\alpha}$$

Thus optimal useful life is in direct proportion to the $1/\alpha$'th power of

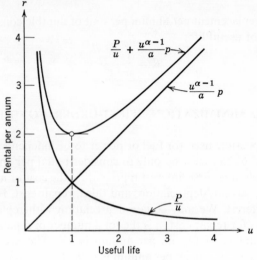

Figure 4.2

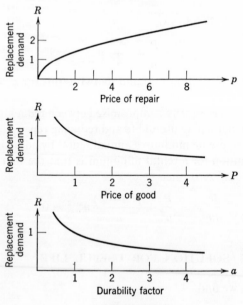

Figure 4.3

price P and durability factor a, and is in inverse proportion to the $1/\alpha$'th power of the price of repair p. Since $\alpha > 1$, the expression in the brackets is positive.

4.6 SOLUTION FOR DEMAND

We really want a demand function. Inserting (4a) into (2) we get the demand function:

$$(5) \qquad R = \left[\frac{p(\alpha - 1)}{Pa} \right]^{1/\alpha}$$

Thus demand is in direct proportion to the $1/\alpha$'th power of the price of repair p, and is in inverse proportion to the $1/\alpha$'th power of the price P of the good and the durability factor a. Figure 4.3 shows the function (5) in three parts and reminds us that, particularly for durables, there are demand curves other than the one showing demand as a function of price.

4.7 SECOND-ORDER CONDITIONS

The second-order condition for a rental minimum is that the second derivative of r with respect to u be positive. By taking the second derivative and simplifying it using (4a), we write it

$$(6) \qquad \frac{d^2r}{du^2} = \alpha \frac{P}{u^3} > 0$$

Under the assumptions made, (6) is clearly satisfied for positive useful life u. Thus the rental materializing when u assumes the value (4a) is indeed a minimum one.

CHAPTER 5

How to Derive a Supply-of-Labor
Function from a Utility Function

5.1 INTRODUCTION

A household spends, works, and saves. We have finished determining its consumption and shall now try to determine the household's supply of hours worked as a response to the wage rate, given the household's utility function. Will the household work longer, shorter, or the same hours if the wage rate rises?

5.2 NOTATION

In a microeconomic theory of labor supply the following notation will be assigned.

Variables

l = hours of leisure per annum
U = utility to the household, resulting from income and leisure
W = wage income per annum
x = hours of work per annum

Parameters

A, B = parameters of a constant-elasticity-of-substitution utility function
α, β = parameters of a Cobb-Douglas utility function
h = total hours available per annum
M = multiplicative factor in the utility functions
ρ = an exponent in a constant-elasticity-of-substitution utility function
w = hourly money wage rate

5.3   UTILITY FUNCTIONS

Suppose that the household has a choice between leisure and working at a fixed hourly money wage rate, thereby earning an income to be spent on consumers' goods purchased at fixed prices. Let the household have no income other than wage income thus earned and derive utility from income as well as from leisure, but from nothing else. The utility function could be of the Cobb-Douglas type.

(1) $$U = MW^{\alpha}l^{\beta}$$

where $0 < \alpha < 1, 0 < \beta < 1$, and $M > 0$. The utility function (1) is adopted with these three restrictions: $W \geq 0, l \geq 0$, and $U \geq 0$. More generally, the utility function could be of the constant-elasticity-of-substitution type.

(1a) $$U = M(AW^{-\rho} + Bl^{-\rho})^{-1/\rho}$$

where $A > 0$, $B > 0$, $M > 0$, $-1 < \rho < 0$ or $0 < \rho$. Equation (1a) is adopted with the same three restrictions as was the Cobb-Douglas utility function (1).

5.4   A TIME-BUDGET CONSTRAINT

By definition, wage income per annum equals the hourly wage rate *times* the number of hours worked per annum. Thus

(2) $$W = wx$$

Also by definition, total hours available represent the sum of working hours and leisure hours.

(3) $$h = x + l$$

where $h > 0$. By inserting (2) into (3), we obtain the time-budget constraint:

(4) $$h = \frac{W}{w} + l$$

The budget referred to is not a budget of how to spend money income but a budget of how to spend time. Time may be spent "purchasing" income at the "price" of $1/w$ hours per dollar's worth of income, or time may be spent "purchasing" leisure at the price one.

5.5 OPTIMAL ALLOCATION OF TIME

Now we may maximize utility (1) or (1a) subject to the time-budget constraint (4). By using (2) and (3) to express wage income W and leisure l, respectively, as functions of hours of work x, and inserting those functions into (1) or (1a), we express utility U as a function of the single variable hours of work x. The first-order condition for a utility maximum is

$$(5) \qquad \frac{dU}{dx} = 0$$

The second-order condition for a maximum of utility is

$$(6) \qquad \frac{d^2U}{dx^2} < 0$$

5.6 SOLUTION FOR THE COBB-DOUGLAS CASE

By using the Cobb-Douglas utility function (1), we carry out the derivation (5), set the derivative equal to zero, solve for x, and find the labor-supply function

$$(7) \qquad x = \frac{\alpha}{\alpha + \beta} h$$

By using (5), the reader may wish to satisfy himself that the second-order condition (6) is satisfied.

Under the assumptions made, labor supply as determined by (7) is positive and unique. However, it is independent of the wage rate: w does not appear in (7). For more richness let us now try the constant-elasticity-of-substitution utility function (1a).

5.7 SOLUTION FOR THE CONSTANT-ELASTICITY-OF-SUBSTITUTION CASE

Again we solve for hours of work x, but this time we use the constant-elasticity-of-substitution utility function (1a) to find the labor-supply function

$$(8) \qquad x = \frac{h}{1 + \left(\dfrac{B}{A} w^\rho\right)^{1/(1+\rho)}}$$

By using (5), the reader may again wish to satisfy himself that the second-order condition (6) is satisfied.

Under the assumptions made, labor supply as determined by (8), is also positive and unique. This time, however, labor supply does depend upon the wage rate, and we can see how by taking the derivative

$$(9) \qquad \frac{\partial x}{\partial w} = - \frac{\dfrac{\rho}{1 + \rho}\left(\dfrac{B}{A}\dfrac{1}{w}\right)^{1/(1+\rho)}}{D^2} h$$

where D stands for the denominator of (8). Since $\rho > -1$, $\rho/(1 + \rho)$ has the same sign as ρ. Consequently, under the assumptions made, the entire partial derivative (9) will be opposite in sign to ρ.

Thus, if $-1 < \rho < 0$, (9) will be positive. This is the case of income and leisure being close substitutes. Here the Hicksian substitution effect overwhelms the income effect, so that an increase in the price w of hours, meaning a reduction in the price $1/w$ of income, will induce the household to spend more time earning income—although income has already increased due to the higher w.

If $\rho > 0$, (9) will be negative. This is where income and leisure are poor substitutes. Here the income effect overwhelms the substitution effect. Income is now such a poor substitute for leisure that the reduced price $1/w$ of income fails to induce the household to spend more time earning income. Indeed, because income has already increased due to the higher w, the household will now spend less time in earning income.

5.8 EMPIRICAL ILLUSTRATION

By using data from the manufacturing sectors of 29 countries during 1953–1960, on hours worked per week and on hourly wage rates expressed in

Figure 5.1. From G. C. Winston, "An International Comparison of Income and Hours of Work," *Rev. Econ. Stat.*, **48**, 35 (February 1966).

United States cents, Winston [1] has found the empirical x-w relationship shown in Fig. 5.1 on a double logarithmic scale. We shall notice that hours worked clearly decline with rising wage rate, and that their elasticity with respect to the wage rate is numerically rather low; it is, roughly -0.1. Suppose we follow Winston in assuming that the response as measured is sufficiently basic in human behavior that it overrides cultural differences. Then typically income does seem to be a poor substitute for leisure: $\rho > 0$, and the income effect does overwhelm the substitution effect.

REFERENCE

[1] Winston, G. C., "An International Comparison of Income and Hours of Work," *Rev. Econ. Stat.*, **48**, 28–39 (February, 1966).

CHAPTER 6

How to Derive a Supply-of-Saving Function from a Utility Function

6.1 INTRODUCTION

The last household activity to be studied is saving. Long ago, Irving Fisher [1] studied savings as a function of the rate of interest. For the simplest possible instance of two-period planning, we shall generalize his model and study savings as a function of the rate of interest, the rate of inflation, the level of income, and the rate of growth of income. The aggregate consumption function in Part 5 will be based directly on what we shall do now.

6.2 NOTATION

In a microeconomic theory of the supply of saving the following notation will be assigned.

Variables

C = quantity consumed
S = money saving
U = utility to the household, resulting from its consumption
Y = overall money income

Parameters

A, B = parameters of a constant-elasticity-of-substitution utility function
α, β = parameters of a Cobb-Douglas utility function
g_P = proportionate rate of change of price of output

47

g_W = proportionate rate of change of money wage income
i = rate of interest
M = multiplicative factor in the utility functions
P = price of output
ρ = exponent in a constant-elasticity-of-substitution utility function
W = money wage income

6.3 THE MODEL

Suppose household consumes only one good, and the quantity of that good consumed in period t is $C(t)$, where $t = 1, 2$. Let the good be perishable, and all saving be loaned. Consequently, the only asset a household can carry over from the first period to the second is a claim in money terms. Let the household be able to lend and borrow at the same rate of interest i. At the beginning of the first period, let the household plan for both periods and derive utility from neither saving per se nor asset-holding per se, but solely from consumption $C(t)$. The utility function may be of Cobb-Douglas form.

$$(1) \qquad\qquad U = M[C(1)]^{\alpha}[C(2)]^{\beta}$$

where $0 < \alpha < 1, 0 < \beta < 1$, and $M > 0$. The utility function (1) is adopted with these three restrictions: $C(1) \geq 0$, $C(2) \geq 0$, and $U \geq 0$. The utility function may also be of the constant-elasticity-of-substitution variety.

$$(1a) \qquad\qquad U = M\{A[C(1)]^{-\rho} + B[C(2)]^{-\rho}\}^{-(1/\rho)}$$

where $A > 0$, $B > 0$, $M > 0$, $-1 < \rho < 0$ or $0 < \rho$. Equation (1a) is adopted with the same three restrictions as was the Cobb-Douglas utility function (1).

Within each period, the household expects to receive the overall money income $Y(t)$, of which some is spent, and some saved.

$$(2, 3) \qquad\qquad Y(t) = P(t)C(t) + S(t) \qquad (t = 1, 2)$$

Within each period, the household expects to be facing prices $P(t)$ of output which are changing at the proportionate rate g_P defined as

$$(4) \qquad\qquad P(2) = (1 + g_P)P(1)$$

Let $1 + g_P > 0$. Prices do not dwindle to zero or below. Within each period, the household expects to be receiving the money wage income $W(t)$, changing at the proportionate rate g_W defined as

$$(5) \qquad\qquad W(2) = (1 + g_W)W(1)$$

Let $1 + g_W > 0$. Wage income does not dwindle to zero or below. Let the household start Period 1 without any assets, then

(6) $$Y(1) = W(1)$$

The savings volume of the first period $S(1)$ may be positive or negative. If positive, it is lent at the rate of interest i, if negative it is borrowed at the same rate of interest. In Period 2, then, assets are $S(1)$, and $iS(1)$ should be added to wage income in order to arrive at overall income. Thus

(7) $$Y(2) = W(2) + iS(1)$$

Let $1 + i > 0$. The interest rate will never swallow up all savings or more. Let the household save only for future consumption. Hence it will conclude Period 2 without any assets. Thus

(8) $$S(2) = -S(1)$$

6.4 A BUDGET-LIKE CONSTRAINT

By inserting (2) through (7) into (8), we may eliminate all variables other than $C(1)$ and $C(2)$ and obtain the counterpart to the familiar budget constraint

(9) $$(2 + g_W + i)\frac{W(1)}{P(1)} = (1 + i)C(1) + (1 + g_P)C(2)$$

6.5 OPTIMAL INTERTEMPORAL ALLOCATION OF CONSUMPTION

Let us now maximize utility (1) or (1a) subject to the budget-like constraint (9). Using (9) to express $C(2)$ as a function of $C(1)$, we insert the result into (1) or (1a). The first-order condition for a utility maximum is then,

(10) $$\frac{dU}{d[C(1)]} = 0$$

And the second-order condition is

(11) $$\frac{d^2U}{d[C(1)]^2} < 0$$

6.6 SOLUTION FOR THE COBB-DOUGLAS CASE

By using the Cobb-Douglas utility function (1), carry out the derivation (10), set the derivative equal to zero, solve for $C(1)$, then use Eq. (2) and find the following savings supply function:

$$(12) \qquad S(1) = \left(1 - \frac{\alpha}{\alpha + \beta} \frac{2 + g_W + i}{1 + i}\right) W(1)$$

By using (10), we may satisfy ourselves that the second-order condition (11) is satisfied.

The first problem to solve is whether the model household will save and lend or dissave and borrow in the first period. From (12) we discover that if $i = (\alpha/\beta)(1 + g_W) - 1$, then $S(1) = 0$. If i is greater than that, $S(1)$ will be positive; if i is less, $S(1)$ will be negative.

The second question to answer is how sensitive savings are to changes in the rate of interest. Therefore take the derivative

$$(13) \qquad \frac{\partial[S(1)]}{\partial i} = \frac{\alpha}{\alpha + \beta} \frac{1 + g_W}{(1 + i)^2} W(1)$$

Thus for positive wage income $W(1)$, (13) is positive. A higher rate of interest induces the household to save more.

Third, how sensitive are savings to an acceleration of inflation? They are entirely insensitive, for g_P does not appear in (12) at all.

Fourth, how sensitive are savings to changes in the level of income? (12) shows savings to have an income elasticity of one:

$$(14) \qquad \frac{\partial[S(1)]}{\partial[W(1)]} \frac{W(1)}{S(1)} = 1$$

Fifth, how sensitive are savings to an acceleration of income? Take the derivative

$$(15) \qquad \frac{\partial[S(1)]}{\partial g_W} = - \frac{\alpha}{\alpha + \beta} \frac{1}{1 + i} W(1)$$

which is always negative. An acceleration of income discourages saving. Why save for an even more abundant future?

For more richness, let us now adopt the constant elasticity-of-substitution utility function (1a).

6.7   SOLUTION FOR THE CONSTANT-ELASTICITY-OF-SUBSTITUTION CASE

Let us once more solve for savings in the first period $S(1)$, but this time by using the constant-elasticity-of-substitution utility function (1a).

$$(16) \qquad S(1) = \left[1 - \frac{2 + g_W + i}{1 + i + (1 + g_P)\left(\dfrac{B}{A}\dfrac{1 + i}{1 + g_P}\right)^{1/(1+\rho)}} \right] W(1)$$

By using (10), we may again satisfy ourselves that the second-order condition (11) is satisfied.

Under the assumptions made, (16) is unique. Is it also positive? Will the model household save or dissave in the first period? From (16) we realize that if

$$i = \frac{A}{B}(1 + g_P)^{-\rho}(1 + g_W)^{1+\rho} - 1$$

then $S(1)$ will be zero. If i is greater than that, $S(1)$ will be positive; if i is less, $S(1)$ will be negative.

Second, how sensitive are savings to changes in the rate of interest? Take the derivative

$$(17)$$

$$\frac{\partial[S(1)]}{\partial i} = - \frac{D - (2 + g_W + i)\left\{1 + \dfrac{1}{1 + \rho}\left[\dfrac{B}{A}\left(\dfrac{1 + g_P}{1 + i}\right)^{\rho}\right]^{1/(1+\rho)}\right\}}{D^2} W(1)$$

where D stands for the denominator of (16). What is the sign of (17)? Will an increase in the rate of interest induce the household to save more or less in the first period? Two cases must be distinguished.

If $-1 < \rho < 0$, (17) is found to be unequivocally positive. This is the situation where present and future outputs are close substitutes; here the Hicksian substitution effect overwhelms the income effect. Thus an increase of the rate of interest induces a saver to further reduce his consumption of present output, hence save more, although his two-period income has increased. (17) will also be positive for values of ρ slightly above zero.

But at some value of ρ above zero, present and future outputs have become such poor substitutes for each other that the Hicksian income effect overwhelms the substitution effect. An increase of the rate of interest still increases his two-period income, but the effect is now too weak to induce the saver to lower his consumption of present output. Future output just is not a good enough substitute for present output to make it worth while for the saver to sacrifice more of the present input. After all, his two-period income has increased. At this value of ρ (17) becomes negative.

Third, how sensitive are savings to an acceleration of inflation? Again the present utility function is richer than was the Cobb-Douglas utility function. Take the derivative

$$(18) \qquad \frac{\partial[S(1)]}{\partial g_P} = \frac{(2 + g_W + i)\dfrac{\rho}{1 + \rho}\left(\dfrac{B}{A}\dfrac{1 + i}{1 + g_P}\right)^{1/(1+\rho)}}{D^2} W(1)$$

Equation (18) has the same sign as ρ. Thus, if $-1 < \rho < 0$, (18) will be negative. This is the instance of present and future consumptions being close substitutes. Here the Hicksian substitution effect overwhelms the income effect. Thus a price increase of future output increases a saver's consumption of present output, hence reduces his savings, although in real terms his two-period income has decreased. If, however, $\rho > 0$, (18) will be positive. This is the case of present and future consumption being poor substitutes. Now the income effect overwhelms the substitution effect. Thus a price increase of future output reduces the consumption of present output, hence increases savings, for in real terms the two-period income has decreased.

Fourth, how sensitive are savings to changes in the level of income in the first period? Equation (16) gives the same simple answer as did (12), that is, that the income elasticity of savings is one.

Fifth, how sensitive are savings to an acceleration of income? Take the derivative

$$(19) \qquad \frac{\partial[S(1)]}{\partial g_W} = -\frac{W(1)}{D}$$

where again D stands for the denominator of (16). Like (15), (19) is always negative. Why save for an even more abundant future?

REFERENCE

[1] Fisher, I., *The Theory of Interest*, New York, 1930.

Part Two

Firm Equilibrium

CHAPTER 7

The Demand Faced by the Firm*

7.1 INTRODUCTION

Before a firm produces anything, it must be facing a demand for it. As an introduction to the theory of the firm, let us examine the demand faced by the firm.

Traditionally, "the demand curve" as used in economic theory has three different meanings. First, there is the demand curve of the individual household, derived from the household's utility function or from its indifference map. Second, there is the *aggregation* of those individual household demand curves into the market demand for the particular product. Third, there is the *disaggregation* of the market demand curve into the demand curves faced by individual firms. Let us avoid confusion by showing precisely how this aggregation and disaggregation are achieved.

7.2 NOTATION

The following notation is assigned.

Variables

C_{hk} = hth output consumed by kth household
η_h = price elasticity of demand for hth output
P_h = price of hth output

Parameters

A_{hk}, B_{hk} = parameters of a constant-elasticity-of-substitution utility function of the kth household

* Chapter 3 is a prerequisite for Chapter 7.

α_{hk}, β_{hk} = parameters of a Cobb-Douglas utility function of the kth household

f = number of firms in an industry

q_{jk} = the probability that the kth household will buy from the jth firm

r_g = annual rental of a unit of the gth durable consumers' good

ρ_k = an exponent of a constant-elasticity-of-substitution utility function of the kth household

s = number of households

Y_k = household budget per annum of the kth household

7.3 THE AGGREGATION OF HOUSEHOLD DEMAND INTO MARKET DEMAND

In Chapter 3 we maximized a household's utility subject to a budget constraint and found demand functions for outputs and capital stocks which were substitutes in consumption but not perfect ones. Suppose the model household is the kth household; then the kth household's demand for the hth output was determined to be

$$C_{hk} = H_{hk} Y_k$$

where H_{hk} is represented alternatively as

(1) $$H_{hk} = \frac{\alpha_{hk}/P_h}{\alpha_{1k} + \cdots + \alpha_{mk} + \beta_{1k} + \cdots + \beta_{nk}},$$

(2) $$H_{hk} = \frac{\left(\dfrac{A_{hk}}{P_h}\right)^{1/(1+\rho_k)}}{(A_{1k}P_1{}^{\rho_k})^{1/(1+\rho_k)} + \cdots + (A_{mk}P_m{}^{\rho_k})^{1/(1+\rho_k)} + (B_{1k}r_1{}^{\rho_k})^{1/(1+\rho_k)} + \cdots + (B_{nk}r_n{}^{\rho_k})^{1/(1+\rho_k)}}$$

The demand function with (1) inserted was derived from a Cobb-Douglas utility function, and the demand function with (2) inserted was derived from a constant-elasticity-of-substitution utility function.

Let there be s households in the market, all facing the same set of prices and rentals $P_1, \ldots, P_m, r_1, \ldots, r_n$. To find the market demand for the hth output we merely sum the household demand function from $k = 1$ to $k = s$.

(3) $$\sum_{k=1}^{s} C_{hk} = H_{h1} Y_1 + \cdots + H_{hs} Y_s$$

The coefficient H_{hk} as defined by (1) or (2) had nothing but taste and price parameters in it. Equation (3) shows market demand to be a weighted sum of the taste and price parameters, the weights being individual incomes $Y_1, \ldots, Y_s$. Income distribution, then, does matter since the same aggregate income may result in different patterns of market demand, depending on how income is distributed among individual households.

In one special instance, however, income distribution does not matter. Assume all households to have identical tastes, then

(4) $$\alpha_{h1} = \cdots = \alpha_{hs} = \alpha_h$$

(5) $$\beta_{g1} = \cdots = \beta_{gs} = \beta_g$$

(6) $$A_{h1} = \cdots = A_{hs} = A_h$$

(7) $$B_{g1} = \cdots = B_{gs} = B_g$$

(8) $$\rho_1 = \cdots = \rho_s = \rho$$

where $h = 1, \ldots, m$ and $g = 1, \ldots, n$. Inserting alternatively either (4) and (5) or (6) through (8) into market demand (3), we find that (3) collapses into

(9) $$\sum_{k=1}^{s} C_{hk} = H_h \sum_{k=1}^{s} Y_k$$

where H_h represents alternatively

$$H_h = \frac{\alpha_h / P_h}{\alpha_1 + \cdots + \alpha_m + \beta_1 + \cdots + \beta_n}$$

$$H_h = \frac{\left(\dfrac{A_h}{P_h}\right)^{1/(1+\rho)}}{(A_1 P_1{}^\rho)^{1/(1+\rho)} + \cdots + (A_m P_m{}^\rho)^{1/(1+\rho)} + (B_1 r_1{}^\rho)^{1/(1+\rho)} + \cdots + (B_n r_n{}^\rho)^{1/(1+\rho)}}$$

Equation (9) indicates that market demand is proportional to aggregate money income and does not depend on the distribution of aggregate money income among households.

7.4 THE PRICE ELASTICITY OF MARKET DEMAND

Having determined market demand as the sum of individual household demands, let us examine its elasticity.

(10) $$\eta_h = \frac{\partial \sum_{k=1}^{s} C_{hk}}{\partial P_h} \frac{P_h}{\sum_{k=1}^{s} C_{hk}} = \frac{\partial C_{h1}}{\partial P_h} \frac{P_h}{C_{h1}} \frac{C_{h1}}{\sum_{k=1}^{s} C_{hk}} + \cdots + \frac{\partial C_{hs}}{\partial P_h} \frac{P_h}{C_{hs}} \frac{C_{hs}}{\sum_{k=1}^{s} C_{hk}}$$

Equation (10) states that the price elasticity of market demand is a weighted sum of all the price elasticities of the demands of the individual households $1, \ldots, s$. In the special instance (9), in which all households were assumed to have identical tastes, (10) collapses into

$$(11) \qquad\qquad \eta_h = -1$$

for a Cobb-Douglas utility function and into

$$(12) \qquad\qquad \eta_h = -\frac{1 + \rho H_h P_h}{1 + \rho}$$

for a constant-elasticity-of-substitution utility function. Thus in both cases the price elasticity of market demand equals the price elasticity of the individual household demands.

Having found market demand and its price elasticity, we must now investigate the demand faced by the individual firm. The fundamental distinction here is between differentiated and nondifferentiated products. Let us begin with the differentiated products, which are easier to analyze.

7.5 PRODUCT DIFFERENTIATION: MARKET DEMAND EQUALS DEMAND FACED BY FIRM

Product differentiation means that the firm has succeeded in setting its product apart from the products of all other firms. Suppose that the hth output just discussed is such a product. Then, by definition, the firm producing it is the *only* firm producing it, and the market demand function just found *is* the demand function faced by the firm.

Nevertheless, the firm does not operate in a vacuum. The other outputs were said to be substitutes in consumption although not perfect ones. This assumption was clearly expressed in the underlying utility functions, and may or may not show in the market and firm demand functions. It does not appear in the special case of an underlying Cobb-Douglas utility function; here, the demand function (3) with (1) inserted into it will contain no price other than P_h, because the income and substitution effects happen to cancel. Here, then, the firm may price its product with the assurance that demand is a function of no other price. An underlying constant-elasticity-of-substitution utility function is different; here, the demand function (3) with (2) inserted into it will contain all prices $P_1, \ldots, P_m$ and all rentals $r_1, \ldots, r_n$. Now if the firm producing the hth output expects prices other than P_h to remain unaffected by its own fixing of P_h, those prices are simply considered parameters, and the firm may still lead an uncomplicated life. This is the assumption underlying all of Part 2. If, however, the firm expects certain prices other than P_h to be affected by its own fixing of P_h, those prices are variables from the point of view of the firm and will have to be recognized by the oligopolistic side-glance. In that case the situation will be quite complicated. However, the time to worry about oligopoly has not come yet; it will come in Part 3 on industry equilibrium. Even there it is still true, of course, that for differentiated products, market demand *is* demand faced by the firm.

7.6 PRICE ELASTICITY OF DEMAND FACED BY FIRM UNDER PRODUCT DIFFERENTIATION

Since for differentiated products market demand is demand faced by the firm, the price elasticity of market demand is the price elasticity of demand faced by the firm.

Will the price elasticity of demand faced by the firm be parametric? In other words, can it be assumed to be the same regardless of price? It cannot in the general case of the elasticity (10) or the special case of the elasticity (12). However, in the special case of the price elasticity (11) it is parametric.

As a first approximation in our models of firm equilibrium we shall often assume the elasticity of demand faced by the firm is parametric. Now we shall examine the more difficult matter of absence of product differentiation.

7.7 NO PRODUCT DIFFERENTIATION: DISAGGREGATION OF MARKET DEMAND INTO DEMANDS FACED BY FIRMS

Absence of product differentiation must mean that a group of firms, call it an "industry," produces the same product. We will try to make this definition more precise. Again, let there be s households. Moreover, let there be f firms each of which maintains an inventory large enough to satisfy all forthcoming demand. No household will be turned away; therefore they may all realize their original purchase plans. Let q_{jk} be the probability that the kth household, when buying the product, buys it from the jth firm; then

$$q_{11} + \cdots + q_{f1} = 1$$

(13)

$$q_{1s} + \cdots + q_{fs} = 1$$

Now one of two things must be true: Either all firms charge the same price or they do not.

7.8 ALL FIRMS CHARGE THE SAME PRICE

Assume that all firms charge the same price. That there is no product differentiation simply must mean that no buyer is any more or less likely to buy from any one firm than from any other; therefore

$$q_{11} = \cdots = q_{f1} = q_1$$

(14)

$$q_{1s} = \cdots = q_{fs} = q_s$$

By taking the systems (13) and (14) together, we obtain

$$(15) \qquad q_1 = \cdots = q_s = \frac{1}{f}$$

Thus, although a single household, the kth household, when making a single purchase chooses at random the firm from which to make it, in making a large number of repeated purchases, the kth household tends to distribute these with $1/f$ purchases to each of the f firms—just as a large number of repeated throws of a single perfect die tends to be distributed with $1/6$ of the throws to each possible outcome. Now what is true of a large number of repeated throws of a single perfect die is also true of the totality of simultaneous throws of s perfect dice, where s is a large number. Similarly, what is true of a large number of repeated purchases by a single household, the kth household, is also true of the totality of simultaneous purchases by s households for which (15) holds, where s is a large number. As a result, each of the f firms gets a $1/f$ share of the market.

7.9 PRICE ELASTICITY OF DEMAND FACED BY FIRM: ALL FIRMS CHARGE THE SAME PRICE

If all firms charge the same price, the demand faced by any of the f firms producing nondifferentiated products was found to be $1/f$ of market demand. Let C be market demand; then clearly if f is a constant,

$$(16) \qquad \eta = \frac{\partial C}{\partial P} \frac{P}{C} = \frac{\partial (C/f)}{\partial P} \frac{P}{C/f}$$

which states that the price elasticity of market demand equals the price elasticity of demand faced by the firm.

7.10 ALL FIRMS DON'T CHARGE THE SAME PRICE

We shall now relax the assumption that all firms charge the same price. Then no household would buy from any firm charging a price higher than that of the firm or firms charging the lowest price, otherwise the firms would not be offering the same product. If several, say n, where $n < f$, firms charge the lowest price, the households will distribute their purchases with a $1/n$ share to each of the n firms.

7.11 PRICE ELASTICITY OF FIRM DEMAND: ALL FIRMS DON'T CHARGE THE SAME PRICE

Let us apply the general rule just given to the case in which $n = 1$. If a single firm, say the jth, reduces its price ever so slightly below that charged by the other firms, it will find itself facing a demand equaling the entire market demand rather than $1/f$ of the latter. Does this mean that if the jth firm becomes smaller and smaller relative to its industry, it finds itself facing a demand elasticity falling without bounds? It does if we follow our mathematics boldly. In the elasticity definition,

$$\eta = \frac{\partial C_j}{\partial P_j} \frac{P_j}{C_j}$$

C_j is demand faced by the jth firm before it cut its price P_j ever so slightly, and that demand was $1/f$ of market demand C. If C is finite, clearly $C_j = C/f$ approaches zero as the number of firms f in the industry rises without bounds. Hence for the finite $\partial C_j/\partial P_j$ the (negative) η does fall without bounds.

CHAPTER 8

The Production Function

8.1 INTRODUCTION

For a given technology a neoclassical production function is a single equation describing the maximum output obtainable from specified inputs and emphasizing their substitutability. A Leontief production function is a system of equations, one for each input, each describing a minimum input required to produce a specified output. Here there is no substitutability at all.

A comprehensive review of the production function, theoretical and econometric, can be found in two recent and lucid surveys [4, 10]. Here, we shall merely examine some simple forms of the production function to be used in the chapters to follow.

We will assign the following notation.

Variables

r = the marginal rate of substitution
σ = the elasticity of substitution
X = output per annum
x_j = absorption of jth input per annum, $j = 1, 2$

Parameters

a_j = absorption of jth input per unit of output, $j = 1, 2$
A, B = parameters of a constant-elasticity-of-substitution production function
α, β = parameters of a Cobb-Douglas production function
M = multiplicative factor in the production functions
ρ = an exponent in a constant-elasticity-of-substitution production function

8.2   THE MARGINAL RATE OF SUBSTITUTION

Let a neoclassical production function be

(1) $$X = X(x_1, x_2)$$

Suppose the firm changes infinitesimally its x_1 by dx_1 and its x_2 by dx_2. The resulting change in output is approximated by the total differential

(2) $$dX = \frac{\partial X}{\partial x_1} dx_1 + \frac{\partial X}{\partial x_2} dx_2$$

An isoquant, such as those shown in Fig. 8.1 for good substitutes and Fig. 8.2 for poor substitutes, is defined by setting (2) equal to zero.

(3) $$dX = 0$$

The marginal rate of substitution is defined as the slope of the isoquant and derived from (2) and (3); thus

(4) $$r = \frac{dx_1}{dx_2} = - \frac{\partial X / \partial x_2}{\partial X / \partial x_1}$$

The marginal rate of substitution is seen to be negative for positive marginal productivities.[1]

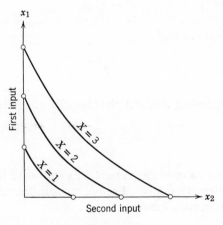

Figure 8.1

[1] We see no good reason to multiply it by *minus* one as was, for example, done by Allen [1] whose exposition we are otherwise following.

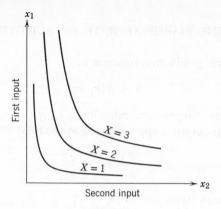

Figure 8.2

8.3   THE ELASTICITY OF SUBSTITUTION

Normally as one moves down an isoquant, the marginal rate of substitution changes with the ratio between the inputs. The rate of substitution may be considered as a function of the input or vice versa.

(5a)
$$r = r\left(\frac{x_1}{x_2}\right)$$

(5b)
$$\frac{x_1}{x_2} = \frac{x_1}{x_2}(r)$$

Take the derivative of (5b):

(6)
$$\frac{d(x_1/x_2)}{dr}$$

and call its corresponding elasticity the elasticity of substitution:

(7)
$$\sigma = \frac{d(x_1/x_2)}{dr}\frac{r}{x_1/x_2}$$

Since (5b) is a function of one variable, its derivative (6) may be thought of as the ratio of two differentials. Each of those differentials may be considered as a total differential, hence

(8)
$$d\left(\frac{x_1}{x_2}\right) = \frac{\partial(x_1/x_2)}{\partial x_1}dx_1 + \frac{\partial(x_1/x_2)}{\partial x_2}dx_2 = \frac{x_2\,dx_1 - x_1\,dx_2}{x_2^2}$$

(9)
$$dr = \frac{\partial r}{\partial x_1}dx_1 + \frac{\partial r}{\partial x_2}dx_2$$

We apply (4) to (8) and (9), insert both into (7), and obtain two alternative forms of (7):

$$(10) \qquad \sigma = \frac{rx_2 - x_1}{r(\partial r/\partial x_1) + (\partial r/\partial x_2)} \frac{r}{x_1 x_2}$$

$$(11) \qquad \sigma = \frac{rx_2 - x_1}{dr/dx_2} \frac{r}{x_1 x_2}$$

The form (11) is most convenient for finding the sign of σ. For positive marginal productivities the marginal rate of substitution r was seen to be negative. Hence for positive x_1 and x_2 the last denominator of (11) as well as the product of its two numerators will be positive. What about its first denominator? Derivative dr/dx_2 indicates how fast r changes as we move down the isoquant, hence measures the latter's curvature. For a convex isoquant that curvature is positive. Negative r increases with increasing x_2. Thus for a convex isoquant, (11) shows its elasticity of substitution to be positive.

The form (11) also shows the elasticity of substitution to be in inverse proportion to the curvature dr/dx_2. If the convex isoquant approaches a straight line, its curvature approaches zero, and the elasticity of substitution will rise without bounds. This is true where the two inputs are very nearly perfect substitutes. However, if the isoquant is bending very sharply at the point in question, its curvature is very high, hence the elasticity of substitution σ will be very low. This is true of poor substitutes. Suppose there is no substitution at all. In Section 8.9 we will examine the extreme case in which inputs must be combined in technologically fixed proportions, and isoquants are L-shaped. Here, in the corner of the L the curvature is undefined, for dr/dx_2 does not approach the same value whether the corner is approached from the left or from the right.

Yet another form of (7) is to be used. If we use (4) to express r in terms of the marginal productivities of x_1 and x_2, insert it into the form (10), and perform the derivations required, we obtain

$$(12) \qquad \sigma = \frac{\dfrac{\partial X}{\partial x_1} \dfrac{\partial X}{\partial x_2} \left(x_1 \dfrac{\partial X}{\partial x_1} + x_2 \dfrac{\partial X}{\partial x_2} \right)}{-\left(\dfrac{\partial X}{\partial x_1}\right)^2 \dfrac{\partial^2 X}{\partial x_2^2} - \left(\dfrac{\partial X}{\partial x_2}\right)^2 \left(\dfrac{\partial^2 X}{\partial x_1^2}\right) + 2 \dfrac{\partial X}{\partial x_1} \dfrac{\partial X}{\partial x_2} \dfrac{\partial^2 X}{\partial x_1 \partial x_2}} \frac{1}{x_1 x_2}$$

8.4 THE PARTICULAR CASE OF A COBB-DOUGLAS PRODUCTION FUNCTION

Let the production function be of a form first written by Wicksell [11] and tested empirically by Cobb and Douglas [3]:

$$(1a) \qquad X = M x_1^{\alpha} x_2^{\beta}$$

where $0 < \alpha < 1$, $0 < \beta < 1$, and $M > 0$. The production function (1a) is considered with these three restrictions: $x_1 \geq 0$, $x_2 \geq 0$, and $X \geq 0$.

If and only if $\alpha + \beta = 1$, the production function (1a) is linearly homogeneous, for then and only then we may replace x_1 by λx_1, x_2 by λx_2, and obtain output λX. Let us not make the assumption that $\alpha + \beta = 1$. We then take the derivatives

$$(13) \qquad \frac{\partial X}{\partial x_1} = \alpha \frac{X}{x_1}$$

$$(14) \qquad \frac{\partial X}{\partial x_2} = \beta \frac{X}{x_2}$$

$$(15) \qquad \frac{\partial^2 X}{\partial x_1^2} = \alpha(\alpha - 1) \frac{X}{x_1^2}$$

$$(16) \qquad \frac{\partial^2 X}{\partial x_2^2} = \beta(\beta - 1) \frac{X}{x_2^2}$$

$$(17) \qquad \frac{\partial^2 X}{\partial x_1\, \partial x_2} = \frac{\partial^2 X}{\partial x_2\, \partial x_1}$$

$$(18) \qquad = \alpha\beta \frac{X}{x_1 x_2}$$

For positive M, x_1, and x_2 (13) and (14) will be positive if and only if α and β are positive, and for positive α and β (15) and (16) will be negative if and only if α and β are both less than one. Thus the marginal productivity of any input has been shown to be positive and diminishing with that input if and only if both α and β lie between zero and one. All this was assumed to be the case. Then (17) and (18) are seen to be positive. Thus the marginal productivity of any one input has been shown to be increasing with the other input.

If (13) through (18) are inserted into (12), then (12) remarkably reduces to

$$(12a) \qquad \sigma = 1$$

Thus, regardless of whether it has increasing, constant, or diminishing returns to scale, that is, regardless of whether $\alpha + \beta > 1$, $\alpha + \beta = 1$, or $\alpha + \beta < 1$, respectively, a Cobb-Douglas production function always has the elasticity of substitution one.

We proceed to study the particular case of a linearly homogeneous production function, whether of the Cobb-Douglas form or some other form.

8.5 THE PARTICULAR CASE OF A LINEARLY HOMOGENEOUS PRODUCTION FUNCTION

The reader will recall that, if in the neoclassical production function (1) x_1 and x_2 underwent the independent changes dx_1 and dx_2, respectively, then the total differential (2) would be an approximation to the increment of output. Since the changes dx_1 and dx_2 were independent, we are free to make them proportional; thus we let λ be a small constant such as $1/1000$ or $1/1,000,000$ and write:

$$(19) \qquad dx_1 = \lambda x_1$$

$$(20) \qquad dx_2 = \lambda x_2$$

Now if the production function were linearly homogeneous, an increase of all inputs by the proportion λ would increase output by that same proportion.

$$(21) \qquad dX = \lambda X$$

Figure 8.2a illustrates this. Let X_1 be a point on the linearly homogeneous surface. Connect X_1 with the origin O and consider the vertical plane containing the heavy connecting line OX_1. This plane intersects the production surface along the entire length of the connecting line OX_1 extended beyond X_1 and intersects the x_1–x_2 plane along the path of proportional expansion of x_1 and x_2. Moving along that path from P_1 to P_2 we find that (21) is true, because the connecting line OX_1 is a tangent to the production surface in X_1; in fact, OX_1 throughout its entire length is contained in that surface.

However, dX, and with it λX, are merely approximations, are they not? In general, if x_1 and x_2 undergo the independent changes dx_1 and dx_2, respectively, then the total differential dX as defined by (2) represents the change in X to the *tangent plane* to the production surface, and ΔX represents the change in X to the production surface *itself*. However, in the linearly homogeneous production function we have special luck: If we follow the path of proportional expansion of x_1 and x_2, the tangent plane and the production surface coincide along the heavy connecting line OX_1, hence the approximation is always perfect, regardless of the size of λ.

By inserting (19), (20), and (21) into (2), we obtain Euler's theorem

$$(22) \qquad X = \frac{\partial X}{\partial x_1} x_1 + \frac{\partial X}{\partial x_2} x_2$$

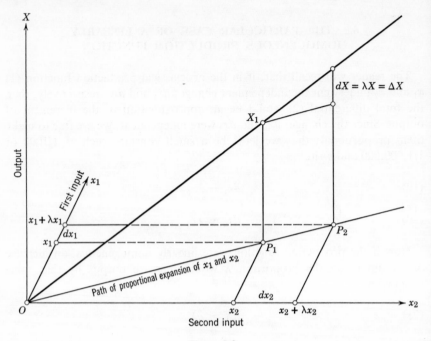

Figure 8.2*a*

Take the partial derivative of (22), first with respect to x_1, then with respect to x_2:

$$(23) \qquad \frac{\partial^2 X}{\partial x_1{}^2} = - \frac{x_2}{x_1} \frac{\partial^2 X}{\partial x_1\, \partial x_2}$$

$$(24) \qquad \frac{\partial^2 X}{\partial x_2{}^2} = - \frac{x_1}{x_2} \frac{\partial^2 X}{\partial x_2\, \partial x_1}$$

If we insert (22), (23), and (24) into (12), then (12) collapses into

$$(12b) \qquad \sigma = \frac{\dfrac{\partial X}{\partial x_1} \dfrac{\partial X}{\partial x_2}}{X \dfrac{\partial^2 X}{\partial x_1\, \partial x_2}}$$

which is valid only for the particular case of a linearly homogeneous production function.

8.6   A CONSTANT-ELASTICITY-OF-SUBSTITUTION PRODUCTION FUNCTION

Now let the production function be of a form[2] first written by Solow [9] and tested empirically by Arrow, Chenery, Minhas, and Solow [2] and Ferguson [6, 7]:

(1b) $$X = M(Ax_1^{-\rho} + Bx_2^{-\rho})^{-(1/\rho)}$$

where $A > 0$, $B > 0$, $M > 0$, $-1 < \rho < 0$ or $0 < \rho$. Equation (1b) is considered with these three restrictions: $x_1 \geq 0$, $x_2 \geq 0$, and $X \geq 0$, as previously. It is linearly homogeneous. If we replace x_1 by λx_1, x_2 by λx_2, then output becomes λX. Consequently, (12b) and (22) will apply. Next we take the derivatives

(25) $$\frac{\partial X}{\partial x_1} = AM^{-\rho}\left(\frac{X}{x_1}\right)^{1+\rho}$$

(26) $$\frac{\partial X}{\partial x_2} = BM^{-\rho}\left(\frac{X}{x_2}\right)^{1+\rho}$$

(27) $$\frac{\partial^2 X}{\partial x_1^2} = AM^{-\rho}(1 + \rho)\left(\frac{X}{x_1}\right)^{\rho}\frac{(\partial X/\partial x_1)x_1 - X}{x_1^2}$$

(28) $$\frac{\partial^2 X}{\partial x_2^2} = BM^{-\rho}(1 + \rho)\left(\frac{X}{x_2}\right)^{\rho}\frac{(\partial X/\partial x_2)x_2 - X}{x_2^2}$$

(29) $$\frac{\partial^2 X}{\partial x_1 \partial x_2} = \frac{\partial^2 X}{\partial x_2 \partial x_1}$$

(30) $$= AB(1 + \rho)M^{-2\rho}X^{1+2\rho}(x_1 x_2)^{-(1+\rho)}$$

From these derivatives, what can we conclude about the marginal productivities? For positive M, x_1, and x_2, (25) and (26) will be positive if and only if A and B are positive. For positive A and B, what will be the signs of (27) and (28)? Since Euler's theorem, Eq. (22), applies, the numerators on the

---

[2] The function was tested empirically in the slightly more elegant (and space-consuming) form obtained by setting

$$M(A + B)^{-1/\rho} = \gamma$$

$$\frac{A}{A + B} = \delta$$

$$\frac{B}{A + B} = 1 - \delta$$

right-hand sides of (27) and (28) will always be negative; hence (27) and (28) will always be opposite in sign to $1 + \rho$. They will be negative, then, if and only if $\rho > -1$, which we assumed to be true. Consequently for positive A and B, the marginal productivity of any input is positive and diminishing with that input. Equations (29) and (30) are both positive; hence the marginal productivity of any input is increasing with the other input.

Finally, (12b) applies. If we insert (25), (26), (29), and (30) into (12b), then we obtain

$$(31) \qquad\qquad \sigma = \frac{1}{1 + \rho}$$

Thus indeed the production function (1b) has a constant elasticity of substitution.

8.7   ONE EXTREME CASE

We shall find it useful to consider two extremes of the linearly homogeneous constant-elasticity-of-substitution production function (1b). In specifying (1b), we stated that $\rho > -1$. To produce the first extreme, let us abandon that restriction and set

$$(32) \qquad\qquad \rho = -1$$

Insert (32) into (1b) and let the (1b) collapse into

$$(33) \qquad X = M(Ax_1 + Bx_2)$$

Take the derivatives of output with respect to inputs and let (25) and (26) collapse into

$$(34) \qquad\qquad \frac{\partial X}{\partial x_1} = MA$$

$$(35) \qquad\qquad \frac{\partial X}{\partial x_2} = MB$$

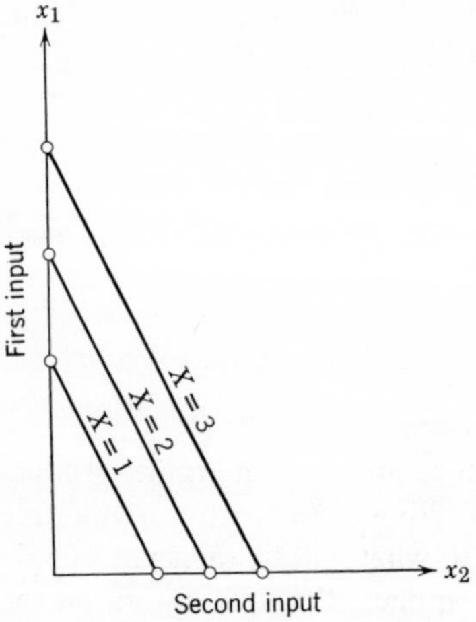

Figure 8.3

Thus marginal productivities are no longer diminishing but constant.

When we try to insert (32) into (31), we find that (31) becomes meaningless. However, we can state that by letting ρ drop close enough to -1, the elasticity of substitution as defined by (31) will become larger than any arbitrarily assignable constant, however large. The extreme case studied here, shown in Fig. 8.3 and representing the case of perfect substitutes, is rarely used in economic theory; therefore let us proceed to examine the widely used opposite extreme.

8.8 THE OTHER EXTREME CASE

Still considering the linearly homogeneous constant-elasticity-of-substitution production function (1b), let us see what happens if we let ρ rise without bounds.

To accomplish this, we must first examine more closely the isoquant map corresponding to (1b). Let the firm change infinitesimally its x_1 by dx_1 and its x_2 by dx_2. The resulting change in output is approximated by the total differential (2), and an isoquant is defined by setting that total differential equal to zero. Therefore insert (3), (25), and (26) into (2) and express the marginal rate of substitution

$$(36) \qquad r = \frac{dx_1}{dx_2} = -\frac{B}{A}\left(\frac{x_1}{x_2}\right)^{1+\rho}$$

Let $\rho > 0$. Then according to (1b) and the restrictions underlying it, we must have $x_1 > 0$ and $x_2 > 0$, for otherwise we would find ourselves trying to divide by zero, a meaningless operation. Consequently, we can set neither x_1 nor x_2 equal to zero. What we can do is the following.

If we let x_1 approach zero closely enough, the absolute difference between (36) and zero will become and remain smaller than any arbitrarily assignable positive constant, however small. Consequently, the isoquants whose slope is defined by (36) have the x_2-axis for an asymptote.

Moreover, if we let x_2 approach zero closely enough, the slope (36) itself will fall without bounds. Consequently, the isoquants also have the x_1-axis for an asymptote.

However large ρ is, the two axes will still be asymptotes. All a very large ρ can do is to make the isoquants approach the axes very slowly. The isoquants look, but are not quite, parallel to the axes.

By inserting large enough values of ρ into (31) it would be possible for the absolute difference between (31) and zero to become and remain less than any arbitrarily assignable positive constant, however small. Thus we are approaching the case of zero elasticity of substitution.

8.9 TECHNOLOGICALLY FIXED INPUT PROPORTIONS

Let us now break completely with the constant-elasticity-of-substitution production function (1b), and let the isoquants actually be, rather than

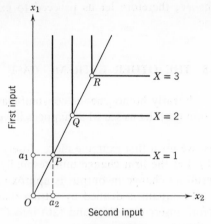

Figure 8.4

merely appear to be parallel to the axes, as shown in Fig. 8.4. The break is complete because, as we have already stated, the curvature of an L-shaped isoquant is undefined: dr/dx_2 does not approach the same value whether the corner of the L is approached from the left or from the right.

How can we express a production function corresponding to L-shaped isoquants? First, allowing for waste of inputs we could express it as a system of inequalities, one for each input, each describing the input required to produce a specified output.

$$(37) \qquad\qquad x_1 \geq a_1 X$$

$$(38) \qquad\qquad x_2 \geq a_2 X$$

where $a_1 \geq 0$, $a_2 \geq 0$, and $X \geq 0$. In Fig. 8.4, a_1 and a_2 are the coordinates of the corner of the L of the isoquant indicating output $X = 1$. Their ratio a_1/a_2 is the technologically fixed input proportion in which the inputs must be combined to avoid waste. The ratio a_1/a_2 is the slope of the straight line $OPQR$ in Fig. 8.4, passing through the corners of the L's.

In a production function described by the system of inequalities (37) and (38) what are marginal productivities like? Imagine a horizontal line drawn through the point Q in Fig. 8.4. Imagine a point on that line immediately to the left of Q. At this point some of the first input is being wasted. Now move the point closer to Q. This means rising from a lower to a higher isoquant; hence incremental output is positive. By contrast, imagine a point on this line immediately to the right of Q. At this point some of the second input is being wasted. Now move this second point closer to Q. This means moving along an isoquant; thus incremental output is zero. Consequently, $\partial X/\partial x_2$ does not approach the same value whether the corner of the L is approached from the left or the right. Just like the curvature dr/dx_2, then, marginal productivity $\partial X/\partial x_2$ is undefined.

Second, avoiding waste of inputs and following the straight line $OPQR$ we could leave the inequality signs out of (37) and (38) and express the production function as a system of equations describing the *minimum* input required to produce a specified output:

(39) $x_1 = a_1 X$

(40) $x_2 = a_2 X$

8.10   THE PROCESS CONCEPT

In the one-output, several-inputs case, a process[3] may be defined as a production program within which every input is in direct proportion to output. Dorfman [5] has very clearly expressed the difference between a process and the neoclassical production function. If we find, when comparing any two points on a production surface, that the ratio of every input to output is the same at the two points, the points represent different levels of the same process. For example, the two points P and Q in Fig. 8.4 represent different levels of the same process. If, on the other hand, the ratios are not the same at the two points, the two points represent two different processes.

8.11   CHOICE AMONG PROCESSES

Modern technology often offers a choice among a finite number of processes. The processes may or may not use the same inputs. For example, the inputs used in an earth-moving job may be (1) shovel hours, (2) pick hours, (3) bulldozer hours, and (4) man hours. Of the two alternative processes, one includes inputs (1), (2), and (4), the other includes (3) and (4). Although, as we have stated, there is no substitution between inputs within a process, there may indeed be substitution between processes. We shall return to this in Chapter 13 on linear programming.

REFERENCES

[1] Allen, R. G. D., *Mathematical Analysis for Economists*, London, 1938, pp. 340–343.
[2] Arrow, K. J., H. B. Chenery, B. S. Minhas, and R. M. Solow, "Capital-Labor Substitution and Economic Efficiency," *Rev. Econ. Stat.*, **43**, 225–250 (August 1961).

[3] The word "activity," formerly used as a synonym of "process," is now used to refer to the level of a process. See Koopmans [8].

[3] Cobb, C. W. and P. H. Douglas, "A Theory of Production," *Am. Econ. Rev.*, **18,** 139–165, Supplement 1928.

[4] Danø, S., *Industrial Production Models*, Vienna and New York, 1966.

[5] Dorfman, R., *Application of Linear Programming to the Theory of the Firm*, Berkeley and Los Angeles, 1951, pp. 14–15.

[6] Ferguson, C. E., "Cross-Section Production Functions and the Elasticity of Substitution in American Manufacturing Industry," *Rev. Econ. Stat.*, **45,** 305–313 (August 1963).

[7] Ferguson, C. E., "Time-Series Production Functions and Technological Progress in American Manufacturing Industry," *Jour. Pol. Econ.*, **73,** 135–146 (April 1965).

[8] Koopmans, T. C., *Three Essays on the State of Economic Science*, New York, 1957, 76–77.

[9] Solow, R. M., "A Contribution to the Theory of Economic Growth," *Quart. Jour. Econ.*, **70,** 77 (February, 1956).

[10] Walters, A. A., "Production and Cost Functions: An Econometric Survey," *Econometrica*, **31,** 1–66 (January–April 1963).

[11] Wicksell, K., *Lectures on Political Economy I*, London, 1934, p. 128.

CHAPTER 9

How to Derive a Cost Function
from a Production Function

9.1 INTRODUCTION

Setting up production functions can have no purpose other than that of explaining firm behavior by stating that a firm behaves in such a way as to maximize something related to the production function, for example, profits.

Now firms produce and sell outputs, purchase and absorb inputs, and invest for the future. If we are merely interested in the determination of optimal output, we could derive a cost function from the production function, define profits as revenue *minus* cost, and find the level of output which maximizes profits. We shall derive such a cost function in this chapter, assuming that the firm's inputs do not affect the prices at which inputs are purchased. In Chapter 11, we shall use the cost function derived here for determining the level of output which maximizes profits.

If we were generally interested in the simultaneous determination of optimal input and output, we might bypass the cost function and determine directly the levels of input and output which maximize profits. We shall do this in Chapters 12 and 13.

9.2 NOTATION

In a microeconomic theory of the firm the following notation is assigned.

Variables

C = cost per annum defined as the money value of all input per annum
X = output per annum
x_j = absorption of jth input per annum

Parameters

A, B = parameters of a constant-elasticity-of-substitution production function

α, β = parameters of a Cobb-Douglas production function

M = multiplicative factor in the production functions

p_j = price of jth input

ρ = an exponent in a constant-elasticity-of-substitution production function

9.3   A COBB-DOUGLAS PRODUCTION FUNCTION

Let the firm have a Cobb-Douglas production function

(1) $X = M x_1{}^\alpha x_2{}^\beta$

where $0 < \alpha < 1$, $0 < \beta < 1$, and $M > 0$. The production function (1) is adopted with these three restrictions: $x_1 \geq 0$, $x_2 \geq 0$, and $X \geq 0$.

The two inputs are substitutes but not perfect ones. If either of the two inputs x_1 or x_2 were zero, output would be zero.

9.4   A FIXED COST BUDGET

For the moment let the firm have the fixed cost budget

(2) $C = p_1 x_1 + p_2 x_2$

where p_j is the price of the jth input, and $p_j > 0, j = 1, 2$.

9.5   MAXIMIZATION OF OUTPUT AT THE GIVEN COST BUDGET: FIRST-ORDER CONDITION

Using (2) to express x_2 as a function of x_1, and inserting the result into (1), we obtain

(3) $X = M x_1{}^\alpha \left(\dfrac{C - p_1 x_1}{p_2} \right)^\beta$

Equation (3) expresses output X as a function of a single variable, the input x_1. Take the first derivative of X with respect to x_1. The first-order condition for an output maximum is that the derivative equal zero.

(4) $\dfrac{dX}{dx_1} = M x_1{}^{\alpha-1} \left(\dfrac{C - p_1 x_1}{p_2} \right)^{\beta-1} \left(\alpha \dfrac{C - p_1 x_1}{p_2} - \beta \dfrac{p_1}{p_2} x_1 \right) = 0$

Since $\alpha - 1$ and $\beta - 1$ are both negative, (4) can be zero only if the expression in the second parentheses is zero. Set this expression equal to zero and solve for x_1; then

(5) $$x_1 = \frac{\alpha}{\alpha + \beta} \frac{C}{p_1}$$

Now insert (5) into (2) and solve for x_2.

(6) $$x_2 = \frac{\beta}{\alpha + \beta} \frac{C}{p_2}$$

9.6 SECOND-ORDER CONDITION

The second-order condition for an output maximum is that the second derivative of output X with respect to the input x_1 be negative. We now take that second derivative, simplify it by using (4), and write it as

(7) $$\frac{d^2 X}{dx_1^2} = -(\alpha + \beta)M \frac{p_1}{p_2} x_1^{\alpha-1} \left(\frac{C - p_1 x_1}{p_2} \right)^{\beta-1} < 0$$

Since α, β, p_1, and p_2 are assumed to be positive, (7) is clearly satisfied for positive values of x_1, x_2, and C. Thus the output materializing when x_1 and x_2 assume the values (5) and (6) is a maximum one.

Divide (5) by (6); then

(8) $$\frac{x_1}{x_2} = \frac{\alpha}{\beta} \frac{p_2}{p_1}$$

and we see that the most efficient proportion in which to apply the two inputs x_1 and x_2 depends solely upon the ratio between the elasticities α and β and the ratio between the prices p_2 and p_1. "Efficient" in what sense? In the sense that the proportion (8) maximizes output within the given cost budget. Notice that the proportion does not depend upon the size of that cost budget, and notice that this is true regardless of whether $\alpha + \beta > 1$ (increasing returns to scale), $\alpha + \beta = 1$ (constant returns to scale), or $\alpha + \beta < 1$ (decreasing returns to scale).

Now we proceed to the derivation of cost curves.

9.7 TOTAL COST

If we insert the input demand functions (5) and (6) into the production function (1), we obtain

(9) $$X = \frac{1}{(\alpha + \beta)^{\alpha+\beta}} \left(\frac{\alpha}{p_1} \right)^{\alpha} \left(\frac{\beta}{p_2} \right)^{\beta} MC^{\alpha+\beta}$$

Equation (9) describes output X as a function of the fixed cost budget C when inputs are always applied in the most efficient proportion (8).

However, the cost budget C typically is not fixed to the firm. Nothing prevents us from thinking of (9) as expressing output as a function of the alternative cost budgets C and of C as a function of X rather than X as a function of C. Therefore we rewrite (9)

(9a) $$C = (\alpha + \beta)\left[\frac{1}{M}\left(\frac{p_1}{\alpha}\right)^{\alpha}\left(\frac{p_2}{\beta}\right)^{\beta}\right]^{1/(\alpha+\beta)} X^{1/(\alpha+\beta)}$$

Here total cost C has been expressed as a function of output X when inputs are always applied in the most efficient proportion (8). Equation (9a) indicates that under increasing returns to scale, that is, $\alpha + \beta > 1$, total cost will rise in less than proportion to output (see Fig. 9.1). Under constant returns to scale, that is, $\alpha + \beta = 1$, total cost will rise in direct proportion to output (see Fig. 9.2). Under decreasing returns to scale, that is, $\alpha + \beta < 1$, total cost will rise in more than proportion to output (see Fig. 9.3).

9.8 UNIT COST

We obtain unit cost by dividing output X into (9a).

(9b) $$\frac{C}{X} = (\alpha + \beta)\left[\frac{1}{M}\left(\frac{p_1}{\alpha}\right)^{\alpha}\left(\frac{p_2}{\beta}\right)^{\beta}\right]^{1/(\alpha+\beta)} X^{1/(\alpha+\beta)-1}$$

From (9b) we see that unit cost declines under increasing returns to scale

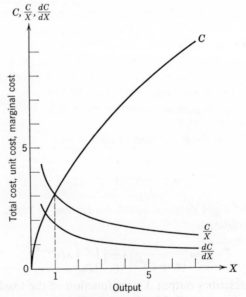

Figure 9.1. $\alpha + \beta > 1$.

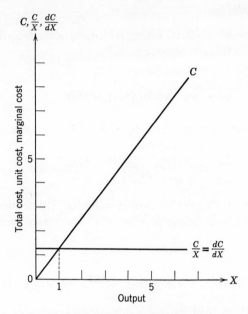

Figure 9.2. $\alpha + \beta = 1$.

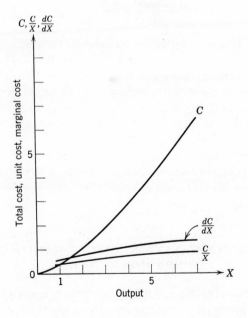

Figure 9.3. $\alpha + \beta < 1$.

(Fig. 9.1), is constant under constant returns to scale (Fig. 9.2), and rises under decreasing returns to scale (Fig. 9.3).

9.9   MARGINAL COST

By taking the derivative of (9a) with respect to X we determine marginal cost.

(9c)
$$\frac{dC}{dX} = \left[\frac{1}{M} \left(\frac{p_1}{\alpha} \right)^{\alpha} \left(\frac{p_2}{\beta} \right)^{\beta} \right]^{1/(\alpha+\beta)} X^{1/(\alpha+\beta)-1}$$

Thus marginal cost (9c) declines under increasing returns to scale, remains constant under constant returns to scale, and rises under decreasing returns to scale.

9.10   THE ELASTICITY OF COST WITH RESPECT TO OUTPUT

If (9c) is divided by (9b), we see that the ratio between marginal and unit cost is the constant:

(9d)
$$\frac{dC}{dX} \frac{X}{C} = \frac{1}{\alpha + \beta}$$

The constant $1/(\alpha + \beta)$ is, of course, merely the elasticity of cost with respect to output, as the left-hand side of (9d) discloses. Thus we have the remarkably simple result that a cost function derived from a Cobb-Douglas production function has a constant elasticity with respect to output. Under increasing returns to scale, that is, $\alpha + \beta > 1$, this elasticity is less than one; hence the marginal cost curve lies below the unit cost curve for any output. Under constant returns to scale, that is, $\alpha + \beta = 1$, the elasticity equals one; hence the marginal cost curve and the unit cost curve coincide for any output. Under decreasing returns to scale, that is, $\alpha + \beta < 1$, the elasticity is greater than one; therefore the marginal cost curve lies above the unit cost curve for any output.

9.11   A CONSTANT-ELASTICITY-OF-SUBSTITUTION PRODUCTION FUNCTION

Equally tidy cost functions will result from a linearly homogeneous production function having constant elasticity of substitution.

(1a)
$$X = M(Ax_1^{-\rho} + Bx_2^{-\rho})^{-(1/\rho)}$$

where $A > 0$, $B > 0$, $M > 0$, $-1 < \rho < 0$ or $0 < \rho$. Equation (1a) is adopted with the same three restrictions, $x_1 \geq 0$, $x_2 \geq 0$, and $X \geq 0$, as before.

Unlike a Cobb-Douglas function, the constant-elasticity-of-substitution production function may or may not permit the firm to operate with one input alone. If $-1 < \rho < 0$ and one of the inputs were zero, output X would be in direct proportion to the other input. Here we have close substitutes and a high elasticity of substitution σ. As we know, if $-1 < \rho < 0$, then $\sigma > 1$. If, however, $\rho > 0$ and one of the inputs x_1 or x_2 were zero, that zero would be raised to a negative power, and (1a) would be meaningless. Here, (1a) does not permit the firm to operate with one input alone. This is the case of poor substitutes and a low elasticity of substitution σ. If $\rho > 0$, then $0 < \sigma < 1$.

9.12 MAXIMIZATION OF OUTPUT AT THE GIVEN COST BUDGET: FIRST-ORDER CONDITION

Using (2) to express x_2 as a function of x_1, we insert the result into (1a) and find

$$(3a) \qquad X = M\left[Ax_1^{-\rho} + B\left(\frac{C - p_1 x_1}{p_2}\right)^{-\rho}\right]^{-(1/\rho)}$$

Equation (3a) again expresses output X as a function of a single variable, the input x_1. Take the first derivative of X with respect to x_1. The first-order condition for an output maximum is that the derivative equal zero. Let x_2 stand for $(C - p_1 x_1)/p_2$ and write

$$(4a) \qquad \frac{dX}{dx_1} = M(Ax_1^{-\rho} + Bx_2^{-\rho})^{-(1+\rho)/\rho}\left(Ax_1^{-\rho-1} - B\frac{p_1}{p_2}x_2^{-\rho-1}\right) = 0$$

Would setting the expression in the first parentheses of (4a) equal to zero make (4a) zero? For the reasons set out in the analogous case of constant-elasticity-of-substitution *utility* functions, it would not. Therefore we set the expression in the second parentheses of (4a) equal to zero, solve for x_1 and x_2, and obtain

$$(5a) \qquad\qquad\qquad x_1 = H_1 C$$

$$(6a) \qquad\qquad\qquad x_2 = H_2 C$$

where H_1 and H_2 represent, respectively,

$$H_1 = \frac{\left(\dfrac{A}{p_1}\right)^{1/(1+\rho)}}{(Ap_1^{\rho})^{1/(1+\rho)} + (Bp_2^{\rho})^{1/(1+\rho)}}$$

and

$$H_2 = \frac{\left(\dfrac{B}{p_2}\right)^{1/(1+\rho)}}{(Ap_1{}^\rho)^{1/(1+\rho)} + (Bp_2{}^\rho)^{1/(1+\rho)}}$$

9.13   SECOND-ORDER CONDITION

Take the second derivative of output X with respect to input x_1, simplify it by using (4a), again let x_2 stand for $(C - p_1x_1)/p_2$, and write

(7a) $\dfrac{d^2X}{dx_1{}^2} = -(1 + \rho)M(Ax_1{}^{-\rho} + Bx_2{}^{-\rho})^{-(1+\rho)/\rho}$

$$\times \left[Ax_1{}^{-\rho-2} + B\left(\frac{p_1}{p_2}\right)^2 x_2{}^{-\rho-2} \right] < 0$$

Under the assumptions made, (7a) is clearly satisfied for positive values of x_1, x_2, and C. Thus the output materializing when x_1 and x_2 assume the values (5a) and (6a) is a maximum one. Now we divide (5a) by (6a):

(8a) $$\frac{x_1}{x_2} = \left(\frac{A}{B}\frac{p_2}{p_1}\right)^{1/(1+\rho)}$$

and see again that the most efficient proportion in which to apply the two inputs depends solely on production-function parameters and relative prices.

9.14   TOTAL COST

After inserting the input demand functions (5a) and (6a) into the constant-elasticity-of-substitution production function (1a), we obtain

(9e) $$C = QX$$

where Q represents

$$Q = \frac{1}{M}\, [(Ap_1{}^\rho)^{1/(1+\rho)} + (Bp_2{}^\rho)^{1/(1+\rho)}]^{(1+\rho)/\rho}$$

Since the production function was a linearly homogeneous one, it is not surprising to find that total cost is in direct proportion to output.

9.15 MARGINAL AND UNIT COST

By dividing (9e) by X and differentiating it with respect to X, we find unit and marginal cost, respectively.

(9f)
$$\frac{C}{X} = Q$$

(9g)
$$\frac{dC}{dX} = Q$$

Divide (9g) by (9f); then

(9h)
$$\frac{dC}{dX}\frac{X}{C} = 1$$

Thus the cost function has unit elasticity with respect to output. Unit and marginal cost coincide. We have, then, a cost function like the one in Fig. 9.2.

9.16 SHORT RUN AND LONG RUN

In this chapter we have considered all inputs—there were only two of them—to be freely variable, and in that sense our total, marginal, and unit cost curves apply to what the economist calls the long run.

As for the short run, economic theory abounds with U-shaped marginal and unit cost curves. We shall not investigate this, for, at least in the manufacturing industry, there is little empirical evidence for the U-shape. The simple reason is, as Massell [1] puts it, that there may be substitution between capital and labor before the capital is in place, but none afterward. Fortunately there exists an empirically relevant alternative to the U-shaped marginal and unit cost curves, that is, linear programming. A prominent feature of linear programming is the existence of input constraints. Some inputs are available in fixed quantities only. For durable plant and equipment this is the situation in the short run. Linear programming is, therefore, excellently suited for the study of the economist's short run, and we shall devote Chapter 13 to it.

REFERENCE

[1] Massell, B. F., "Investment, Innovation and Growth," *Econometrica*, **30**, 240 (April, 1962).

CHAPTER 10

Cost and Indivisibility

10.1 INTRODUCTION

Indivisibility of durable producers' goods is a consequence of certain technological facts of life. If scaled down below a minimum size, the displacements of a machine may become too small relative to surfaces, and surfaces too small relative to lengths. (If we reduce lengths to one-half, then surfaces will be reduced to one-fourth and displacements to one-eighth.)

Two economies of scale follow from indivisibility of durable producers' goods but are rarely distinguished clearly. To do so is the purpose of this chapter.

10.2 NOTATION

The following notation will be assigned.

Variables

C = cost per annum
S_i = physical capital stock of ith durable producers' good held by firm
x_j = absorption of jth input on current account per annum
X = output produced per annum
$\bar{X}_i$ = capacity of physical capital stock of ith durable producers' good held by firm, measured as potential output per annum

Parameters

a_j = absorption of jth input on current account per unit of output
b_i = capital coefficient of ith durable producers' goods
p_j = price of jth input on current account
r_i = rental per annum of a unit of the ith durable producers' good

10.3 INPUT-OUTPUT PROPORTIONALITY

Assume the jth input on current account to be fully divisible and to be in direct proportion to output; then

(1) $$x_j = a_j X$$

where $X \leq \bar{X}_i$ for any i.

Assume that the physical capital stock of the ith durable producers' good held by the firm S_i is an integer. Like Grosse [3] define the capital coefficient as the physical capital stock per unit of capacity. Or, if preferable, define its reciprocal, the capacity of producers' goods, as potential output per physical unit of capital stock.

(2) $$b_i = \frac{S_i}{\bar{X}_i} \quad \text{or} \quad \frac{1}{b_i} = \frac{\bar{X}_i}{S_i}$$

10.4 ISOQUANTS

Production functions are often illustrated by isoquant maps, therefore we will also illustrate our functions in this fashion. Figure 10.1 corresponds to the assumptions (1) and (2). Because durable producers' goods are indivisible, the holding of them must be represented by an integer; hence the vertical parts of the isoquants in Fig. 10.1 must appear as discrete points. The vertical distance between two adjacent points is always one.

By assumption (1) output rises in direct proportion to input on current account until at some point the straight line $OPQR$ is reached. From then

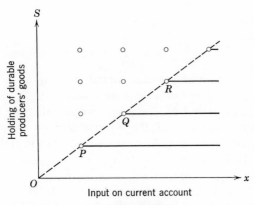

Figure 10.1

on output does not increase at all; hence we shall be following a solid-line isoquant. Everything stated up to now applied to the jth input and the ith durable producers' good. We shall now examine the costs of the firm at large.

10.5 COST

Let the firm absorb m different inputs on current account, hold n different physical capital stocks, and own all capital stocks held. Let the price of the jth input on current account be p_j, and the rental per annum of a unit of the ith durable producers' good be r_i. Rental includes, first, interest representing the cost of money capital to the firm, second, depreciation, and third, repair cost. Define cost per annum as the money value of all input absorbed on current account and rental:

(3) $$C = \sum_{j=1}^{m}(p_j x_j) + \sum_{i=1}^{n}(r_i S_i)$$

where, as we recall, all physical capital stocks S_i were assumed to be integers. Divide (3) by output X, use (1) and (2), and write unit cost as

(4) $$\frac{C}{X} = \sum_{j=1}^{m}(a_j p_j) + \sum_{i=1}^{n}\left(b_i r_i \frac{\overline{X}_i}{X}\right)$$

where $X \leq \overline{X}_i$ for any i.

10.6 THE LAW OF HARMONY

Obviously, unit cost as expressed by (4) is at its minimum if and when

(5) $$\frac{\overline{X}_i}{X} = 1 \qquad \text{for all } i$$

By taking (2) and (5) together, obtain

(5a) $$S_i = \frac{X}{1/b_i}$$

Recalling that we assumed physical capital stock S_i to be an integer, we understand (5a) as stating that to minimize unit cost (4), output X must be a multiple of the capacity $1/b_i$. The lowest output satisfying (5a), then, is the lowest common multiple of all the n capacities $1/b_i$. Outputs equaling any other, and larger, common multiple also satisfy (5a); thus they represent additional unit cost minima.

Imagine, for example, that $m = n = 3$, $r_1 = r_2 = r_3 = 1$, $1/b_1 = 3$, $1/b_2 = 4$, $1/b_3 = 6$, and that $a_1 p_1 + a_2 p_2 + a_3 p_3 = 1$. Then the unit cost curve corresponding to (4) will look like the curve in Fig. 10.2. Here outputs

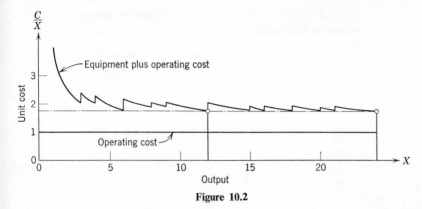

Figure 10.2

12, 24, . . . are the common multiples of the capacities 3, 4, and 6; hence they satisfy (5a) and minimize unit cost. Jantzen [4] called this the Law of Harmony and called the outputs 12, 24, . . . "harmonious" outputs. At all other outputs there would be idling losses. The probability that the output of a large firm will be harmonious is no greater than the chance that the output of a small firm will be. However, since the hyperbolas become flatter for larger outputs, the large firm suffers less by the lack of harmony than does a small firm. In this sense the Law of Harmony is an important economy of scale.

10.7 THE LAW OF TECHNIQUE

Until now we have considered quantitative variations of input and capital stock within the same process. Often, however, it is possible to consider alternative processes. For each process a unit cost curve like that of Fig. 10.2 may be traced. Figure 10.3 indicates this for the three alternative processes

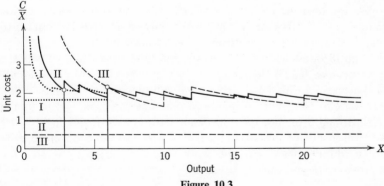

Figure 10.3

Table 10.1 The Characteristics of the Three Processes Shown in Figure 10.3

	Process I	Process II	Process III
r_1	0.2	1.0	5.0
r_2	0.5	1.0	5.0
r_3	–	1.0	–
$1/b_1$	2	3	10
$1/b_2$	3	4	12
$1/b_3$	–	6	–
$\sum_{j=1}^{m}(a_j p_j)$	1.75	1.0	0.5

whose characteristics are shown in Table 10.1. Process II is the same as before, but Processes I and III are new. Process I is what Jantzen [4] called a "low" technique characterized by low-capacity low-rental durable producers' goods and high labor input. Process III Jantzen called a "high" technique characterized by high-capacity high-rental durable producers' goods and low labor input. Jantzen called a diagram like Fig. 10.3 the Law of Technique, and this law expresses another economy of scale, clearly distinct from the Law of Harmony.

10.8   THE LAW OF TECHNIQUE: EXAMPLES

Bressler [1] set up rough designs for six hypothetical milk-pasteurizing plants and plotted the cost curve shown in Fig. 10.4, bearing out Jantzen's Law of Technique. Investment per quart of capacity declines because plant area does not increase as rapidly as capacity, and because construction costs per square foot decrease with floor area. Moreover, hand-operated bottle fillers were specified for the three smallest plants, automatic fillers for the three largest ones. Refrigeration compressors ranged in capacity from 0.5 to 4.5 tons, whereas boilers ranged from 3.5 to 25 horsepower.

Richmond [8] compared the current subsonic intercontinental jet with the future supersonic jet. A hypothetical smaller, but currently profitable, Central European airline now needing two subsonic jets to fly eight round trips per week to New York would need only one supersonic jet to fly the same eight round trips. But one supersonic jet thus used for 45 flight hours per week will cost twice as much as the two subsonic jets taken together, each currently used for 60 flight hours per week. And with only one aircraft, "the airline probably cannot operate dependably and it certainly cannot operate profitably."

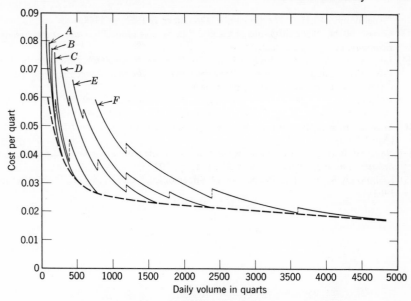

Figure 10.4

According to *The Economist* [2], the level at which economies of scale cease to accrue in the British automobile industry has been set variously at 50,000 to 100,000 cars per annum by the British manufacturers' advisory council.

10.9 CONCLUSIONS

The merits of the Jantzen model are twofold. First, it emphasized very early the absence of substitution between labor and capital within a process and the presence of substitution among processes, as stressed much later by linear programming and some modern contributions by Johansen [5] and Massell [6].

Second, Jantzen assumed the marginal cost curve within a process to be horizontal right up to capacity. Without being logically necessary for his laws, this assumption greatly simplifies them and in addition is often realistic. Twenty years after Jantzen, the Committee on Price Determination of the National Bureau of Economic Research [7] concluded that a "smooth U-shaped curve reflects a bias in economic theory."

REFERENCES

[1] Bressler, R. G., Jr., *City Milk Distribution*, Cambridge, Massachusetts, 1952, pp. 177–227.

90   Firm Equilibrium

[2] "Austin and Morris," *The Economist*, December 1, 1951, p. 1348.
[3] Grosse, R. N., "The Structure of Capital," in *Studies in the Structure of the American Economy*, edited by Leontief, New York, 1953, pp. 185–242.
[4] Jantzen, I., "Voxende Udbytte i Industrien," *Nationalökonomisk Tidsskrift*, 1924, **62**, 1–62. (Translated in I. Jantzen, *Basic Principles of Business Economics and National Calculation*, Copenhagen, 1939, pp. 1–58.)
[5] Johansen, L., "Substitution versus Fixed Production Coefficients in the Theory of Economic Growth: A Synthesis," *Econometrica*, **27**, 157–176 (April 1959).
[6] Massell, B. F., "Investment, Innovation, and Growth," *Econometrica*, **30**, 239–252 (April 1962).
[7] National Bureau of Economic Research, Committee on Price Determination, *Cost Behavior and Price Policy*, New York, 1943, p. 109.
[8] Richmond, S. B., "The Economics of Supersonics," *Challenge*, **12**, 11–15 (October 1963).

CHAPTER 11

Optimum Output

11.1 INTRODUCTION

Firms produce and sell outputs, purchase and absorb inputs, and invest for the future. Much of this activity is ignored by the traditional theory of the firm, and there is nothing wrong in such neglect. If we are merely interested in the determination of optimal output, we may use the cost function just derived from a production function, define profits as revenue *minus* cost, and find the level of output which maximizes profits. We will do that, assuming that the firm's output does affect the price at which output is sold.

11.2 NOTATION

In a theory of the firm the following notation will be assigned.

Variables

C = cost per annum
P = price of output
R = revenue from output sold per annum
X = output produced and sold per annum
Z = profit per annum

Parameters

α = elasticity of output with respect to first input
β = elasticity of output with respect to second input
η = price elasticity of demand faced by firm
M = a multiplicative factor in the production function
N = a multiplicative factor in the demand function
p_j = price of jth input, $j = 1, 2$

11.3 THE MODEL

Define profits as revenue *minus* cost.

(1) $$Z = R - C$$

Define revenue as price of output *times* output sold.

(2) $$R = PX$$

Suppose that the firm is facing a demand curve of the constant-elasticity type

(3) $$X = NP^\eta$$

where $\eta < 0$ and $N > 0$. The demand function (3) is adopted with these two restrictions: $P > 0$ and $X > 0$. Let the firm's cost function be Eq. (9a) found in Chapter 9.

(4) $$C = (\alpha + \beta)\left[\frac{1}{M}\left(\frac{p_1}{\alpha}\right)^\alpha\left(\frac{p_2}{\beta}\right)^\beta\right]^{1/(\alpha+\beta)} X^{1/(\alpha+\beta)}$$

11.4 SOLUTION

Inserting (2), (3), and (4) into (1), we may express profits as

(5) $$Z = \left(\frac{1}{N}\right)^{1/\eta} X^{(1+\eta)/\eta} - (\alpha + \beta)\left[\frac{1}{M}\left(\frac{p_1}{\alpha}\right)^\alpha\left(\frac{p_2}{\beta}\right)^\beta\right]^{1/(\alpha+\beta)} X^{1/(\alpha+\beta)}$$

Take the first derivative of profits with respect to output and set it equal to zero; thus

(6) $$\frac{dZ}{dX} = \frac{1+\eta}{\eta}\left(\frac{1}{N}\right)^{1/\eta} X^{1/\eta} - \left[\frac{1}{M}\left(\frac{p_1}{\alpha}\right)^\alpha\left(\frac{p_2}{\beta}\right)^\beta\right]^{1/(\alpha+\beta)} X^{1/(\alpha+\beta)-1} = 0$$

Solve (6) for output X; then

(7) $$X = \left[\left(\frac{1+\eta}{\eta}\right)^{\alpha+\beta}\left(\frac{1}{N}\right)^{(\alpha+\beta)/\eta} M\left(\frac{\alpha}{p_1}\right)^\alpha\left(\frac{\beta}{p_2}\right)^\beta\right]^{1/[1-(\alpha+\beta)(1+\eta)/\eta]}$$

Since the multiplicative factors M and N, the elasticities α and β, and the input prices p_1 and p_2 were assumed to be positive, the base of (7) will be positive as long as $(1 + \eta)/\eta$ is positive.

If, in the exponent of (7), $1 - (\alpha + \beta)(1 + \eta)/\eta = 0$, that exponent assumes the meaningless form of one divided by zero. If, on the other hand,

$1 - (\alpha + \beta)(1 + \eta)/\eta \gtrless 0$, the exponent is meaningful, and output X will be positive as long as $(1 + \eta)/\eta$ is positive. However, as we shall now see, there will be no profit maximum unless the exponent is positive.

The second-order condition for a profit maximum is that the second derivative of profits with respect to output be negative. Take that second derivative, simplify it by using (6), and write it as

$$(8) \quad \frac{d^2Z}{dX^2} = - \frac{1 - (\alpha + \beta)(1 + \eta)/\eta}{\alpha + \beta} \left[\frac{1}{M}\left(\frac{p_1}{\alpha}\right)^\alpha \left(\frac{p_2}{\beta}\right)^\beta \right]^{1/(\alpha+\beta)} X^{1/(\alpha+\beta)-2} < 0$$

Will (8) be satisfied?

Marshall [3] assumed pure competition, which is defined as η falling without bounds. Then $(1 + \eta)/\eta$ approaches one, output as determined by (7) will be positive, and (8) will be satisfied as long as $\alpha + \beta < 1$. Equation (8) will not be satisfied if $\alpha + \beta \geq 1$; hence, assuming pure competition, only decreasing returns to scale are compatible with a profit maximum. Unwilling to surrender his assumption of pure competition, Marshall [3] went to great lengths to demonstrate the existence of such decreasing returns to scale within the firm. Thinking solely of proprietorships or family corporations, Marshall explained that whatever bounds exist to firm size, growth toward them must always be slow, and alas, after three generations the entrepreneurial spirit will have spent itself: The founder's grandson turns to the fine arts. Or Marshall explained that whatever increasing returns to scale exist are external to the firm; hence they influence industry size but not firm size.

Zeuthen [6], Chamberlin [1], Robinson [4], and Stackelberg [5] took a cue from Cournot [2] and surrendered the assumption of pure competition; hence they found constant and increasing returns to scale fully compatible with a profit maximum. As long as the demand faced by the firm is elastic, that is, $\eta < -1$, then $(1 + \eta)/\eta$ is positive, output determined by (7) is positive, and (8) will be satisfied as long as $1 - (\alpha + \beta)(1 + \eta)/\eta > 0$. The less pure competition is, the farther $(1 + \eta)/\eta$ will fall short of one, and the more room there will be for increasing returns to scale. However, demand must remain elastic, for when $\eta \geq -1$ the second-order condition (8) will no longer be satisfied, because output determined by (7) will have become nonpositive.

REFERENCES

[1] Chamberlin, E. H., *The Theory of Monopolistic Competition*, Cambridge, Massachusetts, 1933.
[2] Cournot, A., *Recherches sur les principes mathématiques de la théorie des richesses*, Paris, 1838.

[3] Marshall, A., *Principles of Economics*, London, 1890.
[4] Robinson, J., *The Economics of Imperfect Competition*, London, 1933.
[5] Von Stackelberg, H., *Marktform und Gleichgewicht*, Vienna and Berlin, 1934.
[6] Zeuthen, F., "Mellem Konkurrence og Monopol," *Nationalökonomisk Tidsskrift*, **67**, 265–305, 1929. (Expanded into *Problems of Monopoly and Economic Warfare*, London, 1930.)

CHAPTER 12

Optimum Input and Output: Neoclassical Model

12.1 INTRODUCTION

Instead of taking the detour via a cost curve, why not determine directly and simultaneously optimal input and optimal output? The purpose of this chapter is to do just that by considering a one-product firm whose output does affect the price at which output is sold but whose inputs do not affect the prices at which inputs are purchased.

12.2 THE GENERAL CASE

In a theory of the firm the following notation will be assigned.

Variables

C = cost per annum
P = price of output
R = revenue from output sold per annum
S_i = physical capital stock of ith durable producers' good held by firm
x_j = absorption of jth input on current account per annum
X = output produced and sold per annum
Z = profit per annum

Parameters

α_j = elasticity of output with respect to x_j
β_i = elasticity of output with respect to S_i
η = price elasticity of demand faced by firm

M = a multiplicative factor in the production function
N = a multiplicative factor in the demand function
p_j = price of jth input on current account
r_i = rental per annum of a unit of the ith durable producers' good

Define profits as revenue *minus* cost:

(1) $$Z = R - C$$

Define revenue as price of output *times* output sold:

(2) $$R = PX$$

Suppose that the individual firm is facing a demand curve:

(3) $$P = P(X)$$

Moreover, let that firm be facing the production function

(4) $$X = X(x_1, \ldots, x_m, S_1, \ldots, S_n)$$

Thus the firm absorbs m different inputs on current account and holds n different physical capital stocks. Let the firm own all capital stocks held. Let the price of the jth input on current account be p_j, and the annual rental of a unit of the ith durable producers' good be r_i. Rental includes first, interest representing the cost of money capital to the firm, second, depreciation, and third, repair cost. Define cost per annum as the money value of all input absorbed on current account and rental:

(5) $$C = \sum_{j=1}^{m} (p_j x_j) + \sum_{i=1}^{n} (r_i S_i)$$

Inserting (2) through (5) into (1) and recalling that

$$\frac{\partial P}{\partial x_h} = \frac{dP}{dX} \frac{\partial X}{\partial x_h} \quad \text{and} \quad \frac{\partial P}{\partial S_g} = \frac{dP}{dX} \frac{\partial X}{\partial S_g}$$

vary the hth input on current account and the gth capital stock and take first partial derivatives of Z with respect to x_h and S_g. The first-order condition for an unconstrained profit maximum is that all such first partial derivatives be zero.

(6) $$\frac{\partial Z}{\partial x_h} = \left(P + X \frac{dP}{dX} \right) \frac{\partial X}{\partial x_h} - p_h = 0 \qquad (h = 1, \ldots, m)$$

(7) $$\frac{\partial Z}{\partial S_g} = \left(P + X \frac{dP}{dX} \right) \frac{\partial X}{\partial S_g} - r_g = 0 \qquad (g = 1, \ldots, n)$$

Thus we see that the derivative of profit with respect to input or capital stock is equal to marginal revenue *times* physical marginal productivity *minus* price or rental. If we rearrange (6) and (7), we obtain the following familiar results.

$$(8) \qquad p_h = \left(P + X \frac{dP}{dX} \right) \frac{\partial X}{\partial x_h} \qquad (h = 1, \ldots, m)$$

$$(9) \qquad r_g = \left(P + X \frac{dP}{dX} \right) \frac{\partial X}{\partial S_g} \qquad (g = 1, \ldots, n)$$

Thus input or capital stock should be hired up to the point where its price or rental equals its marginal revenue productivity. There is also another way of writing (6) and (7), which produces still other familiar results.

$$(10) \qquad P + X \frac{dP}{dX} = \frac{p_h}{\partial X/\partial x_h} \qquad (h = 1, \ldots, m)$$

$$(11) \qquad P + X \frac{dP}{dX} = \frac{r_g}{\partial X/\partial S_g} \qquad (g = 1, \ldots, n)$$

Thus we may also state that by hiring the hth input or the gth capital stock, output should be carried to the point where marginal revenue equals marginal cost. Marginal cost, as we know, equals the input price or the capital stock rental divided by the marginal productivity of the input or the capital stock, respectively.

Consisting of $m + n$ simultaneous equations, one for each input or capital stock, the system (6) and (7) answers the question: How far should each particular input and capital stock be hired?

The second-order conditions are as follows: Form the Hessian $(m + n)$-order determinant of the second derivatives, shown in Table 12.1. Next,

Table 12.1 The Hessian Determinant of the Second Partial Derivatives

$$H = \begin{vmatrix} \dfrac{\partial^2 Z}{\partial x_1{}^2} & \cdots & \dfrac{\partial^2 Z}{\partial x_1\, \partial x_m} & \dfrac{\partial^2 Z}{\partial x_1\, \partial S_1} & \cdots & \dfrac{\partial^2 Z}{\partial x_1\, \partial S_n} \\[2ex] \cdots & & \cdots & \cdots & & \cdots \\[2ex] \dfrac{\partial^2 Z}{\partial x_m\, \partial x_1} & \cdots & \dfrac{\partial^2 Z}{\partial x_m{}^2} & \dfrac{\partial^2 Z}{\partial x_m\, \partial S_1} & \cdots & \dfrac{\partial^2 Z}{\partial x_m\, \partial S_n} \\[2ex] \dfrac{\partial^2 Z}{\partial S_1\, \partial x_1} & \cdots & \dfrac{\partial^2 Z}{\partial S_1\, \partial x_m} & \dfrac{\partial^2 Z}{\partial S_1{}^2} & \cdots & \dfrac{\partial^2 Z}{\partial S_1\, \partial S_n} \\[2ex] \cdots & & \cdots & \cdots & & \cdots \\[2ex] \dfrac{\partial^2 Z}{\partial S_n\, \partial x_1} & \cdots & \dfrac{\partial^2 Z}{\partial S_n\, \partial x_m} & \dfrac{\partial^2 Z}{\partial S_n\, \partial S_1} & \cdots & \dfrac{\partial^2 Z}{\partial S_n{}^2} \end{vmatrix}$$

form principal minors of H. The principal minor formed by deleting the last $m + n - 1$ rows and columns of H must be negative. The principal minor formed by deleting the last $m + n - 2$ rows and columns of H must be positive, etc., the principal minors alternating in sign. When we finally delete no rows and columns, H itself will be positive if $m + n$ is even, negative if $m + n$ is odd. The time has now come to make more specific assumptions.

12.3 A PARTICULAR CASE

Specify the constant-elasticity demand function

(3a) $X = NP^\eta$

where $\eta < -1$ and $N > 0$. The demand function (3a) is adopted with these two restrictions: $P > 0$ and $X > 0$. Furthermore, specify the generalized Cobb-Douglas production function

(4a) $X = M x_1^{\alpha_1} \cdots x_m^{\alpha_m} S_1^{\beta_1} \cdots S_n^{\beta_n}$

where $0 < \alpha_h < 1$, $0 < \beta_g < 1$, and $M > 0$. The production function (4a) is adopted with these $m + n + 1$ restrictions: $x_h \geq 0$, $S_g \geq 0$, and $X \geq 0$, where $h = 1, \ldots, m$ and $g = 1, \ldots, n$. The assumptions about the elasticities α_h and β_g guarantee positive and diminishing marginal productivity of any input. The sum of the elasticities is not assumed to equal one; hence increasing, constant, or diminishing returns to scale may exist.

We can now rewrite (8) and (9) as

(8a) $\dfrac{x_1^{A_1} x_2^{A_2} \cdots x_m^{A_m} S_1^{B_1} S_2^{B_2} \cdots S_n^{B_n}}{x_h} = K_h \qquad (h = 1, \ldots, m)$

and

(9a) $\dfrac{x_1^{A_1} x_2^{A_2} \cdots x_m^{A_m} S_1^{B_1} S_2^{B_2} \cdots S_n^{B_n}}{S_g} = L_g \qquad (g = 1, \ldots, n)$

where A_h, B_g, K_h, and L_g stand for the agglomerations of parameters defined in Table 12.2. Now let us write out the entire system (8a) and (9a) in its logarithmic form:

$$
(A_1 - 1) \log x_1 + A_2 \log x_2 + \cdots + A_m \log x_m
$$
$$
+ B_1 \log S_1 + \cdots + B_n \log S_n = \log K_1
$$

$$
A_1 \log x_1 + (A_2 - 1) \log x_2 + \cdots + A_m \log x_m
$$
(12)
$$
+ B_1 \log S_1 + \cdots + B_n \log S_n = \log K_2
$$

$$
\cdots\cdots\cdots\cdots\cdots\cdots\cdots\cdots\cdots\cdots\cdots\cdots\cdots\cdots
$$

$$
A_1 \log x_1 + A_2 \log x_2 + \cdots + A_m \log x_m
$$
$$
+ B_1 \log S_1 + \cdots + (B_n - 1) \log S_n = \log L_n
$$

Table 12.2 Agglomerations of Parameters

$$A_h = \alpha_h \frac{1 + \eta}{\eta} \qquad (h = 1, \ldots, m)$$

$$B_g = \beta_g \frac{1 + \eta}{\eta} \qquad (g = 1, \ldots, n)$$

$$K_h = \frac{p_h \eta/(1 + \eta)}{\alpha_h M^{(1+\eta)/\eta} N^{-1/\eta}} \qquad (h = 1, \ldots, m)$$

$$L_g = \frac{r_g \eta/(1 + \eta)}{\beta_g M^{(1+\eta)/\eta} N^{-1/\eta}} \qquad (g = 1, \ldots, n)$$

In this form the system (12) is a neat linear system of $m + n$ simultaneous equations in the $m + n$ unknowns $\log x_1, \ldots, \log x_m, \log S_1, \ldots, \log S_n$. Appendix I finds the very tidy solutions to it:

$$(13) \quad \log x_h = \frac{\begin{array}{c} -A_1 \log K_1 - \cdots - A_m \log K_m - B_1 \log L_1 - \cdots \\ - B_n \log L_n + (A_1 + \cdots + B_n - 1) \log K_h \end{array}}{1 - (A_1 + \cdots + A_m + B_1 + \cdots + B_n)}$$

$$(14) \quad \log S_g = \frac{\begin{array}{c} -A_1 \log K_1 - \cdots - A_m \log K_m - B_1 \log L_1 - \cdots \\ - B_n \log L_n + (A_1 + \cdots + B_n - 1) \log L_g \end{array}}{1 - (A_1 + \cdots + A_m + B_1 + \cdots + B_n)}$$

Finally, take the antilogarithm, rearrange, use Table 12.2, and obtain the solutions

$$(15) \qquad\qquad x_h = \frac{\alpha_h}{p_h} Q^q$$

and

$$(16) \qquad\qquad S_g = \frac{\beta_g}{r_g} Q^q$$

where the base Q and the exponent q represent, respectively,

$$Q = \frac{1 + \eta}{\eta} \left(\frac{1}{N}\right)^{1/\eta} \left[M \left(\frac{\alpha_1}{p_1}\right)^{\alpha_1} \cdots \left(\frac{\alpha_m}{p_m}\right)^{\alpha_m} \left(\frac{\beta_1}{r_1}\right)^{\beta_1} \cdots \left(\frac{\beta_n}{r_n}\right)^{\beta_n} \right]^{(1+\eta)/\eta}$$

and

$$q = \frac{1}{1 - (\alpha_1 + \cdots + \alpha_m + \beta_1 + \cdots + \beta_n)(1 + \eta)/\eta}$$

Since the multiplicative factors M and N, the coefficient $(1 + \eta)/\eta$, the elasticities α_h and β_g, the input prices p_h, and the rentals r_g were assumed to be positive, the base Q will be positive.

If in the exponent q, $1 - (\alpha_1 + \cdots + \alpha_m + \beta_1 + \cdots + \beta_n)(1 + \eta)/\eta = 0$, that exponent assumes the meaningless form of one divided by zero. If, on the other hand, $1 - (\alpha_1 + \cdots + \alpha_m + \beta_1 + \cdots + \beta_n)(1 + \eta)/\eta \gtrless 0$, the exponent q is meaningful, and input x_h and capital stock S_g will be positive. However as we shall now see, there will be no profit maximum unless the exponent q is positive.

Are the second-order conditions for a profit maximum satisfied by (15) and (16)? Table 12.3 shows the second-order partial derivatives needed for an evaluation of the Hessian determinant H shown in Table 12.1, and Appendix II shows how to arrive at those derivatives. Appendix III proves that the signs of the principal minors formed from the Hessian determinant H will indeed alternate as required if and only if $1 - (\alpha_1 + \cdots + \alpha_m + \beta_1 + \cdots + \beta_n)(1 + \eta)/\eta > 0$. What is the economic content of this requirement? Under pure competition $(1 + \eta)/\eta$ approaches one, so the requirement collapses into $1 - (\alpha_1 + \cdots + \alpha_m + \beta_1 + \cdots + \beta_n) > 0$, that is, decreasing returns to scale. However, the less pure competition is the more $(1 + \eta)/\eta$ falls short of one, and the more room there will be for increasing returns to scale. This economic content is what we found in Chapter 11.

Equations (15) and (16) express the variables x_h and S_g in terms of parameters alone. How elastic is the input x_h or the capital stock S_g with

Table 12.3 Second Partial Derivatives to Be Used in Hessian Determinant

$$\frac{\partial^2 Z}{\partial x_f\, \partial x_h} = p_h \frac{1 + \eta}{\eta} \frac{\alpha_f}{x_f}$$

$$\frac{\partial^2 Z}{\partial S_g\, \partial x_h} = p_h \frac{1 + \eta}{\eta} \frac{\beta_g}{S_g}$$

$$\frac{\partial^2 Z}{\partial x_h{}^2} = p_h \frac{\alpha_h(1 + \eta)/\eta - 1}{x_h}$$

$$\frac{\partial^2 Z}{\partial S_e\, \partial S_g} = r_g \frac{1 + \eta}{\eta} \frac{\beta_e}{S_e}$$

$$\frac{\partial^2 Z}{\partial x_h\, \partial S_g} = r_g \frac{1 + \eta}{\eta} \frac{\alpha_h}{x_h}$$

$$\frac{\partial^2 Z}{\partial S_g{}^2} = r_g \frac{\beta_g(1 + \eta)/\eta - 1}{S_g}$$

respect to the price p_h or the rental r_g respectively? The answer is seen most easily from the logarithmic forms (13) and (14). Simply take the derivatives with respect to $\log K_h$ and $\log L_g$.

$$(17) \quad \frac{\partial \log x_h}{\partial \log K_h} = -\left[1 + \frac{\alpha_h}{\eta/(1 + \eta) - (\alpha_1 + \cdots + \alpha_m + \beta_1 + \cdots + \beta_n)}\right]$$

$$(18) \quad \frac{\partial \log S_g}{\partial \log L_g} = -\left[1 + \frac{\beta_g}{\eta/(1 + \eta) - (\alpha_1 + \cdots + \alpha_m + \beta_1 + \cdots + \beta_n)}\right]$$

But what are K_h and L_g? According to Table 12.2, the ratios p_h/α_h and r_g/β_g appear in K_h and L_g, respectively, as coefficients multiplied by parameters. Hence the elasticities (17) and (18) *are* merely the elasticities of x_h and S_g with respect to p_h and r_g, respectively. Under conditions necessary for a profit maximum those elasticities are negative and less than *minus* one—just like the price elasticity of the demand for output.

APPENDIX I HOW TO FIND THE SOLUTIONS OF THE SYSTEM (12)

Between x, α, and p on the one hand, and S, β, and r on the other, there is no mathematical difference; hence let us suppress S, β, and r, use Cramer's rule, and write the solution for $A_1 \log x_1$ of the system (12).

$$A_1 \log x_1 = \begin{vmatrix} \log K_1 & 1 & \cdots & 1 \\ \log K_2 & \dfrac{A_2 - 1}{A_2} & \cdots & 1 \\ \cdots\cdots\cdots\cdots\cdots\cdots\cdots\cdots \\ \log K_m & 1 & \cdots & \dfrac{A_m - 1}{A_m} \\ \hline \dfrac{A_1 - 1}{A_1} & 1 & \cdots & 1 \\ 1 & \dfrac{A_2 - 1}{A_2} & \cdots & 1 \\ \cdots\cdots\cdots\cdots\cdots\cdots\cdots\cdots \\ 1 & 1 & \cdots & \dfrac{A_m - 1}{A_m} \end{vmatrix}$$

In both determinants, that of the numerator as well as that of the denominator, multiply the ith column by A_i, $i = 1, \ldots, m$ and subtract the first row from all other rows.

$$A_1 \log x_1 = \frac{\begin{vmatrix} A_1 \log K_1 & A_2 & \cdots & A_m \\ A_1(\log K_2 - \log K_1) & -1 & \cdots & 0 \\ \cdots\cdots\cdots\cdots\cdots\cdots\cdots & & & \\ A_1(\log K_m - \log K_1) & 0 & \cdots & -1 \end{vmatrix}}{\begin{vmatrix} A_1 - 1 & A_2 & \cdots & A_m \\ 1 & -1 & \cdots & 0 \\ \cdots\cdots\cdots\cdots\cdots\cdots\cdots & & & \\ 1 & 0 & \cdots & -1 \end{vmatrix}}$$

In both determinants add A_i times the ith row, $i = 2, \ldots, m$, to their first rows. Then the first element of the first row of the numerator becomes $A_1[\log K_1 + A_2(\log K_2 - \log K_1) + \cdots + A_m(\log K_m - \log K_1)]$, and all other elements of that row become zero. In the denominator, the first element of the first row becomes $A_1 + A_2 + \cdots + A_m - 1$, and all other elements of that row become zero. Hence, dividing away $(-1)^{m-1}$ in numerator and denominator alike, we have

$$\log x_1 = \frac{(A_2 + A_3 + \cdots + A_m - 1) \log K_1 - A_2 \log K_2 - A_3 \log K_3 - \cdots - A_m \log K_m}{1 - (A_1 + A_2 + \cdots + A_m)}$$

In the numerator add and subtract $A_1 \log K_1$, allow for the suppressed S, β, and r, repeat the procedure for $\log x_2$, $\log x_3$, etc., and we obtain the forms (13) and (14).

APPENDIX II HOW TO ARRIVE AT THE DERIVATIVES IN TABLE 12.3

To find the top derivative in Table 12.3, insert the specific demand function (3a) and the specific production function (4a) into (6):

(6a) $$\frac{\partial Z}{\partial x_h} = \frac{\alpha_h}{x_h} N^{-(1/\eta)} \frac{1 + \eta}{\eta} X^{(1+\eta)/\eta} - p_h = 0 \qquad (h = 1, \ldots, m)$$

Differentiate (6a) with respect to x_f and get

$$\frac{\partial^2 Z}{\partial x_f \, \partial x_h} = \frac{\alpha_f}{x_f} \frac{\alpha_h}{x_h} N^{-(1/\eta)} \left(\frac{1 + \eta}{\eta}\right)^2 X^{(1+\eta)/\eta}$$

By utilizing the right-hand half of (6a),

$$\frac{\partial^2 Z}{\partial x_f \, \partial x_h} = \frac{\alpha_f}{x_f} \frac{1 + \eta}{\eta} p_h$$

To find the third derivative in Table 12.3, differentiate (6a) with respect to x_h and get

$$\frac{\partial^2 Z}{\partial x_h{}^2} = \frac{\alpha_h}{x_h} N^{-(1/\eta)} \frac{1 + \eta}{\eta} X^{(1+\eta)/\eta} \frac{\alpha_h(1 + \eta)/\eta - 1}{x_h}$$

By utilizing the right-hand half of (6a),

$$\frac{\partial^2 Z}{\partial x_h{}^2} = p_h \frac{\alpha_h(1 + \eta)/\eta - 1}{x_h}$$

The remaining four derivatives in Table 12.3 are determined similarly.

APPENDIX III PROOF THAT SIGNS OF PRINCIPAL MINORS DO ALTERNATE

As in Appendix I, let us ignore S, β, and r. By using Tables 12.1, 12.2, and 12.3, we may write the m-order Hessian:

$$H = \begin{vmatrix} p_1 \dfrac{A_1 - 1}{x_1} & p_2 \dfrac{A_1}{x_1} & \cdots & p_m \dfrac{A_1}{x_1} \\[2ex] p_1 \dfrac{A_2}{x_2} & p_2 \dfrac{A_2 - 1}{x_2} & \cdots & p_m \dfrac{A_2}{x_2} \\[2ex] \cdots\cdots\cdots\cdots\cdots\cdots\cdots\cdots \\[1ex] p_1 \dfrac{A_m}{x_m} & p_2 \dfrac{A_m}{x_m} & \cdots & p_m \dfrac{A_m - 1}{x_m} \end{vmatrix}$$

First, divide the ith column by p_i; second, multiply the ith row by x_i ($i = 1, \ldots, m$ throughout); third, subtract the first column from all other columns. The Hessian may then be written as

$$H = \frac{p_1 p_2 \cdots p_m}{x_1 x_2 \cdots x_m} \begin{vmatrix} A_1 - 1 & 1 & \cdots & 1 \\ A_2 & -1 & \cdots & 0 \\ \cdots\cdots\cdots\cdots\cdots\cdots \\ A_m & 0 & \cdots & -1 \end{vmatrix}$$

In this determinant add the ith row, $i = 2, \ldots, m$, to the first row. Then the first element of the first row becomes $A_1 + A_2 + \cdots + A_m - 1$, and all other elements of that row become zero; hence

$$H = (-1)^m \frac{p_1 p_2 \cdots p_m}{x_1 x_2 \cdots x_m} [1 - (A_1 + A_2 + \cdots + A_m)]$$

If the expression in brackets is positive, the right-hand side always has the same sign as $(-1)^m$, because input prices $p_1, \ldots, p_m$ have been assumed to be positive, and because the variables $x_1, \ldots, x_m$ have been found to be positive. Hence for $m = 1$ the principal minor is negative, for $m = 2$ it is positive, etc. Thus all conditions for a profit maximum are satisfied.

However, if the expression in the brackets is not positive, they will not be satisfied. After restoring S, β, and r and using Table 12.2, we conclude that the signs of the principal minors will alternate as required if and only if

$$1 - \frac{1 + \eta}{\eta} (\alpha_1 + \cdots + \alpha_m + \beta_1 + \cdots + \beta_n) > 0$$

CHAPTER 13

Optimum Input and Output: Linear Programming

13.1 INTRODUCTION

We now proceed to make use of the practically important case of technologically fixed input proportions, discussed in Sections 8.9, 8.10, and 8.11. Therefore consider a one-product firm whose output does not affect the price at which output is sold and whose input does not affect the price at which inputs are purchased. Suppose there is a choice among n different processes. A process is defined as a production program within which every input is in direct proportion to output. Let the firm absorb m different inputs. In any of the n processes, one or more of the m inputs may be zero.

13.2 THE MODEL

In a linear-programming theory of the firm the following notation will be assigned.

Variables

C = cost per annum
R = revenue from output sold per annum
x_{ij} = absorption of ith input in jth process per annum
X = output produced and sold per annum
z = profit per unit of output sold
Z = profit per annum

Parameters

a_{ij} = absorption of ith input in jth process per unit of output
p = price of input
P = price of output

Define profits as revenue minus cost:

(1) $$Z_j = R_j - C_j   (j = 1, \ldots, n)$$

Define revenue as price of output times output sold:

(2) $$R_j = PX_j   (j = 1, \ldots, n)$$

Within any process, every input is in direct proportion to output:

(3) $$x_{ij} = a_{ij}X_j   (i = 1, \ldots, m; j = 1, \ldots, n)$$

Define cost as the money value of all input:

(4) $$C_j = \sum_{i=1}^{m} (p_i x_{ij})   (i = 1, \ldots, m; j = 1, \ldots, n)$$

Define the profit margin as profit per unit of output sold:

(5) $$Z_j = z_j X_j   (j = 1, \ldots, n)$$

By inserting (1) through (4) into (5), we find that

(5a) $$z_j = P - \sum_{i=1}^{m} (p_i a_{ij})   (i = 1, \ldots, m; j = 1, \ldots, n)$$

For the firm as a whole, profits are defined as the sum total of the profits made within each process:

(6) $$Z = \sum_{j=1}^{n} Z_j$$

Equation (5) permits us to write firm profits as

(6a) $$Z = \sum_{j=1}^{n} (z_j X_j)$$

Thus total profits can be thought of as the total of weighted profit margins of all processes, the weights being the outputs within the respective processes.

13.3 OUTPUT CONSTRAINT BUT NO INPUT CONSTRAINTS

Assume that for some reason the firm is limited to selling the quantity X. Hence the sum of the outputs of all processes must add up to X:

(7) $$X = \sum_{j=1}^{n} X_j$$

Let no other constraints be imposed upon the firm. Specifically, the firm may buy as large quantities as it needs of its inputs at the current prices of inputs. Assume that one of the processes, say the jth process, carries a positive and higher profit margin z_j than any of the remaining $n - 1$ processes. Obviously, the firm maximizes its profits by concentrating all its output in the jth process, setting $X = X_j$ and setting all other X's equal to zero. If two or more processes carry identical, positive, and higher profit margins than any of the remaining processes, the firm will concentrate all its output in those higher-margin processes but will be indifferent to the specific allocation of output within them.

13.4   INPUT CONSTRAINTS BUT NO OUTPUT CONSTRAINT

Suppose there is no constraint on output, but let f out of the m inputs be available in fixed quantities only. For durable plant and equipment this is true in the short run. Let the fixed quantity of the ith input be the parameter x_i, $i = 1, \ldots, f$. The total quantity of the ith input absorbed in all processes must be smaller than or equal to x_i; thus

(8)

$$a_{11}X_1 + a_{12}X_2 + \cdots + a_{1n}X_n \leq x_1$$
$$a_{21}X_1 + a_{22}X_2 + \cdots + a_{2n}X_n \leq x_2$$
$$\cdots\cdots\cdots\cdots\cdots\cdots\cdots\cdots\cdots\cdots\cdots$$
$$a_{f1}X_1 + a_{f2}X_2 + \cdots + a_{fn}X_n \leq x_f$$

In (8) all outputs must be nonnegative. It would now be desirable to transform the system (8) into a system of equations, for equations are easier to handle than inequalities. The introduction of disposal processes will make such a transformation possible.

13.5   DISPOSAL PROCESSES

Let $x_{i(n+i)}$ be the difference between ith input absorbed [on the left-hand side of system (8)] and the fixed quantity available of the input [on the right-hand side of system (8)]. Then $x_{i(n+i)}$ may be disposed of in a new so-called disposal process. In contrast let us call the first n processes active ones. An active process has output as well as input, and its level is measured by its output. A disposal process has one input and no output, and its level cannot be measured in anything else than that input, which must be nonnegative. The system (8) may now be written as

$$
\begin{aligned}
a_{11}X_1 + a_{12}X_2 + \cdots + a_{1n}X_n + x_{1(n+1)} &= x_1 \\
a_{21}X_1 + a_{22}X_2 + \cdots + a_{2n}X_n + x_{2(n+2)} &= x_2 \\
&\cdots\cdots\cdots\cdots\cdots\cdots\cdots\cdots\cdots\cdots\cdots \\
a_{f1}X_1 + a_{f2}X_2 + \cdots + a_{fn}X_n + x_{f(n+f)} &= x_f
\end{aligned}
$$

(9)

Assume that the column of the x's on the right-hand side of (9) is linearly independent of every set of $f - 1$ columns of a's on the left-hand side of (9), an assumption known as the "nondegeneracy assumption." A simple case of degeneracy where $n = 3$ and $f = 2$ would be

$$
4X_1 + 2X_2 + 6X_3 + x_{14} = 20
$$

$$
3X_1 + 5X_2 + 2X_3 + x_{25} = 50
$$

Here the column $(20, 50)$ on the right-hand side is linearly dependent on one column of coefficients on the left-hand side, that is the second column $(2, 5)$: The column $(20, 50)$ could be obtained by multiplying the column $(2, 5)$ by ten.[1]

13.6 BASIC SOLUTIONS

The price paid for transforming inequalities into equations is the introduction of f additional unknowns. Where n is a positive integer, a system of f equations in $n + f$ unknowns will not normally have a unique solution. However, it is the very multiplicity of solutions that makes our problem an optimization problem. Multiplicity provides a choice and thereby an opportunity for profit maximization. How much choice does the firm have?

In a system of f equations in $n + f$ unknowns we could arbitrarily set any n of the unknowns equal to zero, leaving a system of f equations in f unknowns. Under certain circumstances such a system would have a unique solution. The number n can be picked from the number $n + f$ in

$$
\binom{n + f}{n}
$$

different ways, representing the number of possible unique solutions involving f unknowns. Such solutions are called basic ones, and the collection of processes operated at nonzero levels is called a basis.

[1] Degeneracy, ruled out by assumption, does occur in economic problems. For an example, see Charnes, Cooper, and Mellon [1]. For remedies, see Charnes [2].

13.7 BASIC FEASIBLE SOLUTIONS

Some basic solutions may involve negative values of X_j or $x_{i(n+i)}$ and hence be nonfeasible. Rejecting them leaves us with the basic feasible solutions. Basic feasible solutions involve, first, no more processes operated at nonzero levels than there are constraints, and second, no processes operated at negative levels.

13.8 OPTIMIZATION

Let us apply our profits definition, Eq. (1), to the $(n + i)$th process, within which the disposal of the ith input is the sole activity. In Eq. (2) allow for the fact that output equals zero, in Eq. (4) allow for the fact that no input is absorbed other than the one disposed of; then insert (2) and (4) into (1) and find the profits of the disposal process:

(1a) $$Z_{n+i} = -p_i x_{i(n+i)} \qquad (i = 1, \ldots, f)$$

The level of a disposal process can be measured only by the input disposed of; hence its profit margin may be found by dividing (1a) by that input $x_{i(n+i)}$.

(10) $$z_{n+i} = -p_i$$

and firm profits as defined by (6a) may be expressed as

(11) $$Z = \sum_{j=1}^{n} (z_j X_j) + \sum_{i=1}^{f} [z_{n+i} x_{i(n+i)}]$$

This is the amount of profits to be maximized. A fundamental theorem in linear programming now states that no nonbasic feasible solution can be more profitable than the most profitable basic feasible solution. Let us prove it[2] for the simplest possible case in which $m = 2$, $n = 2$, and $f = 1$. In that case we maximize

(11a) $$Z = z_1 X_1 + z_2 X_2 + z_3 x_{13}$$

where

(5a) $$z_1 = P - p_1 a_{11} - p_2 a_{21}$$

(5a) $$z_2 = P - p_1 a_{12} - p_2 a_{22}$$

(10a) $$z_3 = -p_1$$

[2] Adapted from Danø [5]

subject to the constraint

(9a) $$a_{11}X_1 + a_{12}X_2 + x_{13} = x_1$$

Here, a_{11}, a_{12}, p_1, x_1, z_1, and z_2 are assumed to be positive, and X_1, X_2, and x_{13} are assumed to be nonnegative.

Our system is seen to be one with one equation, (9a), in three unknowns, X_1, X_2, and x_{13}. The number of basic solutions is

$$\binom{3}{2} = \frac{3!}{2!\,1!} = 3$$

These three basic solutions are three collections of process levels:

(12) $$X_1 = \frac{x_1}{a_{11}}, \qquad X_2 = 0, \qquad x_{13} = 0$$

(13) $$X_1 = 0, \qquad X_2 = \frac{x_1}{a_{12}}, \qquad x_{13} = 0$$

(14) $$X_1 = 0, \qquad X_2 = 0, \qquad x_{13} = x_1$$

Of nonbasic solutions there are infinitely many, each of which is a collection of process levels:

(15) $$X_1 = \omega_1 \frac{x_1}{a_{11}}, \qquad X_2 = \omega_2 \frac{x_1}{a_{12}}, \qquad x_{13} = \omega_3 x_1$$

where $\omega_1 + \omega_2 + \omega_3 = 1$, ω_1, ω_2, and ω_3 are nonnegative, and at most one of them can equal zero. From the assumptions made, it follows that all basic and nonbasic solutions are feasible. Now use (9a) to express X_1 in terms of X_2, x_{13}, and x_1; then

(16) $$X_1 = \frac{x_1 - a_{12}X_2 - x_{13}}{a_{11}}$$

By inserting (16) into (11a), we obtain

(17) $$Z = \left(z_2 - \frac{z_1 a_{12}}{a_{11}}\right)X_2 + \left(z_3 - \frac{z_1}{a_{11}}\right)x_{13} + \frac{z_1 x_1}{a_{11}}$$

In (16), let us arbitrarily set $X_2 = x_{13} = 0$, so that $X_1 = x_1/a_{11}$, which would constitute the basic solution (12); and according to (17) its profit would be $z_1 x_1/a_{11}$. Can firm profits be raised above $z_1 x_1/a_{11}$ by letting X_2 and x_{13} rise above zero?

We see immediately that x_{13} should not be permitted to rise above zero, for since z_3 is negative, z_1 positive, and a_{11} positive, x_{13} in (17) is multiplied by a negative coefficient.

How about letting X_2 rise above zero then? Three possibilities must be distinguished. First, if $z_2 < z_1 a_{12}/a_{11}$, the coefficient of X_2 in (17) is negative and X_2 should not be permitted to rise above zero. Second, if $z_2 = z_1 a_{12}/a_{11}$, the coefficient of X_2 in (17) is zero and firm profits would neither rise nor fall if X_2 were permitted to rise above zero. Third, if $z_2 > z_1 a_{12}/a_{11}$, the coefficient of X_2 in (17) is positive and X_2 should definitely be permitted to rise above zero. But how far?

From (16) it follows that if X_2 were raised beyond the bound x_1/a_{12}, then X_1 would become negative, which is inadmissible. So that bound is not only as far as X_2 can be raised but also as far as X_2 should be raised, for every rise helps. Consequently, we should set $X_2 = x_1/a_{12}$ and $X_1 = 0$. However, that would be the basic solution (13). Thus we have shown that either the basic solution (12) is best or, if there is anything better, it must be another basic solution, that is, (13). In no case can firm profits be higher than the highest profits in one of the basic solutions (12) or (13). The nonbasic solutions, of which there are infinitely many and which we could never finish examining, need not be examined after all.

This proof was based upon the assumption that $m = 2$, $n = 2$, and $f = 1$, but may easily be generalized.[3]

13.9 THE SIMPLEX CRITERION

We will now return to the simple case in which $m = 2$, $n = 2$, and $f = 1$ and assign the following specific values to our parameters:

$$
\begin{array}{ll}
x_1 = 20 & a_{22} = 5 \\
a_{11} = 4 & p_1 = 2 \\
a_{12} = 2 & p_2 = 3 \\
a_{21} = 3 & P = 20
\end{array}
$$

It follows that the profit margins are as follows:

$$z_1 = 3$$
$$z_2 = 1$$
$$z_3 = -2$$

Equations (11a) and (9a) may now be written.

(11a) $$Z = 3X_1 + X_2 - 2x_{13}$$

(9a) $$4X_1 + 2X_2 + x_{13} = 20$$

[3] For generalization, see Dorfman [6].

Maximize (11a) subject to (9a), X_1, X_2, and x_{13} being nonnegative as usual. First, using (9a) to express x_{13} in terms of X_1 and X_2, we insert the result into (11a), and get

$$(18) \qquad Z = 11X_1 + 5X_2 - 40$$

From (18) we conclude that X_1 and X_2 could profitably be raised above zero, for both have positive coefficients—the basis x_{13} is undesirable.

Second, by using (9a) to express X_2 in terms of X_1 and x_{13}, and inserting the result into (11a), we obtain

$$(19) \qquad Z = X_1 - 2\tfrac{1}{2}x_{13} + 10$$

From (19) we conclude that X_1 could profitably be raised above zero, but that x_{13} should remain zero.

Third, by using (9a) to express X_1 in terms of X_2 and x_{13}, and inserting the result into (11a), we obtain

$$(20) \qquad Z = -\tfrac{1}{2}X_2 - 2\tfrac{3}{4}x_{13} + 15$$

Equation (20) contains all the information in (9a) and (11a); nothing has been lost, no new assumptions added. Thus (20) represents the problem in a nutshell. Combine it with the knowledge that an optimum solution must be found among the basic feasible ones, that is, those solutions which involve only one process, the remaining two processes being operated at zero levels.

The beauty of (20) is that it instantly shows us which processes ought to be operated at zero levels, namely X_2 and x_{13}, for both have negative coefficients. Should either of these two unknowns have values higher than zero, profits according to (20) would surely be lower than if both were zero. Negativity of the coefficients is called the Simplex criterion.

Our luck was bad, and we had to go through all three experiments. Had we reversed their order we should have arrived at (20) at once and would not have needed to find (18) or (19).

13.10 NUMERICAL EXAMPLE

United Motors Corporation is a large producer of passenger cars. Only two models are being considered for the coming model year, the *Puma V8* and the *Nimble Six*. The factory prices after Federal excise tax deduction are $P_1 = \$2200$ and $P_2 = \$1440$, respectively.

United Motors owns eight identical body plants, of which the annual cost of each is $p_1 = \$100,000,000$, and five identical engine plants, of which the annual cost of each is $p_2 = \$200,000,000$. No expansion of these plant facilities is being considered.

At an average price of p_3 = \$0.1 per pound, United Motors can buy as much raw material as it will need. At a money wage rate of p_4 = \$3 per hour, United Motors can buy as many man hours as it will need.

The technologically given input-output coefficients are tabulated as follows.

	Puma V8	Nimble Six
Fraction of one body plant per car	$a_{11} = \dfrac{3}{1,000,000}$	$a_{12} = \dfrac{2}{1,000,000}$
Fraction of one engine plant per car	$a_{21} = \dfrac{2}{1,000,000}$	$a_{22} = \dfrac{1}{1,000,000}$
Pounds of raw material per car	$a_{31} = 4000$	$a_{32} = 3200$
Man hours per car	$a_{41} = 300$	$a_{42} = 200$

Assuming that United Motors wants to maximize its profits within the model year, find the optimal outputs of the two models for the coming model year and the total net profits to be earned.

There are four processes, two active and two disposal. The four profit margins are

$$z_1 = P_1 - (a_{11}p_1 + a_{21}p_2 + a_{31}p_3 + a_{41}p_4) = 200$$
$$z_2 = P_2 - (a_{12}p_1 + a_{22}p_2 + a_{32}p_3 + a_{42}p_4) = 120$$
$$z_3 = -p_1$$
$$z_4 = -p_2$$

Hence total profits equal

(21) $Z = 200X_1 + 120X_2 - 100,000,000x_{13} - 200,000,000x_{24}$

Total profits should be maximized subject to the constraints

$a_{11}X_1 + a_{12}X_2 + x_{13} = x_1$ or $3X_1 + 2X_2 + 1,000,000x_{13} = 8,000,000$

$a_{21}X_1 + a_{22}X_2 + x_{24} = x_2$ or $2X_1 + X_2 + 1,000,000x_{24} = 5,000,000$

Here are two equations in the four unknowns X_1, X_2, x_{13}, and x_{24}. Basic solutions are found by setting any two of those unknowns equal to zero and solving for the remaining two. This can be done in $\binom{4}{2}$ = 6 different ways; hence there are six basic solutions to consider. At this point we might pause to consider the fact that both active processes have positive profit margins, whereas the disposal processes as always have negative profit margins. Hence we have a hunch that x_{13} and x_{24} are the two unknowns which should be set equal to zero. So use the two constraints to express X_1 and X_2 in terms of x_{13} and x_{24}:

$$X_1 = 2,000,000 + 1,000,000x_{13} - 2,000,000x_{24}$$

$$X_2 = 1,000,000 - 2,000,000x_{13} + 3,000,000x_{24}$$

Insert these into the profits equation (21):

(22) $Z = 520,000,000 - 140,000,000x_{13} - 240,000,000x_{24}$

The Simplex criterion is satisfied. Both x_{13} and x_{24} have negative coefficients, and our hunch was correct. Setting x_{13} and x_{24} equal to zero gives us total profits equaling \$520 million.

As for optimal outputs, by setting $x_{13} = x_{24} = 0$ in the two constraints, we obtain

$$X_1 = 2,000,000$$

$$X_2 = 1,000,000$$

13.11   NET VERSUS GROSS PROFITS

Conventional linear programming usually employs the gross profits approach rather than the net profits approach applied here. The conventional approach ignores the cost of the constrained inputs on the grounds that the firm is stuck with them anyway; therefore their magnitude should not affect the decisions to be made. So let us now ignore the cost of the constrained inputs in the disposal as well as in the active processes and write United Motors' *gross* profit margins as

$$z_1 = P_1 - (a_{31}p_3 + a_{41}p_4) = 900$$

$$z_2 = P_2 - (a_{32}p_3 + a_{42}p_4) = 520$$

$$z_3 = z_4 = 0$$

Thus total gross profits now equal

(21a) $Z = 900X_1 + 520X_2$

Total gross profits should be maximized subject to the constraints, which are exactly the same as before. After using those constraints to express X_1 and X_2 in terms of x_{13} and x_{24}, we insert the outcome into the gross profits equation (21a) and get

(22a) $Z = 2,320,000,000 - 140,000,000x_{13} - 240,000,000x_{24}$

Therefore both x_{13} and x_{24} again have negative coefficients, and we notice that those coefficients are exactly the same as in (22) previously, that is, *minus* 140 million and *minus* 240 million, respectively. However, the constant terms of (22) and (22a) differ by $1800 million. This is as it should be: The fixed cost of the eight body plants was $800 million, and the fixed cost of the five engine plants was $1000 million. Thus gross profits $2320 million exceeds net profits $520 million by the amount of fixed cost $1800 million.

Since the constraints are exactly the same as before, setting $x_{13} = x_{24} = 0$ in those constraints gives the same result as before, that is, two million *Puma V8*'s and one million *Nimble Sixes*. Hence fixed cost does not at all affect the decisions to be made.

13.12   COMPUTATION

The search for a profit expression satisfying the Simplex criterion may be a tedious one. We have seen that in a problem involving n active processes and f input constraints, the number of basic solutions is

$$\binom{n + f}{n}$$

To be true, some of them will be nonfeasible. However, shortcuts are badly needed. The most important one is the Simplex method, developed by Dantzig [4] and popularized by Chipman [3]. Here the Simplex criterion is applied at successive stages in such a way that profits improve with every stage.

13.13   A CRITIQUE OF LINEAR PROGRAMMING

Neoclassical theory found certain properties of an optimum; for example that input or capital stock should be hired up to the point where its price or rental equals its marginal revenue productivity. However, since the neoclassicists rarely specified their functions, they rarely found their optima. Linear programming represents an explicit, simple, and workable instruction of how to find the optimum, the simplicity resting on the linearity of the model.

No doubt linearity as expressed in our input-output equations (3) is a very good approximation to production engineering in manufacturing industries. However, it is to be feared that in precisely those industries in which our input-output equations (3) are good approximations, our profit-output equations (5) and (5a) are not, for it is in such industries that competition is nonpure.

However, does not an input-output equation like (3) exclude economies of scale so conducive to nonpure competition? Taken by itself it does, but input constraints reflect the fact that durable plant and equipment are frequently available in a fixed quantity only, hence waste, idling, and disposal processes. In the short run, such a fixed quantity is a trivial fact. But input constraints may also be thought of as reflecting the long-run fact that plant and equipment are only available in certain minimum and larger sizes. If they are scaled down below the minimum size, their displacements may become too small relative to surfaces, and surfaces too small relative to lengths (reduce length to one-half, surfaces will reduce to one-fourth, and displacements will reduce to one-eighth). So if a small firm wishes to employ such plant and equipment, it must accept the minimum size and the waste, idling, and disposal processes that go with it. In this highly realistic sense, linear programming does include economies of scale.

REFERENCES

[1] Charnes, A., W. W. Cooper, and B. Mellon, "Blending Aviation Gasolines—A Study in Programming Interdependent Activities in an Integrated Oil Company," *Econometrica*, **20**, 135–159 (April 1952).

[2] Charnes, A., "Optimality and Degeneracy in Linear Programming," *Econometrica*, **20**, 160–170 (April, 1952).

[3] Chipman, J. S., "Computational Problems in Linear Programming," *Rev. Econ. Stat.*, **35**, 342–349 (November, 1953).

[4] Dantzig, G. B., "Maximization of a Linear Function of Variables Subject to Linear Inequalities," *Activity Analysis of Production and Allocation*, edited by T. C. Koopmans, New York, 1951.

[5] Danø, S., "Lineaer programmering," *Nordisk Matematisk Tidsskrift*, **4**, 121–138 (1956).

[6] Dorfman, R., *Application of Linear Programming to the Theory of the Firm*, Berkeley and Los Angeles, 1951, pp. 28–30.

CHAPTER 14

Optimum Quality of Output

... The modern automobile is impressive evidence that the manufacturers put appearance above safety.

RALPH NADER [1]

14.1 INTRODUCTION

Applied economies implicitly treats product quality as an important variable. When automobile manufacturers are accused of not building enough safety into cars, and when broadcasters are criticized for the low quality of radio and television programs, the implication is obviously that quality of product is a matter of choice to the firm.

Economic theory, however, usually fails to tell us how that choice is made, perhaps because quality is thought of as something nonquantitative or even purely subjective. In this chapter we shall not think of quality that way but instead consider that the physical quality of a product is uniquely determined once all the input and capital coefficients of its production process have been specified. In order to concentrate on quality, we shall suppress price as a variable to the firm. Thus, instead of conforming to usual economic theory, that is, considering price as adjusting to a given quality, we shall think of quality as adjusting to a given price. We shall then set up a simple one-product, one-period model of a potential firm under certainty, solve the model for the optimal values of the input and capital coefficients, and prove that the sufficient first-order and second-order conditions for a profit maximum are met.

14.2 NOTATION

In a microeconomic theory of the firm the following notation will be assigned.

117

Variables

a_j = absorption of jth input per unit of output
b_i = use of ith durable producers' good per unit of output
C = cost per annum
R = revenue from output sold per annum
S_i = physical capital stock of ith durable producers' good held by firm
x_j = absorption of jth input per annum
X = output produced and sold per annum
z = profit per unit of output sold
Z = profit per annum

Parameters

A, B = elasticities of a Cobb-Douglas production function
α, β = elasticities of a particular demand function
M = multiplicative factor of a Cobb-Douglas production function
N = multiplicative factor of a particular demand function
p_j = price of jth input
P = price of output
r_i = rental per annum of a unit of the ith durable producers' good
τ = the quality elasticity of demand

14.3 PHYSICAL QUALITY AS DETERMINED BY INPUT AND CAPITAL COEFFICIENTS

Statistical quality control in mass production is based upon the idea that given the production process, results of quality measurements of the individual units of the product will vary at random between an upper and a lower control limit. If these limits are exceeded the process is not "in control." Ignoring as a first approximation the random variation we may say, then, that the physical quality of the product is uniquely determined once the production process has been completely specified. One such complete specification would be in terms of, first, the time rate of output X, second, the absorption of the physical quantity x_j of the jth input per unit of time, and third, the use of the physical capital stock S_i of the ith durable producers' good, where $j = 1, \ldots, m$, and $i = 1, \ldots, n$.

Once we had specified output X, absorption x_j, and capital stock S_i, we would also by definition have specified the input coefficient a_j and the capital coefficient b_i defined as

(1) $$x_j = a_j X \qquad (j = 1, \ldots, m)$$

(2) $$S_i = b_i X \qquad (i = 1, \ldots, n)$$

In addition to ignoring random quality variations of individual units of the product, we shall ignore increasing and decreasing returns to scale. Then, for a given physical quality of product, the input coefficient a_j and the capital coefficient b_i do not vary with output X_1, and we may specify the production process in terms of a_j and b_i just as completely as we specified it in terms of X, x_j, and S_i. Thus physical quality of product could be said to be uniquely determined once the input coefficient a_j and the capital coefficient b_i had been specified. Is it really impossible for the same set of a_j and b_i to result in different physical qualities of the product? Yes, for otherwise the process must not have been fully specified. The remedy would be further specification, for example, not merely that of inputs and capital use but also when and where to apply them. A specification of when to apply them is clearly called for: Painting an automobile body by first applying baked enamel, then primer, and finally doing the bonderizing would be useless; hence paint applications at different stages of the production process should be considered as different inputs, each with its own input coefficient. A specification of where to apply inputs and capital use is just as clearly called for. Building a house by driving all the nails into its lower section, leaving none for the roof structure, would be useless; hence nails going into different places should be considered as different inputs, each with its own input coefficient.

Although it is in this sense impossible for the same set of a_j and b_i to result in different physical qualities of product, it is quite possible for different sets of a_j and b_i to result in the same physical quality of product. We shall return in Section 14.7 to this very different question.

Our way of looking at quality is realistic. However, and more important to us, it has the theoretical merit of posing unequivocally the optimization problem as seen by the firm. The complete specification of the coefficients a_j and b_i is indeed the ultimate decision the firm must make. A higher labor input coefficient must be decided upon if better workmanship of the product is desired, a higher nylon input coefficient must be decided upon if greater tensile strength is required. In oil refining the firm must decide on a higher capital coefficient reflecting deep rather than shallow cracking if a higher octane rating of gasoline is desired.

14.4 THE DEMAND FUNCTION

The physical quality of the product is uniquely determined once all input coefficients a_j and all capital coefficients b_i of its production process have been specified, where $i = 1, \ldots, n$, and $j = 1, \ldots, m$. However, if physical quality is uniquely determined, then at a given price P of the product, the quantity sold per annum is also uniquely determined. Hence we may write demand faced by the firm as a function of price P and the coefficients a_j and b_i.

(3) $$X = X(P, a_1, \ldots, a_m, b_1, \ldots, b_n)$$

14.5 PROFITS, REVENUE, AND COST

The rest is traditional. Profits are defined as revenue *minus* cost:

(4) $$Z = R - C$$

revenue as price of output *times* output sold:

(5) $$R = PX$$

cost as the money value of all input and rental:

(6) $$C = \sum_{j=1}^{m}(p_j x_j) + \sum_{i=1}^{n}(r_i S_i)$$

and the profit margin as profit per unit of output sold:

(7) $$Z = zX$$

By inserting (1) through (6) into (7),

(7a) $$z = P - \left[\sum_{j=1}^{m}(p_j a_j) + \sum_{i=1}^{n}(r_i b_i) \right]$$

14.6 PROFIT MAXIMIZATION

The conditions for maximum profits Z include first-order and second-order conditions. Let us vary the hth input coefficient a_h or the gth capital coefficient b_g, and let us take first partial derivatives of Z with respect to a_h or b_g. The first-order conditions are that all such first partial derivatives be zero; thus

(8) $$\frac{\partial Z}{\partial a_h} = z\frac{\partial X}{\partial a_h} - p_h X = 0 \qquad (h = 1, \ldots, m)$$

and

(9) $$\frac{\partial Z}{\partial b_g} = z\frac{\partial X}{\partial b_g} - r_g X = 0 \qquad (g = 1, \ldots, n)$$

Let α_h and β_h be the elasticities of demand with respect to the hth input and gth capital coefficient, respectively. By rearranging (8) and (9),

(10)
$$\alpha_h = \frac{\partial X}{\partial a_h} \frac{a_h}{X} = \frac{p_h a_h}{z} \quad (h = 1, \ldots, m)$$

and

(11)
$$\beta_g = \frac{\partial X}{\partial b_g} \frac{b_g}{X} = \frac{r_g b_g}{z} \quad (g = 1, \ldots, n)$$

Consisting of $m + n$ simultaneous equations, one for each input and capital coefficient, the system (10) and (11) tells us how much each particular input and capital coefficient should be raised: namely, until the expenditure per

Table 14.1   The Hessian Determinant of the Second Partial Derivatives

$$H = \begin{vmatrix} \dfrac{\partial^2 Z}{\partial a_1^2} & \cdots & \dfrac{\partial^2 Z}{\partial a_1\, \partial a_m} & \dfrac{\partial^2 Z}{\partial a_1\, \partial b_1} & \cdots & \dfrac{\partial^2 Z}{\partial a_1\, \partial b_n} \\[2ex] \dfrac{\partial^2 Z}{\partial a_m\, \partial a_1} & \cdots & \dfrac{\partial^2 Z}{\partial a_m^2} & \dfrac{\partial^2 Z}{\partial a_m\, \partial b_1} & \cdots & \dfrac{\partial^2 Z}{\partial a_m\, \partial b_n} \\[2ex] \dfrac{\partial^2 Z}{\partial b_1\, \partial a_1} & \cdots & \dfrac{\partial^2 Z}{\partial b_1\, \partial a_m} & \dfrac{\partial^2 Z}{\partial b_1^2} & \cdots & \dfrac{\partial^2 Z}{\partial b_1\, \partial b_n} \\[2ex] \dfrac{\partial^2 Z}{\partial b_n\, \partial a_1} & \cdots & \dfrac{\partial^2 Z}{\partial b_n\, \partial a_m} & \dfrac{\partial^2 Z}{\partial b_n\, \partial b_1} & \cdots & \dfrac{\partial^2 Z}{\partial b_n^2} \end{vmatrix}$$

unit of output sold on that particular input or on rental of that particular producers' good constitutes a fraction of the profit margin equaling the elasticity of demand with respect to that particular input or capital coefficient.

The second-order conditions are as follows: Form the Hessian $(m + n)$-order determinant of the second derivatives (see Table 14.1). Next form its principal minors. The principal minor formed by deleting the last $m + n - 1$ rows and columns must be negative. The principal minor formed by deleting the last $m + n - 2$ rows and columns must be positive, etc., the principal minors always alternating in sign. When, finally, we delete no further rows and columns, the Hessian determinant must be positive if $m + n$ is even, negative if $m + n$ is odd.

That is as much as we can say about the general case. The time has now come to make more specific assumptions, and we shall begin by building up a simple particular demand function from simple, particular, underlying production functions.

14.7 A PARTICULAR DEMAND FUNCTION: NEOCLASSICAL PRODUCTION FUNCTIONS

Specify an arbitrary initial set of input coefficients and capital coefficients, $(\bar{a}_j, \bar{b}_i)$, where $j = 1, \ldots, m$ and $i = 1, \ldots, n$. Once these coefficients have been specified, the physical product has been uniquely determined. If produced, let that quality be demanded in the quantity $\bar{X}$. As for its production function, let us first be neoclassicists and assume that it is the linearly homogeneous Cobb-Douglas production function

(12)
$$X = Mx_1^{A_1} \cdots x_m^{A_m} S_1^{B_1} \cdots S_n^{B_n}$$

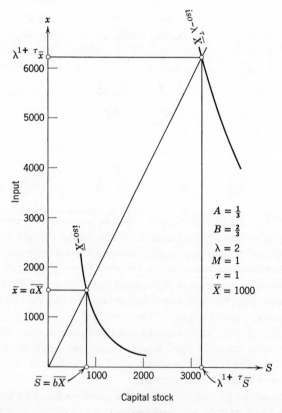

Figure 14.1

where $0 < A_j < 1, 0 < B_i < 1, A_1 + \cdots + A_m + B_1 + \cdots + B_n = 1$, and $M > 0$. The production function (12) is adopted with the usual $m + n + 1$ restrictions: $x_j \geq 0$, $S_i \geq 0$, and $X \geq 0$, where $j = 1, \ldots, m$, and $i = 1, \ldots, n$. Equation (12) defines in x_j-S_i space a family of isoquants each of which describes all possible combinations (x_j, S_i) resulting in the same output. In two-dimensional space one such isoquant is shown as the lower convex curve in Fig. 14.1, arrived at by setting $X = \bar{X}$ in Eq. (12).

Now Fig. 14.1 was a diagram with capital stock S and input x on its axes. Suppose we would rather see a diagram with the capital *coefficient b* and the input *coefficient a* on its axes. We would then use (1) and (2) on (12) and divide by output X:

$$(12a) \qquad 1 = Ma_1{}^{A_1} \cdots a_m{}^{A_m} b_1{}^{B_1} \cdots b_n{}^{B_n}$$

Equation (12a) defines in a_j-b_i space one, and only one, convex hypersurface describing all possible combinations (a_j, b_i) resulting in the same physical quality of product. Since that physical quality was demanded in the quantity $\bar{X}$, the hypersurface might be called an iso-$\bar{X}$ hypersurface. Since the hypersurface has infinitely many points in it, infinitely many different sets (a_j, b_i) will result in the same physical quality of product—which was the very essence of the neoclassical approach. In two-dimensional space the hypersurface is shown as the lower curve in Fig. 14.2.

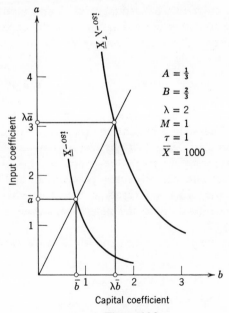

$A = \frac{1}{3}$

$B = \frac{2}{3}$

$\lambda = 2$

$M = 1$

$\tau = 1$

$\bar{X} = 1000$

Figure 14.2

Now let us consider a different physical quality of product. Replace the arbitrary initial set of input and capital coefficients $(\bar{a}_j, \bar{b}_i)$ by a new set $(\lambda \bar{a}_j, \lambda \bar{b}_i)$, where $\lambda > 0$. Once the new input and capital coefficients have been specified, a new physical quality of product has been uniquely determined. If produced, let that quality be demanded in the quantity $\lambda^\tau \bar{X}$, where $\tau > 0$, and let it be produced under the linearly homogeneous Cobb-Douglas production function:

$$(13) \qquad X = \frac{M}{\lambda} (\lambda x_1)^{A_1} \cdots (\lambda x_m)^{A_m} (\lambda S_1)^{B_1} \cdots (\lambda S_n)^{B_n}$$

Let λ pass through all positive numbers, giving an infinite series of physical qualities of product and their production functions, with all of production functions being of the form (13). Equation (13) implies that all such production functions have the same input elasticities (A_j, B_i) but not the same multiplicative factors. The multiplicative factors are in inverse proportion to λ, and they had better be, for if the input changing from x_j to λx_j and the capital stock changing from S_i to λS_i reflect changes in input and capital stock per unit, the number of units being produced must remain unchanged.

Equation (13) defines in λx_j-λS_i space a family of isoquants, each of which describes all possible combinations $(\lambda x_j, \lambda S_i)$ resulting in the same output. In two-dimensional space one such isoquant is shown as the upper curve in Fig. 14.1, plotted by setting $X = \lambda^\tau \bar{X}$ in Eq. (13).

Figure 14.1 was a diagram with capital stock S and input x on its axes. Suppose that we would rather see a diagram with the capital coefficient b and the input coefficient a on its axes. Then we would use (1) and (2) on (13) and divide by X:

$$(13a) \qquad 1 = \frac{M}{\lambda} (\lambda a_1)^{A_1} \cdots (\lambda a_m)^{A_m} (\lambda b_1)^{B_1} \cdots (\lambda b_n)^{B_n}$$

Equation (13a) defines in λa_j-λb_i space one, and only one, convex hypersurface describing all possible combinations $(\lambda a_j, \lambda b_i)$ resulting in the same physical quality of product. Since that physical quality was demanded in the quantity $\lambda^\tau \bar{X}$, the hypersurface might be called an iso-$\lambda^\tau \bar{X}$ hypersurface. Again the hypersurface has infinitely many points in it; and again infinitely many different sets $(\lambda a_j, \lambda b_i)$ will result in the same physical quality of product. In two-dimensional space the new hypersurface is shown as the upper curve in Fig. 14.2.

How will we derive the particular demand function we want? Define some new parameters

$$(14) \qquad N = M^\tau \bar{X}$$

$$(15) \qquad \alpha_j = \tau A_j \qquad (j = 1, \ldots, m)$$

$$(16) \qquad \beta_i = \tau B_i \qquad (i = 1, \ldots, n)$$

and write the desired particular demand function as

(3a) $$X = Na_1^{\alpha_1} \cdots a_m^{\alpha_m} b_1^{\beta_1} \cdots b_n^{\beta_n}$$

From (14), (15), and (16), as well as the restrictions imposed upon A_j, B_i, and M, it follows that $0 < \alpha_j < \tau$, $0 < \beta_i < \tau$, $\alpha_1 + \cdots + \alpha_m + \beta_1 + \cdots + \beta_n = \tau$, and $N > 0$. Let us adopt (3a) with the $m + n + 1$ restrictions; then $a_j \geq 0$, $b_i \geq 0$, and $X \geq 0$.

Does the demand function really contain everything stated in (12a) and (13a)? To verify that it does, we insert (14) through (16) into (12a) and (13a), respectively, and arrive at the following two cases of (3a).

(12b) $$\bar{X} = Na_1^{\alpha_1} \cdots a_m^{\alpha_m} b_1^{\beta_1} \cdots b_n^{\beta_n}$$

(13b) $$\lambda^\tau \bar{X} = N(\lambda a_1)^{\alpha_1} \cdots (\lambda a_m)^{\alpha_m} (\lambda b_1)^{\beta_1} \cdots (\lambda b_n)^{\beta_n}$$

Thus (12a), (13a), and the curves based upon them in Fig. 14.2 are indeed contained in the demand equation (3a). We conclude that (3a) is a function having for its multiplicative factor N the product $M^\tau \bar{X}$, that is, the τth power of the multiplicative factor M of the original production function (12) *times* the quantity $\bar{X}$ demanded of the quality produced under that function. Furthermore, (3a) has for its input and capital *coefficient* elasticities (α_j, β_i) the product of the exponent τ and the *input* and *capital* elasticities (A_j, B_i) of that production function (12).

What is the economic meaning of the exponent τ? We could call it the quality elasticity of demand, for it indicates that if all input and capital coefficients rise in the proportion λ, quantity demanded will rise in the proportion λ^τ. If $\tau < 1$, demand could be called quality inelastic, if $\tau > 1$, demand could be called quality elastic, and if $\tau = 1$, demand could be said to have unitary quality elasticity.

We shall now show that the demand function (3a) could also emerge if the underlying production functions were not neoclassical but of the linear-programming type.

14.8 A PARTICULAR DEMAND FUNCTION: LINEAR-PROGRAMMING TYPE PRODUCTION FUNCTIONS

We shall begin once more by specifying an arbitrary set of input and capital coefficients $(\bar{a}_j, \bar{b}_i)$, where $j = 1, \ldots, m$ and $i = 1, \ldots, n$. Once these input and capital coefficients have been specified, the physical quality of product has been uniquely determined. If produced, again let the latter be demanded in the quantity $\bar{X}$. However, let us no longer be neoclassicists. Let us be linear programmers and consider the initial set $(\bar{a}_j, \bar{b}_i)$ as one defining

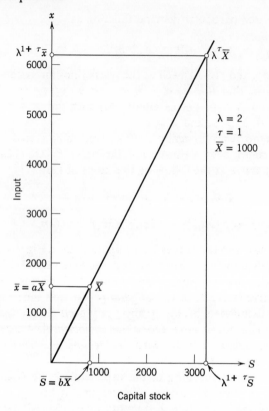

Figure 14.3

in Eqs. (1) and (2) a process within which there is proportionality between output and every input and between output and every capital stock. In two-dimensional space such a process is shown in Fig. 14.3 as a straight line through the origin with the slope $\bar{a}/\bar{b}$.

Conventional linear programming assumes some inputs or capital stocks to be available in fixed quantities only. For each such input a constraint is introduced stating that the total quantity absorbed of that input must be less than or equal to the quantity available. However, other constraints, for example sales constraints, are not introduced. Nevertheless, under nonpure competition, the maximum quantity the market will absorb at fixed price and fixed physical quality of product will be finite. The absence of sales constraints in conventional linear programming must be interpreted either as an implicit assumption of pure competition or as an implicit assumption that the input constraints will limit output anyway, and that the latter bound is narrower than the bound set by the absorption power of the market. We find neither of these assumptions acceptable; therefore we shall replace the conventional input constraints by sales constraints.

For any process, then, a sales constraint should specify the quantity demanded of the product of that process. The quantity demanded of the physical quality produced in the process defined by the input coefficients and capital coefficients $(\bar{a}_j, \bar{b}_i)$ was $\bar{X}$; let us find a point $\bar{X}$ in the two-dimensional Fig. 14.3, which was a diagram with the input x and the capital stock S on its axes. The coordinates of the point $\bar{X}$ must be

$$(\bar{S}, \bar{x}) = (\bar{b}\bar{X}, \bar{a}\bar{X})$$

Suppose we would rather see the point $\bar{X}$ in a diagram with the input coefficient a and the capital coefficient b on its axes. The coordinates of $\bar{X}$ in such a diagram, shown in Fig. 14.4, are found by dividing the coordinates in Fig. 14.3 by $\bar{X}$ and using (1) and (2):

$$\left(\frac{\bar{S}}{\bar{X}}, \frac{\bar{x}}{\bar{X}}\right) = (\bar{b}, \bar{a})$$

Thus the point $\bar{X}$ in Fig. 14.4 lies at a distance from the origin equal to $1/\bar{X}$ of its distance from the origin in Fig. 14.3.

Now consider a different physical quality of product. Replace the arbitrary initial set of input and capital coefficients $(\bar{a}_j, \bar{b}_i)$ by the new set $(\lambda \bar{a}_j, \lambda \bar{b}_i)$,

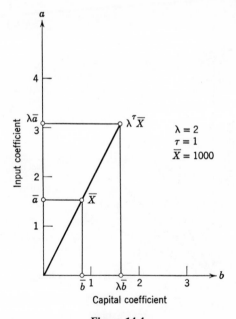

Figure 14.4

where $\lambda > 0$. Once the new input and capital coefficients have been specified, a new physical quality of product has been uniquely determined. If produced, let that quality be demanded in the quantity $\lambda^\tau \bar{X}$, where $\tau > 0$. Let us find a point $\lambda^\tau \bar{X}$ in Fig. 14.3. In such a diagram the coordinates of $\lambda^\tau \bar{X}$ must be

$$(\lambda^{1+\tau} \bar{S},\ \lambda^{1+\tau} \bar{x}) = (\lambda \bar{b} \lambda^\tau \bar{X},\ \lambda \bar{a} \lambda^\tau \bar{X})$$

thus the new point in Fig. 14.3 lies $\lambda^{1+\tau}$ times farther out than did the old point in Fig. 14.3.

Where is the point $\lambda^\tau \bar{X}$ in Fig. 14.4? Its coordinates in Fig. 14.4 are found by dividing the coordinates in Fig. 14.3 by $\lambda^\tau \bar{X}$ and using (1) and (2).

$$\left(\frac{\lambda^{1+\tau} \bar{S}}{\lambda^\tau \bar{X}},\ \frac{\lambda^{1+\tau} \bar{x}}{\lambda^\tau \bar{X}} \right) = (\lambda \bar{b},\ \lambda \bar{a})$$

Thus the new point in Fig. 14.4 lies λ times farther out than did the old point in Fig. 14.4.

Though differing with respect to input coefficients, capital coefficients, and the physical quality of product, the processes considered until now have identical proportions between input coefficients and capital coefficients. In Fig. 14.5, the two processes considered were both contained in straight line I with slope $\bar{a}/\bar{b}$.

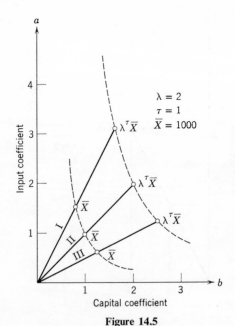

Figure 14.5

Surely processes having different proportions between the input and capital coefficients must exist. Conventional linear programming assumes that there exists a finite number of processes, all of which result in the same physical quality of product. Perhaps it would be more realistic to think of different processes resulting in different physical qualities of product. For example, automation may reduce the random variation of the quality of individual copies of the product, thus producing a "better" product.

Let us remove the conventional constraint that the firm must choose among a finite number of processes, all of which result in the same physical quality of product. Instead, let the firm choose among a number of processes each of which results in a physical quality of product which may or may not be producible by other processes. Removal of a constraint must widen our choice. Figure 14.5 shows four additional processes, two in line II and two in III. Draw a curve through the end points of all processes resulting in physical qualities for which the quantity demanded is the same. Two such iso-X curves have been drawn in Fig. 14.5, one for the quantity demanded $\overline{X}$, the other for the quantity demanded $\lambda^r \overline{X}$. The wider the choice open to the firm, that is, the larger the number of processes available to it, the less objectionable it is to imagine the existence of such a continuous iso-X curve connecting the discrete end points. Let us suppose such a curve exists and that the demand equation containing all such curves is differentiable. Let that equation be, say, of the form (3a).

14.9   THE PARTICULAR DEMAND FUNCTION: A SUMMARY

With its specified restrictions, the demand function (3a) does not permit the same set (a_j, b_i) to result in different values of X. This is as it should be. The physical quality of product is uniquely determined once all input and capital coefficients have been specified. And once the physical quality of product has been uniquely determined so has the quantity demanded of it.

However, for a given value of X, infinitely many sets (a_j, b_i) will satisfy (3a). In a_j-b_i space each such set will form an iso-X hypersurface convex to the origin. Figures 14.2 and 14.5 each showed two such sets. Will physical quality of product be the same at every point of such an iso-X hypersurface? In the neoclassical case treated in Section 14.7 and shown in Fig. 14.2, physical quality will indeed be the same, but in the linear-programming case treated in Section 14.8 and shown in Fig. 14.5, physical quality need not be the same at every point of an iso-X hypersurface. But how can two physical qualities differ, yet be demanded in the same quantity? Very easily. Either the difference in physical quality is too small for the consumer to notice, or if noticed too small for him to care about, or—since all consumers are not alike—the difference in physical quality must attract as much demand as it repels.

14.10 PARTICULAR CASE: SOLUTION

Inserting (3a) into (10) and (11), using (7a), and rearranging, we write the system (10) and (11) as

$$\frac{1 + \alpha_1}{\alpha_1} p_1 a_1 + p_2 a_2 + \cdots + p_m a_m + r_1 b_1 + r_2 b_2 + \cdots + r_n b_n = P$$

$$p_1 a_1 + \frac{1 + \alpha_2}{\alpha_2} p_2 a_2 + \cdots + p_m a_m + r_1 b_1 + r_2 b_2 + \cdots + r_n b_n = P$$

(17)

$$\cdot$$
$$\cdot$$
$$\cdot$$

$$p_1 a_1 + p_2 a_2 + \cdots + p_m a_m + r_1 b_1 + r_2 b_2 + \cdots + \frac{1 + \beta_n}{\beta_n} r_n b_n = P$$

The system (17) is a neat linear system of $m + n$ simultaneous equations in the $m + n$ variables (a_j, b_i). In Appendix I we prove that it has the following very tidy solutions:

$$(18) \quad a_h = \frac{P}{p_h} \frac{\alpha_h}{1 + \alpha_1 + \cdots + \alpha_m + \beta_1 + \cdots + \beta_n} \quad (h = 1, \ldots, m)$$

$$(19) \quad b_g = \frac{P}{r_g} \frac{\beta_g}{1 + \alpha_1 + \cdots + \alpha_m + \beta_1 + \cdots + \beta_n} \quad (g = 1, \ldots, n)$$

The restrictions imposed upon the demand equation (3a) prevented the firm from including any input or capital coefficient with respect to which demand elasticity was nonpositive. We can now see why such restrictions were necessary. In their absence, the solutions (18) and (19) could have become nonpositive. Consequently, such things as imaginary numbers or zero raised to the power zero could have occurred in the demand equation (3a). However, since all elasticities (α_h, β_g) and all prices P, p, and r are assumed to be positive, the solutions (18) and (19) will be positive and unique.

This uniqueness is welcome. As a result of it, if each physical quality of product may be produced in more than one way (see Sections 14.7 and 14.8), (18) and (19) indicate not only which physical quality of product should be produced but also *how* it should be produced. That is a generalization of traditional theory, like that of Chapters 12 and 13, merely stating how a given physical quality of product should be produced.

Are all conditions for a profit maximum satisfied by (18) and (19)? Appendix II indicates how to find the second-order partial derivatives needed for an evaluation of the Hessian determinant H in Table 14.1. Appendix III proves that the signs of the principal minors formed from that determinant do indeed alternate.

Solutions (18) and (19) express the variables a_h and b_g in terms of the price and elasticity parameters alone. The sensitivity of the variables to those parameters can be expressed most simply by the following elasticities:

$$(20) \qquad \frac{\partial a_h}{\partial P} \frac{P}{a_h} = 1$$

$$(21) \qquad \frac{\partial b_g}{\partial P} \frac{P}{b_g} = 1$$

$$(22) \qquad \frac{\partial a_h}{\partial p_h} \frac{p_h}{a_h} = -1$$

$$(23) \qquad \frac{\partial b_g}{\partial r_g} \frac{r_g}{b_g} = -1$$

$$(24) \qquad \frac{\partial a_h}{\partial \alpha_h} \frac{\alpha_h}{a_h} = 1 - \frac{p_h a_h}{P}$$

$$(25) \qquad \frac{\partial b_g}{\partial \beta_g} \frac{\beta_g}{b_g} = 1 - \frac{r_g b_g}{P}$$

Equations (20) and (21) show the elasticity of an input or capital coefficient to be *plus* one with respect to the price of the product. Equations (22) and (23) show the elasticity to be *minus* one with respect to the price of the input or the rental of the producers' good, respectively. Equations (24) and (25) show the elasticity to be positive with respect to the demand elasticities α_h and β_g, respectively. Why is it positive? Because (24) and (25) equal one *minus* the share of the expenditure on that particular input or rental. Expenditure share of what? Share of product price P. However, (10) and (11) showed the share of profit margin z to equal, in equilibrium, the elasticity α_h or β_g, respectively. But all input prices p_h and rentals r_g have been assumed to be positive; hence profit margin z is always less than price P. Consequently, expenditure share of P is always less than expenditure share of z, that is, always less than the elasticity α_h or β_g, already assumed to be positive and less than one. Thus (24) and (25) are indeed positive.

14.11   PARTICULAR CASE, DECISION RULE

By inserting the solutions (18) and (19) into (7a), the one-product firm should determine if the profit margin is positive, zero, or negative. If it is positive, the product should be produced in a physical quality uniquely determined by the solutions (18) and (19) and in a quantity determined by inserting those solutions into the demand equation (3a). If the profit margin is zero, the firm is indifferent between doing the same or doing nothing. If the profit margin is negative, the product should not be produced.

APPENDIX I HOW TO FIND THE SOLUTIONS
OF THE SYSTEM (17)

Since there is no mathematical difference between a, α, and p, on the one hand, and b, β, and r, on the other, let us save space by ignoring the latter three. Solving for p_1a_1 and using Cramer's rule on (17), we obtain

$$p_1a_1 = \frac{\begin{vmatrix} P & 1 & \cdots & 1 \\ P & \dfrac{1+\alpha_2}{\alpha_2} & \cdots & 1 \\ \hdotsfor{4} \\ P & 1 & \cdots & \dfrac{1+\alpha_m}{\alpha_m} \end{vmatrix}}{\begin{vmatrix} \dfrac{1+\alpha_1}{\alpha_1} & 1 & \cdots & 1 \\ 1 & \dfrac{1+\alpha_2}{\alpha_2} & \cdots & 1 \\ \hdotsfor{4} \\ 1 & 1 & \cdots & \dfrac{1+\alpha_m}{\alpha_m} \end{vmatrix}}$$

In both numerator and denominator, we multiply the ith column by α_i, $i = 1, \ldots, m$, and subtract the first row from all other rows:

$$p_1a_1 = \frac{\begin{vmatrix} \alpha_1 P & \alpha_2 & \cdots & \alpha_m \\ 0 & 1 & \cdots & 0 \\ \hdotsfor{4} \\ 0 & 0 & \cdots & 1 \end{vmatrix}}{\begin{vmatrix} 1+\alpha_1 & \alpha_2 & \cdots & \alpha_m \\ -1 & 1 & \cdots & 0 \\ \hdotsfor{4} \\ -1 & 0 & \cdots & 1 \end{vmatrix}}$$

The value of the numerator is $\alpha_1 P$. In the denominator, subtract α_i times the ith row, $i = 2, \ldots, m$, from its first row. Then the first element of its first row becomes $1 + \alpha_1 + \cdots + \alpha_m$, and all other elements of that row become zero; hence

$$p_1 a_1 = \frac{\alpha_1 P}{1 + \alpha_1 + \cdots + \alpha_m}$$

We solve for $p_2 a_2, \ldots, p_m a_m$, in similar fashion; hence (18) and (19) follow.

APPENDIX II SECOND PARTIAL DERIVATIVES TO BE USED IN HESSIAN DETERMINANT

The needed second partial derivatives are

(26)
$$\frac{\partial^2 Z}{\partial a_f \, \partial a_h} = -p_f \frac{\alpha_h}{a_h} X$$

(27)
$$\frac{\partial^2 Z}{\partial b_e \, \partial b_g} = -r_e \frac{\beta_g}{b_g} X$$

(28)
$$\frac{\partial^2 Z}{\partial b_g \, \partial a_h} = -r_g \frac{\alpha_h}{a_h} X$$

(29)
$$\frac{\partial^2 Z}{\partial a_h \, \partial b_g} = -p_h \frac{\beta_g}{b_g} X$$

(30)
$$\frac{\partial^2 Z}{\partial a_h^2} = -p_h \frac{1 + \alpha_h}{a_h} X$$

(31)
$$\frac{\partial^2 Z}{\partial b_g^2} = -r_g \frac{1 + \beta_g}{b_g} X$$

These second partial derivatives have been found as follows: To find derivative (26) take the derivative of (8) with respect to a_f. Then

(8a)
$$\frac{\partial^2 Z}{\partial a_f \, \partial a_h} = z \frac{\partial^2 X}{\partial a_f \, \partial a_h} + \frac{\partial z}{\partial a_f} \frac{\partial X}{\partial a_h} - p_h \frac{\partial X}{\partial a_f}$$

By using (3a) and (7a), we find the various derivatives entering (8a).

$$\frac{\partial X}{\partial a_h} = \frac{\alpha_h}{a_h} X; \qquad \frac{\partial X}{\partial a_f} = \frac{\alpha_f}{a_f} X; \qquad \frac{\partial^2 X}{\partial a_f \, \partial a_h} = \frac{\alpha_h \alpha_f}{a_h a_f} X; \qquad \frac{\partial z}{\partial a_f} = -p_f$$

Inserting all these derivatives into (8a), we obtain

(8b)
$$\frac{\partial^2 Z}{\partial a_f \, \partial a_h} = \frac{\alpha_f}{a_f} X \left(\frac{z \alpha_h}{a_h} - p_h \right) - p_f \frac{\alpha_h}{a_h} X$$

By inserting some of them into (8),

(8c)
$$\frac{\partial Z}{\partial a_h} = X\left(\frac{z\alpha_h}{a_h} - p_h\right) = 0$$

By using (8c) upon (8b) we obtain derivative (26). To find derivative (30), we take the derivative of (8) with respect to a_h:

(8d)
$$\frac{\partial^2 Z}{\partial a_h^{\,2}} = z\frac{\partial^2 X}{\partial a_h^{\,2}} + \frac{\partial z}{\partial a_h}\frac{\partial X}{\partial a_h} - p_h\frac{\partial X}{\partial a_h}$$

Using (3a) and (7a) we find the various derivatives entering (8d):

$$\frac{\partial X}{\partial a_h} = \frac{\alpha_h}{a_h} X; \qquad \frac{\partial^2 X}{\partial a_h^{\,2}} = \frac{\alpha_h(\alpha_h - 1)}{a_h^{\,2}} X; \qquad \frac{\partial z}{\partial a_h} = -p_h$$

Inserting all these derivatives into (8d), we obtain

(8e)
$$\frac{\partial^2 Z}{\partial a_h^{\,2}} = \frac{\alpha_h}{a_h} X\left(\frac{z\alpha_h}{a_h} - p_h\right) - \frac{\alpha_h}{a_h} X\left(\frac{z}{a_h} + p_h\right)$$

Inserting some of the derivatives into (8) we obtain (8c). Using (8c) upon (8e), the first right-hand term of (8e) vanishes. Using (10), the second right-hand term may be written

$$\frac{\partial^2 Z}{\partial a_h^{\,2}} = -p_h\frac{1 + \alpha_h}{a_h} X$$

which is derivative (30). The rest of the derivatives may be similarly derived.

APPENDIX III PROOF THAT SIGNS OF PRINCIPAL MINORS DO ALTERNATE

As in Appendix I, we will ignore b, β, and r. By using Table 14.1 and Appendix II we may write the m-order Hessian determinant:

$$H = \begin{vmatrix} -p_1\dfrac{1 + \alpha_1}{a_1} X & -p_1\dfrac{\alpha_2}{a_2} X & \cdots & -p_1\dfrac{\alpha_m}{a_m} X \\[2ex] -p_2\dfrac{\alpha_1}{a_1} X & -p_2\dfrac{1 + \alpha_2}{a_2} X & \cdots & -p_2\dfrac{\alpha_m}{a_m} X \\[1ex] \cdots\cdots\cdots\cdots\cdots\cdots\cdots\cdots\cdots\cdots\cdots \\[1ex] -p_m\dfrac{\alpha_1}{a_1} X & -p_m\dfrac{\alpha_2}{a_2} X & \cdots & -p_m\dfrac{1 + \alpha_m}{a_m} X \end{vmatrix}$$

First, multiply each row by *minus* one, second, multiply the ith column by a_i, $i = 1, \ldots, m$, third, divide the ith row by $p_i X$, $i = 1, \ldots, m$, fourth, subtract the first row from all other rows. The Hessian determinant may then be written

$$H = (-1)^m \frac{p_1 \cdots p_m}{a_1 \cdots a_m} X^m \begin{vmatrix} 1 + \alpha_1 & \alpha_2 & \cdots & \alpha_m \\ -1 & 1 & \cdots & 0 \\ \cdots\cdots\cdots\cdots\cdots\cdots\cdots \\ -1 & 0 & \cdots & 1 \end{vmatrix}$$

This determinant is the same as that encountered in the denominator of $p_1 a_1$ in Appendix I. As in Appendix I, let us subtract α_i *times* the ith row, $i = 2, \ldots, m$, from its first row. Again the first element of its first row becomes $1 + \alpha_1 + \cdots + \alpha_m$, and all other elements of that row become zero, hence:

$$H = (-1)^m \frac{p_1 \cdots p_m}{a_1 \cdots a_m} X^m (1 + \alpha_1 + \cdots + \alpha_m)$$

The right-hand side always has the same sign as $(-1)^m$, because first, the elasticities $\alpha_1, \ldots, \alpha_m$ and the input prices $p_1, \ldots, p_m$ have been assumed to be positive, second, the variables $a_1, \ldots, a_m$ have been found to be positive, and third from that and (3a) it follows that X is positive. Hence, for $m = 1$ the principal minor is negative, for $m = 2$ it is positive, etc. Thus all conditions for a profit maximum are indeed satisfied.

REFERENCE

[1] Nader, R., *Unsafe at any Speed*, New York, 1966, p. 46.

CHAPTER 15

Optimum Period of Production

15.1 INTRODUCTION

Böhm-Bawerk [1] was the first to set out a rigorous theory of capital, but to him capital always meant circulating capital. Favorite examples used by him and Wicksell [2] were observations of slow biological growth such as maturing wine and growing forests. Here, the key concept was the period of production defined as the lapse of time between the first input of labor and land and the output of the finished product (wine, timber). Such a lapse of time was made possible by capital: Capital "advanced" the wages of labor and the rents of land; this was necessary, for the laborers and landlords cannot wait (if they could they themselves would be capitalists). From this viewpoint, capital was a wages and rent fund. Böhm-Bawerk assumed entrepreneurs to be their own capitalists and showed how they would adjust the variable under their control, that is, the period of production, such as to maximize their internal rate of return.

15.2 NOTATION

In a Böhm-Bawerk microeconomic theory of the firm the following notation will be assigned.

Variables

ι = the internal rate of return per annum
L = number of men employed by firm
τ = the period of production
X = output per annum

Parameters

α = elasticity of output per annum per man with respect to the period of production

M = a multiplicative factor in the production function

P = price of output

w = the money wage rate

15.3 THE MODEL

To simplify things, Böhm-Bawerk assumed land to be a free good, hence rent is zero, and only wages must be advanced. Furthermore, he assumed that the same number of men would work throughout the entire period of production. Let the period of production be τ, and L men work for τ years at the money wage rate w. Total wage payments during the entire period of production are, then, $\tau L w$. Suppose that a man's wages are paid at the beginning of each year. Then at the beginning of the first year the firms' money capital stock is Lw, at the beginning of the second year $2Lw$, ..., and at the beginning of the τth year τLw. Now if the internal rate of return is ι, then profits during the first year are ιLw, during the second year $2\iota Lw$, ..., and during the τth year $\tau \iota Lw$. Over the entire period of production, total wage payments plus total profits equal the total value of output.

(1) $$\tau Lw + \iota Lw(1 + 2 + \cdots + \tau) = \tau PX$$

By using the familiar rule for finding the sum of the first τ terms of an arithmetic progression, dividing away the τ, and rearranging, we may write (1) as

(1a) $$\iota = \frac{2}{1 + \tau}\left(\frac{PX}{Lw} - 1\right)$$

Let annual output per man, X/L, be a rising function of the period of production such that increments are diminishing as, for example, would be true in the function

(2) $$\frac{X}{L} = M\tau^\alpha$$

where $0 < \alpha < 1$, and where M is a positive multiplicative factor. The function (2) is adopted with two restrictions. First, we defined the period of production as the lapse of time between the first input of labor and land and the output of the finished product. A negative period of production would mean, then, that output would precede input, and we can think of no process

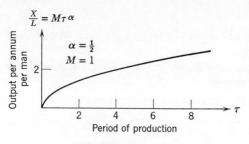

Figure 15.1

in which this would occur. Thus the first restriction is that the period of production must be nonnegative:

(3) $\tau \geq 0$

The second restriction is that annual output per man must be nonnegative.

(4) $\dfrac{X}{L} \geq 0$

Recalling that M was positive, insert (4) into (2) and realize the implication of (4):

(4a) $\tau^\alpha \geq 0$

This implication is important. Suppose, for example, that $\alpha = \frac{1}{2}$ and $M = 1$. Then without the restriction (4), (2) would give us two values of X/L for every positive value of τ, that is, a positive and a negative one.

Thus confined to the first quadrant, the function (2) is illustrated in Fig. 15.1 for the case $\alpha = \frac{1}{2}$ and $M = 1$.

Let there be pure competition in all input and output markets. A potential firm, then, controls neither the wage rate w nor the price P of its output. All it controls is the period of production τ; hence let it adjust the period of production such as to maximize its internal rate of return defined by (1a).

15.4   FIRST-ORDER CONDITION

The first-order condition for a maximum internal rate of return is that the first derivative of (1a) with respect to τ be zero.

(5) $\dfrac{\partial \iota}{\partial \tau} = 0$

By inserting (2) into (1a), we carry out the derivation, set the derivative equal to zero, rearrange, and obtain

$$(6) \qquad\qquad (1 - \alpha)\tau^{\alpha} - \alpha\tau^{\alpha-1} = \frac{1}{M}\frac{w}{P}$$

Does a unique solution for τ exist which is subject to restrictions (3) and (4)? First remember that $0 < \alpha < 1$. Let us examine (6) more closely. In the first left-hand term of (6) τ is raised to the positive power α and multiplied by the positive coefficient $1 - \alpha$; hence for positive τ that term must always be positive and rising with rising τ. When τ equals zero, the term also equals zero. When τ rises without bounds, the term also rises without bounds.

In the second left-hand term of (6) τ is raised to the negative power $\alpha - 1$ and multiplied by the positive coefficient α; hence for positive τ that term must always be positive and falling with rising τ. When τ approaches zero from above, the term rises without bounds. When τ rises without bounds, the term vanishes.

The entire left-hand side of (6) is the difference between the two terms. Consequently, when τ approaches zero from above, the entire left-hand side of (6) falls without bounds, and when τ rises without bounds, the entire left-hand side of (6) rises without bounds. This behavior is illustrated in Fig. 15.2 for the special case $\alpha = \frac{1}{2}$.

Thus subject to our restrictions (3) and (4) a unique solution for τ does exist. If the money wage rate w and the price P are positive, then the right-hand side of (6) is positive and may be represented by a horizontal line at a positive distance from the horizontal τ-axis in Fig. 15.2. Whatever that positive distance is, line and curve must intersect once and once only in the first quadrant.

Furthermore, we can see that the higher the real wage rate w/P, the farther to the right the point of intersection must lie. Consequently, entrepreneurs must respond to a higher real wage rate by expanding their period of production. As we shall see later, this conclusion is crucial for Böhm-Bawerk's general-equilibrium model.

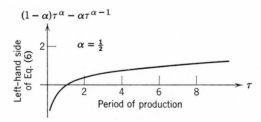

Figure 15.2

15.5 SECOND-ORDER CONDITION

The second-order maximum condition is that the second derivative of (1a) with respect to τ be negative. Use (1a) and write the first derivative

$$\frac{\partial \iota}{\partial \tau} = \frac{2(P/w)M\alpha\tau^{\alpha-1} - \iota}{1 + \tau}$$

Now take the second derivative, use (5), and obtain

(7)
$$\frac{\partial^2 \iota}{\partial \tau^2} = 2\frac{P}{w}\frac{M\alpha(\alpha - 1)\tau^{\alpha-2}}{1 + \tau}$$

On the right-hand side of (7) all factors are positive except $(\alpha - 1)$, which is negative; hence the second derivative (7) is negative, and we have a true maximum.

15.6 POSSIBLE RESTATEMENT?

The acceptance of Böhm-Bawerk's contribution has always been hampered by its narrow confinement to circulating capital. In Chapter 16 we shall see if we can avoid this confinement and yet capture the spirit of Böhm-Bawerk's contribution.

REFERENCES

[1] Von Böhm-Bawerk, Eugen, *Positive Theorie des Kapitales*, Innsbruck 1888. Translated by William Smart as *Positive Theory of Capital*, New York, 1891. Especially Book VII, "The Rate in Market Transactions," and "The Market for Capital in its Full Development," pp. 381–424.
[2] Wicksell, Knut, *Über Wert, Kapital und Rente*, Jena, 1893, especially pp. 90–143.

CHAPTER 16

Optimum Quality of Capital Goods

16.1 INTRODUCTION

Böhm-Bawerk [3] assumed all capital to be circulating. Åkerman [1] and Wicksell [7] were the first to analyze fixed capital, demonstrating how to optimize its useful life. The Åkerman-Wicksell finding, that in the absence of technological progress the lower the rate of interest the longer the optimum useful life, was rediscovered by Blitz and Westfield [2].

We should very much like to determine optimum useful life but would rather do it in the presence of technological progress, and we shall do so in Chapter 17. In the present chapter we shall treat useful life as a parameter and examine a different dimension of fixed capital to be optimized, that is, its degree of automation: Whether one man should operate, say, a pick-and-shovel set or a bulldozer.

16.2 NOTATION

The following notation will be assigned.

Variables

a = minimum labor required to build one unit of producers' goods
b = physical capital stock held by firm per unit of output
K = money value of capital stock held by firm
L = number of men employed by firm
n = present net worth of a new unit of producers' goods
P = price of consumers' goods
p = price of a new unit of producers' goods
S = physical capital stock held by firm
X = output produced and sold per annum

Parameters

β = elasticity of labor requirement with respect to capital coefficient
e = Euler's number, the base of natural logarithms
η = price elasticity of demand faced by firm
i = rate of interest per annum
M = multiplicative factor in the production function
N = multiplicative factor in the demand function
w = the money wage rate
u = useful life of producers' goods

16.3   THE MODEL

Consider a firm facing the constant-elasticity demand function:

(1) $$X = NP^{\eta}$$

where $\eta < -1$ and $N > 0$. The demand function (1) is adopted with these two restrictions: $P > 0$ and $X > 0$.

The firm employs a labor force L and holds a physical capital stock S of producers' goods, all of which are alike. Define a physical unit of producers' goods as the equipment operated by one man; then

(2) $$L = S$$

Define the capital coefficient as the physical capital stock per unit of output

(3) $$b = \frac{S}{X}$$

Or, if preferable, the reciprocal $1/b$ is defined as the output per unit of producers' goods X/S.

All units of producers' goods were said to be alike, but we have not yet said *what* they should be like. We have not yet said whether one man should operate a pick-and-shovel set or a bulldozer. Or whether he should operate an abacus, an adding machine, a desk calculator, or an electronic digital computer. To determine *what* producers' goods should be like is precisely our optimization problem.

For simplicity let the producers' goods industry need no producers' goods for inputs, and let its period of production be of negligible length. Hence it uses only one input, labor.[1] Let a be the minimum labor required to build

---

[1] The assumption that producers' goods are made from labor alone is an extreme one, but according to Gordon [5] it is at least true that "taken as a whole, the capital goods sector is more labor-intensive than that for consumers' goods."

one unit of producers' goods. The minimum labor required to build a bull-dozer greatly exceeds that required to build a pick-and-shovel set, and that required to build a computer greatly exceeds that required to build an abacus. Let the production function for producers' goods express the minimum building labor as a function of the capital coefficient b, and let that function be of the constant-elasticity type

$$(4) \qquad\qquad a = Mb^{\beta}$$

where $M > 0$ and $\beta < -1$. The parameter β is the elasticity of minimum building labor with respect to the capital coefficient and must be assumed to be negative. As previously stated, the minimum building labor required to build the computer exceeds that required to build the abacus. However, to keep trees from growing up to the sky, β must also be assumed to lie on the far side of *minus* one. That is, cutting the capital coefficient in half must more than double building labor. The production function (4) is adopted with the restriction that $b > 0$. Thus restricted, the function is shown in Fig. 16.1 in two alternative ways: Either the capital coefficient b itself or its reciprocal, the capacity $1/b$, is used for an independent variable. Figure 16.2 reproduces from Chenery [4] an empirical counterpart to Fig. 16.1. We notice that for capacities exceeding 80 million cubic feet of gas per day Chenery's curve shows capital to rise more than proportionally to capacity—as we assume that it did.

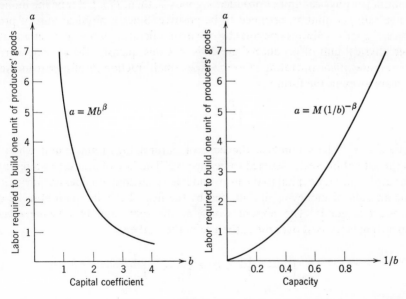

Figure 16.1

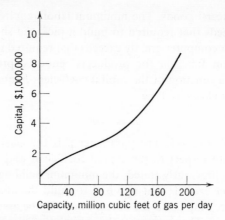

Figure 16.2. From Hollis B. Chenery, "Engineering Production Functions," *Quart. Jour. Econ.*, **63**, 526, Figure 5 (November 1949).

16.4 NET WORTH

In dynamic planning the firm should maximize its net worth; therefore let us carefully define net worth. Let P be the price of output. Revenue per annum per physical unit of producers' goods is, then, P/b. Let w be the money wage rate per annum, assumed to be positive. Since a physical unit of producers' goods is always operated by one man, operating labor cost per annum per physical unit of producers' goods is w. Consequently, the present worth of revenue *minus* operating labor cost per small fraction dt of a year located t years away in the future is

$$\left(\frac{P}{b} - w\right) e^{-it}\, dt$$

where e is Euler's number, the base of natural logarithms,[2] and where i is the rate of interest, assumed to be positive. The rate of interest i represents the cost of money capital to the firm, and it is assumed that i does not vary with the amount of money capital needed by the firm. Let u be the useful life of producers' goods. The present worth of the sum total of revenue *minus* operating labor cost over the entire useful life is, then,

$$\int_0^u \left(\frac{P}{b} - w\right) e^{-it}\, dt = \left(\frac{P}{b} - w\right) \frac{1 - e^{-iu}}{i}$$

[2] We use continuous compounding, and with it Euler's number, in order to profit from the fact that $\int e^x\, dx = e^x$.

Let p be the price of a new unit of producers' goods. The present net worth of the acquisition of one such unit is then defined as

$$(5) \qquad n = \left(\frac{P}{b} - w\right)\frac{1 - e^{-iu}}{i} - p$$

Let firms in the producers' goods industry be fully integrated with our firm in the consumers' goods industry. To its own specification, suppose that our firm orders producers' goods to be delivered at a price p equaling the unit cost of producing them.

$$(6) \qquad p = aw$$

By using (1), (3), (5), and (6), we may write the present net worth of acquiring the entire capital stock S needed to put the firm into business, satisfying the demand for its output.

$$(7) \qquad nS = bNP^\eta w\left[\left(\frac{P}{bw} - 1\right)\frac{1 - e^{-iu}}{i} - a\right]$$

The firm should now adjust the variables under its control b and P such as to maximize (7).

16.5 FIRST-ORDER CONDITION

Vary the capital coefficient b, on the one hand, and the price of output P, on the other, and take first partial derivatives of net worth nS with respect to b and P. The first-order conditions for a net worth maximum are that both first partial derivatives be zero.

$$(8) \qquad \frac{\partial(nS)}{\partial b} = -bNP^\eta w\left[\left(\frac{1 - e^{-iu}}{i} + a\right)\frac{1}{b} + \frac{da}{db}\right] = 0$$

$$(9) \qquad \frac{\partial(nS)}{\partial P} = bNP^{\eta-1}\eta w\left[\left(\frac{1 + \eta}{\eta}\frac{P}{bw} - 1\right)\frac{1 - e^{-iu}}{i} - a\right] = 0$$

By using (4), carry out the derivation required by (8) and express the zero conditions

$$(10) \qquad \frac{1}{a}\frac{1 - e^{-iu}}{i} + 1 = -\beta$$

$$(11) \qquad \left(\frac{1 + \eta}{\eta}\frac{P}{bw} - 1\right)\frac{1 - e^{-iu}}{i} = a$$

16.6   SECOND-ORDER   CONDITION

The second-order conditions for a net worth maximum are as follows:
Form the Hessian second-order determinant of the second derivatives

$$H = \begin{vmatrix} \dfrac{\partial^2(nS)}{\partial b^2} & \dfrac{\partial^2(nS)}{\partial b\,\partial P} \\[2ex] \dfrac{\partial^2(nS)}{\partial P\,\partial b} & \dfrac{\partial^2(nS)}{\partial P^2} \end{vmatrix}$$

This determinant should be positive. Form its principal minor by deleting
its last row and column. This minor should be negative. In the Appendix we
show that these two conditions are satisfied.

Our system of simultaneous equations may now be solved for the optimum
capital coefficient b, the optimum physical capital stock S, and the demand
for money capital K. From such solutions the interest elasticities of b, S, and
K may be determined.

16.7   SOLUTION   FOR   OPTIMUM   CAPITAL   COEFFICIENT b

By combining (4) and (10), we find

(12)
$$b = \left(-\frac{1}{1+\beta}\frac{1-e^{-iu}}{i}\frac{1}{M} \right)^{1/\beta}$$

The quantity $1 + \beta$ is negative, hence the expression in parentheses is
positive and b is real and positive. To see how the optimum capital coefficient
varies with the rate of interest, find the elasticity of b with respect to i.

(13)
$$\frac{\partial b}{\partial i}\frac{i}{b} = \frac{1}{\beta}\frac{iu - e^{iu} + 1}{e^{iu} - 1}$$

The expression $(iu - e^{iu} + 1)/(e^{iu} - 1)$ is mapped in Fig. 16.3, and for
relevant values of i and u we see that it lies between zero and *minus* one. The
elasticity β is negative and less than *minus* one. Hence the elasticity (13) will
lie between zero and *plus* one. The optimum capital coefficient b will fall with
falling rate of interest i but will be inelastic with respect to the interest rate.
Its elasticity will be higher, the higher are the negative elasticity β, and the
rate of interest i, and the longer is useful life u. The solution (12) contains
neither w nor η, so the optimal capital coefficient varies with neither the
money wage rate nor with the price elasticity of demand.[3]

[3] The complete insensitivity of the capital coefficient b to the money wage rate w is
explained by the result that according to (14) price of output P is in direct proportion to
w. The insensitivity is a beautiful example of Samuelson's [6] Nonsubstitution Theorem.

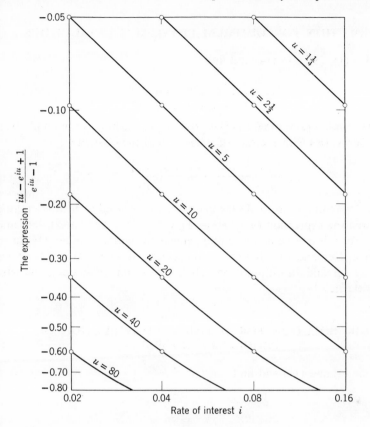

The expression $\dfrac{iu - e^{iu} + 1}{e^{iu} - 1}$

Rate of interest i

Figure 16.3

16.8 SOLUTION FOR OPTIMUM PRICE OF OUTPUT P

Combine (10) and (11) and find

$$(14) \qquad P = \frac{\beta}{1 + \beta} \frac{\eta}{1 + \eta} \, bw$$

Since both elasticities β and η were assumed to be negative and less than *minus* one, since the optimum capital coefficient b was found to be positive, and since the money wage rate w was assumed to be positive, (14) must be positive. For a known capital coefficient b, (14) shows the price of output P to be in direct proportion to the money wage rate w and the capital coefficient b.

16.9 SOLUTION FOR OPTIMUM PHYSICAL CAPITAL STOCK S

Combine (1), (3), and (14) and find

(15)
$$S = N\left(\frac{\beta}{1+\beta}\frac{\eta}{1+\eta}w\right)^{\eta}b^{1+\eta}$$

Under the assumptions made (15) is positive. To see how optimum physical capital stock varies with the rate of interest, find the elasticity

(16)
$$\frac{\partial S}{\partial i}\frac{i}{S} = \frac{1+\eta}{\beta}\frac{iu - e^{iu} + 1}{e^{iu} - 1}$$

Under the assumptions made the expression $(1 + \eta)/\beta$ is positive. Figure 16.3 showed the expression $(iu - e^{iu} + 1)/(e^{iu} - 1)$ to lie between zero and *minus* one for relevant values of i and u. Hence the entire elasticity (16) must be negative. Demand for physical capital stock will be inelastic if the price elasticity of demand for output is only slightly less than *minus* one, otherwise it will be elastic.

16.10 SOLUTION FOR OPTIMUM CONSTRUCTION OF PRODUCERS' GOODS a

Combine (4) and (12) and find

(17)
$$a = -\frac{1}{1+\beta}\frac{1 - e^{-iu}}{i}$$

Since the elasticity β was assumed to be less than *minus* one, (17) will be positive.

16.11 SOLUTION FOR PRICE OF PRODUCERS' GOODS p

Combine (6) and (17) and find

(18)
$$p = -\frac{1}{1+\beta}\frac{1 - e^{-iu}}{i}w$$

For the assumed values $1 + \beta < 0$ and $w > 0$, (18) is positive.

16.12 SOLUTION FOR THE DEMAND FOR MONEY CAPITAL K

Having now solved for optimum physical capital stock S and its price p, we may now find their product $K = pS$, the money value of optimum capital stock. Use (12), (15), and (18) and find

$$(19) \quad K = \left(\frac{1}{M}\right)^{(1+\eta)/\beta} N \left(\frac{\beta}{1+\beta}\frac{\eta}{1+\eta}\right)^\eta w^{1+\eta} \left(-\frac{1}{1+\beta}\frac{1-e^{-iu}}{i}\right)^{(1+\beta+\eta)/\beta}$$

The elasticity of the demand for money capital K with respect to the rate of interest i is

$$(20) \quad \frac{\partial K}{\partial i}\frac{i}{K} = \frac{1+\beta+\eta}{\beta}\frac{iu-e^{iu}+1}{e^{iu}-1}$$

Under the assumptions made the expression $(1+\beta+\eta)/\beta$ is positive. Figure 16.3 showed the expression $(iu-e^{iu}+1)/(e^{iu}-1)$ to lie between zero and *minus* one for relevant values of i and u. Hence the entire elasticity (20) must be negative. Demand for money capital will be inelastic if the price elasticity of demand for output is only slightly less than *minus* one, otherwise it may be elastic.

Comparing (20) and (16) we notice that the only difference between them is the addition of β in the numerator of (20). Consequently, the demand for money capital K is more interest-elastic than was the demand for physical capital stock S. This is natural: The demand for money capital K rises with falling rate of interest i, not only because the demand for physical capital stock S rises but also because more automatic producers' goods with a lower capital coefficient b and a higher price tag p now become optimal.

16.13 CONCLUSIONS

To handle the difficult problem of the optimum quality of producers' goods we have made the following simplifying assumptions. The firm considers useful life to be a parameter. Throughout this useful life the firm expects to be facing the same price-elastic demand curve for its output and to be paying the same money wage rate. The firm uses only one kind of producers' goods, built from labor alone. Building labor varies with the quality of producers' goods, and cutting the capital coefficient in half more than doubles building labor.

By assuming that the firm maximized its net worth we found optimum values of the capital coefficient b, the physical capital stock S, and demand for money capital K. The interest elasticity of the capital coefficient b was found to lie between zero and *plus* one. The interest elasticities of physical capital stock S and money capital K were both found to be negative, and both could lie on either side of *minus* one. However, the demand for money capital K was always more elastic than the demand for physical capital stock S, because a lower rate of interest i not only induces firms to use *more* producers' goods, but also induces them to use *better* ones, that is, more automatic ones having a lower capital coefficient and carrying a higher price tag.

Examining the quality optimization problem as we have done here yields, perhaps, better insight into the automation phenomenon than does the standard approach. Automation has a twofold effect. First, it raises minimum building labor required to build one unit of producers' goods a. Second, it reduces the capital coefficient b. We have defined a physical unit of producers' goods as the equipment operated by one man; consequently, a reduction of b means fewer such physical units, and with them fewer men, required to produce a given output. The essence of automation, then, is to increase the demand for building labor but to reduce the demand for operating labor. Only by distinguishing as sharply between building and operating labor as we have done can we capture this essence.

APPENDIX PROOF THAT SECOND-ORDER CONDITIONS ARE SATISFIED

Equations (8) and (9) are the first derivatives of the present net worth of the acquisition of the entire capital stock with respect to the capital coefficient b and the price of output P. By using them the second derivatives entering the Hessian determinant are found to be

(21)
$$\frac{\partial^2(nS)}{\partial b^2} = -bNP^n w \left(\frac{2}{b} \frac{da}{db} + \frac{d^2a}{db^2} \right)$$

(22)
$$\frac{\partial^2(nS)}{\partial P \, \partial b} = 0$$

(23)
$$\frac{\partial^2(nS)}{\partial b \, \partial P} = 0$$

(24)
$$\frac{\partial^2(nS)}{\partial P^2} = bNP^n w(1 + \eta) \frac{1}{bw} \frac{1}{P} \frac{1 - e^{-iu}}{i}$$

From (4) we obtain the following:

(25)
$$\frac{da}{db} = \frac{a}{b} \beta$$

(26)
$$\frac{d^2a}{db^2} = \frac{a}{b^2} \beta(\beta - 1)$$

By using (10), insert (25) and (26) into (21) and derive

(27)
$$\frac{\partial^2(nS)}{\partial b^2} = \frac{\beta}{b} NP^n w \frac{1 - e^{-iu}}{i}$$

By using (14), we write (24) as

(28)
$$\frac{\partial^2(nS)}{\partial P^2} = \frac{1}{b} NP^\eta w \frac{1 - e^{-iu}}{i} \frac{1 + \beta}{\beta} \frac{1}{\eta} \left(\frac{1 + \eta}{w}\right)^2$$

Inserting (27) and (28) into the Hessian determinant, we write it as

$$H = \left(-\frac{1}{b} NP^\eta w \frac{1 - e^{-iu}}{i}\right)^2 \begin{vmatrix} -\beta & 0 \\ 0 & -\frac{1 + \beta}{\beta} \frac{1}{\eta} \left(\frac{1 + \eta}{w}\right)^2 \end{vmatrix}$$

This determinant is positive, for a square has been factored out and is always positive, and β and η are both less than *minus* one.

Form the principal minor of this determinant by deleting its last row and column. What has now been factored out is no longer a square but a negative number raised to the first power, and the only element left inside is $-\beta$, which is positive. Hence the principal minor is negative, and the second-order conditions for a maximum present net worth of the entire capital stock are indeed satisfied.

REFERENCES

[1] Åkerman, G., *Realkapital und Kapitalzins*, Stockholm, 1923.

[2] Blitz, R. C., "Capital Longevity and Economic Development," and F. M. Westfield, "A Mathematical Note on Optimum Longevity," *Am. Econ. Rev.*, **48**, 313–332 (June 1958).

[3] Von Böhm-Bawerk, E., *Positive Theorie des Kapitales*, Innsbruck, 1888.

[4] Chenery, H. B., "Engineering Production Functions," *Quart. Jour. Econ.*, **63**, 526, Fig. 5 (November 1949).

[5] Gordon, R. A., "Differential Changes in the Prices of Consumers' and Capital Goods," *Am. Econ. Rev.*, **51**, 937–957 (December 1961).

[6] Samuelson, P. A., "A New Theorem on Nonsubstitution," in *Money, Growth, and Methodology and Other Essays in Economics in Honor of Johan Åkerman*, edited by H. Hegeland, Lund, Sweden, 1961, pp. 407–423.

[7] Wicksell, K., "Realkapital och kapitalränta," *Ekonomisk Tidskrift*, **25**, 145–180 (1923). Translated as the second appendix to *Lectures on Political Economy*, **1**, London, 1934.

CHAPTER 17

Optimum Replacement of Capital Goods

17.1 INTRODUCTION

In Chapters 12 and 16 we found optimum capital stocks of durable producers' goods to be held by the firm. Clearly, the determination of optimum stock is one thing and the determination of the optimum flow of durable producers' goods required to maintain such a stock is quite another. To proceed from optimum stock to optimum flow we need a model of optimum replacement of durable producers' goods. The purpose of this chapter is to provide such a model.

Assume realistically that designing and maintenance standards of durable producers' goods permit a useful life far in excess of what is economically optimal under technological obsolescence. This does not mean that the designing and maintenance standards mentioned are mistaken or wasteful. Lesser standards could indeed shorten potential useful life, but probably only by jeopardizing the trouble-free daily operation so vital to the firm.

Exactly which useful life is optimal under technological obsolescence? Durable producers' goods should not be replaced too soon, or the cost of acquiring them occurs too frequently. They should not be replaced too late either, or the falling price of their output catches up with them: Once in place they have irreducible operating costs, while new producers' goods of later vintages and higher efficiency become available to the firm as well as to potential entrants into the industry. To protect itself against this entry the firm must, then, plan for the price of its output to be falling steadily. As retirement is postponed, the efficiency of the old producers' goods is more and more at odds with the falling price of output; hence the pressure for retirement builds up.

Avoiding the assumption of pure competition, in this chapter we try to

152

find the optimum useful life of producers' goods and to examine its sensitivity to their price, the rate of interest, and the rate of technological progress.

17.2 NOTATION

In a microeconomic theory of the firm the following notation will be assigned.

Variables

A = present net worth of the endless stream of all future acquisitions of producers' goods by the firm

L = number of men employed by the firm

n = present net worth of a new unit of producers' goods

P = price of consumers' goods

p = price of a new unit of producers' goods

S = physical capital stock held by firm

X = output produced and sold per annum

u = useful life of producers' goods

Parameters

a = minimum labor required to build one unit of producers' goods

b = physical capital stock held by firm per unit of output

e = Euler's number, the base of natural logarithms

η = price elasticity of demand faced by firm

i = rate of interest per annum

μ = rate of technological progress

N = multiplicative factor in the demand function

w = the money wage rate

17.3 DEMAND FACED BY FIRM

Consider a firm facing at time v the constant-elasticity demand function

$$(1) \qquad X(v) = N(v)[P(v)]^{\eta}$$

where $\eta < -1$ and $N(v) > 0$. The demand function (1) is adopted with these two restrictions: $P(v) > 0$ and $X(v) > 0$.

17.4 THE PHYSICAL CAPITAL COEFFICIENT DEFINED

At time v let the firm employ a labor force $L(v)$ operating a physical capital stock $S(v)$ of newly built producers' goods of vintage v. Define a physical unit of producers' goods as the equipment operated by one man.

(2) $L(v) = S(v)$

All producers' goods of the same vintage are exactly alike. The physical capital coefficient $b(v)$ of newly built producers' goods of vintage v is defined as the physical capital stock of such goods held at time v per unit of their output per annum.

(3) $b(v) = \dfrac{S(v)}{X(v)}$

17.5   TECHNOLOGICAL PROGRESS DEFINED

Producers' goods of different vintages are not alike. Let technological progress manifest itself in a steady reduction of the physical capital coefficient $b(t)$ of newly built producers' goods of vintage t, where $v < t$; then

(4) $b(t) = e^{\mu(t-v)}b(v)$

where μ is the proportionate rate of technological progress per annum with continuous compounding and $\mu < 0$.

17.6   TECHNOLOGICAL PROGRESS REFLECTED IN THE PRICE POLICY OF THE FIRM

At time v let the firm acquire the newest available producers' goods, that is, producers' goods of vintage v. During the useful life of those producers' goods, other firms may at any time t, where $v < t < v + u$, enter the industry by acquiring new producers' goods of vintage t. Let them do so whenever the net worth $n(t)$ of acquisition of a new unit of producers' goods of vintage t, as seen at time t, exceeds the net worth $n(v)$ of a new unit of vintage v, as seen at time v. As we shall prove in Section 17.7, the firm may protect itself from such entry by reducing its price steadily such that

(5) $P(t) = e^{\mu(t-v)}P(v)$

where again μ is the rate of technological progress, defined by Eq. (4), and $P(v)$ is price of output at time v. Let the firm adopt the policy of steady price reduction defined by Eq. (5).

17.7   FINDING THE NET WORTH OF A NEW UNIT OF PRODUCERS' GOODS

The physical capital coefficient of producers' goods of vintage v is $b(v)$. That capital coefficient remains frozen for the entire useful life u of producers' goods. At time t, $P(t)$ is the price of output, therefore revenue per annum per physical unit of producers' goods is $P(t)/b(v)$. Since $P(t)$ is steadily declining according to (5) but $b(v)$ is frozen, revenue is steadily declining during useful life. Let w be the money wage rate per annum, assumed to be positive. Since a physical unit of producers' goods is always operated by one man, operating labor cost per annum per physical unit of producers' goods is w. At time v the worth of revenue *minus* operating labor cost per small fraction dt of a year located at time t is, then

(6)
$$\left[\frac{P(t)}{b(v)} - w\right]e^{-i(t-v)}\, dt$$

where e is Euler's number, the base of natural logarithms, and i is the rate of interest, assumed to be positive. The rate of interest i represents the cost of money capital to the firm and is assumed not to vary with the amount of money needed by the firm. Insert (5) into (6) and write (6) as

(7)
$$\left[\frac{P(v)}{b(v)}e^{\mu(t-v)} - w\right]e^{-i(t-v)}\, dt$$

At time v the worth of the sum total of revenue *minus* operating labor cost over the entire useful life u of the unit of producers' good is, then

$$\int_{v}^{v+u}\left[\frac{P(v)}{b(v)}e^{\mu(t-v)} - w\right]e^{-i(t-v)}\, dt = \frac{P(v)}{b(v)}\frac{1 - e^{(\mu-i)u}}{i - \mu} - w\frac{1 - e^{-iu}}{i}$$

Let p be the price of a new unit of producers' good. Assume the salvage value of the unit when retired to be zero. The *net* worth of the acquisition of a new unit of producers' good of vintage v, as seen at time v, is then

(8)
$$n(v) = \frac{P(v)}{b(v)}\frac{1 - e^{(\mu-i)u}}{i - \mu} - w\frac{1 - e^{-iu}}{i} - p$$

For simplicity let the producers' goods industry need no producers' goods for inputs, and let its period of construction be of negligible length. Hence it uses only one input, labor. Let a be the minimum labor required to build one unit of durable producers' goods, and suppose firms in the producers' goods industry to be fully integrated with firms in the consumers' goods industry. To their own specification, the consumers' goods firms order producers' goods from the producers' goods firms, to be delivered at an accounting price p equaling the unit cost of producing producers' goods. Then

(9)
$$p = aw$$

regardless of vintage. Inserting (9) into (8),

(10) $$n(v) = \frac{P(v)}{b(v)} \frac{1 - e^{(\mu-i)u}}{i - \mu} - w \frac{1 - e^{-iu} + ai}{i}$$

Equation (10) defines the net worth of the acquisition of a new unit of producers' good of vintage v, as seen at time v. However, it follows from (4) and (5) that

(11) $$\frac{P(t)}{b(t)} = \frac{P(v)}{b(v)}$$

Thus we have proved that under our price policy assumption (5) the net worth of acquisition of a new unit of producers' goods of vintage t, as seen at time t, will indeed equal that of a new unit of vintage v, as seen at time v. This is not surprising, for the lower output price P of producers' goods of later vintage is exactly offset by their lower capital coefficient b, so their revenue is stationary. Moreover, everything else is stationary; the building labor of new producers' goods is still a, the goods are still operated by one man, and the money wage rate is still w.

17.8 HOW FREQUENTLY SHOULD REPLACEMENT TAKE PLACE?

The substitution that we shall now study is that between new producers' goods and old ones on the verge of retirement: How frequently should a stock of old producers' goods be replaced by a stock of new ones? A new stock of what capacity? This problem is a problem of pure replacement and should be purged of everything else. Consequently, at replacement time old stock should be replaced by new stock of the same capacity, or the choice would no longer be purely between new and old stock but would also be a choice between expansion of capacity and no expansion.

Thus let a capital stock be forever replaced every u years, maintaining constant capacity. At time $t = 0$ let the firm acquire the vintage zero capital stock $S(0) = b(0)X(0)$. At time $t = u$ this vintage zero capital stock is retired and replaced by vintage u capital stock. But vintage u capital stock is more efficient than was vintage zero capital stock. According to (4), $b(u) = e^{\mu u}b(0)$, where $\mu < 0$, so the physical capital stock needed for replacement is less, that is, $S(u) = b(u)X(0) = e^{\mu u}b(0)X(0)$.

At time $t = 2u$ the second replacement takes place, and again the physical capital stock needed for replacement is less, that is, $S(2u) = b(2u)X(0) = e^{2\mu u}b(0)X(0)$. Every u years another replacement takes place, and at time

$t = ju$ the physical capital stock required for the jth replacement is

$$(12) \qquad S(ju) = e^{j\mu u}b(0)X(0)$$

17.9 NET WORTH OF FUTURE PHYSICAL CAPITAL STOCKS REQUIRED FOR REPLACEMENT

By using (10), (11), and (12) we find that at time $t = ju$, the net worth of the acquisition of the $S(ju)$ new units required for the jth replacement is

$$(13) \qquad n(ju)S(ju) = e^{j\mu u}b(0)n(0)X(0)$$

This net worth of the acquisition of the $S(ju)$ new units required for the jth replacement is seen at time $t = ju$. Let us see it instead from time $t = 0$. Discounting net worth from $t = ju$ to $t = 0$, we multiply it by e^{-iju}, so that it shrinks to $e^{(\mu - i)ju}b(0)n(0)X(0)$. Let us now find the net worth as seen from $t = 0$ not only of the jth replacement but of all the $j + 1$ acquisitions $S(0)$, $S(u)$, $S(2u)$, . . . , $S(ju)$, ending with the jth replacement. That sum is

$$b(0)n(0)X(0)[1 + e^{(\mu - i)u} + e^{(\mu - i)2u} + \cdots + e^{(\mu - i)ju}]$$

The expression in brackets is a geometrical progression of $j + 1$ terms, and each term equals the preceding one *times* $e^{(\mu - i)u}$. Notice that the exponent $(\mu - i)u < 0$. Now let $j + 1$ rise without bounds and find the net worth of such an endless series of generations $S(0)$, $S(u)$, $S(2u)$, . . . , as seen at time $t = 0$; then

$$(14) \qquad A(0) = \frac{b(0)n(0)X(0)}{1 - e^{(\mu - i)u}}$$

In (1) and (10) set $v = 0$ throughout and insert (1) and (10) into (14); thus

$$(15) \qquad A(0) = b(0)N(0)[P(0)]^n \left[\frac{P(0)}{b(0)} \frac{1}{i - \mu} - \frac{w}{i} \frac{1 - e^{-iu} + ai}{1 - e^{(\mu - i)u}} \right]$$

The firm should adjust the two variables under its control, that is, initial price $P(0)$ and useful life u such as to maximize (15).

17.10 FIRST-ORDER CONDITIONS

Vary the price of output $P(0)$, on the one hand, and the useful life u, on the other, and take first partial derivatives of the net worth $A(0)$ with respect to $P(0)$ and u. The first-order conditions for a net worth maximum are that both first partial derivatives be zero.

(16) $\dfrac{\partial A(0)}{\partial P(0)} = b(0)N(0)[P(0)]^{\eta-1}\left[\dfrac{P(0)}{b(0)}\dfrac{1+\eta}{i-\mu} - \eta\dfrac{w}{i}\dfrac{1-e^{-iu}+ai}{1-e^{(\mu-i)u}}\right] = 0$

(17) $\dfrac{\partial A(0)}{\partial u} = -b(0)N(0)[P(0)]^{\eta}\dfrac{w}{i}$

$$\times \dfrac{[1-e^{(\mu-i)u}]ie^{-iu} + [1-e^{-iu}+ai](\mu-i)e^{(\mu-i)u}}{[1-e^{(\mu-i)u}]^2}$$

$$= 0$$

Solve (16) for $P(0)$ and (17) for u, respectively; then

(18) $$P(0) = \dfrac{\eta}{1+\eta}\dfrac{i-\mu}{i}\dfrac{1-e^{-iu}+ai}{1-e^{(\mu-i)u}}b(0)w$$

(19) $$ie^{-\mu u} - \mu e^{-iu} = (ai+1)(i-\mu)$$

Equation (18) is an explicit solution for $P(0)$. Equation (19) is beautiful but does not permit an explicit solution for u. We can prove, however, that one and only one positive solution for u exists. First set $u = 0$ and see that the left-hand side of (19) turns into $i - \mu$. Next let u rise above zero and take the derivative:

$$\dfrac{\partial(ie^{-\mu u} - \mu e^{-iu})}{\partial u} = -\mu ie^{-iu}[e^{(i-\mu)u} - 1]$$

For $i > 0$, $\mu < 0$, and $u > 0$ this derivative is positive, which means that the left-hand side of (19) always rises with rising u. Furthermore, it rises without bounds. The first term of (19) has e raised to the positive power $-\mu u$ and multiplied by the positive coefficient i; thus when u rises without bounds the first term also does so. The second term has e raised to the negative power $-iu$ and multiplied by the positive coefficient $-\mu$; therefore when u rises without bounds the second term vanishes. Consequently, the left-hand side of (19) rises without bounds, because it is the sum of a term rising without bounds and a vanishing term. For $a = 8$, $i = 0.08$, and $\mu = -0.02$, Fig. 17.1 shows the left-hand side of (19) as a function of u.

Now for $i > 0$ and $a > 0$ the right-hand side of (19) is greater than $i - \mu$; hence it may be represented by a horizontal line at a positive distance greater than $i - \mu$ from the horizontal axis in Fig. 17.1. Therefore, in the first quadrant, line and curve must intersect once and only once.

Equation (18) shows that for $a > 0$, $b > 0$, $i > 0$, $\mu < 0$, $u > 0$, $w > 0$, and elastic demand, one and only one positive solution for $P(0)$ exists.

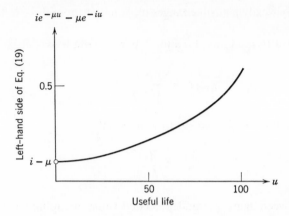

Figure 17.1. Conditions: $a = 8$, $i = 0.08$, $\mu = -0.02$.

For the purpose of Chapter 48 we shall find it useful to express optimal price $P(0)$ as a function of optimal useful life u; therefore insert (19) into (18).

$$(20) \qquad P(0) = \frac{\eta}{1 + \eta}\, e^{-\mu u} b(0) w$$

17.11   SECOND-ORDER CONDITIONS

Form the Hessian second-order determinant of the second derivatives:

$$(21) \qquad H = \begin{vmatrix} \dfrac{\partial^2 A(0)}{\partial [P(0)]^2} & \dfrac{\partial^2 A(0)}{\partial P(0)\, \partial u} \\[2ex] \dfrac{\partial^2 A(0)}{\partial u\, \partial P(0)} & \dfrac{\partial^2 A(0)}{\partial u^2} \end{vmatrix}$$

This determinant should be positive. Form its principal minor by deleting its last row and column. This minor should be negative. In the Appendix we see that these two conditions are satisfied.

17.12   EMPIRICALLY PLAUSIBLE RANGES OF VALUES OF a, i, AND μ

The solution (19) expresses optimum useful life u as a function of minimum building labor a, the rate of interest i, and the rate of technological progress

μ. What are empirically plausible ranges of values of those three independent variables?

First, in regard to minimum building labor a, write it as

$$a = \frac{awS(v)}{wS(v)}$$

Then take advantage of (2) and (9) to write it as

$$a = \frac{pS(v)}{wL(v)}$$

or the ratio between aggregate undepreciated value of capital stock and the consumers' goods industry's annual wage bill. In the real world, some capital stock is used by the producers' goods industry, so let us look for the ratio between aggregate undepreciated value of capital stock and the aggregate wage bill. In developed and underdeveloped economies respectively, the aggregate undepreciated value of capital stock is from 6 to 3 times net national product, and labor's share is from $\frac{4}{5}$ to $\frac{3}{4}$, respectively. Consequently, an empirically plausible value for a would be from 8 to 4 in developed and underdeveloped economies, respectively.

Second—the rate of interest i—in the United States the actual rate of return on reproducible depreciated capital stock has been around 0.08 [2, pp. 983, 943].

Finally, for the rate of technological progress μ, it follows from (2) and (3) that $1/b(v) = X(v)/L(v)$: The reciprocal of the physical capital coefficient equals average labor productivity in the consumers' goods industry. Ignoring the fact that labor productivity rises faster in the consumers' goods industry than in the producers' goods industry, let us look for labor productivity in the economy as a whole. In the United States between 1900 and 1949 real income per man hour tripled, [2, p. 937] corresponding to an annual proportionate rate with continuous compounding of 0.0224. So if the real world's rise in real income per man hour had been due to technological progress alone, and if technological progress had been the same in the consumers' and the producers' goods industries, our μ would be -0.0224.

17.13 SOLUTIONS FOR EMPIRICALLY PLAUSIBLE RANGES OF VALUES OF a, i, AND μ

Let minimum building labor vary from 4 to 16 man years, let the rate of interest i vary from 0.04 to 0.16 per annum, and let the rate of technological

Table 17.1 Values of Useful Life u as Computed
from Equation (19)

$$(a = 4)$$

μ \ i	0.04	0.08	0.12	0.16
−0.01	32	40	48	56
−0.02	21	24	27	31
−0.03	17	19	21	22
−0.04	15	15	17	19

progress μ vary from −0.01 to −0.04. Tables 17.1 through 17.4 show 64 solutions of Eq. (19) within these ranges. For example, for $a = 8$, $i = 0.08$, and $\mu = -0.03$, useful life u is found to be 26 years, a not implausible value.[1] To obtain these 64 solutions, binary chopping and the Newton-Raphson root approximation method were used on an I.B.M. 7094 digital computer. The computer produced the 64 solutions in 12 seconds.

On a double-logarithmic scale, Figs. 17.2 through 17.7 map some of the results of Tables 17.1 through 17.4. Double-logarithmic scale was preferred, because on such a scale the elasticities of u with respect to a, i, and μ will appear visibly as the slope of the curve. And only elasticities can measure the sensitivity of u to a, i, and μ, as long as u does not have the same

Table 17.2 Values of Useful Life u as Computed
from Equation (19)

$$(a = 8)$$

μ \ i	0.04	0.08	0.12	0.16
−0.01	48	62	75	89
−0.02	30	36	42	48
−0.03	23	26	30	33
−0.04	19	22	24	26

[1] Goldsmith [1] makes the point that under static conditions the current (depreciated) value of capital stock is equal to the current value of total output multiplied by one-half the average life of total output. In the United States the depreciated capital to net output ratio is 3.1, gross national product is $\frac{35}{32}$ *times* net national product, and four-fifths of the gross national product consists of consumers' goods. Set the useful life of consumers' goods equal to zero; then the average useful life of the rest of the gross national product, that is, producers' goods output, must be 28 years.

Table 17.3 Values of Useful Life u as Computed from Equation (19)

$(a = 12)$

i μ	0.04	0.08	0.12	0.16
−0.01	60	79	97	112
−0.02	38	44	52	60
−0.03	28	32	38	42
−0.04	24	26	30	32

Table 17.4 Values of Useful Life u as Computed from Equation (19)

$(a = 16)$

i μ	0.04	0.08	0.12	0.16
−0.01	71	95	114	133
−0.02	44	52	62	69
−0.03	32	38	44	48
−0.04	26	30	34	38

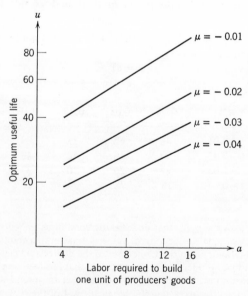

Figure 17.2. Condition: $i = 0.08$.

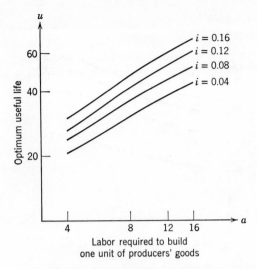

Figure 17.3. Condition: $\mu = -0.02$.

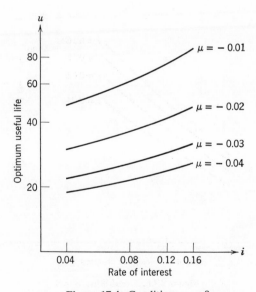

Figure 17.4. Condition: $a = 8$.

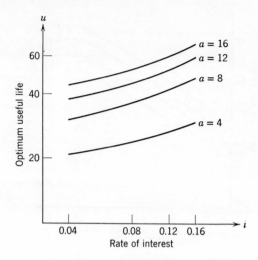

Figure 17.5. Condition: $\mu = -0.02$.

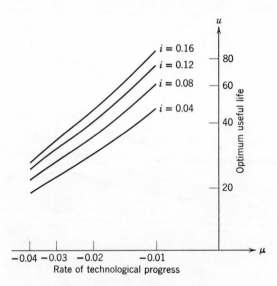

Figure 17.6. Condition: $a = 8$.

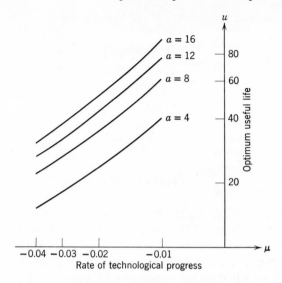

Figure 17.7. Condition: $i = 0.08$.

dimension as a, i, and μ. Very roughly, in the ranges examined, Figs. 17.2 through 17.7 show the elasticity of optimum useful life u with respect to minimum building labor a to be around $\frac{1}{2}$, the elasticity with respect to the rate of interest i to be around $\frac{1}{3}$, and the elasticity with respect to the rate of technological progress μ to be around $-\frac{2}{3}$.

17.14   CONCLUSION

We have found the optimum useful life of durable producers' goods to be longer the costlier are the producers' goods, the higher is the rate of interest, and the slower is technological progress. Intuitively, these results make sense: The costlier the producers' goods and the higher the rate of interest, the more urgent it becomes to save capital cost by lengthening the useful life of producers' goods. The slower the technological progress, the less difference between the efficiencies of producers' goods of consecutive vintages, hence the lower the pressure for retirement.

APPENDIX   PROOF THAT SECOND-ORDER CONDITIONS ARE SATISFIED

The first derivatives of the net worth $A(0)$ with respect to $P(0)$ and u have already been found as (16) and (17). Using these, the second derivatives entering the Hessian determinant H are found to be

(22)
$$\frac{\partial^2 A(0)}{\partial [P(0)]^2} = N(0)[P(0)]^{\eta-1} \frac{1+\eta}{i-\mu}$$

(23)
$$\frac{\partial^2 A(0)}{\partial P(0)\, \partial u} = 0$$

(24)
$$\frac{\partial^2 A(0)}{\partial u\, \partial P(0)} = 0$$

(25)
$$\frac{\partial^2 A(0)}{\partial u^2} = b(0)N(0)[P(0)]^{\eta} \frac{w}{i} i\mu e^{-iu}$$

Under the assumptions made, all factors of (22) are positive except $1 + \eta$, which is negative, hence (22) is negative. All factors of (25) are positive except μ, which is negative, hence (25) is negative. Thus the Hessian determinant H is positive. Form its principal minor by deleting its last row and column. This principal minor consists of (22) alone, which was negative. Thus the second-order conditions for a maximum net worth $A(0)$ are indeed satisfied.

REFERENCES

[1] Goldsmith, R., "The Growth of Reproducible Wealth of the United States of America from 1805 to 1950," in *Income and Wealth of the United States*, edited by S. Kuznets, Cambridge, England, 1952, p. 290 and p. 293 n.
[2] Kravis, I. B., "Relative Income Shares in Fact and Theory," *Am. Econ. Rev.*, **49**, (December 1959).

Part Three

Industry Equilibrium

CHAPTER 18

Industry Equilibrium under Pure Competition*

18.1 ASSUMPTIONS

Let cost to the firm be the money value of all input and rental as defined in Chapter 12, that is, as including interest representing the cost of money capital to the firm. Suppose that there is freedom of entry and exit in all industries, then ultimately the cost of money capital to the firm is what money capital could earn in other industries.

Let a group of firms, called an industry, produce the same product in the sense defined in Chapter 7, and let all firms within the industry, established as well as potential, be facing the same production function and the same input prices and rentals. Potential firms, then, will enter the industry whenever profits are positive, and established firms will leave the industry whenever profits are negative. Finally, let medium-sized firms operate under constant returns to scale, larger firms under decreasing returns to scale, and smaller firms under increasing returns to scale. The equilibrium number of firms accommodated may then be determined as follows.

18.2 THE GENERAL CASE

In Chapter 12 we found the condition for a profit maximum that input or capital stock should be hired up to the point where their price or rental

* Chapters 7, 11, and 12 are prerequisites for Chapter 18.

169

equaled their marginal-revenue productivity:

(1) $$p_h = \left(P + X\frac{dP}{dX}\right)\frac{\partial X}{\partial x_h} \qquad (h = 1, \ldots, m)$$

(2) $$r_g = \left(P + X\frac{dP}{dX}\right)\frac{\partial X}{\partial S_g} \qquad (g = 1, \ldots, n)$$

Now from a point satisfying those two conditions, on the production surface in $(m + n + 1)$-dimensional space

(3) $$X = X(x_1, \ldots, x_m, S_1, \ldots, S_n)$$

let all inputs and capital stocks be increased simultaneously by the small differentials $dx_h = \Delta x_h$ and $dS_g = \Delta S_g$. Then the total differential

(4) $$dX = \frac{\partial X}{\partial x_1}dx_1 + \cdots + \frac{\partial X}{\partial x_m}dx_m + \frac{\partial X}{\partial S_1}dS_1 + \cdots + \frac{\partial X}{\partial S_n}dS_n$$

will be an approximation to the increment ΔX of output: We recall that if x_h and S_g undergo the independent changes dx_h and dS_g, respectively, then the differential dX represents the change in X to *the tangent plane* to the production surface (3), whereas ΔX represents the change in X to the production surface (3) *itself*.

Since the changes dx_h and dS_g were independent, we are free to make them proportional, so let λ be a small constant like $1/1000$ or $1/1,000,000$ and write

(5) $$dx_h = \lambda x_h \qquad (h = 1, \ldots, m)$$

(6) $$dS_g = \lambda S_g \qquad (g = 1, \ldots, n)$$

Insert (1), (2), (5), and (6) into (4); then

(7) $$dX = \frac{\lambda}{P + X(dP/dX)}(p_1 x_1 + \cdots + p_m x_m + r_1 S_1 + \cdots + r_n S_n)$$

Now let competition be pure; therefore

(8) $$\frac{dP}{dX} = 0$$

And let us distinguish between constant, decreasing, and increasing returns.

18.3 CONSTANT RETURNS TO SCALE

Initially, let the number of firms accommodated within the industry be such as to permit the individual firm to be medium-sized, hence operating

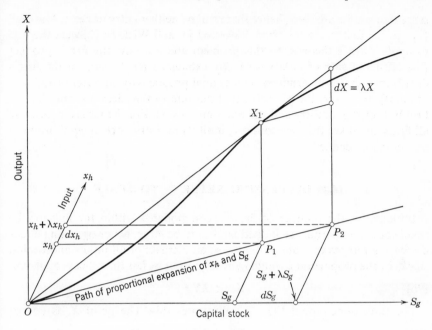

Figure 18.1

under constant returns to scale. In that case an increase of all inputs and capital stocks by the proportion λ would increase output by that same proportion:

$$(9a) \qquad dX = \lambda X$$

Figure 18.1 illustrates this for $h = g = 1$, giving us merely three dimensions instead of $m + n + 1$. The point X_1 on the production surface is one of constant returns to scale and satisfies the conditions (1) and (2). Connect X_1 with the origin O and consider the vertical plane containing the connecting line OX_1. This plane intersects the production surface along the heavy S-shaped curve and intersects the x_h-S_g plane along the path of proportional expansion of x_h and S_g. Moving along that path from P_1 to P_2 we find that (9a) is true, because the connecting line OX_1 is a tangent to the heavy S-shaped curve in X_1.

Insert (8) and (9a) into (7); then

$$(10a) \qquad PX = p_1 x_1 + \cdots + p_m x_m + r_1 S_1 + \cdots + r_n S_n$$

or, in the notation of Chapter 12, $R = C$ or $Z = 0$.

Since all firms, established as well as potential, have been assumed to be alike, (10a) holds for any of them, and the industry is in equilibrium in the sense that profits are zero; hence there will be neither entry nor exit. Marshall [1] was the first to see this, but Wicksteed [3] and Wicksell [2] were the first to apply Euler's theorem to this problem and see how the firm's product [the left-hand side of (10a)] is exactly exhausted by the sum of the firm's distributive shares determined by marginal productivity [the right-hand side of (10a)]. However, the pie will equal the sum of the slices not only for the firm but for the industry and the economy as well. For the industry, because all firms are alike; for the economy, if all its industries are in equilibrium in the sense just defined.

18.4 DECREASING RETURNS TO SCALE

Initially, let the number of firms accommodated within the industry be small enough to permit the individual firm to be large, hence operating under decreasing returns to scale. In that case an increase of all inputs and capital stocks by the proportion λ would increase output by less than that proportion.

(9b) $dX < \lambda X$

The three-dimensional Fig. 18.2 illustrates this. The point X_2 is one of

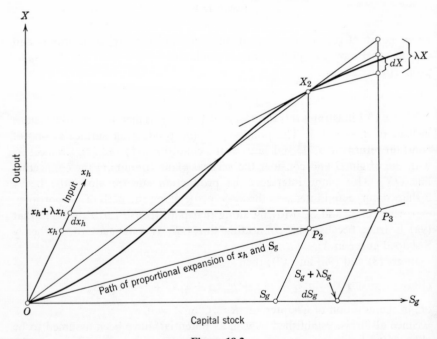

Figure 18.2

decreasing returns to scale and satisfies conditions (1) and (2). Connect X_2 with the origin O and consider the vertical plane containing the connecting line OX_2. The plane intersects the production surface along the heavy S-shaped curve and intersects the x_h-S_g plane along the path of proportional expansion of x_h and S_g. Moving along that path from P_2 to P_3 we find that (9b) is true, because the connecting line OX_2 is steeper than the tangent to the heavy S-shaped curve in X_2.

Insert (8) and (9b) into (7).

(10b) $$PX > p_1 x_1 + \cdots + p_m x_m + r_1 S_1 + \cdots + r_n S_n$$

So profits are positive, for the firm's product now exceeds the sum of the firm's distributive shares determined by the marginal-productivity principle. That principle seems in danger, then, but the situation will remedy itself: Positive profits attracts new firms to the industry, thereby decreasing the size of the firm until returns to scale become constant. Then (10a) holds, the industry is in equilibrium, and the marginal-productivity principle is salvaged.

18.5 INCREASING RETURNS TO SCALE

Initially, let the number of firms accommodated within the industry be large enough to force the individual firm to be small, hence operating under increasing returns to scale. In that case an increase of all inputs and capital stocks by the proportion λ would increase output by more than that proportion.

(9c) $$dX > \lambda X$$

The three-dimensional Fig. 18.3 illustrates this. The point X_3 is one of increasing returns to scale and satisfies conditions (1) and (2). Connect X_3 with the origin O and consider the vertical plane containing the connecting line OX_3. The plane intersects the production surface along the heavy S-shaped curve and intersects the x_h-S_g plane along the path of proportional expansion of x_h and S_g. Moving along that path from P_3 to P_4 we find that (9c) is true, because the connecting line OX_3 is less steep than the tangent to the heavy S-shaped curve in X_3.

Insert (8) and (9c) into (7).

(10c) $$PX < p_1 x_1 + \cdots + p_m x_m + r_1 S_1 + \cdots + r_n S_n$$

So profits are negative, for the firm's product now falls short of the sum of the firm's distributive shares determined by the marginal-productivity principle. Is that principle in danger, then? Would this situation remedy itself, too? Wicksell [2] was not so sure. True enough, firms having to pay

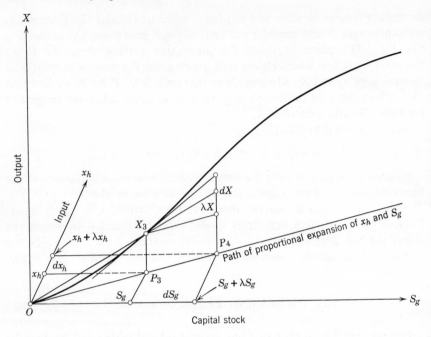

Figure 18.3

more for their inputs than warranted by the value of their product would succumb. With fewer firms left in the industry, the size of the individual firm might increase until returns to scale became constant. However, before all that had happened, might not the number of firms have become too small for pure competition to survive? It might, and we shall examine that possibility in Chapter 19.

18.6 NUMBER OF FIRMS UNDETERMINED

In Section 18.1 we assumed that medium-sized firms operated under constant returns to scale, larger firms under decreasing returns to scale, and small firms under increasing returns to scale. Obviously, if "medium-sized" is not a unique scale but a short range of scales, the model loses some of its precision. The number of firms to be accommodated within the industry becomes a short range of numbers rather than a unique number.

It is worse still, if the production function is such that constancy, decrease, or increase in the returns to scale, respectively, holds universally for any scale. Indeed the production functions used elsewhere in this volume are of that type. For example, let the production function be the one used in the particular case of Chapter 12:

$$(11) \qquad X = M x_1^{\alpha_1} \cdots x_m^{\alpha_m} S_1^{\beta_1} \cdots S_n^{\beta_n}$$

with the restrictions mentioned there. Furthermore, let the demand function be one used in the particular case of Chapter 12:

$$(12) \qquad X = NP^{\eta}$$

with the restrictions mentioned there. By using (11) and (12), the first-order conditions (1) and (2) collapse into

$$(13) \qquad p_h = P \frac{1 + \eta}{\eta} \frac{\alpha_h}{x_h} X \qquad (h = 1, \ldots, m)$$

$$(14) \qquad r_g = P \frac{1 + \eta}{\eta} \frac{\beta_g}{S_g} X \qquad (g = 1, \ldots, n)$$

After multiplying (13) by x_h and (14) by S_g and summing, we find

$$(15) \quad (\alpha_1 + \cdots + \alpha_m + \beta_1 + \cdots + \beta_n) \frac{1 + \eta}{\eta} PX$$
$$= p_1 x_1 + \cdots + p_m x_m + r_1 S_1 + \cdots + r_n S_n$$

Let us now make two specific assumptions. First, let the production function (11) be a linearly homogeneous one. In other words,

$$\alpha_1 + \cdots + \alpha_m + \beta_1 + \cdots + \beta_n = 1$$

Furthermore, let us assume pure competition. So $(1 + \eta)/\eta$ approaches one. This combination of assumptions plays havoc with firm as well as industry equilibrium. With regard to firm equilibrium, in Chapters 11 and 12 we found that the second-order conditions for maximum profits were unsatisfied by the combination of constant returns to scale and pure competition. In Chapter 11, the second derivative of profits with respect to output became zero for that combination, and in Chapter 12 the Hessian became zero for that combination; this did not permit the signs of its principal minors to alternate.

With regard to industry equilibrium, everything stated in Section 18.2 as well as Eq. (10a) could now hold at any scale. Consequently, the number of firms accommodated within the industry can no longer be determined by the condition that profits be zero.

However, not everything is lost. Given the input prices p_h and r_g we could still determine two things. First, we could determine the best proportions in which to combine inputs. Divide (13) by (14),

$$(16) \qquad \frac{x_h}{S_g} = \frac{\alpha_h}{\beta_g} \frac{r_g}{p_h}$$

which is our old acquaintance Eq. (8) in Chapter 9 revealing the most efficient proportion in which to apply inputs. "Efficient" in what sense? In the sense that the proportion described maximizes output within a given cost budget. As we saw, the proportion did not depend upon the size of that cost budget, and that was true regardless of whether returns to scale were increasing, constant, or decreasing.

Once we know the proportion in which to apply inputs we can determine the output price P at which firms could just break even and hang onto the industry by obeying (16): Arbitrarily fix one input, say x_h. Then let (16) determine all others. Insert all inputs thus determined into the production function (11) and find output X. Insert output X and all inputs into (15), now collapsing into (10a), and find price P.

Thus while the number of firms would remain undetermined, the most efficient input proportions and the break-even price would not. We shall make use of this fact in Chapters 25 and 26.

REFERENCES

[1] Marshall, A., *Principles of Economics*, London, 1890, Book V.
[2] Wicksell, K., *Föreläsningar i nationalekonomi*, Lund, Sweden, 1901. (Translated by E. Classen and edited by Lionel Robbins as *Lectures on Political Economy*, London, 1934, Vol. I, pp. 124–133.)
[3] Wicksteed, P. H., *An Essay on the Co-ordination of the Laws of Distribution*, London, 1894.

CHAPTER 19

Nonpure Competition*

19.1 NO PRODUCT DIFFERENTIATION

Assuming product differentiation to be absent, in Section 18.5 we examined the case of increasing returns to scale. Initially the number of firms accommodated within the industry was assumed to be large enough to force the individual firm to be small, hence operating under increasing returns to scale. It was shown how firms having to pay more for their inputs than was warranted by the value of the firm's product would succumb. With fewer firms left, let the size of the individual firm increase such as to permit it to operate under constant returns to scale. However, let the firms now be too few for pure competition to survive. In that case (8) of Chapter 18 must be written as

$$(8a) \qquad \frac{dP}{dX} < 0$$

However, Eq. (7) of Chapter 18 would still apply, therefore insert (8a) and (9a) of Chapter 18 into it, then

$$(10d) \qquad PX > p_1 x_1 + \cdots + p_m x_m + r_1 S_1 + \cdots + r_n S_n$$

Therefore profits are positive and will attract new firms, thus decreasing the size of the individual firm and forcing it to operate under increasing returns to scale. Its monopolistic profits would then be swallowed up by the costs of operating at a less efficient scale. Or would they?

We are still assuming product differentiation to be absent. In Chapter 7 we defined such absence as follows: If all firms charge the same price, no buyer is any more or less likely to buy from any one firm than from any

* Chapter 18 is a prerequisite for Chapter 19.

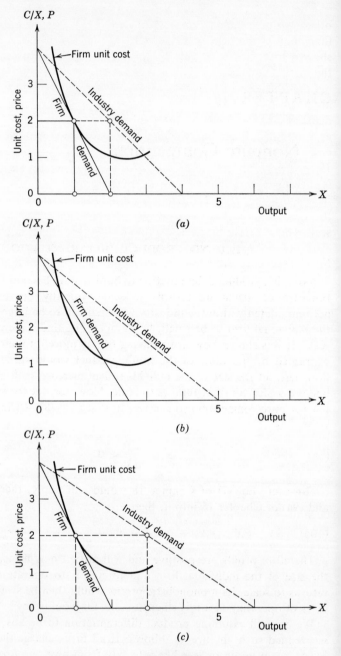

Figure 19.1

178

other. No household is going to buy from any firm charging a price higher than that of the firm or firms charging the lowest price. As a result, we showed that each of f firms charging the same price would get a share of the market equaling $1/f$.[1]

Consequently, each of f such firms is facing a firm demand curve whose abscissa at any common price equals $1/f$ of the abscissa of the industry demand curve at the same price. Figure 19.1 shows the firm demand curve as a solid line, the industry demand curve as a broken line, and the firm unit cost curve as a U-shaped solid curve. Figure 19.1 has three parts. In Fig. 19.1a $f = 2$ with each duopolist just breaking even. Since industry demand is growing, there will eventually be room for the triopoly shown in Fig. 19.1c in which $f = 3$ with each triopolist just breaking even. In both (a) and (c) then, profits are swallowed up by the costs of operating at a less efficient scale. However, in Fig. 19.1b there is room for more than two firms breaking even but not yet for three, so each duopolist can make positive profits, because his unit cost curve lies partly below his firm demand curve. Exactly how much profits he can make depends upon how cozy the duopoly situation is and need not concern us here.

19.2 PRODUCT DIFFERENTIATION

Product differentiation means that the firm has succeeded in setting its product apart from the products of all other firms. By definition the firm producing such a product is the *only* firm producing it, and the market demand function is the demand function faced by the firm. If within the demand function the firm can make positive profits, the firm should exist, if it cannot, it should not. Whether or not the firm can find such a niche within which to exist depends, of course, upon the production function for the product variety chosen, as well as upon the input prices.

The statements just made do not take us very far, especially not for the class of products in which product differentiation is most important, that is, the class of consumer durables. Here industry equilibrium is closely related to the relative strength of expansion demand and replacement demand. The purpose of the remainder of this chapter is to illustrate this relationship, and let us exemplify the consumer durable by automobiles.

---

[1] Our definition of absence of product differentiation rules out what Modigliani [3] called Sylos' [4] postulate, supposedly holding under such absence, that is, that established firms can maintain their original output vis-a-vis an entrant. Under our definition, a firm entering an industry hitherto inhabited by f firms will automatically inflict upon each of them a reduction of market share from $1/f$ to $1/(1 + f)$. Clearly, then, the resulting output of established firms is not up to them alone. Thus we cannot rely on the Sylos-Modigliani model, and our own differs strikingly from it.

19.3 NOTATION

The following notation will be assigned.

Variables

C = number of automobiles demanded per annum
R = number of automobiles retired per annum
S = stock of automobiles

Parameters

g = proportionate rate of growth of stock of automobiles
u = useful life of an automobile

Let t be the time coordinate dating variables. Thus, a flow variable like C or R marked (t) refers to period t; a stock variable like S marked (t) refers to time t. Let period t be the period beginning at time t, ending at time $t + 1$.

19.4 THE EQUILIBRIUM FLOW-STOCK RELATIONSHIP IN AUTOMOBILE DEMAND

The expansion-replacement relationship is part of the more fundamental flow-stock relationship in a growing stock of consumers' durables. Let us find that flow-stock relationship as follows.

Express the change in automobile stock from time t to time $t + 1$ as the difference between the flow of new-car demand and the flow of retirement.

$$(1) \qquad S(t + 1) - S(t) = C(t) - R(t)$$

Let automobile stock be growing smoothly at the annual proportionate rate of growth g.

$$(2) \qquad S(t + 1) = (1 + g)S(t)$$

Let the useful life of all automobiles be u, then the flow of retirement during period t equals the flow of new-car demand during period $t - u$.

$$(3) \qquad R(t) = C(t - u)$$

Combine (1), (2), and (3); then

$$(4) \qquad C(t) = gS(t) + C(t - u)$$

In (4) go back u periods, replacing t throughout by $t - u$; thus

$$(4a) \qquad C(t - u) = gS(t - u) + C(t - 2u)$$

In the same way, keep going back u periods at a time n times, keep inserting results like (4a) into (4), use (2), and find

$$C(t) = gS(t)[1 + (1 + g)^{-u} + (1 + g)^{-2u} + \cdots + (1 + g)^{-nu}] + C(t - nu)$$

Upon this, use the rule for finding the sum of the first n terms of a geometric progression, let n rise without bounds, divide both sides by $S(t)$, and find the equilibrium flow–stock relationship

(5)
$$\lim_{n \to \infty} \frac{C(t)}{S(t)} = \frac{g}{1 - (1 + g)^{-u}}$$

19.5 THE EQUILIBRIUM EXPANSION-REPLACEMENT RELATIONSHIP IN AUTOMOBILE DEMAND

The equilibrium flow–stock ratio (5) makes it possible to find very simple expressions for expansion demand and replacement demand. Expansion demand is $S(t + 1) - S(t)$; divide it by $C(t)$ to express its share of demand, insert (2) and (5), and find

(6)
$$\frac{S(t + 1) - S(t)}{C(t)} = 1 - (1 + g)^{-u}$$

Replacement demand is $R(t)$; divide it by $C(t)$ to express its share of demand, insert (1) and (6), and find

(7)
$$\frac{R(t)}{C(t)} = (1 + g)^{-u}$$

19.6 EMPIRICAL ILLUSTRATION

For an empirical illustration, let us compare the expansion–replacement relationship in the United States around 1960 to that of the European Economic Community at the same time, and we shall see a striking difference between the setting of the automobile industry on the two sides of the Atlantic.

In the United States around 1960 the flow–stock ratio was 0.10, which is what Eq. (5) would give us for such empirically plausible American values as a proportionate rate of growth of stock $g = 0.045$ and a useful life $u = 13$ years.

In the European Economic Community around 1960 the flow–stock ratio was 0.25. Although the lower durability of European low-displacement, high-revolution engine designs must be somewhat offset by higher European maintenance standards, we would expect the useful life of European automobiles to be shorter than that of American ones, and the limited information we have on useful lives[2] bears us out. The European flow–stock ratio of 0.25 is what Eq. (5) would give us for such empirically plausible European values as a proportionate rate of growth of stock $g = 0.22$ and a useful life $u = 11$ years.

Inserting these American and European values of g and u into (6) and (7) we find the following American and European shares:

	U.S.	E.E.C.
Expansion share of demand	0.43	0.88
Replacement share of demand	0.56	0.12

It seems clear, then, that the American and the European automobile industries around 1960 were in different stages of development. At this point it will be useful to distinguish three stages of the growth of a consumer durables industry.

19.7 THREE STAGES OF A CONSUMER DURABLES INDUSTRY

In the first stage of the industry's growth, lack of production know-how makes the product very costly. Only the very rich can afford it, and the very rich are small in number. This is the "pioneering" stage, exemplified by both the United States and the European automobile industries in the first decade of the twentieth century.

In the second stage, accumulated production know-how *plus* new technological progress rapidly reduce unit cost. Because of the shape of the income-distribution curve in capitalist society, very small price reductions at this stage may expand the market considerably. Hence firms will cut price along with unit cost in an attempt to capture a big slice of the new uncultivated markets. Uncultivated markets are easier to invade than cultivated ones, because no brand loyalties exist in them as yet. The second stage, then, is characterized by fierce price competition. This is the "bonanza" stage at which demand is almost wholly expansion demand.

The bonanza stage inevitably produces its own ending. In the third stage almost every household can afford to own the consumer durable and does so. This is the "saturation" stage at which replacement demand has become a very large part of total demand. Here a producer meets two kinds of

---

[2] Define the average useful life of a generation of automobiles as that age at which half the generation has been scrapped. That age has been estimated by Boulding [1] at 13.6 years for the United States and by Wallander [5] at 11.5 years for Sweden.

competition: first, rival brands which he may consider relatively harmless to him if his customers have a high degree of brand loyalty and second, and less harmless, the existing stock of durables already in use:

"In other words, Frigidaire's principal competitor for commercial refrigeration today is not ice but old-style mechanical equipment, *including its own early models . . . ."* [2]

In the United States automobile market, the historical transition point from bonanza to saturation is not difficult to identify. Using semilogarithmic scale, Fig. 19.2 shows the United States stock of automobiles from 1900 to 1965. In semilogarithmic scale a constant proportionate rate of growth of stock will manifest itself as a straight-line time path of stock. Figure 19.2 could be rather well approximated by two such lines, that is, a very steep one (1900–1925) and a much flatter one (1925–1965). The sharp corner where the two lines meet is 1925.

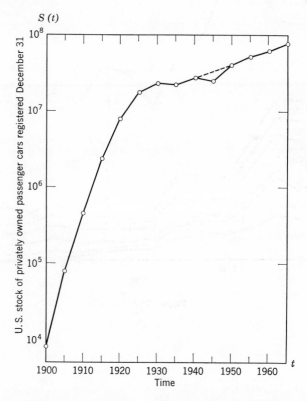

Figure 19.2. From *Automobile Facts and Figures*, Detroit, Michigan, 1966, p. 18.

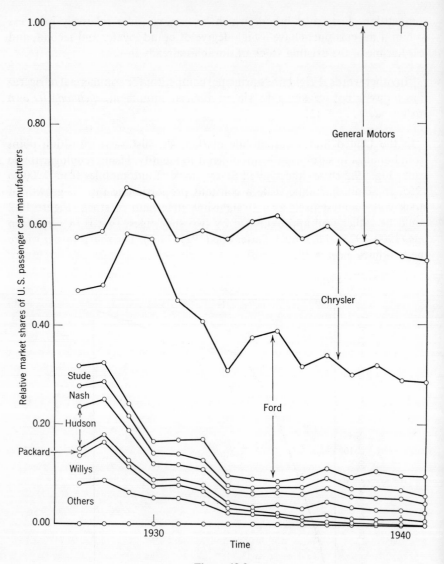

Figure 19.3

184

19.8   SIGNIFICANCE FOR INDUSTRY EQUILIBRIUM

Once the sharp corner has been passed, that is, once replacement demand has become a very large part of total demand, a firm's optimal sales approach is bound to change. Facing the vast stock of existing consumer durables, mostly in excellent working condition, the firm must make their owners dissatisfied with what they have. Thus the firm must adopt a policy of frequent style changes. The large United States automobile firms adopted the annual model shift in the late 1920's—immediately after they had passed the sharp corner in Fig. 19.2.

Once the large firms have adopted the annual model shift, the small ones find themselves caught in a vicious circle: They cannot join the annual model-shift pattern, because they lack the volume over which to spread the very high annual overhead costs of tools, jigs, and dies retired every two to three years because of obsolescence. And because they cannot join the annual model-shift pattern, they keep losing volume to their bigger rivals who have adopted the pattern. The small United States automobile firms found themselves in this vicious circle after the large ones had adopted the annual model shift in the late 1920's. Figure 19.3 is a close-up of the market shares from 1927 to 1941.

As for Europe, the beginnings of a European bonanza stage were noticeable in the 1920's, but depression and war postponed its continuation until 1950. In the mid-sixties there are signs that the European bonanza is coming to an end, and even the reduced number of firms in the European automobile industry surviving by 1966 may well prove too large for a fully integrated European Economic Community.

REFERENCES

[1] Boulding, K. E., "An Application of Population Analysis to the Automobile Popula - tion of the United States," *Kyklos*, **8** (1955).

[2] Markham, T. W., Sales Promotion Manager of the Frigidaire Corporation, "New Sales to Old Owners," *Printer's Ink*, July 16, 1936, p. 15.

[3] Modigliani, F., "New Developments on the Oligopoly Front," *Jour. Pol. Econ.*, **66**, 215–232 (June 1958).

[4] Sylos-Labini, P., *Oligopolio e progresso tecnico*, Milan, 1957. (Translated by E. Henderson as *Oligopoly and Technical Progress*, Cambridge, Massachusetts, 1962.)

[5] Wallander, J., *Studier i bilismens ekonomi*, Stockholm, 1958, Appendix F, 330–333.

CHAPTER 20

Duopoly Price in the Absence of Product Differentiation*

20.1 INTRODUCTION

Where returns to scale are nondecreasing, such as in manufacturing, transportation, and mass retailing, the number of firms in an industry will often be very small. The fewer the firms, and the less product differentiation there is among them, the more vitally each firm's actions will affect its rivals' profits.

We shall confine our study of oligopoly to duopoly and begin with the case of duopoly price formation for a given product produced at constant unit costs, identical or different between the duopolists. We shall examine alternative price solutions and find the circumstances under which duopoly is likely to give way to monopoly. We shall also find what incentives are inherent in the model and what social performance is likely to result from responses to them.

20.2 NOTATION

The following notation will be assigned.

Variables

B_{hi} = bribe paid to ith firm in hth industry
C_{hi} = cost per annum of ith firm in hth industry
P_{hi} = price charged by ith firm in hth industry
R_{hi} = revenue from output sold per annum by ith firm in hth industry
X_{hi} = output produced and sold per annum by ith firm in hth industry
Z_{hi} = profits per annum of ith firm in hth industry

* Chapter 7 is a prerequisite for Chapter 20.

186

Parameters

A_h = coefficient in constant-elasticity-of-substitution utility function
e = Euler's number, the base of natural logarithms
i = rate of interest
J = agglomeration of utility and price parameters outside the duopoly
j = firm horizon
Q_{hi} = unit cost of ith firm in hth industry
ρ = exponent in constant-elasticity-of-substitution utility function
t = time
τ = length of war of attrition
Y = household budget per annum

20.3 PROFITS AND COST

Within the ith firm in the hth industry, define profits as revenue *minus* cost.

$$(1) \qquad Z_{hi} = R_{hi} - C_{hi} \qquad (h = 1, i = 1, 2)$$

Define revenue as price *times* output sold.

$$(2) \qquad R_{hi} = P_{hi}X_{hi} \qquad (h = 1, i = 1, 2)$$

Let the firm operate under constant returns to scale, so its costs are in direct proportion to its output; thus

$$(3) \qquad C_{hi} = Q_{hi}X_{hi} \qquad (h = 1, i = 1, 2)$$

Until Section 20.20 on the Bertrand solution, let the duopolists charge the same price:

$$(4) \qquad P_{11} = P_{12} = P_1$$

20.4 THE MONOPOLY SOLUTION

In a chapter on duopoly it might seem strange to start out with monopoly, but such a start will facilitate our presentation. Therefore, for the time being, let seller 1 be a monopolist. A monopolist is facing market demand; hence let us look for a market demand function. In accordance with the synthetic approach underlying this book, we should very much like to derive our market demand function from the household utility function. This has indeed already been done. In Chapter 3 we maximized a household's utility, subject to a budget constraint, and found household demand functions for outputs and capital stocks which were substitutes in consumption but not perfect ones. In Chapter 7 we utilized these household demand functions to find market demand functions. Assuming s households to have identical constant-elasticity-of-substitution utility functions, we wrote market demand for the output of the hth industry as Eq. (9) of Chapter 7. In that equation, set $h = 1$, so our monopoly is a monopoly in the first industry of the economy. Furthermore, set market demand equal to the monopolist's output and use the following abbreviations:

$$\sum_{k=1}^{s} C_{hk} = X_h$$

$$\sum_{k=1}^{s} Y_k = Y$$

$$(A_2 P_2{}^\rho)^{1/(1+\rho)} + \cdots + (A_m P_m{}^\rho)^{1/(1+\rho)} + (B_1 r_1{}^\rho)^{1/(1+\rho)} + \cdots$$
$$+ (B_n r_n{}^\rho)^{1/(1+\rho)} = J,$$

permitting us to write market demand as

$$(5) \qquad X_1 = \frac{(A_1/P_1)^{1/(1+\rho)}}{(A_1 P_1{}^\rho)^{1/(1+\rho)} + J} Y$$

In summary, (5) is the demand faced by the monopolist producing the first product of an economy consisting of households having identical constant-elasticity-of-substitution individual utility functions and having an aggregate budget Y per annum.

Let us make (5) more manageable by fixing a specific value for ρ. Which value? We want other goods in the economy to be close substitutes for the monopolized one, and to make this true, $-1 < \rho < 0$. A particularly manageable demand function would result from setting $\rho = -\tfrac{1}{2}$; Equation (5) would then collapse into

$$(6) \qquad X_1 = \frac{1}{P_1} \frac{Y}{1 + (J/A_1{}^2)P_1}$$

Insert the market demand function (6) into the revenue function (2) and the cost function (3), then insert both into (1) and express monopoly profits as

$$(7) \qquad Z_{11m} = \frac{P_1 - Q_{11}}{P_1} \frac{Y}{1 + (J/A_1{}^2)P_1}$$

where m stands for monopoly. The monopolist will now adjust his price so as to maximize his profits Z_{11m} as expressed by (7). The first-order condition for such a maximum is

$$\frac{\partial Z_{11m}}{\partial P_1} = 0$$

Carry out the derivation, arrive at a quadratic equation in P_1, solve it, and let the resulting value of P_1 be P_{1m}.

$$(8) \qquad P_{1m} = Q_{11} \pm \sqrt{Q_{11}^2 + Q_{11}\frac{A_1^2}{J}}$$

Since the last term under the square root sign is positive, one solution is positive, the other negative. Of these, we reject the latter. For the special case of $A_1^2/J = \frac{1}{9}$ and $Q_{11} = 1$, the monopoly solution for price is

$$P_{1m} = 2.05$$

Insert that value of P_1 into (7) and find the monopoly solution for profits. For the special case of $Y = 1000$, profits will be

$$Z_{11m} = 26.33$$

Now we shall examine duopoly.

20.5   DUOPOLY

In Chapter 7, we found that as long as all f firms producing nondifferentiated products charge the same price, the demand faced by each of them would be $1/f$ of market demand.

Applying this to duopoly we would say, then, that the demand faced by each duopolist would be one-half of market demand. But is this not too simple? Doesn't recent analysis of duopoly price abound with U-shaped unit cost curves or even absolute supply restrictions? One duopolist, it is said, can supply only so much, and this restriction will have to be carefully incorporated into the demand curve faced by his rival, called by Shubik [7] a "contingent" demand curve.

To us, supply restrictions, either absolute or in the form of decreasing returns to scale, are unnecessary complications of, nay alien to, the duopoly problem. Pure competition, to be sure, may depend for its survival upon the existence of decreasing returns to scale beyond a scale so small that a large number of firms operating at that scale can be accommodated within the industry, as we saw in Chapter 18. This is not true under duopoly. It is the very absence of such decreasing returns or other supply restrictions which leads to duopoly in the first place, and such absence ought to be gratefully accepted by the theorist studying duopoly. Therefore let each duopolist be perfectly capable of satisfying whatever demand comes his way. If so, that will be one-half of market demand.

$$(9) \qquad X_{11} = X_{12}$$

$$(10) \qquad = \frac{X_1}{2} = \frac{1}{P_1}\frac{1}{1 + (J/A_1^2)P_1}\frac{Y}{2}$$

Insert (2) through (4) into (1), then insert (9) and (10) and write the profits of the duopolists as

$$(11) \qquad Z_{11d} = \frac{P_1 - Q_{11}}{P_1} \frac{1}{1 + (J/A_1^2)P_1} \frac{Y}{2}$$

$$(12) \qquad Z_{12d} = \frac{P_1 - Q_{12}}{P_1} \frac{1}{1 + (J/A_1^2)P_1} \frac{Y}{2}$$

where d stands for duopoly.

20.6 VON NEUMANN-MORGENSTERN SOLUTION

Bertrand [1] hinted[1] and von Neumann-Morgenstern [8] proved that duopolists 1 and 2 will form a coalition against the consumers. The coalition will maximize its combined profits $Z_{11d} + Z_{12d}$. Does this mean that the duopolists 1 and 2 are no longer pursuing their self-interest but have somehow become altruistic? Not at all; duopolists can always be bribed into accepting the maximizing price P_{1d}, for at maximum $Z_{11d} + Z_{12d}$, each duopolist can get what he could have gotten at any other common price *plus* a bribe. The first-order condition for such a maximum is

$$\frac{\partial (Z_{11d} + Z_{12d})}{\partial P_1} = 0$$

Carry out the derivation, arrive at a quadratic equation in P_1, solve it, and let the resulting value of P_1 be P_{1d}, where d stands for duopoly:

$$(13) \qquad P_{1d} = \frac{Q_{11} + Q_{12}}{2} \pm \sqrt{\left(\frac{Q_{11} + Q_{12}}{2} \right)^2 + \frac{Q_{11} + Q_{12}}{2} \frac{A_1^2}{J}}$$

Since the last term under the square root sign is positive, one root is positive, the other negative. Of these we reject the latter.

20.7 SPLITTING THE PROFITS OF THE VON NEUMANN-MORGENSTERN SOLUTION

It was said that duopolists could always be bribed into accepting the maximizing von Neumann-Morgenstern price P_{1d}, but on the size of the bribe von Neumann and Morgenstern were silent. However, something can, be said, and we shall try to say it.

---

[1] "Leur intérêt serait de s'associer ou tout au moins de fixer le prix commun, de manière à prélever sur l'ensemble des acheteurs la plus grande recette possible..."

20.8 EQUAL UNIT COSTS

As long as the duopolists have equal unit costs Q_{11} and Q_{12}, then (11) and (12) show Z_{11d} and Z_{12d} to be equal. For the special case of $A_1{}^2/J = \frac{1}{9}$ and $Q_{11} = Q_{12} = 1$, the von Neumann-Morgenstern price solution is

$$P_{1d} = 2.05$$

Insert that value of P_1 into (11) and (12) and find the von Neumann-Morgenstern profits solutions. For the special case of $Y = 1000$ they are

$$Z_{11d} = 13.17 \qquad Z_{12d} = 13.17 \qquad Z_{11d} + Z_{12d} = 26.33$$

Along the axes of Fig. 20.1 are plotted the two prices P_{11} and P_{12}, required by Eq. (4) to be equal. The von Neumann-Morgenstern price solution is shown as the point N on the 45° line through zero, representing Eq. (4).

Since under equal unit costs, profits Z_{11d} and Z_{12d} are equal, the common price maximizing $Z_{11d} + Z_{12d}$ is at the same time the common price maximizing Z_{11d} and Z_{12d} separately. Figure 20.2 illustrates this: Both Z_{11d} and Z_{12d} peak at $P_{1d} = 2.05$, the von Neumann-Morgenstern point. Consequently, both duopolists are quite happy with the latter. Really, neither needs to be bribed into accepting something otherwise unpalatable. On the other hand, neither wants to pass up a bribe if one could be had.

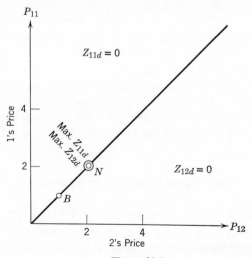

Figure 20.1

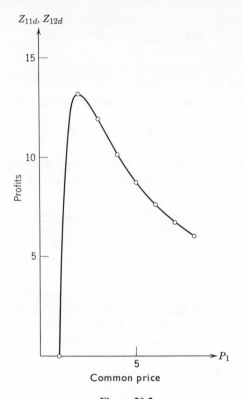

Figure 20.2

Can a bribe be had? A duopolist secures a bribe for himself by making his rival submit to a threat. Under nondifferentiated duopoly a threat must be a threat of price cutting. Relative bargaining power is a matter of relative vulnerability. But price, and hence quantity sold, being the same for the duopolists, and unit cost and hence profit margin being also the same, relative vulnerability to price cutting is the same. Consequently, bargaining power is the same, and a bribe is unlikely to be secured. If both realize this, neither may try.

20.9 DIFFERENT UNIT COSTS

Let us now turn to the more dramatic case of different unit costs. Let one of the duopolists, say 1, possess patents or secret know-how not possessed by the other. If unit costs Q_{11} and Q_{12} differ, (11) and (12) show Z_{11d} and Z_{12d} to differ. For the special case of $A_1{}^2/J = \frac{1}{9}$, $Q_{11} = 1$, and $Q_{12} = 2$, the von

Neumann-Morgenstern duopoly price solution will be

$$P_{1d} = 3.05$$

Insert that value of P_1 into (11) and (12) and find the von Neumann Morgenstern duopoly profits solution. For the special case of $Y = 1000$, profits will be:

$$Z_{11d} = 11.79 \qquad Z_{12d} = 6.04 \qquad Z_{11d} + Z_{12d} = 17.83$$

The von Neumann-Morgenstern point is shown as the point N in Fig. 20.3, using the same axes as Fig. 20.1.

Since under different unit costs Z_{11d} and Z_{12d} are different, the common price maximizing $Z_{11d} + Z_{12d}$ will no longer at the same time maximize Z_{11d} and Z_{12d} separately. Figure 20.4 illustrates this: A maximum $Z_{11d} = 13.17$ occurs at $P_1 = 2.05$, whereas a maximum $Z_{12d} = 6.76$ occurs at $P_1 = 4.05$. These points and the von Neumann-Morgenstern point are shown in Fig. 20.3 as well as in Table 20.1.

At first sight, then, the von Neumann-Morgenstern price $P_{1d} = 3.05$ appeals to neither duopolist, and it will take some bribing to secure it. Who is going to be bribed by whom? The answer lies in the difference in vulnerability between duopolists 1 and 2. As before, price charged and quantity sold by the duopolists are the same, but unit cost and hence profit margin are no longer the same. Consequently, relative vulnerability to price cutting is not the same, and this difference in vulnerability will manifest itself in an upper and a lower bound to a bribe B_{11d} per annum paid by 2 to 1.

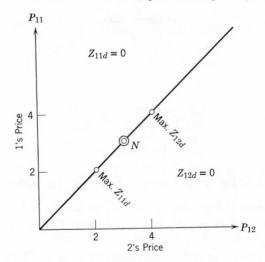

Figure 20.3

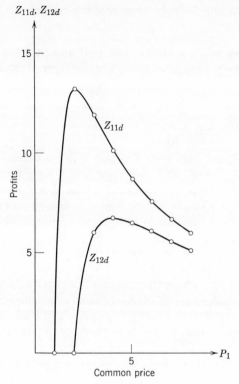

Figure 20.4

Table 20.1 Some Crucial Profit Points

P_1	Z_{11d}	Z_{12d}
2.05	13.17	0.63
3.05	11.79	6.04
4.05	10.05	6.76

20.10   UPPER AND LOWER BOUNDS TO BRIBE B_{11d}

The upper bound to the bride B_{11d} is 5.41, for a bribe of 5.41 would leave 2 with merely $6.04 - 5.41 = 0.63$, or the same payoff as he would be earning after a unilateral price cut by 1 to 2.05.

The lower bound to the bribe B_{11d} is 1.38, for a bribe of 1.38 would leave 1 with merely $11.79 + 1.38 = 13.17$, or the same payoff as he would be earning after his unilateral price cut to 2.05.

Can 1 always get away with such a unilateral price cut? Yes, for at a price of 2.05, 2 is selling at merely 0.05 above unit cost, making merely $Z_{12d} =$ 0.63, hence is in no position to threaten 1 with further, disciplinary price cutting. We conclude that

$$(14) \qquad\qquad 1.38 \leq B_{11d} \leq 5.41$$

So there is plenty of room for bargaining skill, indeed the very width of the gap between the upper and the lower bound reflects the superiority of the von Neumann-Morgenstern solution over the alternative solution $P_1 = 2.05$, and is a measure of the incentive to establish the von Neumann-Morgenstern solution.

Having established the bounds, can we say more about the size of the bribe? We can certainly say that the bribe actually agreed upon is likely to be neither 5.41 nor 1.38.

First, a bribe equaling its upper bound 5.41 would leave 2 indifferent, for in the absence of a bribing agreement he could be equally well off. However, at a suggested bribe of 5.41 much is at stake for 1. Agreement leaves him with $11.79 + 5.41 = 17.20$, whereas his unilateral price cut to 2.05 would leave him with merely 13.17. So 1 is far more anxious than 2 to secure an agreement and will have to pare down the bribe to shake 2 out of his indifference. Consequently, very high bribe suggestions at or close to 5.41 will be abandoned in favor of lower ones.

Second, a bribe equaling its lower bound 1.38 would leave 1 indifferent, for in the absence of a bribing agreement he would be equally well off. However, at a suggested bribe of 1.38 much is at stake for poor 2. Agreement leaves him with $6.04 - 1.38 = 4.66$, whereas 1's unilateral price cut to 2.05 would leave 2 with merely 0.63. Therefore 2 is far more anxious than 1 to secure an agreement and will have to raise the bribe to shake 1 out of his indifference. Consequently, very low bribe suggestions at or close to 1.38 will be abandoned in favor of higher ones.

20.11 BRIBING NONFEASIBLE

Suppose a country's antitrust laws rule out such elaborate bribes splitting the profits of a von Neumann-Morgenstern solution. Then duopolists cannot bargain for a bribe, all they can bargain for is a common price, and perhaps even that can be done only implicitly. Now if unit costs are equal, neither party really needs to be bribed. Also they have the same relative vulnerability, hence the same relative bargaining power. Everything points to the von Neumann-Morgenstern solution.

However, if unit costs differ, there is a violent conflict of interest, and since it cannot be patched up by bribing, it may have to be fought out. Price cutting by 1 to 2.05 seems likely, and 2 cannot help it.

At this point duopoly theory usually ends. However, we cannot take duopoly for granted; we must also examine the viability of duopoly itself. Could duopoly turn into monopoly?

20.12 THE MONOPOLY AND THE VON NEUMANN-MORGENSTERN SOLUTIONS COMPARED

Let us compare the industry's profits under the two solutions found. First, into Eq. (7) insert P_{1m} for P_1 and write monopoly profits as

$$(15) \qquad Z_{11m} = \frac{P_{1m} - Q_{11}}{P_{1m}} \frac{Y}{1 + (J/A_1^2)P_{1m}}$$

Second, into Eqs. (11) and (12) insert P_{1d} for P_1, add them, rearrange, and write duopoly profits as

$$(16) \qquad Z_{11d} + Z_{12d} = \frac{P_{1d} - (Q_{11} + Q_{12})/2}{P_{1d}} \frac{Y}{1 + (J/A_1^2)P_{1d}}$$

Are (15) and (16) equal or different?

20.13 EQUAL UNIT COSTS

Assume unit costs to be equal between the duopolists:

$$(17) \qquad\qquad Q_{11} = Q_{12}$$

Insert (17) into (13), compare with (8), and see that monopoly price equals duopoly price:

$$(18) \qquad\qquad P_{1m} = P_{1d}$$

Insert (17) and (18) into (16) and see that monopoly profits equal duopoly profits:

$$(19) \qquad\qquad Z_{11m} = Z_{11d} + Z_{12d}$$

Thus the monopoly and the von Neumann-Morgenstern solutions differ with respect to neither price nor profits. Consequently, there will be no inherent tendency for monopoly to replace duopoly. Duopoly is viable.

20.14 DIFFERENT UNIT COSTS

Assume duopolist 1 to have lower unit costs than duopolist 2; thus

(20) $$Q_{11} < Q_{12}$$

In (20), add Q_{11} and divide by 2 on both sides:

(21) $$Q_{11} < \frac{Q_{11} + Q_{12}}{2}$$

Equations (8), (13), and (21) combined show monopoly price to be lower than duopoly price; thus

(22) $$P_{1m} < P_{1d}$$

Now insert the monopoly price solution (8) into the first factor of the right-hand side of the monopoly profits solution (15).

(23) $$\frac{P_{1m} - Q_{11}}{P_{1m}} = \frac{1}{\dfrac{Q_{11}}{\sqrt{Q_{11}^2 + Q_{11}(A_1^2/J)}} + 1}$$

Then transform the inequality (21) into the equality

(24) $$\lambda Q_{11} = \frac{Q_{11} + Q_{12}}{2}$$

where $$\lambda > 1$$

Insert (24) into the duopoly price solution (13); then insert (13) into the first factor of the right-hand side of the duopoly profits solution (16), then:

(25) $$\frac{P_{1d} - (Q_{11} + Q_{12})/2}{P_{1d}} = \frac{1}{\dfrac{Q_{11}}{\sqrt{Q_{11}^2 + Q_{11}(A_1^2/\lambda J)}} + 1}$$

Comparing (23) and (25) and recalling that $\lambda > 1$, we can see that

(26) $$\frac{P_{1m} - Q_{11}}{P_m} > \frac{P_{1d} - (Q_{11} + Q_{12})/2}{P_{1d}}$$

So the first factor of the right-hand side of (15) is greater than that of (16). It follows from the inequality (22) that so is the second factor on the right-hand side. Consequently,

(27) $$Z_{11m} > Z_{11d} + Z_{12d}$$

Thus, although the monopoly charges a lower price than does the duopoly, its lower unit cost permits it to make a larger amount of profits than does the duopoly. This result may spell the doom of duopoly. True enough, a monopoly maintaining the price P_{1m} as determined by (8) and maximizing Z_{11m} makes the former duopolist 1 better off and the former duopolist 2 worse off than would a duopoly coalition maintaining the common price P_{1d} as determined by (13) and maximizing $Z_{11d} + Z_{12d}$. However, because of the inequality (27), the better-off duopolist 1 can always bribe the worse-off duopolist 2 into accepting the monopoly and still remain better off himself.

We have found, then, an inherent tendency for monopoly to replace duopoly; because of the cost disparity, duopoly is no longer viable. In our numerical example, the von Neumann-Morgenstern solution was $P_{1d} = 3.05$, at which duopolist 1 could be sure of earning $Z_{11d} = 11.79$ *plus* a bribe the lower bound of which was $B_{11d} = 1.38$, a total payoff of 13.17. But as a monopolist 1 could be making $Z_{11m} = 26.33$, or twice as much. What stands between 1 and his monopoly is 2. Vulnerable as 2 may be, he is still there and denies 1 half the market at any common price. How could 1 dislodge 2? There are two ways: War of attrition and bribing.

20.15   WAR OF ATTRITION FORCING DUOPOLIST 2 INTO WITHDRAWAL

For a period whose length τ is calculated to be long enough to drive duopolist 2 out of business, let duopolist 1 consider maintaining a cutthroat price $P_{1w} \leq Q_{12}$, where w stands for war. During this war 1's profits will be Z_{11w}. After the lapse of the period τ, when 2 has withdrawn, 1's profits will be Z_{11m}, as determined by the monopoly solution (15). Let 1's horizon be j. and let j rise without bounds; then the present worth of the flow of 1's future profits is

$$(28) \quad \int_0^\tau Z_{11w} e^{-it}\, dt + \lim_{j \to \infty} \int_\tau^j Z_{11m} e^{-it}\, dt = \frac{(1 - e^{-i\tau})Z_{11w} + e^{-i\tau}Z_{11m}}{i}$$

where e is Euler's number, the base of natural logarithms, i is the rate of interest representing the cost of money capital to the firm and assumed not to vary with the amount of money capital needed, and t is time. The integral (28) represents the worth to duopolist 1 of monopoly by conquest, allowing for the cost of conquest.

For the moment we ignore the possibility of bribing duopolist 2 into withdrawal; this will be examined presently. The alternative to war would then be for 1 and 2 to agree upon the von Neumann-Morgenstern duopoly price as determined by (13), under which duopolist 1 would be earning Z_{11d} as determined by (11) *plus* a bribe B_{11d} as determined by (14). The present worth of the flow of 1's future payoffs would have been

$$(29) \qquad \lim_{j \to \infty} \int_0^j (Z_{11d} + B_{11d})e^{-it}\, dt = \frac{Z_{11d} + B_{11d}}{i}$$

The integral (29) represents the worth to 1 of duopoly in peace. Clearly a necessary condition for 1 to decide on a war of attrition is that monopoly by conquest is at least as valuable to him as duopoly in peace, that is, (28) $\geq$ (29) or

$$(30) \qquad (1 - e^{-i\tau})Z_{11w} + e^{-i\tau}Z_{11m} \geq Z_{11d} + B_{11d}$$

Examine (30) more closely. A higher rate of interest i or a longer period of attrition τ would at the same time raise $1 - e^{-i\tau}$ and reduce $e^{-i\tau}$, that is, raise the weight of Z_{11w}, which is low, and reduce the weight of Z_{11m}, which is high. Thus the left-hand side of (30) would be reduced and a war of attrition perhaps discouraged.

We said that (30) was a necessary condition for duopolist 1 to decide on a war of attrition. However, it is not a sufficient condition, for war may be made redundant by an agreement reflecting the outcome of war but saving the cost of war, as we shall now see.

20.16 BRIBING 2 INTO WITHDRAWAL

The second way of dislodging 2 would be to pay him a lump-sum bribe B_{12m} for his peaceful and immediate withdrawal from the industry. We have already said that because of the inequality (27) such a bribe can be paid by duopolist 1 and still leave him better off than under duopoly. What are the upper and lower bounds of such a bribe?

20.17 UPPER AND LOWER BOUNDS TO BRIBE B_{12m}

The upper bound to the bribe B_{12m} is whichever of the following two upper bounds is the lower. First, the bribe cannot exceed what it is worth to 1 to be alone. What is it worth to him to be alone? At time zero let 2 be bribed into withdrawal from the industry. Again let 1's horizon be j, and let j rise without bounds; then the present worth of the flow of 1's future profits is

$$(31) \qquad \lim_{j \to \infty} \int_0^j Z_{11m} e^{-it}\, dt = \frac{Z_{11m}}{i}$$

If 1 had not been alone, he and 2 would have agreed upon the von Neumann-Morgenstern duopoly price as determined by (13), under which duopolist 1 would be earning Z_{11d} as determined by (11) *plus* a bribe B_{11d} as determined by (14). Under such a duopoly the present worth of the flow of 1's future payoffs would have been (29). The difference between (31) and (29) is the difference between the present worth of 1's future payoffs when alone and when not alone, hence is the worth to him of being alone. That difference must be an upper bound to the bribe B_{12m}:

$$(32) \qquad\qquad B_{12m} \leq \frac{Z_{11m} - (Z_{11d} + B_{11d})}{i}$$

The upper bound (32) is higher the lower the rate of interest i, and the lower the duopoly bribe B_{11d}. In our numerical example in which $A_1^2/J = \frac{1}{9}$, $Q_{11} = 1$, and $Y = 1000$, let the rate of interest be $i = 0.05$; then the upper bound (32) is 263.3.

Second, however much it is worth to 1 to be alone, the bribe B_{12m} cannot exceed the cost of a war of attrition dislodging 2. What is this cost? At time zero let 2 be bribed into withdrawal from the industry. The present worth of the flow of 1's future profits is (31), but let us write it a little differently:

$$(31) \qquad \lim_{j \to \infty} \int_0^j Z_{11m} e^{-it} \, dt = \frac{Z_{11m}}{i} = \frac{(1 - e^{-i\tau})Z_{11m} + e^{-i\tau}Z_{11m}}{i}$$

The integral (28) represented the worth to duopolist 1 of monopoly by conquest. The difference between (31) and (28) is the difference between the present worth of 1's future profits when alone from the outset and when alone only after conquest, hence represents the cost of conquest. That difference must be an upper bound to the bribe B_{12m}:

$$(33) \qquad\qquad B_{12m} \leq \frac{1 - e^{-i\tau}}{i} (Z_{11m} - Z_{11w})$$

The upper bound (33) is higher the longer the duration τ, the lower the cutthroat price P_{1w}, and the lower the rate of interest i. In our numerical example in which $A_1^2/J = \frac{1}{9}$, $Q_{11} = 1$, $Y = 1000$, and $i = 0.05$, let 1 adopt the cutthroat price $P_{1w} = 1$, so $Z_{11w} = 0$. At this price let it last five years before 2 succumbs, hence $\tau = 5$. The upper bound (33) is, then, 116.5.

The upper bound (33) is lower than the upper bound (32) then, and becomes the ultimate upper bound to B_{12m}.

What is the lower bound to the bribe B_{12m}?

If 2 does not agree to withdraw, one of two things will happen. If condition (30) is not satisfied, 1 and 2 will agree upon the von Neumann-Morgenstern duopoly solution with its bribe B_{11d} per annum paid by 2 to 1 as determined by (14). If condition (30) is satisfied, 1 will start his war of attrition.

In our numerical example in which $A_1^2/J = \frac{1}{9}$, $Q_{11} = 1$, $Y = 1000$, $i = 0.05$, $P_{1w} = 1$, $Z_{11w} = 0$, and $\tau = 5$, condition (30) is indeed satisfied. For $B_{11d} = 5.41$ and $B_{11d} = 1.38$, (30) turns into, respectively

(30a) $\qquad\qquad\qquad 20.51 \geq 17.20 \qquad 20.51 \geq 13.17$

Consequently, 1 will start his war of attrition. Assuming 2 to hold out for the duration τ of the war, the present worth of the flow of 2's future profits is:

(34) $$\int_0^\tau Z_{12w}e^{-it}\, dt = \frac{1 - e^{-i\tau}}{i} Z_{12w}$$

The present worth (34) will be the lower bound to B_{12m}:

(35) $$B_{12m} \geq \frac{1 - e^{-i\tau}}{i} Z_{12w}$$

Add to the numerical values given above that $Q_{12} = 2$, then $Z_{12w} = -50$, and the right-hand side of (35) will be -221.2. Summarizing,

(36) $$-221.2 \leq B_{12m} \leq 116.5$$

Thus there is plenty of room for bargaining skill; indeed the very width of the gap between the upper and the lower bound reflects the superiority of the monopoly solution over its alternatives and is a measure of the incentive to establish it. Reasoning as we did in Section 20.10, we can certainly say that the bribe actually agreed upon is likely to be neither 116.5 nor -221.2; it is more likely to be well within those extremes.

20.18   BRIBING NONFEASIBLE

Dislodging duopolist 2 by bribe will often take the form of simple purchase of his plant by duopolist 1. Under the Clayton Act such a merger would be illegal in the United States whenever it would substantially lessen competition—as it indeed intends to do. Therefore, 1 would be left with his war of attrition as the only way of dislodging 2.

20.19   INHERENT INCENTIVES AND SOCIAL PERFORMANCE

The high-cost duopolist clearly has a very strong incentive to avoid finding himself in the predicament just described, under which he may be facing defeat in a war of attrition or may survive as a duopolist only by paying a rather heavy bribe out of his already meager profits. The only way to avoid such prospects is to prevent the cost disadvantage from arising in the first place. It follows that duopolists have at least as much incentive to keep their costs low and to pursue process innovation as have pure competitors.

In fact, they have more such incentive than pure competitors. For its survival, pure competition depends upon the existence of decreasing returns to scale beyond a scale so small that a large number of firms operating at that scale can be accommodated within the industry. Under pure competition, then, his scale alone will keep a low-cost producer from threatening others with extinction. Indeed, the purpose of Marshall's [5] Particular Expenses Curve was to show the peaceful coexistence under pure competition of high-cost and low-cost producers, the latter owing their low costs to some exclusive, natural advantage. Not so under duopoly. It is the absence of such decreasing returns to scale which leads to duopoly, and the absence itself makes threats of extinction very real ones.

If, on the other hand, the high-cost duopolist fails to respond to the inherent incentive, he is likely to be punished by elimination, either through a war of attrition or peacefully through bribing. By eliminating the high-cost source of supply and concentrating all output on the low-cost source, the monopoly serves the consumers better than did the duopoly. After all, in our numerical example monopoly price was 2.05, whereas the von Neumann-Morgenstern duopoly price was 3.05. But does not monopoly exploit consumers more cruelly than does duopoly? Is not market demand, faced by the monopolist, less elastic than $1/f$ of it, faced by any of f firms in an industry? In Eq. (16) of Chapter 7 we found the price elasticity of market demand to equal the price elasticity of demand faced by any of f firms in an industry; hence monopoly does not exploit consumers more cruelly than does duopoly. In the numerical example in which $A_1^2/J = \frac{1}{9}$, solutions (8) and (13) showed monopoly and duopoly price alike to be roughly twice unit cost, reflecting a demand elasticity of roughly -2.

20.20 THE BERTRAND SOLUTION

Bertrand [1] grossly misrepresented Cournot [2] by saying:

"Cournot suppose que l'un des concurrents baissera ses prix pour attirer à lui les acheteurs, et que l'autre, pour les ramener, les baissant à son tour davantage, ils ne s'arrêteront dans cette voie que lorsque chacun d'eux, lors même que son concurrent renoncerait à la lutte, ne gagnerait plus rien à abaisser ses prix."

Although Cournot had said no such thing, it was worth saying. Machlup [4] has expressed the difference between Bertrand and Cournot very elegantly:

"[In Bertrand] the competitors do not—as in Cournot—sell what they produce, but they produce what they sell. That is to say, . . . they first name a price and then fill all the orders they receive."

In naming their price, Bertrand duopolists assume the price charged by their rival to remain constant. Assuming as Bertrand did "qualité identique," that is, absence of product differentiation, any seller who lowers his price ever so slightly below the common price will get the entire market to himself, doubling his sales:

"Si l'un des concurrents abaisse seul le sien, il attire à lui, en négligeant des exceptions sans importance, la totalité de la vente, et il doublera sa recette si son concurrent le laisse faire."

This would go on until the profit margin of one or both duopolists had become zero. Thus for our numerical example in which $A_1{}^2/J = \frac{1}{9}$, and $Q_{11} = Q_{12} = 1$, the Bertrand price solution is

$$P_{1d} = 1.00$$

Insert that value of P_1 into (11) and (12) and find the Bertrand profits solution. For the special case of $Y = 1000$ it is

$$Z_{11d} = 0 \qquad Z_{12d} = 0 \qquad Z_{11d} + Z_{12d} = 0$$

The Bertrand price solution is shown as the point B in Fig. 20.1. Price in the Bertrand solution is slightly less than half the price of the von Neumann-Morgenstern solution. Profits have been entirely wiped out.

Duopolists may be unlikely to engage in Bertrand price-cutting. Indeed, in the absence of product differentiation the very idea of a disparity of prices struck us as being weird enough to be ruled out by Eq. (4).

But are duopolists rational? Giving the participants a pecuniary payoff from a duopoly game, Fouraker and Siegel [3] have conducted experiments in which Bertrand outcomes turned out to be very common. But improving the realism of the Fouraker-Siegel experiment, Murphy [6] found Bertrand outcomes much less common.

Be that as it may, a duopolist may after all engage in Bertrand price-cutting. In the absence of product differentiation his rival has no protection against it, he is at the mercy of his foolish rival. In Chapter 21 we shall examine the protection offered by product differentiation.

REFERENCES

[1] Bertrand, J., "Théorie mathématique de la richesse sociale" (book review) *Journal des savants*, 499–508 (September 1883).
[2] Cournot, A., *Recherches sur les principes mathématique de la théorie des richesses*, Paris, 1838.
[3] Fouraker, L. E., and S. Siegel, *Bargaining Behavior*, New York, 1963.
[4] Machlup, F., *The Economics of Sellers' Competition*, Baltimore, Maryland, 1952, p. 377.
[5] Marshall, A., *Principles of Economics*, London, 1961, Appendix H, pp. 805–812.
[6] Murphy, J. L., "Effects of the Threat of Losses on Duopoly Bargaining," *Quart. Jour. Econ.*, **80**, 296–313 (May 1966).
[7] Shubik, M., *Strategy and Market Structure*, New York, 1959, pp. 80–117.
[8] Von Neumann, J., and O. Morgenstern, *Theory of Games and Economic Behavior*, Princeton, 1944.

CHAPTER 21

Duopoly Price under Product Differentiation*

21.1 INTRODUCTION

Chapter 20 ended with the hazards of Bertrand price-cutting in the absence of product differentiation. In this chapter we will introduce product differentiation and examine duopoly price formation for a pair of given, differentiated products produced at constant unit costs, equal between the duopolists. We shall find a new incentive inherent in the model and examples of the social performance resulting from responses to it.

21.2 NOTATION

The introduction of product differentiation simplifies our notation. Under product differentiation there is only one firm producing each product constituting, as it were, its own industry; thus our firm subscript i may be dropped, and only the industry subscript h is left. The following notation will be assigned.

Variables

C_h = cost per annum of firm in hth industry
P_h = price charged by firm in hth industry
R_h = revenue from output sold per annum by firm in hth industry
X_h = output produced and sold per annum by firm in hth industry
Z_h = profits per annum of firm in hth industry

Parameters

A_h = coefficients in constant-elasticity-of-substitution utility function
J = agglomeration of utility and price parameters outside the duopoly

* Chapter 7 is a prerequisite for Chapter 21.

Q_h = unit cost of firm in hth industry
ρ = exponent in constant-elasticity-of-substitution utility function
Y = household budget per annum

21.3 PROFITS AND COST

Within the firm of the hth industry, define profits as revenue *minus* cost:

$$(1) \qquad Z_h = R_h - C_h \qquad (h = 1, 2)$$

and revenue as price *times* output sold:

$$(2) \qquad R_h = P_h X_h \qquad (h = 1, 2)$$

Let the firm operate under constant returns to scale; thus costs are in direct proportion to output:

$$(3) \qquad C_h = Q_h X_h \qquad (h = 1, 2)$$

In Chapter 20, the emphasis was on unit cost differences. In this chapter the emphasis is on product differences; therefore let the duopolists have the same unit cost.

$$(4) \qquad Q_1 = Q_2 = Q$$

21.4 DEMAND FACED BY DUOPOLISTS

In Chapter 20, we considered a duopoly in product 1 of the economy. Both duopolists produced it, so there was no product differentiation. Now imagine that each duopolist has succeeded in setting his product apart from all other products in the economy. Then, by definition, the firm producing this product is the only firm producing it; this firm constitutes, as it were, its own industry and faces the market demand function for that product. Therefore we now need two market demand functions. Again, in accordance with the synthetic approach underlying this book, we should very much like to derive those two market demand functions from the household utility function, and indeed have already done so: Assuming s households to have identical constant-elasticity-of-substitution individual utility functions, we have expressed market demand for the output of the hth industry as Eq. (9) of Chapter 7. Now all we have to do is to set $h = 1, 2$, and our duopoly will be one of products 1 and 2 of the economy. Furthermore, in (9) of Chapter 7 set

$$\sum_{k=1}^{s} C_{hk} = X_h$$

$$\sum_{k=1}^{s} Y_k = Y$$

$$(A_3 P_3{}^\rho)^{1/(1+\rho)} + \cdots + (A_m P_m{}^\rho)^{1/(1+\rho)} + (B_1 r_1{}^\rho)^{1/(1+\rho)} + \cdots$$
$$+ (B_n r_n{}^\rho)^{1/(1+\rho)} = J$$

The symbol J, then, represents an agglomeration of price and utility parameters of the economy outside the duopoly. Let nothing have changed there; thus J is the same as it was in Chapter 20, but the number m is up by one. The use of J permits us to write the demand functions faced by the duopolists as

$$(5) \qquad X_1 = \frac{(A_1/P_1)^{1/(1+\rho)}}{(A_1 P_1{}^\rho)^{1/(1+\rho)} + (A_2 P_2{}^\rho)^{1/(1+\rho)} + J} \, Y$$

$$(6) \qquad X_2 = \frac{(A_2/P_2)^{1/(1+\rho)}}{(A_1 P_1{}^\rho)^{1/(1+\rho)} + (A_2 P_2{}^\rho)^{1/(1+\rho)} + J} \, Y$$

In summary, (5) and (6) are the demands faced by duopolists producing the first and second product, respectively, of an economy consisting of households having identical constant-elasticity-of-substitution individual utility functions and having an aggregate budget Y per annum.

Our use of the constant-elasticity-of-substitution utility function, common to all households, implies an extreme success in product differentiation. Thus differentiation is implied to have created an elasticity of substitution

$$\sigma = \frac{1}{1+\rho}$$

between products 1 and 2, produced by the duopolists, equal to that existing between any of the products 1 or 2 on the one hand, and any product outside the duopoly, on the other. As a result, the duopolists have become largely independent, as we shall see in Section 21.7.

Let us make (5) and (6) more manageable. First, let us fix a specific value for ρ, the same one used in Chapter 20, that is, $\rho = -\frac{1}{2}$. Second, let us set $A_1 = A_2 = A$. Equations (5) and (6) will then collapse into

$$(7) \qquad X_1 = \frac{1}{P_1} \frac{Y P_2}{P_1 + P_2 + (J/A^2) P_1 P_2}$$

$$(8) \qquad X_2 = \frac{1}{P_2} \frac{Y P_1}{P_1 + P_2 + (J/A^2) P_1 P_2}$$

By taking the partial derivatives of any X with respect to its own price and the other price, the reader may convince himself that the quantity demanded of any duopolist's product falls with rising price of his own and rises with rising price charged by the other duopolist. We would certainly expect close substitutes to behave in no other way.

We now have all we need to find the duopolists' profits functions. Insert (2) through (4), and (7) and (8) into (1):

$$(9) \qquad Z_1 = \frac{P_1 - Q}{P_1} \frac{YP_2}{P_1 + P_2 + (J/A^2)P_1P_2}$$

$$(10) \qquad Z_2 = \frac{P_2 - Q}{P_2} \frac{YP_1}{P_1 + P_2 + (J/A^2)P_1P_2}$$

For this new system, let us now find both the von Neumann-Morgenstern and the Bertrand price and profits solutions.

21.5   VON NEUMANN-MORGENSTERN SOLUTION

Again let duopolists 1 and 2 form a von Neumann-Morgenstern [7] coalition against the consumers. The coalition will maximize its combined profits $Z_1 + Z_2$. The two first-order conditions for such a maximum are

$$(11) \qquad \frac{\partial(Z_1 + Z_2)}{\partial P_1} = 0$$

$$(12) \qquad \frac{\partial(Z_1 + Z_2)}{\partial P_2} = 0$$

Carry out these partial derivations, deduct (12) from (11), and find

$$(13) \qquad (P_1 - P_2)\left(P_1 + P_2 + \frac{J}{A^2}P_1P_2\right) = 0$$

For positive prices, the expression in the second parentheses must be positive; hence (13) can be satisfied only by

$$(14) \qquad P_1 = P_2 = P$$

Insert (14) into (11):

$$(15) \qquad P = Q \pm \sqrt{Q^2 + 2Q\frac{A^2}{J}}$$

Since the last term under the square root sign is positive, one solution is positive, the other negative. Of these we reject the latter.

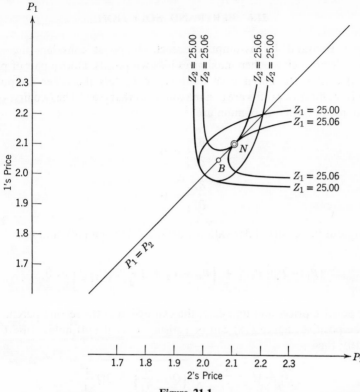

Figure 21.1

We assumed J to be the same as it was in Chapter 20, so let us examine the special case of $A^2/J = \frac{1}{9}$ and $Q = 1$. For these values the von Neumann-Morgenstern price solution is

$$P = 2.11$$

Insert that value of P into (9) and (10) and find the von Neumann-Morgenstern profits solutions. For the special case of $Y = 1000$ the solutions are

$$Z_1 = 25.06 \qquad Z_2 = 25.06 \qquad Z_1 + Z_2 = 50.12$$

Figure 21.1 is a close-up of the area around the von Neumann-Morgenstern point N in a diagram with the two prices P_1 and P_2 plotted on the axes. Now that the products are differentiated, the duopolists may sell at different prices and are no longer confined to the 45° line through zero. The von Neumann-Morgenstern point, however, according to (14) is still located on that line. For illustration, two isoprofits curves are shown for each duopolist, that is, $Z_h = 25.00$ and $Z_h = 25.06$, $h = 1, 2$.

21.6 BERTRAND SOLUTION

Under Bertrand [1] assumptions, each duopolist considers the other duopolist's price given, then maximizes his own profits. Does a pair of prices (P_1, P_2) exist such that if each duopolist considers the other duopolist's price given, his own profits are at a maximum at that pair? The two first-order conditions for such a maximum are

(16)
$$\frac{\partial Z_1}{\partial P_1} = 0$$

(17)
$$\frac{\partial Z_2}{\partial P_2} = 0$$

Carry out these partial derivations, deduct (17) from (16), and find

(18)
$$(P_1 - P_2)\left[P_1P_2 + \left(P_1 + P_2 + 2\frac{J}{A^2}P_1P_2\right)Q\right] = 0$$

For positive prices and unit cost, the expression in the second parentheses must be positive; hence (18) can be satisfied only if (14) holds. Insert (14) into (16); then

(19)
$$P = Q - \frac{A^2}{2J} \pm \sqrt{\left(Q - \frac{A^2}{2J}\right)^2 + 3Q\frac{A^2}{J}}$$

Since the last term under the square root sign is positive, as usual one solution is positive, the other negative, and we reject the latter solution.

For the special case of $A^2/J = \frac{1}{9}$ and $Q = 1$, the Bertrand price solution is

$$P = 2.05$$

Insert that value of P into (9) and (10) and find the Bertrand profits solutions. For the special case of $Y = 1000$ they are

$$Z_1 = 25.05 \qquad Z_2 = 25.05 \qquad Z_1 + Z_2 = 50.10$$

Far from being zero, Bertrand profits are practically the same as von Neumann-Morgenstern profits; indeed this is a striking difference between absence and presence of product differentiation.

The Bertrand point, too, according to (14) is still located on the 45° line through zero and is shown as B in Fig. 21.1.

21.7 THE MANIFESTATION OF SUCCESS IN PRODUCT DIFFERENTIATION

We said that our use of the constant-elasticity-of-substitution utility function, common to all households, implies an extreme success in product differentiation. This success can now be seen to pay off in two distinct ways.

First, it pays off in the sense that the highest profits under product differentiation are much higher than the highest profits in the absence of product differentiation. In Chapter 20 the economy had m goods, and we were considering a duopoly in one of them, product 1. The duopolists considered the prices of the remaining $m - 1$ goods given and could at best make a combined profit of 26.33 at a price of 2.05. In this chapter, the economy has $m + 1$ goods, and we are considering a duopoly in two of them, products 1 and 2. Everything outside the duopoly is the same as before; the duopolists still consider the prices of the remaining $m - 1$ goods given, but can now at best make a combined profit of 50.12 at a price of 2.11. This is almost twice as much profits as before.

Second, success pays off in the sense that the lowest profits under product differentiation are also much higher than the lowest profits in the absence of product differentiation. The Bertrand solution in Chapter 20 was zero combined profits at a price of 1.00. In this chapter, the Bertrand solution yields a combined profit of 50.10 at a price of 2.05. Here, then, a lapse from the von Neumann-Morgenstern solution into the Bertrand solution is nothing much to worry about: It would reduce price by less than 3 per cent and reduce profits hardly at all. No duopolist is at the mercy of his rival any more; each has found a protected niche for himself.

21.8 INCENTIVES INHERENT IN THE MODEL

The extreme success in product differentiation assumed in this chapter constitutes an inherent incentive to product differentiation. Firms are promised a haven protected from the hazards of Bertrand price-cutting. Actual results may fall short of such a haven, but even where they do not, the haven is a temporary one. To be sure, the rival may have to wait for one's patent to expire, or he may have to wait until he has accumulated enough know-how. Tooling-up also takes time. However, sooner or later anything successful will be imitated. Kaplan and Kahn [4] observe that "losses of business and diminishing profit margins on traditional lines, like heavy chemicals and heavy steels, finally forced companies like Allied Chemical & Dye and U.S. Steel to catch up with the caravan. The old-line locomotive companies were swept off their feet when General Motors introduced diesel engines." To keep up product differentiation, a never-ending succession of product innovations is necessary.

When not introducing wholly new products, firms still have an incentive to keep improving established ones, and such improvements do add up over the years. Studies of the social performance of oligopolistic industries often show impressive proportionate rates of growth of product quality resulting, no doubt, from such incentives. Table 21.1 and Fig. 21.2, which uses semi-logarithmic scale, summarize some examples. Such proportionate rates of growth of product quality are hardly unusual, for oligopoly not only provides

Table 21.1 Quality Improvement under Oligopoly

Source	Product	Period	Quality	Average Rate of Growth of Quality, per Cent per Year
[6]	Incandescent lamp	1906–1937	Lumens per watt	$4\frac{3}{4}$
[3]	Fluorescent lamp	1938–1942	Lumens per watt	10
			Useful life	13
[5]	Tire	1920–1948	Mileage	6
[2]	General Electric refrigerator	1927–1950	Ice freezing rate	$6\frac{1}{4}$
			Useful life	5
			Refrigerating capacity	3
			Kw hours per month	−4
			Noise level	−7
[2]	Chevrolet automobile	1928–1950	Horsepower	$4\frac{1}{2}$
			Maximum speed	$2\frac{1}{8}$
			Miles per gallon at 30 mph	$\frac{7}{8}$
[8]	Ford automobile	1949–1958	Distance covered in 4 seconds after standing start	$4\frac{1}{4}$
			Weight	$\frac{3}{4}$
			Miles per gallon at 30 mph	$\frac{3}{4}$

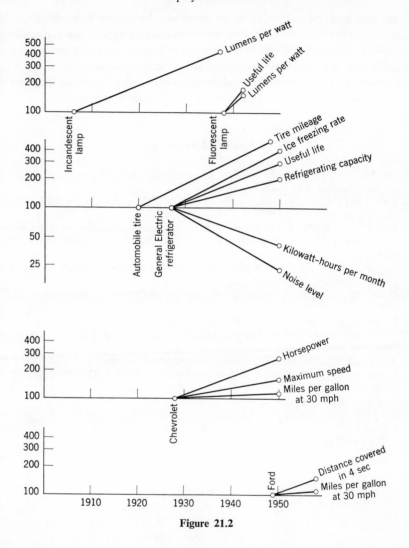

Figure 21.2

the incentive for them but, unlike pure and monopolistic competition, oligopoly also provides the profits necessary to respond to the incentive. Profits
are high enough to finance product innovation as well as process innovation
(producing same output with less input).

Such product and process innovation must be far more important to
society than the hypothetical, and probably petty, price reductions obtainable
from the purification of price competition. Admittedly, there would still be
incentives to process innovation under pure competition. However, with

profits low under freedom of entry there would not be enough funds to finance such innovation. United States experience in agriculture is a striking example. If the spectacular postwar growth of productivity in agriculture is a triumph, it is a triumph of socialism, not pure competition, for the bulk of agricultural research in the United States is sponsored by either the United States Department of Agriculture or the large state universities.

REFERENCES

[1] Bertrand, J., "Théorie mathématique de la richesse sociale" (book review) *Journal des savants*, September 1883, 499–508.

[2] Brems, H., *Product Equilibrium under Monopolistic Competition*, Cambridge, Massachusetts, pp. 16–17.

[3] Bright, A. A., and W. R. MacLaurin, "Economic Factors Influencing the Development and Introduction of the Fluroescent Lamp," *Jour. Pol. Econ.*, **51**, 429–450 (October 1943).

[4] Kaplan, A. D. H., and A. E. Kahn, "Big Business in a Competitive Society," *Fortune*, February 1953, 4.

[5] Owen, W., *Automotive Transportation, Trends, and Problems*, Washington, D.C., 1949, p. 28.

[6] Stigler, G. J., *Trends in Output and Employment*, New York, 1947, p. 11.

[7] Von Neumann, J., and O. Morgenstern, *Theory of Games and Economic Behavior*, Princeton, 1944.

[8] Yntema, T. O., *Statement Before the Subcommittee on Antitrust and Monopoly of the Committee of the Judiciary, U.S. Senate, February 4–5, 1958*, Dearborn, Michigan, 1958, p. 29.

CHAPTER 22

Duopoly Quality of Output

22.1 INTRODUCTION

A comparison between the duopoly models of Chapters 20 and 21 showed a considerable payoff from, and a resulting incentive for, product differentiation. As in almost all economic theory, the two chapters treated the absence or presence of product differentiation as a datum. Yet, if product differentiation is really that important it ought to be treated as a key variable in the theory of duopoly. Therefore instead of examining duopoly price formation for a pair of given products, as we did in Chapter 21, we shall now examine duopoly product quality formation for a pair of given prices. In other words, instead of finding von Neumann-Morgenstern and Bertrand solutions for duopoly price, we shall now find such solutions for duopoly quality. Having done that, we shall know how much product differentiation to expect under duopoly. Will duopolists disperse, qualitywise, or will they cluster, as Hotelling [3] said they would:

"Buyers are confronted everywhere with an excessive sameness . . . . Methodist and Presbyterian churches are too much alike; cider is too homogeneous."

22.2 NOTATION

The following notation will be assigned.

Variables

α = value of product quality offered by duopolist 1
β = value of product quality offered by duopolist 2

215

C_h = cost per annum of firm in hth industry
R_h = revenue from output sold per annum by firm in hth industry
X_h = output produced and sold per annum by firm in hth industry
x = value of product quality
Z_h = profits per annum of firm in hth industry

Parameters

e = Euler's number, the base of natural logarithms
$\Phi(\cdot)$ = the normal distribution function
$\phi(\cdot)$ = the normal density function
P_h = price charged by firm in hth industry
π = 3.14159
Q_h = unit cost of firm in hth industry
q = a density
σ^2 = the variance of the function (6)
$\sigma_1{}^2$ = the variance of the functions (7) and (8)

22.3   PROFITS AND COST

Since under product differentiation there is only one firm producing each product and constituting, as it were, its own industry, the firm subscript i may be dropped, and only the industry subscript h is left. Consequently, the first three equations here are the same as the first three equations of Chapter 21.

(1) $$Z_h = R_h - C_h \qquad (h = 1, 2)$$

(2) $$R_h = P_h X_h \qquad (h = 1, 2)$$

(3) $$C_h = Q_h X_h \qquad (h = 1, 2)$$

In Chapters 20 and 21 the emphasis was on cost and price. In this chapter the emphasis is on neither, so let duopolists have the same unit cost and charge the same price. Let both unit cost and price be parameters, and let us fix some simple values for them.

(4) $$Q_1 = Q_2 = 1$$

(5) $$P_1 = P_2 = 2$$

22.4   CONSUMER PREFERENCES

Let product quality be one-dimensional, quantitative, and capable of continuous variation. Let its value be x. In previous chapters, all consumers

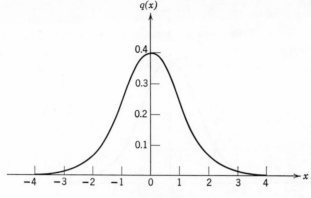

Figure 22.1

were assumed to have the same tastes. In this chapter let us assume tastes with respect to x to differ among consumers, and let the variation of tastes among consumers be described by the normal probability density function

(6) $$q(x) = \frac{1}{\sigma\sqrt{2\pi}} e^{-\frac{1}{2}(\frac{x}{\sigma})^2}$$

having the mean 0 and the variance σ^2. Thus 50 per cent of the consumers prefer a value of x within the interval $-0.67\sigma < x < 0.67\sigma$, 68.3 per cent a value within the interval $-\sigma < x < \sigma$, 95 per cent a value within the interval $-1.96\sigma < x < 1.96\sigma$, and 99 per cent a value within the interval $-2.58\sigma < x < 2.58\sigma$. For $\sigma^2 = 1$ the function (6) is shown in Fig. 22.1.

22.5 SELLER 1 ALONE

For the time being, let seller 1 be alone, offering one product quality only. Let the value of that quality be α. Now consider all consumers who prefer some specific value x. Let the proportion of those consumers preferring x but nevertheless willing to buy α be the function

(7) $$f(x \mid \alpha, \sigma_1) = e^{-\frac{1}{2}(\frac{x-\alpha}{1})^2}$$

Here $x - \alpha$ is the gap between what is preferred x and what is being offered α, and σ_1 is a measure of the tolerance of the consumers, that is, their willingness to accept a given gap $x - \alpha$. If the gap $x - \alpha = 0$, then (7) collapses into $f(x \mid \alpha, \sigma_1) = 1$; hence everybody preferring x will buy α. For any value of the the gap $x - \alpha$ other than zero, some consumers preferring x will refuse to

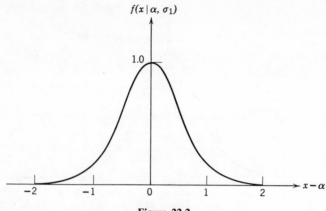

Figure 22.2

buy α, and $f(x \mid \alpha, \sigma_1) < 1$. For gaps much wider than $3\sigma_1$, virtually all consumers preferring x will refuse to buy α. For the special case of $\sigma_1^2 = \frac{1}{3}$, the function (7) is shown in Fig. 22.2.

22.6 SELLER 2 ALONE

Instead of seller 1, let seller 2 be alone, offering one product quality only. Let the value of that quality be β. Again consider all consumers who prefer some specific value x. Let the proportion of those consumers preferring x but nevertheless willing to buy β be the function

$$(8) \qquad f(x \mid \beta, \sigma_1) = e^{-\frac{1}{2}(\frac{x-\beta}{\sigma_1})^2}$$

22.7 SELLERS 1 AND 2 BOTH PRESENT

Finally, let sellers 1 and 2 both be present, offering product qualities α and β, respectively. Assume $\alpha \leq \beta$. First consider the case $\alpha = \beta$. Here, (7) and (8) are equal for all x, there is no product differentiation at all, and consumers are indifferent as between sellers 1 and 2. Then consider the case $\alpha < \beta$. There will now be many consumers who would have been willing to buy α had seller 1 been alone, and who would also have been willing to buy β had seller 2 been alone. From whom will such consumers buy? Now (7) and (8) are no longer equal for all x, so assume that consumers for whom $f(x \mid \alpha, \sigma_1) > f(x \mid \beta, \sigma_1)$ will buy α and consumers for whom $f(x \mid \alpha, \sigma_1) < f(x \mid \beta, \sigma_1)$ will buy β. Equations (7) and (8) are still, however, equal for one

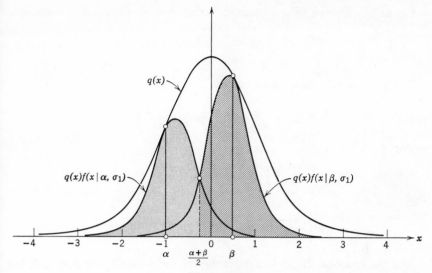

Figure 22.3

specific value of x, that is, $x = (\alpha + \beta)/2$. Consumers preferring that particular value of x will, then, be indifferent as between sellers 1 and 2.

It follows that consumers buying α constitute the following proportion of all consumers.

$$(9) \qquad \int_{-\infty}^{(\alpha+\beta)/2} q(x)f(x \mid \alpha, \sigma_1)\, dx$$

The integral (9) is shown as the left-hand shaded area in Fig. 22.3.
Consumers buying β constitute the following proportion of all consumers.

$$(10) \qquad \int_{(\alpha+\beta)/2}^{\infty} q(x)f(x \mid \beta, \sigma_1)\, dx$$

The integral (10) is shown as the right-hand shaded area in Fig. 22.3.
The Appendix to this chapter shows how to carry out these integrations.

$$(11) \quad \int_{-\infty}^{(\alpha+\beta)/2} q(x)f(x \mid \alpha, \sigma_1)\, dx$$

$$= \sigma_1\sqrt{2\pi}\; \phi\!\left(\frac{\alpha}{\sqrt{\sigma^2 + \sigma_1^2}}\right)\Phi\!\left[\frac{\sqrt{\sigma^2 + \sigma_1^2}}{\sigma\sigma_1}\left(\frac{\alpha + \beta}{2} - \frac{\alpha\sigma^2}{\sigma^2 + \sigma_1^2}\right)\right]$$

and

$$(12) \quad \int_{(\alpha+\beta)/2}^{\infty} q(x)f(x \mid \beta, \sigma_1)\, dx$$

$$= \sigma_1\sqrt{2\pi}\; \phi\!\left(\frac{\beta}{\sqrt{\sigma^2 + \sigma_1^2}}\right)\Phi\!\left[\frac{\sqrt{\sigma^2 + \sigma_1^2}}{\sigma\sigma_1}\left(\frac{\alpha + \beta}{2} - \frac{\beta\sigma^2}{\sigma^2 + \sigma_1^2}\right)\right]$$

Let us now choose some convenient values for our variances; for example

$$\sigma^2 = 1$$

$$\sigma_1{}^2 = \tfrac{1}{3}$$

The integral (11) then collapses into

(13)
$$X_1 = \sqrt{\tfrac{2}{3}\pi}\ \phi\!\left(\frac{\alpha}{\sqrt{\tfrac{4}{3}}}\right)\Phi\!\left(\frac{2\beta - \alpha}{2}\right),$$

where

$$\phi\!\left(\frac{\alpha}{\sqrt{\tfrac{4}{3}}}\right) = \frac{1}{\sqrt{\tfrac{8}{3}\pi}}\,e^{-(3/8)\alpha^2}$$

and

$$\Phi\!\left(\frac{2\beta - \alpha}{2}\right) = \frac{1}{\sqrt{2\pi}}\int_{-\infty}^{(2\beta-\alpha)/2} e^{-(1/2)y^2}\,dy$$

The last function $\Phi[(2\beta - \alpha)/2]$ is shown, for $\alpha = -1$ and $\beta = \tfrac{1}{2}$, as the shaded area in Fig. 22.4.

And the integral (12) collapses into

(14)
$$X_2 = \sqrt{\tfrac{2}{3}\pi}\ \phi\!\left(\frac{\beta}{\sqrt{\tfrac{4}{3}}}\right)\Phi\!\left(-\frac{2\alpha - \beta}{2}\right),$$

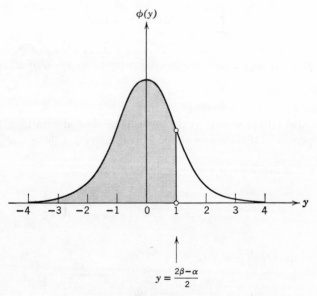

$$y = \frac{2\beta - \alpha}{2}$$

Figure 22.4

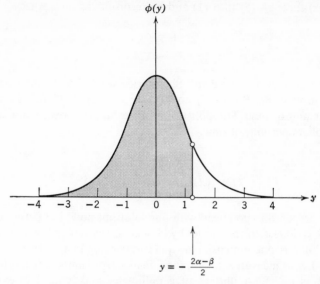

$$y = -\frac{2\alpha - \beta}{2}$$

Figure 22.5

where

$$\phi\left(\frac{\beta}{\sqrt{\frac{4}{3}}}\right) = \frac{1}{\sqrt{\frac{8}{3}\pi}}\, e^{-(3/8)\beta^2}$$

and

$$\Phi\left(-\frac{2\alpha - \beta}{2}\right) = \frac{1}{\sqrt{2\pi}} \int_{-\infty}^{-(2\alpha-\beta)/2} e^{-(1/2)y^2}\, dy$$

The last function $\Phi[-(2\alpha - \beta)/2]$ is shown, for $\alpha = -1$ and $\beta = \frac{1}{2}$, as the shaded area in Fig. 22.5.

22.8 DEMANDS FACED BY DUOPOLISTS

Let there be one million consumers in the market. Some of them are not going to buy the product at all, because neither α nor β comes close enough to their preferred value x. Let those who do buy, buy one unit of the product per unit of time from either duopolist 1 or duopolist 2. As defined by (13) and (14), X_1 and X_2 are measured, then, in millions of units sold per unit of time. For example, if the integral (13) equals 0.355, this means that 0.355 million consumers are going to buy one unit each per unit of time from duopolist 1. His sales will then be 0.355 million units per unit of time.

Insert (2) through (5) into (1) and write profits as

(15) $Z_1 = X_1$

(16) $Z_2 = X_2$

What are profits measured in? Since price was $2 and unit cost $1, the profit per unit is $1. Profits Z_1 and Z_2 are measured, then, in millions of dollars per unit of time. Duopolist 1, in the example above, will make 0.355 million dollars per unit of time.

22.9 COLOR AS QUALITY

We are prepared to go ahead with our solutions now, but before doing so, let us add vividness to the model by choosing, say, color for an example of quality. Color is one-dimensional, quantitative, and capable of continuous variation. Let us measure α and β, then, in angstrom units. The angstrom unit is defined as one ten-millionth of a millimeter and is used to express the length of very short waves. Radiations having a wavelength below 4000 or above 8000 angstroms are invisible. Therefore, let -2 on our quality scale correspond to 4000 angstroms and 2 correspond to 8000 angstroms. Now we can let our duopolists move their α and β around in the visible part of the spectrum and find their equilibria. It follows from our assumption $\alpha \leq \beta$, however, that they will merely be operating in the shaded part of Fig. 22.6.

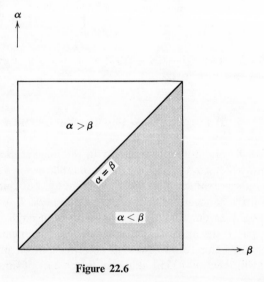

Figure 22.6

22.10   VON NEUMANN-MORGENSTERN SOLUTION

Once again let us apply the von Neumann-Morgenstern [5] theory of games to duopoly. Let duopolists 1 and 2 form a coalition against the consumers, and let the coalition maximize its combined profits $Z_1 + Z_2$. The two first-order conditions for such a maximum are

(17)
$$\frac{\partial(Z_1 + Z_2)}{\partial\alpha} = 0$$

(18)
$$\frac{\partial(Z_1 + Z_2)}{\partial\beta} = 0$$

Carry out these derivations, add (17) and (18), and find

(19) $$-\frac{3}{8}\left[\alpha\Phi\left(\frac{2\beta - \alpha}{2}\right)e^{-(3/8)\alpha^2} + \beta\Phi\left(-\frac{2\alpha - \beta}{2}\right)e^{-(3/8)\beta^2}\right] = 0$$

Equation (19) is seen to be satisfied by

(20) $$\alpha = -\beta$$

Insert (20) into (17) and find

(21) $$e^{-(1/2)[-(3/2)\alpha]^2} = -\frac{\alpha}{2}\int_{-\infty}^{-(3/2)\alpha} e^{-(1/2)y^2}\, dy$$

Using a table of the area under the normal density function, we apply a bit of trial and error, and find

(22) $$\alpha = -0.62$$

Insert (22) into (20);

(23) $$\beta = 0.62$$

The von Neumann-Morgenstern solutions (22) and (23) are shown as the point N in Fig. 22.7. We see that duopolist 1 will offer a green product and duopolist 2 a red one. There is, in other words, a considerable quality dispersion. Insert (22) and (23) into (15) and (16) and find the von Neumann-Morgenstern profits solutions

$$Z_1 = 0.357 \quad Z_2 = 0.357 \quad Z_1 + Z_2 = 0.714$$

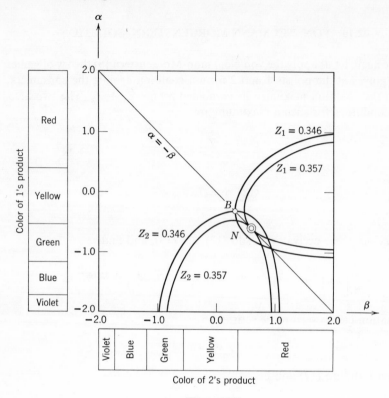

Figure 22.7

22.11 BERTRAND SOLUTION

Bertrand [1] never thought of anything else than price policy, but let us generalize his reasoning: Each duopolist considers the other duopolist's product quality given, then maximizes his own profits. Does a pair of product qualities (α, β) exist such that if each duopolist considers the other duopolist's product quality given, his own profits are at a maximum at that pair? The two first-order conditions for such a maximum are

(24) $$\frac{\partial Z_1}{\partial \alpha} = 0$$

(25) $$\frac{\partial Z_2}{\partial \beta} = 0$$

Carry out these derivations, add (24) and (25), and find

$$(26) \quad \frac{1}{\sqrt{2\pi}} \left[e^{-\frac{1}{2}\left(-\frac{2\alpha-\beta}{2}\right)^2} - e^{-\frac{1}{2}\left(\frac{2\beta-\alpha}{2}\right)^2} \right]$$

$$-\frac{3}{2}\left[\alpha\Phi\left(\frac{2\beta-\alpha}{2}\right) + \beta\Phi\left(-\frac{2\alpha-\beta}{2}\right) \right] = 0$$

Equation (26) is seen to be satisfied by

$$(27) \qquad\qquad \alpha = -\beta$$

Insert (27) into (24), then

$$(28) \qquad e^{-(1/2)[-(3/2)\alpha]^2} = -\tfrac{3}{2}\alpha \int_{-\infty}^{-(3/2)\alpha} e^{-(1/2)y^2}\, dy$$

Again by using a table of the area under the normal density function, we apply trial and error, and find

$$(29) \qquad\qquad \alpha = -0.34$$

Insert (29) into (27), hence

$$(30) \qquad\qquad \beta = 0.34$$

The Bertrand solutions (29) and (30) are shown as the point B in Fig. 22.7. We see that duopolist 1 will offer a greenish yellow product and duopolist 2 a reddish yellow one. Here, then, the duopolists will disperse less than they did in the von Neumann-Morgenstern solution. Insert (29) and (30) into (15) and (16) and find the Bertrand profits solutions

$$Z_1 = 0.346 \qquad Z_2 = 0.346 \qquad Z_1 + Z_2 = 0.692$$

22.12 CONCLUSION: COMPARISON WITH HOTELLING

We have found the offerings of the two duopolists, α and β, to be 1.24 angstroms apart in the von Neumann-Morgenstern solution but merely 0.68 angstrom apart in the Bertrand solution. Neither result validates Hotelling's result, arrived at under Bertrand assumptions, that duopolists would cluster completely.

Burns [2] has called attention to the assumption which produces the complete clustering in Hotelling's model:

"If there is a tendency for all cider to be of medium sweetness, those who prefer very sweet and those who prefer very acid cider buy just as much of the medium type as they would if the cider available were of precisely the grade which they prefer."

By contrast, in our model consumers lose interest in the offerings α and β as the gap between preferred and nearest offered value of x widens. Consequently, any move by a duopolist towards the densely populated center, that is, any move involving heavier clustering of duopolists, will be accompanied by loss of business at the outer fringe. It is this loss which keeps the duopolist from going all the way to the center.

Another difference between Hotelling's model and ours is that Hotelling's center was no more densely populated than the fringes. Hotelling assumed consumers to be equally distributed in their tastes.

In summary: Even without any clustering of consumer tastes, Hotelling found duopolists clustering completely. By contrast, even with a pronounced clustering of consumer tastes (see Fig. 22.1), we have found duopolists to cluster completely neither in the von Neumann-Morgenstern solution nor in the Bertrand solution.

22.13   CONCLUSION: COMPARISON WITH PRICE EQUILIBRIUM

We now notice a difference between quality equilibrium and price equilibrium under duopoly. In both Chapters 20 and 21 we found the von Neumann-Morgenstern price to be higher than the Bertrand price (although in Chapter 21 it was not very much higher). Thus the consumers were better off pricewise in Bertrand equilibrium.

By contrast, in this chapter we have found the quality offerings α and β to be 1.24 angstroms apart in the von Neumann-Morgenstern solution, but merely 0.68 angstrom apart in the Bertrand solution. Under which of the two solutions are the consumers better off? Remember Eqs. (15) and (16) stating that profits equaled sales (because there was a one-dollar profit on each unit sold). Thus paying the same price \$2, 0.714 million consumers felt it worthwhile to buy from either duopolist 1 or 2 in the von Neumann-Morgenstern solution, whereas merely 0.692 million consumers felt it worthwhile to buy in the Bertrand solution. We conclude that the von Neumann-Morgenstern dispersal pleases more consumers than the Bertrand clustering. The consumers are better off qualitywise, then, in the von Neumann-Morgenstern solution.

The remarkable result that the more competitive Bertrand solution is the better pricewise but the worse qualitywise than the more cooperative von Neumann-Morgenstern solutions, warns us against generalizing from price equilibrium to quality equilibrium. Quality equilibrium is important enough to justify special treatment—all too rarely received.

APPENDIX HOW TO TAKE INTEGRALS (9) AND (10)

Insert (6) and (7) into (9), consolidate the exponents, and find e raised to the power

$$- \frac{1}{2}\left[\left(\frac{x}{\sigma}\right)^2 + \left(\frac{x-\alpha}{\sigma_1}\right)^2 \right]$$

Let us write the expression in brackets as

$$\frac{x^2(\sigma^2 + \sigma_1^2)}{\sigma^2\sigma_1^2} + \frac{\alpha^2\sigma^2(\sigma^2 + \sigma_1^2)}{\sigma^2\sigma_1^2(\sigma^2 + \sigma_1^2)} - \frac{2\alpha x\sigma^2}{\sigma^2\sigma_1^2}$$

$$= \left[\frac{\sqrt{\sigma^2 + \sigma_1^2}}{\sigma\sigma_1}\left(x - \frac{\alpha\sigma^2}{\sigma^2 + \sigma_1^2}\right) \right]^2 + \frac{\alpha^2}{\sigma^2 + \sigma_1^2}$$

This permits us to write our integral (9) as

(9) $$\frac{1}{\sigma\sqrt{2\pi}} e^{-\frac{1}{2}\left(\frac{\alpha}{\sqrt{\sigma^2+\sigma_1^2}}\right)^2} \int_{-\infty}^{(\alpha+\beta)/2} e^{-\frac{1}{2}\left[\frac{\sqrt{\sigma^2+\sigma_1^2}}{\sigma\sigma_1}\left(x-\frac{\alpha\sigma^2}{\sigma^2+\sigma_1^2}\right)\right]^2} dx$$

Now let us first define an auxiliary normal density function:

$$\phi\left(\frac{\alpha}{\sqrt{\sigma^2 + \sigma_1^2}}\right) = \frac{1}{\sqrt{\sigma^2 + \sigma_1^2}\sqrt{2\pi}} e^{-\frac{1}{2}\left(\frac{\alpha}{\sqrt{\sigma^2+\sigma_1^2}}\right)^2}$$

Second, we write for short:

$$\sigma_2 = \frac{\sigma\sigma_1}{\sqrt{\sigma^2 + \sigma_1^2}} \qquad m = \frac{\alpha\sigma^2}{\sigma^2 + \sigma_1^2}$$

and define an auxiliary normal distribution function as

$$\frac{1}{\sigma_2\sqrt{2\pi}} \int_{-\infty}^{(\alpha+\beta)/2} e^{-\frac{1}{2}\left(\frac{x-m}{\sigma_2}\right)^2} dx = \frac{1}{\sigma_2\sqrt{2\pi}} \int_{-\infty}^{x} e^{-\frac{1}{2}\left(\frac{y-m}{\sigma_2}\right)^2} dy$$

$$= \frac{1}{\sqrt{2\pi}} \int_{-\infty}^{(x-m)/\sigma_2} e^{-(1/2)u^2} dy = \Phi\left(\frac{x-m}{\sigma_2}\right)$$

These two auxiliary functions $\phi(\cdot)$ and $\Phi(\cdot)$ permit us to write our integral (9) in the form (11). The integral (10) is treated analogously and written in the form (12).

The reader in need of help may consult a good text in probability theory such as Parzen [4].

REFERENCES

[1] Bertrand, J., "Théorie mathématique de la richesse sociale" (book review) *Journal des savants*, (September 1883) 499–508.
[2] Burns, A. R., *The Decline of Competition*, New York, 1936, pp. 404–405.
[3] Hotelling, H., "Stability in Competition," *Econ. Jour.*, **39**, 41–57 (March 1929).
[4] Parzen, E., *Modern Probability Theory and Its Applications*, New York, 1960, pp. 188–189.
[5] von Neumann, J., and O. Morgensten, *Theory of Games and Economic Behavior*, Princeton, 1944.

CHAPTER 23

Labor-Management Bargaining

23.1 INTRODUCTION

In Chapters 20 and 21 we examined the price formation in output markets under duopoly. What about the price formation in input markets, especially the most important input market, that of labor? Serious work on wage determination under collective bargaining began with Zeuthen [2] whose model still seems important enough to warrant a brief restatement.

23.2 NOTATION

The following notation will be assigned.

Variables

q = probability of conflict
w = money wage rate
U = utility

Parameter

c = net outcome of conflict defined as money wage rate after conflict with due allowance for costs of conflict

Let the subscripts L and M stand for labor and management, respectively.

23.3 POINT OF DEPARTURE

Zeuthen began with the outcome of a conflict as expected by labor and management, respectively. As seen by labor, the outcome c_L is defined as the

229

money wage rate after conflict reduced by the costs of conflict. As seen by management, the outcome c_M is defined as the money wage rate after conflict raised by the costs of conflict. Labor's expectation of the gross outcome of conflict need not coincide with management's expectation, and labor's cost of conflict (lost wages) may be very different from management's cost (lost orders).

23.4   UPPER AND LOWER BOUNDS TO NEGOTIATED MONEY WAGE RATE

The upper bound to the negotiated money wage rate is c_M, for that is what management would have to live with after a conflict, the costs of which have been allowed for.

The lower bound to the negotiated money wage is c_L, for that is what labor can expect after a conflict, the costs of which have been allowed for.

We conclude that

(1) $$c_L < w(t) < c_M$$

23.5   THE HIGHEST PROBABILITY OF CONFLICT TO WHICH LABOR WILL EXPOSE ITSELF

At the tth round in the bargaining process, let management offer a wage rate $w_M(t)$ and let labor demand the (higher) wage rate $w_L(t)$. Thus labor faces the choice between the certain prospect of $w_M(t)$ to be had by accepting management's offer, on the one hand, and on the other hand the uncertain prospect of either succeeding in raising the wage rate to $w_L(t)$ with peace whose probability is $1 - q_L(t)$, or failing to do so and facing the outcome c_L of a conflict whose probability is $q_L(t)$. Notice at this point that if labor rejects management's offer, the sum of the probabilities $1 - q_L(t)$ and $q_L(t)$ is one: There is no alternative to $w_L(t)$ and c_L.

Now let labor find the value of $q_L(t)$ which leaves it indifferent. Indifference must mean equality between the utilities of the two possible lines of action open to labor, each utility being multiplied by its probability:

(2) $$[1 - q_L(t)]U_L[w_L(t)] + q_L(t)U_L(c_L) = U_L[w_M(t)]$$

or

(3) $$q_L(t) = \frac{U_L[w_L(t)] - U_L[w_M(t)]}{U_L[w_L(t)] - U_L(c_L)}$$

In rejecting management's offer and holding out for $w_L(t)$, labor will expose itself to no probability of conflict higher than $q_L(t)$ as defined by (3), for such a higher probability would make the left-hand side of (2) less than the right-hand side, hence call for acceptance of management's offer.

23.6 THE HIGHEST PROBABILITY OF CONFLICT TO WHICH MANAGEMENT WILL EXPOSE ITSELF

Still at the tth round, on the other side of the bargaining table, management faces the choice between the certain prospect of $w_L(t)$, to be had by surrendering to labor's demand, on the one hand, and on the other hand the uncertain prospect of either succeeding in having management's original offer $w_M(t)$ accepted with peace whose probability is $1 - q_M(t)$, or failing to do so and facing the outcome c_M of a conflict whose probability is $q_M(t)$. Notice again that if management does not surrender to labor's demand, the sum of the probabilities $1 - q_M(t)$ and $q_M(t)$ is one: There is no alternative to $w_M(t)$ and c_M.

Now let management find the value of $q_M(t)$ which leaves it indifferent. Indifference must mean equality between the utilities of the two possible lines of action open to management, each utility being multiplied by its probability:

(4) $$[1 - q_M(t)]U_M[w_M(t)] + q_M(t)U_M(c_M) = U_M[w_L(t)]$$

or

(5) $$q_M(t) = \frac{U_M[w_M(t)] - U_M[w_L(t)]}{U_M[w_M(t)] - U_M(c_M)}$$

In refusing to surrender to labor's demand and holding out for $w_M(t)$, management will expose itself to no probability of conflict higher than $q_M(t)$ as defined by (5), for such a higher probability would make the left-hand side of (4) less than the right-hand side, hence call for surrender to labor's demand.

23.7 A SUGGESTED WAGE RATE AT WHICH $q_L(t)$ AND $q_M(t)$ ARE EQUAL

Zeuthen concluded that if at the tth round, $q_L(t)$ as defined by (3) differs from $q_M(t)$ as defined by (5), the party with the lower maximum probability to which he is willing to expose himself, will give in to the other party. However, he will not necessarily give in by accepting the other party's standing offer or surrendering to his standing demand. He may also revise his own offer or demand, thus starting a $(t + 1)$st round of the bargaining process.

Such new rounds will be initiated as long as $q_L(t)$ and $q_M(t)$ differ. In this way Zeuthen visualizes the parties drifting toward a money wage rate suggested at the xth round at which $q_L(x)$ and $q_M(x)$ are equal.

23.8   A FLAW?

In Zeuthen's model the tth round must be the *last* round. For we have noticed that when labor rejects management's offer, there is no alternative to $w_L(t)$ and c_L. And when management refuses to surrender to labor's demand, there is no alternative to $w_M(t)$ and c_M. Neither party anticipates anything other than either conflict or unconditional acceptance of the party's own terms. The possibility that the adversary revises his offer or demand is not anticipated, or it would have had a probability greater than zero attached to it and would have been included in (2) and (4).

Or, if the tth round is not the last round, Zeuthen must have considered his parties as shortsighted as Bertrand duopolists who are constantly observing the very thing happening which their expectations rule out.

23.9   AVOIDING THE FLAW: A SIMPLE RESTATEMENT

We may avoid the flaw—and sacrifice the precision—of Zeuthen's model by searching for a narrowed-down area of the bargaining result rather than a precise point. What we can safely say is this.

First, a negotiated money wage rate equal to its upper bound c_M would leave management indifferent, for after a conflict whose costs to management had been allowed for, management would be equally well off. However, at such a wage rate equal to c_M much is at stake for labor: Agreement leaves it with c_M, conflict would have left it with c_L. Thus labor is far more anxious than management to secure an agreement and will have to pare down the suggested wage rate to shake management out of its indifference. Consequently, very high wage suggestions at or near c_M will be abandoned in favor of lower ones.

Second, a negotiated wage rate equal to its lower bound c_L would leave labor indifferent, for after a conflict whose costs to labor had been allowed for, labor would be equally well off. However, at such a wage rate equal to c_L much is at stake for management: Agreement leaves it with c_L, conflict would have left it with c_M. Hence management is far more anxious than labor to secure an agreement and will have to raise the suggested wage rate to shake labor out of its indifference. Consequently, very low wage suggestions at or near c_L will be abandoned in favor of higher ones.

We conclude that the negotiated wage rate is likely to be neither c_M nor c_L. However, it cannot be pinned down by Zeuthen's equality between $q_L(x)$ and $q_M(x)$ either. For a brilliant modern analysis of the imponderables of bargaining, refer to Schelling [1].

REFERENCES

[1] Schelling, T. C., "Bargaining, Communication, and Limited War," *Conflict Resolution* **1,** 19–36 (March 1957).

[2] Zeuthen, F., *Den økonomiske Fordeling*, Copenhagen, 1928; or *Economic Theory and Method*, Cambridge, Massachusetts, 1955, pp. 286–298.

Part Four

General Equilibrium

CHAPTER 24

An Austrian Model without Capital*

24.1 INTRODUCTION

The Austrians wanted to isolate the hard core of economizing. Economizing means having scarce resources and having to choose what to do with them. Ignoring what they called the money veil, the Austrians visualized directly the physical quantities of input, output, exchange, and consumption. They began with a Robinson Crusoe economy and later expanded it to become a multiperson economy. Let us apply modern tools of analysis to the simplest possible Menger-Wieser [2, 6] case of an equilibrium of two inputs, two outputs, and two persons. Production does not take time, no durable producers' goods are used, hence no capital is needed.

I. ONE-PERSON ECONOMY

24.2 NOTATION

In our one-person model, the following notation will be assigned.

Variables

U = utility to Robinson resulting from his consumption
X_j = jth output per annum, $j = 1, 2$
x_{ij} = ith input absorbed by jth output per annum, $i = j = 1, 2$

Parameters

A = elasticity of utility with respect to first output
B = elasticity of utility with respect to second output

* Chapters 1 and 8 are prerequisites for Chapter 24.

237

α_j = elasticity of jth output with respect to first input, $j = 1, 2$
β_j = elasticity of jth output with respect to second input, $j = 1, 2$
M_j = multiplicative factor in the production function for jth output, $j = 1, 2$
N = multiplicative factor in the utility function

24.3 THE EDGEWORTH-BOWLEY BOX

Let Robinson's production functions for the two outputs be linearly homogeneous and of Cobb-Douglas form

(1) $$X_1 = M_1 x_{11}{}^{\alpha_1} x_{21}{}^{\beta_1}$$

(2) $$X_2 = M_2 x_{12}{}^{\alpha_2} x_{22}{}^{\beta_2}$$

where α_j and β_j are parameters lying between zero and one, $\alpha_j + \beta_j = 1$, and M_j is a multiplicative factor depending upon the units of measurement $j = 1, 2$.

As a starting point, let Robinson consider producing an arbitrary quantity of the first output. In a diagram like Fig. 24.1 with the first input on the vertical axis and the second input on the horizontal axis, draw the isoquant for that arbitrary quantity. As we know, for a production function like (1), the isoquant will be convex to the origin.

The Austrians assumed the total available quantity of each input to be given. Let us take advantage of that assumption and turn our diagram in Fig. 24.1 into the celebrated Edgeworth-Bowley box, that is, a rectangle whose height measures the total available quantity of the first input and whose

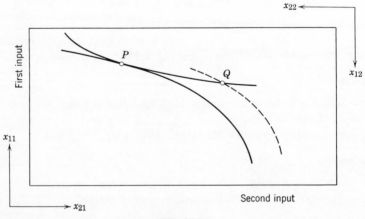

Figure 24.1

base measures the total available quantity of the second input. Begin at the northeastern corner of this rectangle and plot the first input absorbed by the second output downward, and plot the second input absorbed by the second output leftward. With this new origin, there must exist a system of isoquants for the second output. For a production function like (2), as we know, these isoquants will be convex to the northeastern corner of the rectangle. One of them must be in a position of tangency with the isoquant we drew originally for the first output. As long as Robinson wants to produce the arbitrary fixed amount of the first input, he should obviously be in the tangency point P in Fig. 24.1. Were he, for example, to produce in the point Q, we would get the same quantity of the first output but less of the second.

24.4 THE EDGEWORTH-BOWLEY CURVE

We should now very much like to derive the locus of all such tangency points, that is the Edgeworth-Bowley curve. To derive it, proceed as follows. Let Robinson change infinitesimally his x_{11} by dx_{11}, his x_{21} by dx_{21}, his x_{12} by dx_{12}, and his x_{22} by dx_{22}. His two isoquants are then defined by the requirement that output remains unaffected:

$$(3) \qquad dX_1 = \frac{\partial X_1}{\partial x_{11}} dx_{11} + \frac{\partial X_1}{\partial x_{21}} dx_{21} = 0$$

$$(4) \qquad dX_2 = \frac{\partial X_2}{\partial x_{12}} dx_{12} + \frac{\partial X_2}{\partial x_{22}} dx_{22} = 0$$

Use the production functions (1) and (2), carry out the derivations ordered by (3) and (4), and find the slopes of the two isoquants

$$(5) \qquad \frac{dx_{11}}{dx_{21}} = - \frac{\beta_1}{\alpha_1} \frac{x_{11}}{x_{21}}$$

$$(6) \qquad \frac{dx_{12}}{dx_{22}} = - \frac{\beta_2}{\alpha_2} \frac{x_{12}}{x_{22}}$$

In a tangency point, the slopes (5) and (6) are equal, hence

$$(7) \qquad \frac{x_{11}/x_{21}}{x_{12}/x_{22}} = \frac{\beta_2/\alpha_2}{\beta_1/\alpha_1}$$

Figure 24.2 shows seven possible Edgeworth-Bowley curves, one for each of the seven values 8, 4, 2, 1, $\frac{1}{2}$, $\frac{1}{4}$, and $\frac{1}{8}$ of the ratio (7). Thus we have found that if the ratio (7) is greater than one, the curve is convex to the northwestern corner of the box, if the ratio (7) equals one, the curve is simply a diagonal

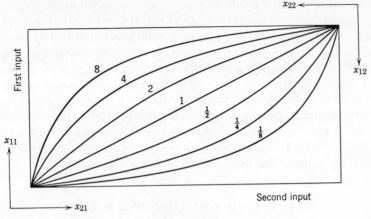

Figure 24.2

of the box, and if the ratio (7) is less than one, the curve is convex to the southeastern corner of the box.

24.5 THE PRODUCTION POSSIBILITIES CURVE

As Robinson passes along his Edgeworth-Bowley curve from southwest to northeast, he has increasing quantities of his first output and decreasing quantities of his second. We might wish to plot his two quantities of output X_1 and X_2 for each tangency point in the Edgeworth-Bowley box, and we could do that in a new diagram having the two outputs on its axes rather than the two inputs. That would give us the Samuelson production possibilities curve. We should very much like to derive it and find out if it is convex, a straight line, or concave. Define its slope by dividing (3) by (4); thus

$$(8) \qquad \frac{dX_1}{dX_2} = \frac{(\partial X_1/\partial x_{11})\, dx_{11} + (\partial X_1/\partial x_{21})\, dx_{21}}{(\partial X_2/\partial x_{12})\, dx_{12} + (\partial X_2/\partial x_{22})\, dx_{22}}$$

However, remember we are moving along the Edgeworth-Bowley curve all the time. Along this curve two things are true: Eq. (7) holds and all inputs remain exhausted:

$$(9) \qquad\qquad\qquad\qquad dx_{11} = -dx_{12}$$

$$(10) \qquad\qquad\qquad\qquad dx_{21} = -dx_{22}$$

Carry out the derivations ordered by (8), insert (7) several times, then (9) and (10) into the result, and obtain

$$(11) \qquad \frac{dX_1}{dX_2} = -\frac{\alpha_1}{\alpha_2} \frac{X_1}{x_{11}} \frac{x_{12}}{X_2} = -\frac{\partial X_1/\partial x_{11}}{\partial X_2/\partial x_{12}}$$

$$(12) \qquad \frac{dX_1}{dX_2} = -\frac{\beta_1}{\beta_2} \frac{X_1}{x_{21}} \frac{x_{22}}{X_2} = -\frac{\partial X_1/\partial x_{21}}{\partial X_2/\partial x_{22}}$$

Thus we have two alternative expressions for the slope of the production possibilities curve: Equation (11) is the ratio between the marginal productivities of the *first* input in X_1 and X_2. Equation (12) is the ratio between the marginal productivities of the *second* input; also in X_1 and X_2. One expression is as good as the other, but let us consider (12). Using nothing but the two production functions (1) and (2), we may write

$$(13) \qquad \frac{X_1}{x_{21}} = M_1 \left(\frac{x_{11}}{x_{21}}\right)^{\alpha_1}$$

$$(14) \qquad \frac{x_{22}}{X_2} = \frac{1}{M_2} \left(\frac{x_{12}}{x_{22}}\right)^{-\alpha_2}$$

Insert (13) and (14) into (12); thus

$$\frac{dX_1}{dX_2} = -\frac{\beta_1}{\beta_2} \frac{M_1}{M_2} \frac{(x_{11}/x_{21})^{\alpha_1}}{(x_{12}/x_{22})^{\alpha_2}}$$

Finally, write the exponent α_1 as $\alpha_1 - \alpha_2 + \alpha_2$, use (7) again, and obtain

$$(15) \qquad \frac{dX_1}{dX_2} = -\frac{\beta_1}{\beta_2} \frac{M_1}{M_2} \left(\frac{x_{11}}{x_{21}}\right)^{\alpha_1-\alpha_2} \left(\frac{\beta_2/\alpha_2}{\beta_1/\alpha_1}\right)^{\alpha_2}$$

Equation (15) is well worth all the trouble taken in deriving it, for it permits us to see that what happens to the slope of the production possibilities curve really boils down to what happens to the ratio x_{11}/x_{21} as we move along the Edgeworth-Bowley curve. There are three possibilities, illustrated in Figs. 24.3 through 24.5.

Figure 24.3 shows the case in which the ratio (7) is greater than one. Recalling that $\alpha_j + \beta_j = 1$, such a situation occurs whenever α_1 is greater than α_2. Figure 24.3 shows the ratio x_{11}/x_{21} to be declining as Robinson moves from the southwestern to the northeastern corner of his Edgeworth-Bowley box. Since that ratio is raised to the positive power $\alpha_1 - \alpha_2$, (15) is negative and rising (or numerically falling). The production possibilities curve, then, has the concave appearance shown in the small diagram in the lower right-hand corner of Fig. 24.3.

Figure 24.4 shows the case in which the ratio (7) equals one. This occurs whenever $\alpha_1 = \alpha_2$. Here, (15) turns into a constant; hence the production

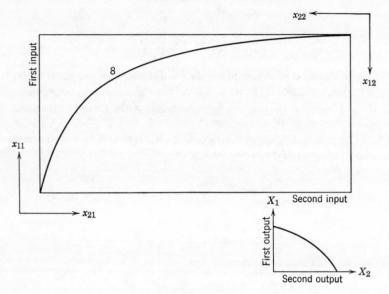

Figure 24.3

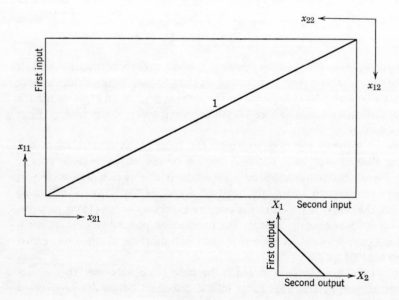

Figure 24.4

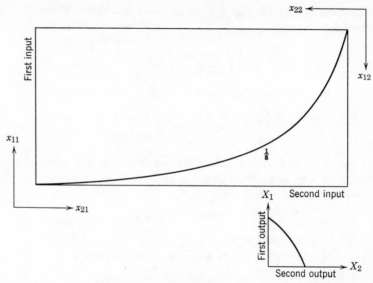

Figure 24.5

possibilities curve is a straight line having the slope $-M_1/M_2$, as shown in the small diagram in the lower right-hand corner of Fig. 24.4.

Figure 24.5 shows the case in which the ratio (7) is less than one. Recalling that $\alpha_j + \beta_j = 1$, such a case occurs whenever α_1 is less than α_2. Figure 24.5 shows the ratio x_{11}/x_{21} to be rising as Robinson moves from the southwesten to the northeastern corner of his Edgeworth-Bowley box. Since that ratio is raised to the negative power $\alpha_1 - \alpha_2$, (15) is negative and rising (or numerically falling). The production possibilities curve, then, has the concave appearance shown in the small diagram in the lower right-hand corner of Fig. 24.5.

Thus we have satisfied ourselves that the production possibilities curve is always nonconvex, that is, it is either concave or a straight line.

24.6 ROBINSON'S INDIFFERENCE MAP

Let Robinson have a utility function of the Cobb-Douglas form

$$(16) \qquad\qquad U = N X_1{}^A X_2{}^B$$

where A and B are parameters lying between zero and one, and where N is a multiplicative factor dependent upon the units of measurement.

Let Robinson change infinitesimally his X_1 by dX_1 and his X_2 by dX_2. His indifference curve is defined by the requirement that the resulting change in utility be zero.

(17) $$dU = \frac{\partial U}{\partial X_1} dX_1 + \frac{\partial U}{\partial X_2} dX_2 = 0$$

Use (16) and (17) to find Robinson's marginal rate of substitution:

(18) $$\frac{dX_1}{dX_2} = -\frac{B}{A}\frac{X_1}{X_2} = -\frac{\partial U/\partial X_2}{\partial U/\partial X_1}$$

Thus the slope of Robinson's indifference curve, or his marginal rate of substitution, is seen to be equal to the ratio between the marginal utilities to him of the outputs X_2 and X_1.

24.7   INDIFFERENCE MAP AND PRODUCTION POSSIBILITIES CURVE CONFRONTED

In the same X_1-X_2 diagram draw Robinson's indifference map and his production possibilities curve. One of his indifference curves must be in a position of tangency with his production possibilities curve. This follows from our finding that the production possibilities curve is always nonconvex. As we know, for a utility function like (16) the indifference curves will always be convex to the origin. The tangency point is Robinson's optimum, indicating how much he should produce (and consume) of each output. The tangency point is shown as the point C in Fig. 24.6. Here, the slope of the production possibilities curve as expressed by (11) and (12) must equal the slope of the indifference curve as expressed by (18). Hence we may say that rational

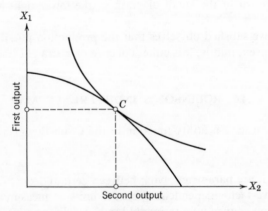

Figure 24.6

allocation of Robinson's resources implies that

(19)
$$\frac{\partial X_1/\partial x_{11}}{\partial X_2/\partial x_{12}} = \frac{\partial X_1/\partial x_{21}}{\partial X_2/\partial x_{22}} = \frac{\partial U/\partial X_2}{\partial U/\partial X_1}$$

or in words that the ratio between the marginal productivities of the *first* input in the two "industries" must be equal to the ratio between the marginal productivities of the *second* input in the two "industries." That ratio, in turn, must be equal to the inverse of the ratio between the marginal utilities of the outputs of the two "industries." So much for Robinson Crusoe.

II. TWO-PERSON ECONOMY

24.8   NOTATION

Now let a second person (Friday) arrive on the stage, necessitating an expansion of our notation as follows.

Variables

C_{jk} = jth output consumed by kth person, $k = 1, 2$
E = exchange rate, in number of physical units of first output exchanging for one physical unit of second output
U_k = utility to kth person resulting from his consumption, $k = 1, 2$
X_{jk} = jth output produced by kth person, $k = 1, 2$
x_{ijk} = ith input absorbed by jth output produced by kth person, $k = 1, 2$

24.9   THE EXCHANGE RATE

Let the two persons be endowed with different quantities of the same two inputs; then their production possibilities curves are different. Let the two persons have different tastes with respect to the same two outputs, then their indifference maps are different. Figure 24.7 shows the production possibilities curve and the indifference map for each person. In such a situation trade will normally result. For each person, Fig. 24.7 also shows a straight line whose slope E is the same for the two persons. This slope represents the exchange rate defined as the number of physical units of first output exchanging for one physical unit of second output. This exchange rate is supposed to have emerged in a purely competitive market; how it emerges will become clear presently. No person thinks he can affect it by withholding some of his own output: It is beyond his control. In Fig. 24.7 the straight line whose slope E is the

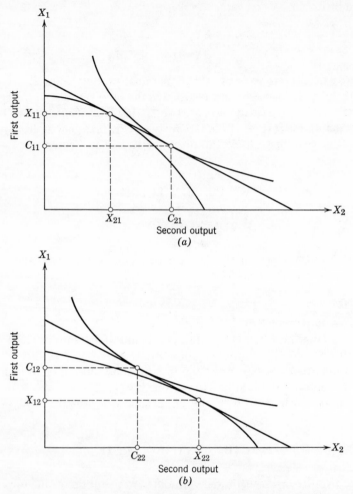

Figure 24.7. (*a*) First person. (*b*) Second person.

exchange rate has always been drawn in such a way that it is a tangent to the person's production possibilities curve. Let us look at each of the two persons in turn.

24.10 EQUILIBRIUM OF FIRST PERSON

As the diagram in Fig. 24.7 is drawn, the first person should clearly produce X_{11} and X_{21} and consume C_{11} and C_{21}, thus trading away the quantity $X_{11} - C_{11}$ of the first output in return for the quantity $C_{21} - X_{21}$ of the second output. This would lift him to the highest indifference curve he could possibly reach, passing through the tangency point (C_{21}, C_{11}).

From the fact that the straight line whose slope E is the exchange rate is a tangent to the production possibilities curve, and from Eqs. (11) and (12) it follows that

$$(20) \qquad E = \frac{dX_{11}}{dX_{21}} = - \frac{\partial X_{11}/\partial x_{111}}{\partial X_{21}/\partial x_{121}} = - \frac{\partial X_{11}/\partial x_{211}}{\partial X_{21}/\partial x_{221}}$$

And from the fact that the straight line whose slope E is the exchange rate is also a tangent to the indifference curve, and from Eq. (18) it follows that

$$(21) \qquad E = \frac{dC_{11}}{dC_{21}} = - \frac{\partial U_1/\partial C_{21}}{\partial U_1/\partial C_{11}}$$

24.11 EQUILIBRIUM OF SECOND PERSON

As the diagram in Fig. 24.7 is drawn, the second person should clearly produce X_{12} and X_{22} and consume C_{12} and C_{22}, thus trading away the quantity $X_{22} - C_{22}$ of the second output in return for the quantity $C_{12} - X_{12}$ of the first output. This would lift him to the highest indifference curve he could possibly reach, passing through the tangency point (C_{22}, C_{12}).

From the fact that the straight line whose slope E is the exchange rate is a tangent to the production possibilities curve, and from Eqs. (11) and (12) it follows that

$$(22) \qquad E = \frac{dX_{12}}{dX_{22}} = - \frac{\partial X_{12}/\partial x_{112}}{\partial X_{22}/\partial x_{122}} = - \frac{\partial X_{12}/\partial x_{212}}{\partial X_{22}/\partial x_{222}}$$

From the fact that the straight line whose slope E is the exchange rate is also a tangent to the indifference curve, and from Eq. (18) it follows that

$$(23) \qquad E = \frac{dC_{12}}{dC_{22}} = - \frac{\partial U_2/\partial C_{22}}{\partial U_2/\partial C_{12}}$$

24.12 MARKET EQUILIBRIUM

For the exchange rate E to be in equilibrium, the first person's supply of the first output must equal the second person's demand for it, that is,

$$(24) \qquad X_{11} - C_{11} = C_{12} - X_{12}$$

Would not also the first person's demand for the second output have to equal the second person's supply of it?

(25) $$C_{21} - X_{21} = X_{22} - C_{22}$$

Of course it would, but Eq. (25) is not a new and independent one; it may be derived from (24) as follows. If at the exchange rate E the first person supplies $X_{11} - C_{11}$, that is the same thing as *demanding*

$$\frac{X_{11} - C_{11}}{E} = X_{21} - C_{21}$$

And if at the same exchange rate E the second person demands the quantity $C_{12} - X_{12}$, that is the same thing as *supplying*

$$\frac{C_{12} - X_{12}}{E} = C_{22} - X_{22}$$

The simple reason is that one output can be paid for only with the other. Multiply through by *minus* one and thus derive (25) from (24). What we have encountered here is an example of Walras' law with which we shall presently become better acquainted.

Thus in market equilibrium each person is willing to give up of each output exactly the quantity the other person wants. If this were not true, the exchange rate would modify itself until it was, as the reader can verify for himself. The exchange rate thus established has an impressive array of properties which may be found by combining (20) through (23); that is,

$$E = -\frac{\partial X_{11}/\partial x_{111}}{\partial X_{21}/\partial x_{121}} = -\frac{\partial X_{11}/\partial x_{211}}{\partial X_{21}/\partial x_{221}} = -\frac{\partial X_{12}/\partial x_{112}}{\partial X_{22}/\partial x_{122}}$$

(26)
$$= -\frac{\partial X_{12}/\partial x_{212}}{\partial X_{22}/\partial x_{222}} = -\frac{\partial U_1/\partial C_{21}}{\partial U_1/\partial C_{11}} = -\frac{\partial U_2/\partial C_{22}}{\partial U_2/\partial C_{12}}$$

or in words that the exchange rate equals the ratio between the marginal productivities of the *first* input in the two "industries," and equals the ratio between the marginal productivities of the *second* input in the two "industries," and does so for both persons. Furthermore, the exchange rate equals the inverse of the ratio between the marginal utilities of the two outputs, and does so for both persons.

24.13   THE SPECIAL CASE OF NO TRADE

We said that in the situation described, trade will normally result. However, we have already found in the case of a one-person economy that the production possibilities curve is always nonconvex, that is, it is either concave or a straight line. Until now we have drawn it as a concave curve, and now is the time to examine the special case in which it is a straight line. We recall that

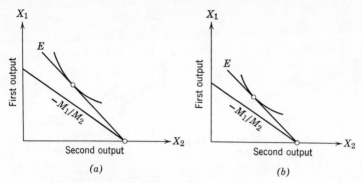

Figure 24.8. (a) First person. (b) Second person.

if $\alpha_1 = \alpha_2$, (15) turned into the constant

$$(15a) \qquad \frac{dX_1}{dX_2} = - \frac{M_1}{M_2}$$

If both persons have the same technological knowledge, then if $\alpha_1 = \alpha_2$ for one of them, this is true for the other as well. Consequently, (15a) holds for both persons, that is, their production possibilities curves are both straight lines, and the straight lines have the same slope. Notice that this will occur even if the inputs with which the two persons are endowed differ greatly with respect to quantities. Three possibilities should be examined. First, in Fig. 24.8 the exchange rate line is steeper than the production possibilities lines. This would induce both persons to specialize completely in the production of the second output, so there can be no trade. Second, in Fig. 24.9 the exchange rate line has the same slope as the production possibilities lines, making both persons indifferent to trade. Third, in Fig. 24.10 the exchange rate line is less steep than the production possibilities lines, inducing both persons to

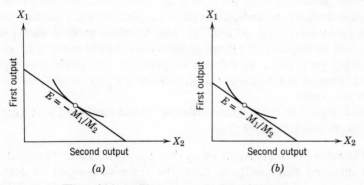

Figure 24.9. (a) First person. (b) Second person.

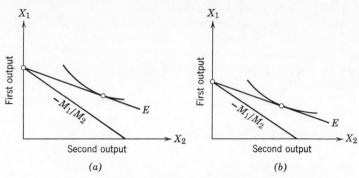

Figure 24.10. (a) First person. (b) Second person.

specialize completely in the production of the first input, so again there can be no trade.

24.14 COMPARISON WITH RICARDO

To Ricardo [1, 3, 4] the relative value of two commodities equaled their relative marginal labor requirements [3, pp. 36–37]. Ricardo's "relative value" is the reciprocal of the Austrian exchange rate between the two outputs, and the Ricardian "relative marginal labor requirements" is the reciprocal of the Austrian relative marginal productivities of labor in the two "industries." Thus Ricardo's labor theory of value is simply expressed by the equality of the first two ratios of (26). That was all there was to Ricardo, but it was far from all there was to the Austrians. The rest is apparent in the equality between the first two and the remaining five ratios of (26).

First, Ricardo never made sure that the relative marginal labor requirements between two commodities would be the same in all firms, at most he implied it.

Second, Ricardo's labor and capital were nonsubstitutable within the same output and would be combined in the same technologically fixed proportion in all industries [3, pp. 30 and 38]. The Austrians avoided such patently unrealistic assumptions. To them, all inputs were substitutable in all outputs, and input proportions in different outputs not only could, but typically would, have to differ in order to satisfy the marginal conditions (26). So much for capital.

Third, regarding land, Ricardo thought he had eliminated it as a determinant of relative values, for:

"The value of corn is regulated by the quantity of labour bestowed on its production on that quality of land [the extensive margin], or with that portion of capital [the intensive margin], which pays no rent [3, p. 74]."

Exit rent. However, the Austrian conditions (26) clearly show the ratio between the marginal productivities of labor to be no more important than the ratio between the marginal productivities of any other input, land for example. Really, then, Ricardo might as well have said that the relative value of two commodities equaled their relative marginal *land* requirements. Such a "land" theory of value would have been neither worse nor better than Ricardo's "labor" theory of value. Notice that the latter is not salvaged by the Ricardian assumption of a fixed supply of land. To the Austrians the supply of land, too, is fixed, as is indeed the supply of any input—or we could not have drawn our box diagram.

Fourth, like all of us Ricardo was hunting for things technologically fixed or otherwise objective, and his relative marginal labor requirement may have sounded to him like a technology parameter. But a cornerstone in his model was the law of diminishing returns in agriculture. As labor input on a fixed quantity of land was rising, the marginal productivity of labor would decline. This is nothing but saying that as the margins of cultivation are pushed outward, the marginal labor requirements of agricultural products will rise. Hence marginal labor requirements are not technology parameters; on the contrary, they cannot be known until the margins of cultivation themselves are known for all inputs, all outputs, and all persons, that is, until the entire general-equilibrium model has been solved, for example, as we have done geometrically by finding our tangency points in Fig. 24.7. Notice that no such general-equilibrium solution would have been possible on the basis of technology alone. We need the "want" parameters (our indifference curves) every bit as much as we need the "technology" parameters (our isoquants).[1]

[1] Thus Ricardo had no want parameters, hence had no general-equilibrium solution, and did not realize he needed one. The Austrians, in contrast, had one without realizing it. That they did not realize it is seen from their belief that their system was superior to that of Walras by being "causal," whereas his was merely "functional" [5, p. 957 n.]

REFERENCES

[1] Brems, H., "An Attempt at a Rigorous Restatement of Ricardo's Long-run Equilibrium," *Can. Jour. Econ. Pol. Sci.*, **26**, 74–86 (February 1960).
[2] Menger, C., *Grundsätze der Volkswirtschaftslehre*, Vienna, 1871.
[3] *The Works and Correspondence of David Ricardo, I*, edited by P. Sraffa, New York, 1951.
[4] Samuelson, P. A., "A Modern Treatment of the Ricardian Economy," *Quart. Jour. Econ.*, **73**, 1–35 and 217–231 (February and May 1959).
[5] Schumpeter, J. A., *History of Economic Analysis*, New York, 1954.
[6] von Wieser, F., *Der natürliche Werth*, Vienna, 1889.

CHAPTER 25

One-Country General Equilibrium*

25.1 INTRODUCTION

The Austrian model of general equilibrium was a model of pure production and barter between individuals. No firms charged money prices for output, paid money prices for input, or maximized money profits. No household earned or spent money income.

Let us now move one step closer to reality by separating households from firms, thus introducing money prices, money profits, and money incomes. But let the economy remain a stationary one.

Assuming linearly homogeneous production functions and pure competition, consider the simple case of two inputs, two outputs, and two households. How many firms? Well, as we know, under linearly homogeneous production functions and pure competition, large and small firms alike would have zero profits. The size and therefore the number of firms would remain indeterminate.

25.2 NOTATION

In our general equilibrium model the following notation will be assigned.

Variables

$C_{jk} = j$th output consumed by kth person
$P_j =$ price of jth output
$p_i =$ price of ith input
$U_k =$ utility to kth person, resulting from his consumption
$X_j = j$th output

* Chapters 2, 12, and 18 are prerequisites for Chapter 25.

x_{ij} = ith input absorbed by jth output
Y_k = money income of kth person

Parameters

A = elasticity of utility with respect to first output
B = elasticity of utility with respect to second output
α_j = elasticity of jth output with respect to first input
β_j = elasticity of jth output with respect to second input
M_j = multiplicative factor in the production function for jth output
N = multiplicative factor in the utility function
x_i = total available quantity of ith input

25.3 PRODUCTION FUNCTIONS

Let the production functions for the two outputs be linearly homogeneous and of Cobb-Douglas form.

(1) $$X_1 = M_1 x_{11}{}^{\alpha_1} x_{21}{}^{\beta_1}$$
(2) $$X_2 = M_2 x_{12}{}^{\alpha_2} x_{22}{}^{\beta_2}$$

where $0 < \alpha_j < 1$, $0 < \beta_j < 1$, $M_j > 0$, and $\alpha_j + \beta_j = 1$. The production functions (1) and (2) are adopted with these six restrictions: $x_{ij} \geq 0$, and $X_j \geq 0$, $i = j = 1, 2$. It is unnecessary to assume that $\alpha_1 \gtrless \alpha_2$.

25.4 PROFIT MAXIMIZATION UNDER PURE COMPETITION

In Eq. (8) of Chapter 12 we expressed the first-order condition for an unconstrained profit maximum that any input should be hired up to the point where its price equaled its marginal revenue productivity. Apply this general condition to the special case of pure competition and Cobb-Douglas production functions. As a result, write the following four first-order conditions:

(3) $$p_1 = P_1 \frac{\alpha_1}{x_{11}} X_1$$

(4) $$p_2 = P_1 \frac{\beta_1}{x_{21}} X_1$$

(5) $$p_1 = P_2 \frac{\alpha_2}{x_{12}} X_2$$

(6) $$p_2 = P_2 \frac{\beta_2}{x_{22}} X_2$$

Rearrange (3) and (4) and add them. Rearrange (5) and (6) and add them; then

(3a) $$P_1X_1 = p_1x_{11} + p_2x_{21}$$

(5a) $$P_2X_2 = p_1x_{12} + p_2x_{22}$$

Equations (3a) and (5a) are merely our familiar Eq. (10a) of Chapter 18 (Euler's theorem applied to the distributive shares).

25.5 UTILITY FUNCTIONS AND BUDGET CONSTRAINTS

Let both persons have the same utility function, and let it be of Cobb-Douglas form

$$U_1 = NC_{11}{}^A C_{21}{}^B$$

$$U_2 = NC_{12}{}^A C_{22}{}^B$$

where A and B are parameters lying between zero and one, and where N is a positive multiplicative factor dependent upon the units of measurement. It is unnecessary to assume that $A + B = 1$.

Let no person save; hence his budget constraints are

$$Y_1 = P_1C_{11} + P_2C_{21}$$

$$Y_2 = P_1C_{12} + P_2C_{22}$$

25.6 UTILITY MAXIMIZATION

In Chapter 2 we found that under utility functions of Cobb-Douglas form, utility maximization will lead to demand functions whose budget elasticities are *plus* one, whose price elasticities are *minus* one, and whose cross elasticities are zero. By applying the method to this case, we obtain the following four demand functions:

(7) $$C_{11} = \frac{A}{A + B}\frac{Y_1}{P_1}$$

(8) $$C_{21} = \frac{B}{A + B}\frac{Y_1}{P_2}$$

(9) $$C_{12} = \frac{A}{A + B}\frac{Y_2}{P_1}$$

(10) $$C_{22} = \frac{B}{A + B}\frac{Y_2}{P_2}$$

25.7 PERSONAL INCOMES

Let the first person own the first input and the second person own the second input. Who are the entrepreneurs? It does not matter, for under linearly homogeneous production functions and pure competition there will be zero profits in each and every firm, hence zero profits in each industry. Consequently, the only incomes we need consider are

(11) $$Y_1 = p_1 x_1$$

(12) $$Y_2 = p_2 x_2$$

25.8 EQUILIBRIUM IN INPUT MARKETS

In the Austrian tradition let the total available quantity of the ith input be a positive parameter x_i. Prices of both inputs adjust in such a way that the total available quantity of each input is fully absorbed.

(13) $$x_1 = x_{11} + x_{12}$$

(14) $$x_2 = x_{21} + x_{22}$$

25.9 EQUILIBRIUM IN OUTPUT MARKETS

The price of the first output adjusts in such a way that output equals demand.

(15) $$X_1 = C_{11} + C_{12}$$

Does the price of the second output not adjust as well in such a way that output equals demand? Indeed it does, but not as a new and independent condition. Combine (3a), (5a), (11), (12), (13) and (14) and obtain

$$P_1 X_1 + P_2 X_2 = Y_1 + Y_2$$

Combine (7) through (10), use (15), and obtain

$$P_1 X_1 + P_2(C_{21} + C_{22}) = Y_1 + Y_2$$

Thus it follows that for the second output, too, output equals demand.

(15a) $$X_2 = C_{21} + C_{22}$$

Once again, then, we have encountered Walras' [2] law. As a result, we have merely 15 equations to determine 16 variables:

$C_{11}, C_{12}, C_{21}, C_{22}$ X_1, X_2

P_1, P_2 $x_{11}, x_{12}, x_{21}, x_{22}$

p_1, p_2 Y_1, Y_2

Like a Walras system, then, our system is in some sense indeterminate. In which sense? Suppose the system to be satisfied by a certain set of prices P_j and p_i and money incomes Y_k. Now if in this set each variable were multiplied by the same arbitrary constant, all equations would still hold. However, suppose the system to be satisfied by a certain set of quantities C_{jk}, X_j, and x_{ij}. If in this set each variable were multiplied by the same arbitrary constant, Eqs. (13) and (14) would no longer hold, for x_1 and x_2 are not variables but parameters.

Thus, if in an attempt to bring the number of variables down to the number of equations a variable must be eliminated, that variable should be a price, not a quantity. Let it be, say, p_1 assumed to be positive. Divide all equations containing prices or money incomes by p_1, the Walrasian *numéraire*. That eliminates one variable from the system and leaves us with prices and money incomes that are relative to p_1, rather than absolute, as our variables.

25.10 SOLUTIONS

First let us solve for the four inputs x_{ij}. Use (3a), (5a), (7) through (10), (15), and (15a), obtaining

$$A(p_1 x_{12} + p_2 x_{22}) = B(p_1 x_{11} + p_2 x_{21})$$

From (3) through (6) find

$$\frac{p_1}{p_2} = \frac{\alpha_1}{\beta_1} \frac{x_{21}}{x_{11}} = \frac{\alpha_2}{\beta_2} \frac{x_{22}}{x_{12}}$$

Inserting this, we take the outcomes together with (13) and (14), and obtain the solutions for the allocation of inputs:

$$(16) \qquad\qquad x_{11} = \frac{\alpha_1 A}{\alpha_1 A + \alpha_2 B} x_1$$

$$(17) \qquad\qquad x_{12} = \frac{\alpha_2 B}{\alpha_1 A + \alpha_2 B} x_1$$

$$(18) \qquad\qquad x_{21} = \frac{\beta_1 A}{\beta_1 A + \beta_2 B} x_2$$

$$(19) \qquad\qquad x_{22} = \frac{\beta_2 B}{\beta_1 A + \beta_2 B} x_2$$

Once the allocation of input has been determined, the rest is easy. Combine (1) through (6) with (16) through (19) and obtain the solutions for relative prices, that is, prices relative to the *numeraire* p_1:

$$(20) \qquad \frac{p_2}{p_1} = \frac{\beta_1 A + \beta_2 B}{\alpha_1 A + \alpha_2 B} \frac{x_1}{x_2}$$

$$(21) \qquad \frac{P_1}{p_1} = \frac{1}{M_1 \alpha_1{}^{\alpha_1} \beta_1{}^{\beta_1}} \left(\frac{\beta_1 A + \beta_2 B}{\alpha_1 A + \alpha_2 B} \frac{x_1}{x_2} \right)^{\beta_1}$$

$$(22) \qquad \frac{P_2}{p_1} = \frac{1}{M_2 \alpha_2{}^{\alpha_2} \beta_2{}^{\beta_2}} \left(\frac{\beta_1 A + \beta_2 B}{\alpha_1 A + \alpha_2 B} \frac{x_1}{x_2} \right)^{\beta_2}$$

Direct insertion of (16) through (19) into (1) and (2) will give the solutions for outputs.

$$(23) \qquad X_1 = M_1 \left(\frac{\alpha_1 A x_1}{\alpha_1 A + \alpha_2 B} \right)^{\alpha_1} \left(\frac{\beta_1 A x_2}{\beta_1 A + \beta_2 B} \right)^{\beta_1}$$

$$(24) \qquad X_2 = M_2 \left(\frac{\alpha_2 B x_1}{\alpha_1 A + \alpha_2 B} \right)^{\alpha_2} \left(\frac{\beta_2 B x_2}{\beta_1 A + \beta_2 B} \right)^{\beta_2}$$

Direct insertion of (11), (12), and (20) through (22) into (7) through (10) gives us the solutions for the allocation of outputs:

$$(25) \qquad C_{11} = \frac{A}{A + B} M_1 \alpha_1{}^{\alpha_1} \beta_1{}^{\beta_1} \left(\frac{\alpha_1 A + \alpha_2 B}{\beta_1 A + \beta_2 B} \frac{x_2}{x_1} \right)^{\beta_1} x_1$$

$$(26) \qquad C_{21} = \frac{B}{A + B} M_2 \alpha_2{}^{\alpha_2} \beta_2{}^{\beta_2} \left(\frac{\alpha_1 A + \alpha_2 B}{\beta_1 A + \beta_2 B} \frac{x_2}{x_1} \right)^{\beta_2} x_1$$

$$(27) \qquad C_{12} = \frac{A}{A + B} M_1 \alpha_1{}^{\alpha_1} \beta_1{}^{\beta_1} \left(\frac{\beta_1 A + \beta_2 B}{\alpha_1 A + \alpha_2 B} \frac{x_1}{x_2} \right)^{\alpha_1} x_2$$

$$(28) \qquad C_{22} = \frac{B}{A + B} M_2 \alpha_2{}^{\alpha_2} \beta_2{}^{\beta_2} \left(\frac{\beta_1 A + \beta_2 B}{\alpha_1 A + \alpha_2 B} \frac{x_1}{x_2} \right)^{\alpha_2} x_2$$

Finally, by combining (11), (12), and (20) find the money incomes relative to the *numéraire* p_1; thus

$$(29) \qquad \frac{Y_1}{p_1} = x_1$$

$$(30) \qquad \frac{Y_2}{p_1} = \frac{\beta_1 A + \beta_2 B}{\alpha_1 A + \alpha_2 B} x_1$$

and find the distributive shares

(29a)
$$\frac{Y_1}{Y_1 + Y_2} = \frac{\alpha_1 A + \alpha_2 B}{A + B}$$

(30a)
$$\frac{Y_2}{Y_1 + Y_2} = \frac{\beta_1 A + \beta_2 B}{A + B}$$

25.11   CONCLUSIONS

We have solved the general-equilibrium model explicitly for both outputs produced by firms, both inputs absorbed by firms, both outputs consumed by persons, all relative prices, and both relative money incomes. The reader may easily convince himself that under the assumptions made about the values of the parameters used, all solutions are positive and unique. Hence both outputs will be produced, each output will absorb some of each input, and each person will consume some of each output. All inputs and outputs will be economic goods.

Ultimately, the solutions depend upon four categories of parameters: First, engineering supplies the technology parameters α_j and β_j. Second, physiology and psychology supply the want parameters A and B. Third, nature supplies the resource parameters x_1. Fourth, legal institutions establish private ownership to those resources, making it possible for private persons to earn an income from them. None of the four would suffice in itself to determine the system—as the classical school, the marginal utility school, or the institutionalist school have believed that one or the other of them would. Economics is nothing less than the interaction of technology, wants, resources, and legal institutions.

25.12   PUBLIC-POLICY IMPLICATIONS, IF ANY

Each decision-making unit in our general-equilibrium model pursues its own interest exclusively. Every firm maximizes its profits, every household maximizes its utility. Yet, as a collective result, all these individual pursuits produce a price solution, Eqs. (21) and (22), under which each output is produced at its lowest possible unit cost, sold at that cost, and produced in exactly the quantity households desire when given a free choice in disposing of their incomes. All waste in production and consumption having been thus eliminated, it is impossible to raise one household's utility without lowering any other household's utility. The solution of our general-equilibrium model represents, then, a Pareto [1] optimum. Who could possibly want government to interfere with such a solution?

First, somebody unwilling to accept the income distribution expressed in Eqs. (29) and (30) might desire government interference. As analysts, we cannot make interpersonal utility comparisons, hence can neither condone nor condemn the income distribution expressed in Eqs. (29) and (30). But United States farmers, hospital patients, magazine publishers, import substitute producers, steamship companies, social-security beneficiaries, state-university students, transit riders, and others have persuaded government to interfere with income distribution in their favor. The grounds on which this is being done are plainly political, which takes the subject right out of this book.

Second, although nobody might wish to interfere with our general-equilibrium model as set out above, the actual United States economy is a different matter. In the latter there is patently not pure competition. Consequently, goods may not be produced at their lowest possible unit cost (see Fig. 19.1), and even if they are they will not sell at that cost. Cases may then be made for antitrust action, regulation of public utilities, or nationalization. Furthermore, the utility functions specified in Section 25.5 assumed a household's utility to depend solely upon that household's consumption. However, in the actual United States economy a household may be bothered by the congestion, noise, or pollution resulting from other households' consumption. Such effects are allowed for in nobody's maximization and government must allow for what nobody else will allow for.

REFERENCES

[1] Pareto, V., *Manuel d'économie politique* 2nd ed., Paris, 1927, Chapter VI.
[2] Walras, L., *Eléments d'économie politique pure*, Lausanne, 1874. (Translated by W. Jaffe as *Elements of Pure Economics*, Homewood, Illinois, 1954.)

CHAPTER 26

Two-Country General Equilibrium*

26.1 INTRODUCTION

The need for a particular theory of international trade arises from two facts. First, factor mobility among countries is much lower than factor mobility within countries. Second, different countries have different monetary units.

Let us extend our general equilibrium to two countries, then, assuming, first, that outputs move freely from one country to the other, transportation costs being zero; second, that inputs do not move at all from one country to the other; and third, that each country has its own Walrasian *numéraire*. Moreover, let those *numéraires* be—arbitrarily—the prices of the first input in the first and the second country, respectively.

Again assuming linearly homogeneous production functions and pure competition, consider the simple case of two inputs, two outputs, and two households in each country. How many firms? Again, under linearly homogeneous production functions and pure competition large and small firms alike would have zero profits. The size and therefore the number of firms would remain indeterminate.

26.2 NOTATION

In the two-country general-equilibrium model the following notation will be assigned.

Variables

C_{hjk} = jth output consumed by kth person in hth country
E = exchange rate, in number of monetary units of Country 1 equivalent to one monetary unit of Country 2

* Chapter 25 is a prerequisite for Chapter 26.

P_{hj} = price of jth output in hth country
p_{hi} = price of ith input in hth country
U_{hk} = utility to kth person in hth country, resulting from his consumption
X_{hj} = jth output produced by hth country
x_{hij} = ith input absorbed by jth output produced by hth country
Y_{hk} = money income of kth person in hth country

Parameters

A_h = elasticity of utility with respect to first output in hth country
B_h = elasticity of utility with respect to second output in hth country
α_j = elasticity of jth output with respect to first input
β_j = elasticity of jth output with respect to second input
M_j = multiplicative factor in the production function of jth output
N_h = multiplicative factor in the utility functions in hth country
x_{hi} = total available quantity of ith input in hth country

26.3   PRODUCTION FUNCTIONS

Suppose both countries are capable of producing both outputs—we shall see later whether or not it will be economical for them to do so. For each output let the two countries have the same production function; let that function be linearly homogeneous, and of Cobb-Douglas form. The first country's production functions for the two outputs are, then

$$(1) \qquad X_{11} = M_1 x_{111}{}^{\alpha_1} x_{121}{}^{\beta_1}$$

$$(2) \qquad X_{12} = M_2 x_{112}{}^{\alpha_2} x_{122}{}^{\beta_2}$$

The second country's production functions are

$$(3) \qquad X_{21} = M_1 x_{211}{}^{\alpha_1} x_{221}{}^{\beta_1}$$

$$(4) \qquad X_{22} = M_2 x_{212}{}^{\alpha_2} x_{222}{}^{\beta_2}$$

where $0 < \alpha_j < 1$, $0 < \beta_j < 1$, $M_j > 0$, $\alpha_j + \beta_j = 1$, and $\alpha_1 \gtrless \alpha_2$ (hence $\beta_2 \gtrless \beta_1$). The production functions (1) through (4) are adopted with these twelve restrictions: $x_{hij} \geq 0$, and $X_{hj} \geq 0$, $h = i = j = 1, 2$.

26.4   PROFIT MAXIMIZATION UNDER PURE COMPETITION

In Eq. (8) of Chapter 12 we expressed the first-order condition for an unconstrained profit maximum that any input should be hired up to the point where its price equaled its marginal revenue productivity. Apply this general condition to our special case of pure competition and Cobb-Douglas production functions. As a result, write the following eight first-order conditions, four for the first country:

(5)
$$p_{11} = P_{11} \frac{\alpha_1}{x_{111}} X_{11}$$

(6)
$$p_{12} = P_{11} \frac{\beta_1}{x_{121}} X_{11}$$

(7)
$$p_{11} = P_{12} \frac{\alpha_2}{x_{112}} X_{12}$$

(8)
$$p_{12} = P_{12} \frac{\beta_2}{x_{122}} X_{12}$$

For the second country there are the following four conditions:

(9)
$$p_{21} = P_{21} \frac{\alpha_1}{x_{211}} X_{21}$$

(10)
$$p_{22} = P_{21} \frac{\beta_1}{x_{221}} X_{21}$$

(11)
$$p_{21} = P_{22} \frac{\alpha_2}{x_{212}} X_{22}$$

(12)
$$p_{22} = P_{22} \frac{\beta_2}{x_{222}} X_{22}$$

By rearranging and adding (5) and (6), (7) and (8), (9) and (10), and (11) and (12) we may produce four versions of Eq. (10a) of Chapter 18 (Euler's theorem applied to the distributive shares), that is, for the first country:

(5a)
$$P_{11}X_{11} = p_{11}x_{111} + p_{12}x_{121}$$

(7a)
$$P_{12}X_{12} = p_{11}x_{112} + p_{12}x_{122}$$

and for the second country:

(9a)
$$P_{21}X_{21} = p_{21}x_{211} + p_{22}x_{221}$$

(11a)
$$P_{22}X_{22} = p_{21}x_{212} + p_{22}x_{222}$$

26.5 UTILITY FUNCTIONS AND BUDGET CONSTRAINTS

Within each country let both persons have the same utility function, and let the latter be of Cobb Douglas form. However, the utility functions may differ between countries. The utility functions of the two persons in the first country are

$$U_{11} = N_1 C_{111}{}^{A_1} C_{121}{}^{B_1}$$

$$U_{12} = N_1 C_{112}{}^{A_1} C_{122}{}^{B_1}$$

and the utility functions of the two persons in the second country are

$$U_{21} = N_2 C_{211}{}^{A_2} C_{221}{}^{B_2}$$

$$U_{22} = N_2 C_{212}{}^{A_2} C_{222}{}^{B_2}$$

where A_h and B_h are parameters lying between zero and one and N_h is a positive multiplicative factor dependent upon the units of measurement. It is unnecessary to assume that $A_1 \gtrless A_2$, that $B_2 \gtrless B_1$, or that $A_h + B_h = 1$, $h = 1, 2$.

Let no person save, so the budget constraints of the two persons in the first country are

$$Y_{11} = P_{11} C_{111} + P_{12} C_{121}$$

$$Y_{12} = P_{11} C_{112} + P_{12} C_{122}$$

and the budget constraints of the two persons in the second country are

$$Y_{21} = P_{21} C_{211} + P_{22} C_{221}$$

$$Y_{22} = P_{21} C_{212} + P_{22} C_{222}$$

26.6   UTILITY MAXIMIZATION

In Chapter 2 we found that under utility functions of Cobb-Douglas form, utility maximization will lead to demand functions whose budget elasticities are *plus* one, price elasticities are *minus* one, and cross-elasticities are zero. Applying the method here gives us the following four such demand functions of the two persons in the first country:

(13)
$$C_{111} = \frac{A_1}{A_1 + B_1} \frac{Y_{11}}{P_{11}}$$

(14)
$$C_{121} = \frac{B_1}{A_1 + B_1} \frac{Y_{11}}{P_{12}}$$

(15)
$$C_{112} = \frac{A_1}{A_1 + B_1} \frac{Y_{12}}{P_{11}}$$

(16)
$$C_{122} = \frac{B_1}{A_1 + B_1} \frac{Y_{12}}{P_{12}}$$

In the second country, the four demand functions of the two persons are

$$(17) \qquad C_{211} = \frac{A_2}{A_2 + B_2} \frac{Y_{21}}{P_{21}}$$

$$(18) \qquad C_{221} = \frac{B_2}{A_2 + B_2} \frac{Y_{21}}{P_{22}}$$

$$(19) \qquad C_{212} = \frac{A_2}{A_2 + B_2} \frac{Y_{22}}{P_{21}}$$

$$(20) \qquad C_{222} = \frac{B_2}{A_2 + B_2} \frac{Y_{22}}{P_{22}}$$

26.7 PERSONAL INCOMES

Let the first person own the first input and the second person own the second input. Who are the entrepreneurs? It does not matter, for under linearly homogeneous production functions and pure competition there will be zero profits in each and every firm, hence zero profits in each industry in each country. Consequently, the only incomes in the first country are

$$(21) \qquad Y_{11} = p_{11}x_{11}$$

$$(22) \qquad Y_{12} = p_{12}x_{12}$$

and the only incomes in the second country are

$$(23) \qquad Y_{21} = p_{21}x_{21}$$

$$(24) \qquad Y_{22} = p_{22}x_{22}$$

26.8 EQUILIBRIUM IN INPUT MARKETS

Inputs have been assumed not to move at all from one country to the other. Consequently, the markets for inputs are enclosed national markets. In the Austrian tradition, let the total available quantity of the ith input in the hth country be a positive parameter x_{hi}. In the first country, prices of inputs adjust in such a way that the total available quantity of each input is fully absorbed; thus

$$(25) \qquad x_{11} = x_{111} + x_{112}$$

$$(26) \qquad x_{12} = x_{121} + x_{122}$$

Similarly, in the second country,

(27) $$x_{21} = x_{211} + x_{212}$$

(28) $$x_{22} = x_{221} + x_{222}$$

26.9   EQUILIBRIUM IN OUTPUT MARKETS

Unlike inputs, outputs move freely from one country to the other, transportation costs being zero. Therefore the markets for outputs are world markets rather than national markets. The world market prices of either output adjust in such a way that for each output, world output equals world demand.

(29) $$X_{11} + X_{21} = C_{111} + C_{112} + C_{211} + C_{212}$$

(30) $$X_{12} + X_{22} = C_{121} + C_{122} + C_{221} + C_{222}$$

26.10   THE EXCHANGE RATE

Precisely because outputs move freely from one country to the other, transportation costs being zero, the first output must command the same price, when measured in the same monetary unit, everywhere in the world market; hence

(31) $$P_{11} = EP_{21}$$

For the same reason, must not the second output, too, command the same price everywhere in the world market?

(31a) $$P_{12} = EP_{22}$$

Indeed it must, but as we shall see in a moment, (31a) is not a new and independent equation.

26.11   THE BALANCES OF PAYMENT

We are now tempted to conclude our collection of equations by saying that for each country, the balance of payment, when measured in the country's own monetary unit, equals zero; thus

(29a) $$P_{11}(C_{111} + C_{112} - X_{11}) + P_{12}(C_{121} + C_{122} - X_{12}) = 0$$

(30a) $$P_{21}(C_{211} + C_{212} - X_{21}) + P_{22}(C_{221} + C_{222} - X_{22}) = 0$$

Although they are undeniably true, (29a) and (30a) are not new and independent equations. To see this, we combine Euler's theorem (5a) through

(11a) with (21) through (28) and obtain for the two countries

$$P_{11}X_{11} + P_{12}X_{12} = Y_{11} + Y_{12}$$

$$P_{21}X_{21} + P_{22}X_{22} = Y_{21} + Y_{22}$$

But from (13) through (20) it follows that

$$P_{11}(C_{111} + C_{112}) + P_{12}(C_{121} + C_{122}) = Y_{11} + Y_{12}$$

$$P_{21}(C_{211} + C_{212}) + P_{22}(C_{221} + C_{222}) = Y_{21} + Y_{22}$$

From these two pairs of equations taken together, (29a) and (30a) follow directly. Moreover, we can now see why (31a) is not a new and independent equation, either. Just insert (29) and (30) into (29a) and (30a) and find

(29b) $$\frac{P_{11}}{P_{21}} = \frac{P_{12}}{P_{22}}$$

therefore if (31) is true, (31a) follows.

26.12   NUMBER OF EQUATIONS AND VARIABLES

It is clear, then, that we have only 31 equations to determine our 33 variables:

$C_{111}, C_{112}, C_{121}, C_{122}, C_{211}, C_{212}, C_{221}, C_{222}$
E
$P_{11}, P_{12}, P_{21}, P_{22}$
$p_{11}, p_{12}, p_{21}, p_{22}$
$X_{11}, X_{12}, X_{21}, X_{22}$
$x_{111}, x_{112}, x_{121}, x_{122}, x_{211}, x_{212}, x_{221}, x_{222}$
$Y_{11}, Y_{12}, Y_{21}, Y_{22}$

However, for each country separately we may divide all equations containing prices or money incomes by the same price, say p_{11} and p_{21}, respectively, using those prices for Walrasian *numéraires*. Assume that both *numéraires* p_{11} and p_{21} are positive. This would eliminate two variables from the system, and we would be left with relative prices and money incomes rather than absolute ones as variables.

26.13   NONNEGATIVE SOLUTIONS

All variables to be solved for, that is, $C_{hjk}, E, P_{hj}, p_{hi}, X_{hj}, x_{hij}$, and Y_{hk}, must be nonnegative. Possible emerging negative solutions are to be rejected in favor of setting the variable in question equal to zero.

26.14 A WEAK FACTOR PRICE EQUALIZATION THEOREM

After dividing (6) by (5), (8) by (7), (10) by (9), and (12) by (11), we obtain

(5b)
$$\frac{p_{12}}{p_{11}} = \frac{\beta_1}{\alpha_1} \frac{x_{111}}{x_{121}}$$

(7b)
$$\frac{p_{12}}{p_{11}} = \frac{\beta_2}{\alpha_2} \frac{x_{112}}{x_{122}}$$

(9b)
$$\frac{p_{22}}{p_{21}} = \frac{\beta_1}{\alpha_1} \frac{x_{211}}{x_{221}}$$

(11b)
$$\frac{p_{22}}{p_{21}} = \frac{\beta_2}{\alpha_2} \frac{x_{212}}{x_{222}}$$

Use these upon (5), (7), (9), and (11), inserting (1) through (4); thus

(5c)
$$\frac{P_{11}}{P_{21}} = \frac{p_{11}}{p_{21}} \left(\frac{x_{111}/x_{121}}{x_{211}/x_{221}}\right)^{\beta_1} = \frac{p_{11}}{p_{21}} \left(\frac{p_{12}/p_{11}}{p_{22}/p_{21}}\right)^{\beta_1}$$

(7c)
$$\frac{P_{12}}{P_{22}} = \frac{p_{11}}{p_{21}} \left(\frac{x_{112}/x_{122}}{x_{212}/x_{222}}\right)^{\beta_2} = \frac{p_{11}}{p_{21}} \left(\frac{p_{12}/p_{11}}{p_{22}/p_{21}}\right)^{\beta_2}$$

The reader should take notice of the steps taken in (5c) and (7c), for this is where the reasoning breaks down in the case of complete specialization. For the moment we ignore complete specialization, remember the important assumption that $\alpha_1 \gtrless \alpha_2$ (hence $\beta_2 \gtrless \beta_1$), use (29b), and arrive at a weak factor price equalization theorem

(29c)
$$\frac{p_{12}}{p_{11}} = \frac{p_{22}}{p_{21}}$$

Thus, although inputs do not move at all from one country to the other, the relative prices of the first and the second inputs are the same in the two countries. Precisely how high the ratio between them, (29c), is, we do not know as yet. Nor do we know how high are the purchasing powers of input prices in the two countries. In due time, however, we shall find the answers to both questions.

26.15 THE ALLOCATION OF INPUTS

Now we use (5b) and (7b) upon (25), combine the result with (26), and express x_{121} and x_{122} in terms of the price ratio p_{12}/p_{11}. Similarly, we use (9b)

and (11b) upon (27), take the result together with (28), and express x_{221} and x_{222} in terms of the price ratio p_{22}/p_{21}. Finally, we use (5b) through (11b) to express x_{111}, x_{112}, x_{211}, and x_{212} in terms of x_{121}, x_{122}, x_{221}, and x_{222}, respectively. As a result, we obtain the following four expressions for the allocation of the inputs of the first country:

$$(32) \qquad x_{111} = \frac{\alpha_1}{\beta_1} \frac{x_{11} - \dfrac{\alpha_2}{\beta_2} \dfrac{p_{12}}{p_{11}} x_{12}}{D}$$

$$(33) \qquad x_{121} = \frac{p_{11}}{p_{12}} \frac{x_{11} - \dfrac{\alpha_2}{\beta_2} \dfrac{p_{12}}{p_{11}} x_{12}}{D}$$

$$(34) \qquad x_{112} = \frac{\alpha_2}{\beta_2} \frac{\dfrac{\alpha_1}{\beta_1} \dfrac{p_{12}}{p_{11}} x_{12} - x_{11}}{D}$$

$$(35) \qquad x_{122} = \frac{p_{11}}{p_{12}} \frac{\dfrac{\alpha_1}{\beta_1} \dfrac{p_{12}}{p_{11}} x_{12} - x_{11}}{D}$$

For the second country, the results are

$$(36) \qquad x_{211} = \frac{\alpha_1}{\beta_1} \frac{x_{21} - \dfrac{\alpha_2}{\beta_2} \dfrac{p_{22}}{p_{21}} x_{22}}{D}$$

$$(37) \qquad x_{221} = \frac{p_{21}}{p_{22}} \frac{x_{21} - \dfrac{\alpha_2}{\beta_2} \dfrac{p_{22}}{p_{21}} x_{22}}{D}$$

$$(38) \qquad x_{212} = \frac{\alpha_2}{\beta_2} \frac{\dfrac{\alpha_1}{\beta_1} \dfrac{p_{22}}{p_{21}} x_{22} - x_{21}}{D}$$

$$(39) \qquad x_{222} = \frac{p_{21}}{p_{22}} \frac{\dfrac{\alpha_1}{\beta_1} \dfrac{p_{22}}{p_{21}} x_{22} - x_{21}}{D}$$

where all the denominators are

$$D = \frac{\alpha_1}{\beta_1} - \frac{\alpha_2}{\beta_2}$$

Again we see how important it was to assume that $\alpha_1 \gtrless \alpha_2$ (hence $\beta_2 \gtrless \beta_1$); otherwise, the denominators D could have been zero and then no input x_{hij} could have been meaningful.

Equations (32) through (35) contain ratio p_{12}/p_{11}, and (36) through (39) contain the ratio p_{22}/p_{21}. From (29c) the two ratios are known to be equal, but as long as we do not know what their value is, Eqs. (32) through (39) cannot be considered solutions for the allocation of inputs. Therefore let us solve for that value.

26.16 SOLUTION FOR RELATIVE PRICES OF INPUTS

Upon the equilibrium condition for the first output market, Eq. (29), use the demand equations (13), (15), (17), and (19) and the income equations (21) through (24) and find

$$X_{11} + X_{21} = \frac{A_1}{A_1 + B_1} \frac{1}{P_{11}} (p_{11}x_{11} + p_{12}x_{12}) + \frac{A_2}{A_2 + B_2} \frac{1}{P_{21}} (p_{21}x_{21} + p_{22}x_{22})$$

From (5c), (7c), (29c), and (31) it follows that

(31b) $$\frac{P_{11}}{P_{21}} = \frac{p_{11}}{p_{21}} = \frac{p_{12}}{p_{22}} = E$$

Insert (31b) and Euler's theorem (5a) and (9a) as well as (5b) and (9b), in order to express the price ratio p_{12}/p_{11} in terms of x_{111} and x_{211}. Take the outcome together with (32) and (36) and finally arrive at the solution for p_{12}/p_{11}, which according to (29c) is also the solution for p_{22}/p_{21}.

(40) $$\frac{p_{12}}{p_{11}} = \frac{p_{22}}{p_{21}}$$

(41) $$= \frac{\dfrac{\beta_1 A_1 + \beta_2 B_1}{A_1 + B_1} x_{11} + \dfrac{\beta_1 A_2 + \beta_2 B_2}{A_2 + B_2} x_{21}}{\dfrac{\alpha_1 A_1 + \alpha_2 B_1}{A_1 + B_1} x_{12} + \dfrac{\alpha_1 A_2 + \alpha_2 B_2}{A_2 + B_2} x_{22}}$$

Under the assumptions made about the value of our parameters, (40) and (41) are always positive, for all parameters were assumed to be positive.

Now that we possess a solution for the ratios p_{12}/p_{11} and p_{22}/p_{21}, Eqs. (32) through (39) can be considered solutions for the allocation of inputs, for had we had the space we could have inserted (40) and (41) into (32) through (39) and obtained only parameters on the right-hand sides of (32) through (39).

The possibility clearly arises that some of the solutions (32) through (39) are negative. To this possibility we shall return at length in Section 26.22.

26.17 A STRONG FACTOR PRICE EQUALIZATION THEOREM

To add vividness to our conclusions, let the first country be Britain, the second Australia. Let the first input be labor, the second land. Let the first output be clothing, the second food.

Instead of solving for price ratios having the *numéraire* in their denominators, we shall find it useful to solve for the reciprocals of such ratios. From (5) through (12), with (1) through (4) inserted, we find the following solutions for real wage rates in Britain and Australia.

$$(42) \qquad \frac{p_{11}}{P_{11}} = M_1 \alpha_1{}^{\alpha_1} \beta_1{}^{\beta_1} \left(\frac{p_{11}}{p_{12}}\right)^{\beta_1}$$

$$(43) \qquad \frac{p_{21}}{P_{21}} = M_1 \alpha_1{}^{\alpha_1} \beta_1{}^{\beta_1} \left(\frac{p_{21}}{p_{22}}\right)^{\beta_1}$$

Because of the weak factor price equalization theorem (29c), (42) and (43) are equal: The British and the Australian real wage rates are equal, both in terms of clothing. But furthermore we find

$$(44) \qquad \frac{p_{11}}{P_{12}} = M_2 \alpha_2{}^{\alpha_2} \beta_2{}^{\beta_2} \left(\frac{p_{11}}{p_{12}}\right)^{\beta_2}$$

$$(45) \qquad \frac{p_{21}}{P_{22}} = M_2 \alpha_2{}^{\alpha_2} \beta_2{}^{\beta_2} \left(\frac{p_{21}}{p_{22}}\right)^{\beta_2}$$

Again because of the weak factor price equalization theorem (29c), (44) and (45) are equal: The British and the Australian real wage rates are also equal in terms of food.

Furthermore we find the following solutions for real rental rates in Britain and Australia.

$$(46) \qquad \frac{p_{12}}{P_{11}} = M_1 \alpha_1{}^{\alpha_1} \beta_1{}^{\beta_1} \left(\frac{p_{12}}{p_{11}}\right)^{\alpha_1}$$

$$(47) \qquad \frac{p_{22}}{P_{21}} = M_1 \alpha_1{}^{\alpha_1} \beta_1{}^{\beta_1} \left(\frac{p_{22}}{p_{21}}\right)^{\alpha_1}$$

Because of the weak factor price equalization theorem (29c), (46) and (47) are equal: The British and the Australian real rental rates are equal, both in terms of clothing. But furthermore we find

$$(48) \qquad \frac{p_{12}}{P_{12}} = M_2 \alpha_2{}^{\alpha_2} \beta_2{}^{\beta_2} \left(\frac{p_{12}}{p_{11}}\right)^{\alpha_2}$$

$$(49) \qquad \frac{p_{22}}{P_{22}} = M_2 \alpha_2{}^{\alpha_2} \beta_2{}^{\beta_2} \left(\frac{p_{22}}{p_{21}}\right)^{\alpha_2}$$

Again because of the weak factor price equalization theorem (29c), (48) and (49) are equal: The British and the Australian real rental rates are also equal in terms of food.

In Section 26.14 we found the weak factor price equalization theorem that the relative prices of the first and the second inputs are the same in the two countries [see Eq. (29c)]. Equations (42) through (49) strengthen (29c) into the statement that in the two countries, each of the two inputs has the same real wage rate, or real rental rate, defined in terms of either output. This is the famous *factor price equalization theorem* developed by Heckscher [1], Ohlin [2], [3], and [4], and Samuelson [5] and [6].

The strong factor price equalization theorem expressed in the form (42) through (49) may be considered solutions for all relative prices, for had we had the space we could have inserted (40) and (41) into (42) through (49) and obtained only parameters on the right-hand sides of (42) through (49).

26.18 SOLUTION FOR THE EXCHANGE RATE

In the process of finding (40) and (41) we found in passing the solution for the exchange rate, that is, (31b), according to which the exchange rate simply equals the ratio between the two *numéraires*.

$$(50) \qquad \frac{p_{11}}{p_{21}} = E$$

26.19 SOLUTIONS FOR OUTPUT

Once we possess the solutions for the allocation of input, (32) through (39) with (40) and (41) inserted in them, we could insert those solutions into our output equations (1) through (4) and obtain only parameters on the right-hand sides of (1) through (4).

26.20 SOLUTION FOR THE ALLOCATION OF OUTPUT

Insert (21) through (24) into (13) through (20), use (42) through (49), and find the allocation of output between the two persons of the first country.

$$(51) \qquad C_{111} = \frac{A_1}{A_1 + B_1}\, M_1 \alpha_1{}^{\alpha_1} \beta_1{}^{\beta_1} \left(\frac{p_{11}}{p_{12}}\right)^{\beta_1} x_{11}$$

$$(52) \qquad C_{121} = \frac{B_1}{A_1 + B_1}\, M_2 \alpha_2{}^{\alpha_2} \beta_2{}^{\beta_2} \left(\frac{p_{11}}{p_{12}}\right)^{\beta_2} x_{11}$$

$$(53) \qquad C_{112} = \frac{A_1}{A_1 + B_1}\, M_1 \alpha_1{}^{\alpha_1} \beta_1{}^{\beta_1} \left(\frac{p_{12}}{p_{11}}\right)^{\alpha_1} x_{12}$$

$$(54) \qquad C_{122} = \frac{B_1}{A_1 + B_1}\, M_2 \alpha_2{}^{\alpha_2} \beta_2{}^{\beta_2} \left(\frac{p_{12}}{p_{11}}\right)^{\alpha_2} x_{12}$$

Similarly, we obtain the allocation of output between two persons of the second country.

$$(55) \qquad C_{211} = \frac{A_2}{A_2 + B_2}\, M_1 \alpha_1{}^{\alpha_1} \beta_1{}^{\beta_1} \left(\frac{p_{21}}{p_{22}}\right)^{\beta_1} x_{21}$$

$$(56) \qquad C_{221} = \frac{B_2}{A_2 + B_2}\, M_2 \alpha_2{}^{\alpha_2} \beta_2{}^{\beta_2} \left(\frac{p_{21}}{p_{22}}\right)^{\beta_2} x_{21}$$

$$(57) \qquad C_{212} = \frac{A_2}{A_2 + B_2}\, M_1 \alpha_1{}^{\alpha_1} \beta_1{}^{\beta_1} \left(\frac{p_{22}}{p_{21}}\right)^{\alpha_1} x_{22}$$

$$(58) \qquad C_{222} = \frac{B_2}{A_2 + B_2}\, M_2 \alpha_2{}^{\alpha_2} \beta_2{}^{\beta_2} \left(\frac{p_{22}}{p_{21}}\right)^{\alpha_2} x_{22}$$

26.21 SOLUTION FOR PERSONAL INCOMES

From (21) through (24) we find the money incomes relative to the *numéraires* p_{11} and p_{21}:

$$(59) \qquad \frac{Y_{11}}{p_{11}} = x_{11}$$

$$(60) \qquad \frac{Y_{12}}{p_{11}} = \frac{p_{12}}{p_{11}} x_{12}$$

$$(61) \qquad \frac{Y_{21}}{p_{21}} = x_{21}$$

$$(62) \qquad \frac{Y_{22}}{p_{21}} = \frac{p_{22}}{p_{21}} x_{22}$$

We also find the distributive shares.

$$
\text{(63)} \qquad \frac{Y_{11}}{Y_{11} + Y_{12}} = \frac{1}{1 + \dfrac{p_{12}}{p_{11}} \dfrac{x_{12}}{x_{11}}}
$$

$$
\text{(64)} \qquad \frac{Y_{12}}{Y_{11} + Y_{12}} = \frac{1}{1 + \dfrac{p_{11}}{p_{12}} \dfrac{x_{11}}{x_{12}}}
$$

$$
\text{(65)} \qquad \frac{Y_{21}}{Y_{21} + Y_{22}} = \frac{1}{1 + \dfrac{p_{22}}{p_{21}} \dfrac{x_{22}}{x_{21}}}
$$

$$
\text{(66)} \qquad \frac{Y_{22}}{Y_{21} + Y_{22}} = \frac{1}{1 + \dfrac{p_{21}}{p_{22}} \dfrac{x_{21}}{x_{22}}}
$$

26.22   COMPLETE SPECIALIZATION

Now is the time to examine the possibility, hinted at in Section 26.16, that some of the input solutions (32) through (39) become negative and consequently must be rejected in favor of setting those inputs equal to zero.

From our choice of Britain as the first country and Australia as the second it follows that

$$
\frac{x_{11}}{x_{12}} > \frac{x_{21}}{x_{22}}
$$

for Britain is more richly endowed with labor and less richly endowed with land than Australia.

From our choice of clothing as the first output and food as the second it follows that

$$
\frac{\alpha_1}{\beta_1} > \frac{\alpha_2}{\beta_2}
$$

for clothing is more labor-intensive than food. It follows that the denominator D of the input solutions (32) through (39) is positive. But could any of their numerators now be negative?

The numerators of (34) and (35) are possible candidates for negativity. To be sure, it follows from (40) that the ratio p_{12}/p_{11} rises with rising x_{11} and falling x_{12}. But it rises in less than proportion to the rise in x_{11} and the fall in x_{12}. Consequently, there is a distinct possibility that in Britain labor is so abundant and land so scarce that

(67) $$\frac{\alpha_1}{\beta_1}\frac{p_{12}}{p_{11}} x_{12} - x_{11} \leq 0$$

If this is true, the input solutions (34) and (35) become negative or zero. If they become negative, they will have to be rejected in favor of setting

(34a) $$x_{112} = x_{122}$$
(35a) $$= 0$$

Equations (34a) and (35a) state that Britain should allocate neither labor nor land to the production of food—almost her actual situation by 1914. However, if $x_{112} = x_{122} = 0$, then (7c) will have the ratio 0/0 in it; it will thus become meaningless and play havoc with even the weak factor price equalization theorem (29c). We can no longer derive (29c), let alone the strong theorem (42) through (49), in whose derivation the weak theorem (29c) was instrumental.

Instead, Britain should allocate all its labor and land to the production of clothing. For it follows from (67) *plus* the assumption that $\alpha_1/\beta_1 > \alpha_2/\beta_2$ that the numerator of (32) and (33) will be positive.

(67a) $$x_{11} - \frac{\alpha_2}{\beta_2}\frac{p_{12}}{p_{11}} x_{12} > 0$$

Thus under the assumptions (67) and (67a) there is complete specialization as far as Britain is concerned.

The numerators of (36) and (37) are other possible candidates for negativity. To be sure, it follows from (41) that the ratio p_{22}/p_{21} falls with falling x_{21} and rising x_{22}. But it falls in less than proportion to the fall in x_{21} and the rise in x_{22}. Consequently, there is a distinct possibility that in Australia land is so abundant and labor so scarce that

(68) $$x_{21} - \frac{\alpha_2}{\beta_2}\frac{p_{22}}{p_{21}} x_{22} \leq 0$$

If so, the input solutions (36) and (37) become negative or zero. If they become negative, they will have to be rejected in favor of setting

(36a) $$x_{211} = x_{221}$$
(37a) $$= 0$$

Equations (36a) and (37a) state that Australia should allocate neither labor nor land to the production of clothing. However, if $x_{211} = x_{221} = 0$, then (5c) will have the ratio 0/0 in it; it will thus become meaningless and—as (7c) did previously—play havoc with even the weak factor price equalization theorem (29c) and with it the strong theorem (42) through (49) as well.

Instead, Australia should allocate all its labor and land to the production of food. For it follows from (68) *plus* the assumption that $\alpha_1/\beta_1 > \alpha_2/\beta_2$ that the numerators of (38) and (39) will be positive:

(68a)
$$\frac{\alpha_1}{\beta_1} \frac{p_{22}}{p_{21}} x_{22} - x_{21} > 0$$

Thus under the assumptions (68) and (68a) there is complete specialization as far as Australia is concerned.

26.23 SOLUTIONS UNDER COMPLETE SPECIALIZATION

We see now that the factor price equalization theorem collapses under complete specialization, but what *are* the solutions for prices and quantities in that case? If we assume complete specialization in both countries and insert (34a) through (37a) into (25) through (28), we obtain the following simple input solutions:

(69)
$$x_{111} = x_{11}$$

(70)
$$x_{121} = x_{12}$$

(71)
$$x_{112} = 0$$

(72)
$$x_{122} = 0$$

(73)
$$x_{211} = 0$$

(74)
$$x_{221} = 0$$

(75)
$$x_{212} = x_{21}$$

(76)
$$x_{222} = x_{22}$$

26.24 SOLUTIONS FOR RELATIVE PRICES OF INPUTS UNDER COMPLETE SPECIALIZATION

Not even the weak factor price equalization theorem holds any more, but the relative prices of inputs may still be found, of course. Inserting (69) and (70) into (5b), and (75) and (76) into (11b), we find

(77)
$$\frac{p_{12}}{p_{11}} = \frac{\beta_1}{\alpha_1} \frac{x_{11}}{x_{12}}$$

(78)
$$\frac{p_{22}}{p_{21}} = \frac{\beta_2}{\alpha_2} \frac{x_{21}}{x_{22}}$$

26.25 SOLUTION FOR THE EXCHANGE RATE UNDER COMPLETE SPECIALIZATION

The only solution which looks more complicated in the case of complete specialization is that for the exchange rate. Equations (5c) and (7c) have lost their meaning; therefore (31b) can no longer be derived. However, outputs still move freely from one country to the other—that is one of the encouragements to complete specialization—thus (31) and (31a) still hold. Hence in (29), we set $X_{21} = 0$, use (5a), (13), (15), (17), (19), (21) through (24), (31), (69), (70), (77), and (78) upon it, and arrive at the solution for the exchange rate

$$(79) \qquad E = \frac{\alpha_2}{\alpha_1} \frac{B_1}{A_2} \frac{A_2 + B_2}{A_1 + B_1} \frac{x_{11}}{x_{21}} \frac{p_{11}}{p_{21}}$$

Thus under complete specialization the exchange rate is no longer merely the ratio between the two *numéraires* p_{11} and p_{21}. Rather it is that ratio multiplied by several others to be interpreted as follows. In our example, the exchange rate is the price of Australian dollars expressed in British pounds. Equation (79), then, tells us that that price is the higher, the more labor-intensive is food, the less labor-intensive is clothing, the more intensively British consumers desire food, the less intensively Australian consumers desire clothing, the more richly endowed with labor is Britain, and the less richly endowed with labor is Australia.

26.26 RELATIVE PRICES OF INPUTS AND OUTPUTS UNDER COMPLETE SPECIALIZATION

The strong factor price equalization theorem does not hold any more either, but we can still find, for each country, the real wage rate and the real rental rate, defined in terms of either of the two outputs. The four easy ones to find are a country's input prices relative to the price of the output produced by that country under complete specialization. The system of Eqs. (5) through (12) has now collapsed into only (5), (6), (11), and (12). Combine them with (1), (4), (69), (70), (75), and (76) and obtain

$$(80) \qquad \frac{p_{11}}{P_{11}} = M_1 \alpha_1 \left(\frac{x_{12}}{x_{11}} \right)^{\beta_1}$$

$$(81) \qquad \frac{p_{12}}{P_{11}} = M_1 \beta_1 \left(\frac{x_{11}}{x_{12}} \right)^{\alpha_1}$$

determining Britain's real wage rate and real rental rate, respectively, both in terms of the output produced at home, that is, clothing. Furthermore, find

$$(82) \qquad \frac{p_{21}}{P_{22}} = M_2 \alpha_2 \left(\frac{x_{22}}{x_{21}}\right)^{\beta_2}$$

$$(83) \qquad \frac{p_{22}}{P_{22}} = M_2 \beta_2 \left(\frac{x_{21}}{x_{22}}\right)^{\alpha_2}$$

determining Australia's real wage and real rental rate, respectively, both in terms of the output produced at home, that is, food.

The next four equations determining relative prices of inputs and outputs are a little harder to derive. They determine a country's input prices relative to the price of the output imported by that country under complete specialization. Production equations like (5), (6), (11), and (12) alone will no longer do. However, from (31), (31a), (77), (78), and (80) through (83), we find

$$(84) \qquad \frac{p_{11}}{P_{12}} = M_2 \alpha_2 \left(\frac{x_{22}}{x_{21}}\right)^{\beta_2} \frac{1}{E} \frac{p_{11}}{p_{21}}$$

$$(85) \qquad \frac{p_{12}}{P_{12}} = \frac{\beta_1}{\alpha_1} \frac{x_{11}}{x_{12}} M_2 \alpha_2 \left(\frac{x_{22}}{x_{21}}\right)^{\beta_2} \frac{1}{E} \frac{p_{11}}{p_{21}}$$

determining Britain's real wage rate and real rental rate, respectively, both in terms of the output which is imported, that is, food. Furthermore, we find

$$(86) \qquad \frac{p_{21}}{P_{21}} = M_1 \alpha_1 \left(\frac{x_{12}}{x_{11}}\right)^{\beta_1} E \frac{p_{21}}{p_{11}}$$

$$(87) \qquad \frac{p_{22}}{P_{21}} = \frac{\beta_2}{\alpha_2} \frac{x_{21}}{x_{22}} M_1 \alpha_1 \left(\frac{x_{12}}{x_{11}}\right)^{\beta_1} E \frac{p_{21}}{p_{11}}$$

determining Australia's real wage and real rental rate, respectively, both in terms of the output which is imported, that is, clothing.

26.27 SOLUTIONS FOR OUTPUT AND ITS ALLOCATION UNDER COMPLETE SPECIALIZATION

In regard to outputs, insertion of our input solutions (69) through (76) into Eqs. (1) through (4) would give us the desired, very simple solutions. To obtain the allocation of output among consumers, we use (21) through

(24), (31), (31a), and (77) through (83) upon (13) through (20) and find

$$(88) \qquad C_{111} = \frac{A_1}{A_1 + B_1} M_1 \alpha_1 \left(\frac{x_{12}}{x_{11}}\right)^{\beta_1} x_{11}$$

$$(89) \qquad C_{121} = \frac{A_2}{A_2 + B_2} M_2 \alpha_1 \left(\frac{x_{22}}{x_{21}}\right)^{\beta_2} x_{21}$$

$$(90) \qquad C_{112} = \frac{A_1}{A_1 + B_1} M_1 \beta_1 \left(\frac{x_{11}}{x_{12}}\right)^{\alpha_1} x_{12}$$

$$(91) \qquad C_{122} = \frac{A_2}{A_2 + B_2} M_2 \beta_1 \left(\frac{x_{22}}{x_{21}}\right)^{\beta_2} x_{21}$$

$$(92) \qquad C_{211} = \frac{B_1}{A_1 + B_1} M_1 \alpha_2 \left(\frac{x_{12}}{x_{11}}\right)^{\beta_1} x_{11}$$

$$(93) \qquad C_{221} = \frac{B_2}{A_2 + B_2} M_2 \alpha_2 \left(\frac{x_{22}}{x_{21}}\right)^{\beta_2} x_{21}$$

$$(94) \qquad C_{212} = \frac{B_1}{A_1 + B_1} M_1 \beta_2 \left(\frac{x_{12}}{x_{11}}\right)^{\beta_1} x_{11}$$

$$(95) \qquad C_{222} = \frac{B_2}{A_2 + B_2} M_2 \beta_2 \left(\frac{x_{21}}{x_{22}}\right)^{\alpha_2} x_{22}$$

26.28 SOLUTION FOR PERSONAL INCOMES UNDER COMPLETE SPECIALIZATION

Finally, by inserting (77) and (78) into (21) through (24) we could solve for personal incomes and distributive shares. Distributive shares become particularly simple, that is, α_1 and β_1 for Britain and α_2 and β_2 for Australia—as we would indeed expect them to be in a one-output economy whose production function is of Cobb-Douglas form.

REFERENCES

[1] Heckscher, E. F., "Utrikeshandelns verkan på inkomstfördelningen," *Ekonomisk Tidskrift*, **21**, 2, 1–32 (1919). (Translated as "The Effect of Foreign Trade on the Distribution of Income," in *Readings in the Theory of International Trade*, edited by H. S. Ellis and L. A. Metzler, Philadelphia and Toronto, 1949, pp. 272–300.

[2] Ohlin, B., *Handelns teori*, Stockholm, 1924.

[3] Ohlin, B., *Interregional and International Trade*, Cambridge, Massachusetts, 1933.

[4] Ohlin, B., "Utrikeshandelsteorin—ett forsök till 'Ehrenrettung'," *Ekonomisk Tidskrift*, **63**, 73–92 (June 1961).
[5] Samuelson, P. A., "International Trade and Equalization of Factor Prices," *Econ. Jour.*, **58**, 163–184 (June 1948).
[6] Samuelson, P. A., "International Factor Price Equalization Once Again," *Econ. Jour.*, **59**, 181–197 (June 1949).

CHAPTER 27

An Austrian Model of Labor And Capital*

27.1 INTRODUCTION

In Eq. (6) in Chapter 15 on Böhm-Bawerk's model, we found the optimum period of production τ to be the following function of the real wage rate w/P:

$$(6) \qquad (1 - \alpha)\tau^{\alpha} - \alpha\tau^{\alpha-1} = \frac{1}{M}\frac{w}{P}$$

In the Austrian tradition let us now transform this theory of the firm into a general equilibrium theory of labor and capital in a stationary economy producing consumers' goods by applying labor inputs to a time-consuming process of production. All capital is circulating and consists of a wage fund. To the economy, the available quantities of labor and capital are given. A Böhm-Bawerk general-equilibrium theory, then, would determine the real wage rate and the internal rate of return to firms.

27.2 NOTATION

In our Böhm-Bawerk general-equilibrium model the following notation will be assigned.

Variables

ι = the internal rate of return per annum in firms
L = number of men employed by all firms
τ = the period of production
P = price of output

* Chapter 15 is a prerequisite for Chapter 27.

Parameters

α = elasticity of output per annum per man with respect to the period of production

F = available labor force

K = available money capital

M = a multiplicative factor in the production function

w = the money wage rate—the *numeraire*

27.3 THE MODEL

As we saw in Böhm-Bawerk's theory of the firm, the money capital stock of the firm at the beginning of the first year was Lw, at the beginning of the second year $2Lw, \ldots$, and at the beginning of the τth year τLw. Hence the average desired money capital stock of the firm was $[(1 + \tau)/2]Lw$. Now let L be the number of men employed by *all* firms rather than by a single firm. Freeze the money wage rate w once and for all—use it for a *numeraire*. At the frozen money wage rate let the value of available accumulated capital be K, a parameter, and let average desired money capital stock of all firms be equal to the value of available accumulated capital, a parameter; then

$$(1) \qquad K = \frac{1 + \tau}{2} Lw$$

Furthermore, let the number of men all firms desire to employ be equal to the available labor force, a parameter; thus

$$(2) \qquad L = F$$

By combining (1) and (2) we obtain

$$(3) \qquad K = \frac{1 + \tau}{2} Fw$$

27.4 SOLUTION FOR EQUILIBRIUM REAL WAGE RATE

An interpretation of the system (3) and (6) is as follows. The money wage rate was fixed once and for all—used for a *numeraire*. To find the real wage rate, we would have to divide the money wage rate w by the price of output P, one of our variables. Suppose now that we fix some arbitrary value of the price of output P. Then the real wage rate w/P is known, and Eq. (6) will give us the corresponding optimal period of production τ. Three alternatives appear.

Either the now-determined optimal period of production happens to satisfy (3). In that case the arbitrarily fixed value of the price of output P happened to be the equilibrium value.

Or, at the now-determined optimal period of production τ, the available accumulated capital K would be too small to employ the entire available labor force. The resulting unemployment would then depress the real wage rate w/P by raising P, hence encourage a shorter period of production. Remember that (6) of Chapter 15 required the period of production τ to fall with falling real wage rate w/P. The price of output P would keep rising, that is, the real wage rate w/P would keep falling until Eq. (3) was satisfied.

Or, finally, at the now-determined period of production τ, the available accumulated capital K would be capable of employing more than the available labor force. The resulting labor shortage would then raise the real wage rate w/P by depressing P, hence encourage a longer period of production. Remember that (6) of Chapter 15 required the period of production τ to rise with rising real wage rate w/P. The price of output P would keep falling, that is, the real wage rate would keep rising until (3) was satisfied.

27.5 SOLUTION FOR THE EQUILIBRIUM INTERNAL RATE OF RETURN

Once the equilibrium values of the period of production τ and the real wage rate w/P have been found, Eqs. (1a), (2), and (6) in Chapter 15 combined will determine the equilibrium internal rate of return:

(4)
$$\iota = \frac{2\alpha}{\tau(1 - \alpha) - \alpha}$$

Is (4) positive? From Chapter 15 we recall that subject to the restrictions mentioned there Eq. (6) gave us a positive and unique solution for τ. Now the right-hand side of (6) was always positive, therefore the left-hand side had to be.

(6a)
$$(1 - \alpha)\tau^{\alpha} - \alpha\tau^{\alpha-1} > 0$$

Now multiply by $\tau^{1-\alpha}$, which is positive because τ was positive:

(6a)
$$(1 - \alpha)\tau - \alpha > 0$$

Apply this to (4) and see that in equilibrium the internal rate of return is indeed positive. How does it vary with the period of production? Take the derivative of (4) with respect to τ

(5)
$$\frac{\partial \iota}{\partial \tau} = - \frac{2\alpha(1 - \alpha)}{[\tau(1 - \alpha) - \alpha]^2}$$

Since $0 < \alpha < 1$, (5) is always negative; hence the internal rate of return ι falls with rising τ.

27.6 CONCLUSION

Böhm-Bawerk determined the equilibrium real wage rate and the equilibrium internal rate of return in a stationary economy in which entrepreneurs respond to a higher real wage rate by expanding their period of production. He found that the higher the value of available accumulated money capital, the longer will be the period of production, the lower will be the equilibrium internal rate of return and the higher will be the equilibrium real wage rate.

Böhm-Bawerk's solution for the equilibrium internal rate of return will be the point of departure in Chapter 39 on the Wicksellian model of inflation.

27.7 POSSIBLE RESTATEMENT

Still, Böhm-Bawerk's narrow confinement to circulating capital is of concern to us. Just as we restated his theory of the firm and avoided that confinement, let us see if we can do the same for his general-equilibrium theory. We shall devote Chapter 28 to this task.

The Equilibrium Rate of Interest in a Stationary Economy*

28.1 INTRODUCTION

Let us now abandon Böhm-Bawerk's assumption that all capital is circulating and adopt the opposite but far more realistic assumption that all capital is fixed. We may then extend our theory of the optimum quality of capital goods, stated in Chapter 16, into a general-equilibrium theory of wages and interest in a stationary economy producing two goods, that is, consumers' and producers' goods.

To the firm the interest rate and the money wage rate were parameters. To the economy as a whole the interest rate is a variable that we should like to determine. In regard to the money wage rate, we shall simplify things by freezing it—using it for a Walrasian *numeraire*. Then the real wage rate will be the variable we should like to determine. The two new variables, the interest rate and the real wage rate, will be determined by the two equilibrium conditions that supply and demand be equal in the markets for labor and money capital.

28.2 NOTATION

The following notation will be assigned.

Variables

a = minimum labor required to build one unit of producers' goods

---

* Chapter 16 is a prerequisite for Chapter 28.

b = physical capital stock held by consumers' goods industry per unit of output

C = consumption demand per annum

c = propensity to consume net income

D = depreciation per physical unit of producers' goods

f = labor's share of net income

h = gross investment to gross output ratio

I = output of producers' goods per annum

i = rate of interest per annum

k = worth of a unit of producers' goods, determined as the sum of the discounted revenue *minus* operating labor cost over its remaining useful life

L = number of men employed by consumers' goods industry

l = number of men employed by producers' goods industry

n = present net worth of a new unit of producers' goods

P = price of consumers' goods

p = price of a new unit of producers' goods

π = net income to gross output ratio, the "payout" ratio

R = retirement of producers' goods per annum

S = physical capital stock held by consumers' goods industry

V = money interest bill per annum

W = money wage bill per annum

X = output of consumers' goods per annum

Y_{gross} = money gross output per annum

Y_{net} = money net income per annum

Parameters

β = elasticity of labor requirement with respect to capital coefficient

e = Euler's number, the base of natural logarithms

η = price elasticity of demand faced by firms in the consumers' goods industry

F = available labor force

K = available money capital

M = a multiplicative factor in the production function

N = a multiplicative factor in the demand function

u = useful life of producers' goods

w = the money wage rate—the *numeraire*

All flow variables are instantaneous rates measured per annum. How can an instantaneous rate be measured per annum? It can, in much the same way in which the speedometer of an automobile measures the instantaneous rate of speed in miles per *hour*.

28.3 MICROECONOMICS

Assuming a new firm to use only one kind of producers' goods and determining what that kind should be, Chapter 16 examined the quality optimization problem of capital goods in its purest and simplest form.

This chapter is firmly based upon the microeconomics developed in Chapter 16, hence let us collect in one place and in their original numbering the equations we need from Chapter 16. First, the firm was facing the constant-elasticity demand function

(1) $$X = NP^{\eta}$$

Second, we defined a physical unit of producers' goods as the equipment operated by one man, hence

(2) $$L = S$$

Third, we defined the capital coefficient as the physical capital stock per unit of output.

(3) $$b = \frac{S}{X}$$

Fourth, we expressed the minimum building labor as a function of the capital coefficient b.

(4) $$a = Mb^{\beta}$$

Fifth, we defined the net worth of the acquisition of a new unit of producers' goods as seen at the time of acquisition.

(5) $$n = \left(\frac{P}{b} - w\right)\frac{1 - e^{-iu}}{i} - p$$

Sixth, we found the net worth of the acquisition of the entire capital stock needed to satisfy the demand faced by the firm. Maximizing that net worth, we found the following solutions for optimum construction of producers' goods a, optimum capital coefficient b, optimum price of output P, and optimum price of producers' goods p:

(17) $$a = -\frac{1}{1 + \beta}\frac{1 - e^{-iu}}{i}$$

(12) $$b = \left(-\frac{1}{1 + \beta}\frac{1 - e^{-iu}}{i}\frac{1}{M}\right)^{1/\beta}$$

(14) $$P = \frac{\beta}{1 + \beta}\frac{\eta}{1 + \eta}bw$$

(18) $$p = -\frac{1}{1 + \beta}\frac{1 - e^{-iu}}{i}w$$

We shall find it useful to insert (14) and (18) into (5) and express optimum net worth as

(5a)
$$n = - \frac{\beta}{(1 + \beta)(1 + \eta)} \frac{1 - e^{-iu}}{i} w$$

28.4 PURE COMPETITION

Let us simplify our macroeconomics by confining ourselves to the special case of pure competition. Let the price elasticity of demand faced by the firm η approach *minus* infinity and use the approximation

(29)
$$\frac{\eta}{1 + \eta} = 1$$

We deduct one on both sides of (29), insert the result into (5a), and find

(5b) $n = 0$

28.5 MACROECONOMICS

Let us now turn from microeconomics to macroeconomics. Let the economy consist of firms, of which all are exactly like the one described in Chapter 16. Consequently, the economy will produce only two goods, consumers' goods and producers' goods. The quality of the consumers' goods is given, but as shown in Chapter 16 the quality of producers' goods is a function of the rate of interest, hence is determined within our model simultaneously with the rate of interest.

Furthermore, the economy includes households whose propensity to consume net income will be found to be one, as is mandatory in a stationary economy. A nonstationary economy somewhat similar to the economy analyzed here will be analyzed in Chapter 48.

Finally, the economy includes a money capital market in which firms may borrow and savers may lend funds at the rate of interest i per annum with continuous compounding. The government is ignored.

28.6 PHYSICAL CAPITAL STOCK AND RETIREMENT

Let capital stock remain stationary, so gross investment always equals retirement; thus

(30) $I = R$

Let gross investment remain stationary; hence at the fixed useful life u, retirement is always $1/u$ of physical capital stock.

$$(31) \qquad\qquad R = \frac{S}{u}$$

28.7 FULL EMPLOYMENT

The number of men employed by the producers' goods industry equals the labor required per unit *times* output of producers' goods.

$$(32) \qquad\qquad l = aI$$

A physical unit of producers' goods was defined as the equipment operated by one man, hence the number of men employed by the consumers' goods industry equals the physical capital stock of producers' goods held by the consumers' goods industry.

$$(33) \qquad\qquad L = S$$

Let the number of men firms desire to employ equal the available labor force, a parameter; hence

$$(34) \qquad\qquad L + l = F$$

28.8 THE MONEY VALUE OF PRODUCERS' GOODS OUTPUT

The money value of producers' goods output is pI. Use (18), (30), and (31) to write it as

$$(35) \qquad\qquad pI = - \frac{1}{1+\beta} \frac{1 - e^{-iu}}{iu} wS$$

28.9 THE MONEY VALUE OF CONSUMERS' GOODS OUTPUT

The money value of consumers' goods output is PX. Use (3), (14), and (29) to write it as

$$(36) \qquad\qquad PX = \frac{\beta}{1+\beta} wS$$

28.10 THE MONEY VALUE OF GROSS OUTPUT

Since producers' and consumers' goods are measured in different physical units we cannot add their physical outputs but merely the money value of their outputs; therefore

$$Y_{\text{gross}} = pI + PX$$

Into this insert (35) and (36):

(37)
$$Y_{\text{gross}} = \frac{\beta - (1 - e^{-iu})/iu}{1 + \beta} \, wS$$

28.11 THE GROSS INVESTMENT TO GROSS OUTPUT RATIO

How large a proportion of its gross output will the economy have to allocate to investment in order to maintain itself? We divide (35) by (37) and find the gross investment to gross output ratio

(38)
$$h = \frac{pI}{Y_{\text{gross}}} = - \frac{(1 - e^{-iu})/iu}{\beta - (1 - e^{-iu})/iu}$$

The gross investment to gross output ratio h as expressed by (38) is a function of the rate of interest i. For example, let $\beta = -2.09$ and $u = 28$. Then let the rate of interest be, say, $i = 0.08$ and 0.20 in a developed and an underdeveloped economy, respectively. The gross investment to gross output ratio will then be $h = 0.160$ and 0.078, respectively.

28.12 THE NET INCOME PER UNIT OF PRODUCERS' GOODS

Aggregate demand seemingly played no role in the Böhm-Bawerk general-equilibrium model. In our own model let us therefore be very specific in determining consumption demand. Consumption demand must depend upon net income; therefore we are forced to study net income formation. Let us begin with the net income flowing from one physical unit of producers' goods of vintage v. Revenue per annum from such a unit is P/b. The money wage rate per annum is w. Since by definition the unit is operated by one man, operating labor cost per annum per unit is w. Revenue *minus* operating labor cost, then, is $P/b - w$.

At time τ, where $v \le \tau \le v + u$, the worth of revenue *minus* operating labor cost per small fraction dt of a year located at time t is

$$\left(\frac{P}{b} - w\right) e^{-i(t-\tau)} \, dt$$

and at time τ the worth of the sum total of revenue *minus* operating labor cost over the entire remaining useful life of the unit is

$$(39) \qquad k(v, \tau) = \int_\tau^{v+u} \left(\frac{P}{b} - w \right) e^{-i(t-\tau)} \, dt$$

By using (39) we may define depreciation and net income. Depreciation on the unit of producers' goods of vintage v during the year from time τ to time $\tau + 1$ is defined as the deterioration of its worth during that year.

$$(40) \qquad D(v, \tau) = k(v, \tau) - k(v, \tau + 1)$$

Economists often fail to define their income concept, but let us follow Lindahl [1] who did not fail to do this. Define net income at time τ from the physical unit of producers' goods of vintage v as the interest[1] on its worth. Thus

$$(41) \qquad V(v, \tau) = ik(v, \tau)$$

Therefore let us take the integral (39) and obtain

$$(42) \qquad k(v, \tau) = \left(\frac{P}{b} - w \right) \frac{1 - e^{-i(v+u-\tau)}}{i}$$

28.13   THE AGGREGATE INTEREST BILL

Just as the interest bill on one unit of producers' goods was the interest on its worth, so the aggregate interest bill is the interest on the worth of the aggregate capital stock. To find that worth, we proceed as follows.

Producers' goods of vintage v, like those of any other vintage, were produced at the rate I per annum. Producers' goods of vintages from v to $v + dv$, where dv is a small fraction of a year located at time v, were produced

---

[1] Our net income definition (41) tells us to multiply $k(v, \tau)$ by the rate of interest i to get net income $V(v, \tau)$. Is such simple multiplication correct for the case of continuous compounding, or should we not rather multiply by $e^i - 1$?

No, we should not; for remember that like all flow variables, net income is an instantaneous rate measured per annum. First, let us examine the case of discontinuous compounding. Deposit a sum K at the beginning of a period equal to one-mth of a year, and let interest be compounded m times a year at the rate i/m per one-mth of a year. Interest income earned on K during the period equal to one-mth of a year is Ki/m per one-mth of a year. For example, let $i = 0.08$ and $m = 12$. Monthly income is, then, $0.00666 \cdots K$ per month. But nothing keeps us from measuring this monthly income on a per annum basis and saying that it is earned at the rate Ki per annum. We can still measure on a per annum basis even if we let m rise without bounds, thus adopting continuous compounding. We would then say that interest income is flowing at an instantaneous rate measured as Ki per annum.

within that fraction of a year dv; hence the number of physical units of such producers' goods existing now is $I\,dv$, and as seen at time τ their worth is

$$k(v, \tau)I\,dv$$

As seen at time τ the worth of all producers' goods existing at that time, that is, of vintages from $\tau - u$ to τ, is

(43)
$$\int_{\tau-u}^{\tau} k(v, \tau)I\,dv$$

Insert (42) into (43) and evaluate the integral; thus

(43a)
$$\int_{\tau-u}^{\tau} k(v, \tau)I\,dv = \left(\frac{P}{b} - w\right)\frac{I}{i} \int_{\tau-u}^{\tau} [1 - e^{-i(v+u-\tau)}]\,dv$$

$$= \left(\frac{P}{b} - w\right)\frac{I}{i}\,Q$$

where

$$Q = \frac{iu + e^{-iu} - 1}{i}$$

A table of powers of e will show that Q is positive for any $iu > 0$. Insert (14), (29), (30), and (31) into (43a); then

(43b)
$$\int_{\tau-u}^{\tau} k(v, \tau)I\,dv = -\frac{1}{1+\beta}\frac{w}{i}\frac{Q}{u}\,S$$

What have we found? Equation (43b) is the worth at any time of aggregate depreciated capital stock in a stationary economy. Net income from that stock is the interest on it. Hence multiply (43b) by i and get the aggregate interest bill in the economy:

(44)
$$V = -\frac{1}{1+\beta}\frac{Q}{u}\,wS$$

28.14   THE AGGREGATE WAGE BILL

At full employment the aggregate wage bill is

$$W = wF$$

Into this insert (17), (30), (31), (32), (33), and (34):

(45)
$$W = \left(1 - \frac{1}{1+\beta}\frac{1 - e^{-iu}}{iu}\right)wS$$

28.15 AGGREGATE NET INCOME

Aggregate net income is the sum of the aggregate interest and wage bills.

$$Y_{net} = V + W$$

Into this insert (44) and (45) and write it simply as

(46) $$Y_{net} = \frac{\beta}{1 + \beta}\, wS$$

28.16 THE NET INCOME PAYOUT RATIO

Define the net income payout ratio as the ratio between net income and gross output, then insert (37) and (46).

(47) $$\pi = \frac{Y_{net}}{Y_{gross}} = \frac{\beta}{\beta - (1 - e^{-iu})/iu}$$

The net income payout ratio π as expressed by (47) is a function of the rate of interest. For example, again let $\beta = -2.09$ and $u = 28$. Let the rate of interest be $i = 0.08$ and 0.20 in a developed and an underdeveloped economy, respectively. The net income payout ratio is then $\pi = 0.840$ and 0.922, respectively.

28.17 CONSUMPTION DEMAND

Let wage earners and capitalists alike have the propensity c to consume net real income. Aggregate consumption demand is, then

$$C = c\, \frac{Y_{net}}{P}$$

Into this insert (46):

(48) $$PC = c\, \frac{\beta}{1 + \beta}\, wS$$

28.18 EQUILIBRIUM IN THE CONSUMERS' GOODS MARKET

Equilibrium in the consumers' goods market requires output and demand to be equal:

(49) $$PX = PC$$

Into (49), we insert (36) and (48); then

(50) $$c = 1$$

In other words, for equilibrium in the consumers' goods market to prevail, the propensity to consume net real income must be one. This is natural. If there were nonzero net saving, the economy would be decaying or growing and could not be stationary.

28.19 EQUILIBRIUM IN THE MONEY CAPITAL MARKET

We have frozen the money wage rate w, therefore we may use it for a Walrasian *numeraire*. At this frozen money wage rate, let the money value of available accumulated capital be K, a parameter. Now all units of producers' goods were assumed to be alike, but *what* they are going to be like depends upon the rate of interest: A lower rate of interest will induce firms to use higher priced, more automatic producers' goods with a lower capital coefficient, say bulldozers rather than pick-and-shovel sets. But whatever producers' goods are like, in equilibrium the worth of aggregate depreciated capital stock as expressed by (43b) must equal available money capital:

(51) $$- \frac{1}{1+\beta} \frac{w}{i} \frac{Q}{u} S = K$$

28.20 SOLUTION FOR EQUILIBRIUM RATE OF INTEREST

By inserting (17) and (30) through (34) into (51),

(52) $$- \frac{1}{i} \frac{1}{1 + \beta u/Q} = \frac{K}{wF}$$

The right-hand side of (52) does not contain i. The left-hand side is positive for any $iu > 0$ and is falling with rising i. Consequently the equilibrium rate of interest will be the lower the higher is the available money capital.

For example, consider first a developed economy in which the available money capital to money wage bill ratio K/wF is, say, 5. Still assuming $\beta = -2.09$ and $u = 28$ we find that according to (52) $i = 0.08$.

Second, consider an underdeveloped economy in which the available money capital to money wage bill ratio K/wF is, say, 3.2. Still assuming $\beta = -2.09$ and $u = 28$ we now find $i = 0.20$.

28.21 STABILITY OF EQUILIBRIUM

If the rate of interest were greater than its equilibrium value, the optimum quality of producers' goods would be too low. Optimum building labor a as determined by (17) would be too low; hence price p as determined by (18) would be too low for demand for money capital to exhaust the entire available money capital K at full employment. For such a high rate of interest only a lower K could bring about equilibrium, as (52) shows. The excess supply of money capital must depress the rate of interest.

If the rate of interest were less than its equilibrium value, the optimum quality of producers' goods would be too high. Optimum building labor a as determined by (17) would be too high; hence price p as determined by (18) would be too high to enable all borrowers to be satisfied out of the given available money capital K at full employment. For such a low rate of interest only a higher K could bring about equilibrium, as (52) shows. The excess demand for money capital must raise the interest rate. We conclude that the equilibrium is a stable one.

28.22 SOLUTION FOR EQUILIBRIUM REAL WAGE RATE

Use (12), (14), and (29) to solve for the equilibrium real wage rate

$$(53) \qquad \frac{w}{P} = \frac{1+\beta}{\beta}\left(-\frac{1}{1+\beta}\frac{1-e^{-iu}}{i}\frac{1}{M}\right)^{-1/\beta}$$

As shown in Fig. 28.1, $(1 - e^{-iu})/i$ is rising with falling i. According to (52) the equilibrium rate of interest was the lower the higher was available money capital. Consequently, the equilibrium real wage rate is the higher the higher is available money capital. The positive effect of capital accumulation under stationary technology upon the real wage rate is referred to as the Wicksell effect.

28.23 LABOR'S SHARE

To find labor's share of aggregate net income divide (45) by (46), obtaining

$$(54) \qquad f = \frac{W}{Y_{\text{net}}} = \frac{1 + \beta - (1 - e^{-iu})/iu}{\beta}$$

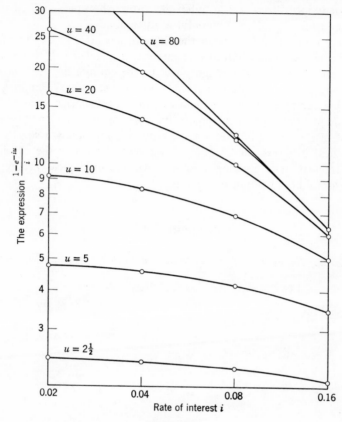

Figure 28.1

Labor's share f as expressed by (54) is a function of the rate of interest. For example, again let $\beta = -2.09$ and $u = 28$. Then let the rate of interest be $i = 0.08$ and 0.20 in a developed and an underdeveloped economy, respectively. Labor's share is then $f = 0.712$ and 0.607, respectively.

28.24   CONCLUSION

Avoiding Böhm-Bawerk's concept of the period of production but explicitly incorporating net income and aggregate demand, we hope to have captured the spirit of his contribution. We have determined the equilibrium rate of interest and the equilibrium real wage rate in a stationary economy in which the quality of producers' goods adjusts to the rate of interest. A lower rate of interest induces firms to use bulldozers rather than pick-and-shovel sets, to use electronic digital computers rather than abaci.

We have found that the higher the value of available money capital, the lower will be the equilibrium rate of interest, the higher will be the quality of producers' goods, and the higher will be the equilibrium real wage rate.

However, there is something artificial about the stationary economy. How was all that capital accumulated, and why did accumulation suddenly stop? We should very much like to replace the concept of a stationary economy with that of a growing one. However, growth is intimately associated with technological progress. In Chapter 48 we shall determine the equilibrium rate of interest in a growing economy with technological progress and variable useful life of producers' goods.

REFERENCE

[1] Lindahl, E., *Studies in the Theory of Money and Capital*, London, 1939, pp. 99–101, 143–146.

CHAPTER 29

The Static Open Leontief Model

Each of the industries . . . has its own peculiar input requirements, characteristic of that industry not only in the United States and in Europe but also wherever it happens to be in operation. The recipes for satisfying the appetite of a blast furnace, a cement kiln, or a thermoelectric power station will be the same in India or Peru as it is, say, in Italy or California. In a sense the input-coefficient matrix derived from the U.S.-European input-output table represents a complete cookbook of modern technology.

WASSILY LEONTIEF [5, p. 49]

29.1 INTRODUCTION

In its original Walrasian [6] form the theory of general equilibrium was characterized by a very large number of variables, among which possibly nonlinear relationships were postulated but not specified. Only in one respect was the theory simple, that is, input-output coefficients were parameters.

Walras himself perhaps never thought of putting his model to practical use by estimating its parameters empirically. Before Leontief [3, 4, 5] could succeed in such a venture, drastic simplification was necessary. All supply limitations had to be ignored, and all nonindustry demand had to be made parametric, thus ignoring specifically the relationship between household demand and household income.

29.2 THE MODEL

Consider an $(m + 1)$-sector model of stationary equilibrium. Let the $(m + 1)$st sector be entrepreneur households; let the mth sector be labor households; and let the remaining $m - 1$ sectors be industries. Each industry produces one product. This product is demanded, first, by industries using

297

it for an input and second, by the household sectors consuming it. For each product, equilibrium requires output to equal demand. The labor household sector is selling man-hours to the $m - 1$ industry sectors. Labor supply limitations are ignored. Labor's remuneration, the wage bill, constitutes the income of the labor households. To any industry, the difference between its revenue and its cost constitutes its profits. Profits are fully distributed and constitute the income of the entrepreneur households. However, labor income and entrepreneur income are not allowed to affect consumption demand and are, in this sense, open ends of the model, hence its name.

29.3   NOTATION

The static open Leontief model is assigned the following notation.

Variables

C_j = cost of jth industry defined as its money expenditure on input, $j = 1, \ldots, m - 1$

x_{ij} = output of sector i absorbed by sector j, $i = 1, \ldots, m; j = 1, \ldots, m - 1$

X_j = output of jth industry. $j = 1, \ldots, m - 1$

Z_j = profits of jth industry. $j = 1, \ldots, m - 1$

Parameters

a_{ij} = output of sector i absorbed per unit of output by sector j, $i = 1, \ldots, m; j = 1, \ldots, m - 1$

P_j = price of output of jth industry, $j = 1, \ldots, m - 1$

w = money wage rate

x_{jm} = autonomous labor household consumption. $j = 1, \ldots, m - 1$

$x_{j(m+1)}$ = autonomous entrepreneur household consumption. $j = 1, \ldots, m - 1$

y_j = shorthand for all autonomous household consumption. $y_j = x_{jm} + x_{j(m+1)}$

29.4   EQUATIONS

Let us begin with the production equations. They all assume a direct proportionality between input and output, the factor of proportionality being the input-output coefficient (Walras' "coefficient de fabrication"). First, let any industry absorb inputs from all industries, including itself; then

(1) $$x_{ij} = a_{ij}X_j \qquad (i, j = 1, \ldots, m - 1)$$

Of such equations we have $(m-1)^2$. Second, let any industry absorb inputs from the labor household sector; thus

(2) $$x_{mj} = a_{mj}X_j \qquad (j = 1, \ldots, m-1)$$

Of such equations we have $m-1$. Third, let any industry absorb inputs of entrepreneur services from the entrepreneur household sector. In quantitative terms, such inputs can be expressed only as the profits distributed in return to the entrepreneur households; hence

(3) $$x_{(m+1)j} = Z_j \qquad (j = 1, \ldots, m-1)$$

Of such equations we have $m-1$. Profits are defined as revenue minus cost:

(4) $$Z_j = P_j \sum_{i=1}^{m+1} x_{ji} - C_j \qquad (j = 1, \ldots, m-1)$$

Of such equations we have $m-1$. Cost, in turn, is defined as the money expenditure on all inputs, including labor input:

(5) $$C_j = \sum_{i=1}^{m-1} (P_i x_{ij}) + w x_{mj} \qquad (j = 1, \ldots, m-1)$$

Of such equations we have $m-1$. Finally in equilibrium, output in any industry must equal demand for it.

(6) $$X_j = \sum_{i=1}^{m+1} x_{ji} \qquad (j = 1, \ldots, m-1)$$

Of such equations we have $m-1$; hence we have a total of $(m-1)^2 + 5(m-1)$ equations. As for variables there are $(m-1)^2$ interindustry transactions x_{ij}, $m-1$ labor inputs x_{mj}, and $m-1$ entrepreneur inputs $x_{(m+1)j}$. Furthermore, there are $m-1$ outputs X_j, $m-1$ profits Z_j, and $m-1$ costs C_j. Hence our total is $(m-1)^2 + 5(m-1)$ variables, or the same number as the number of equations.

29.5 SOLUTION

Using Eq. (1) and the parameters x_{jm} and $x_{j(m+1)}$ upon Eq. (6), we may write (6) as the system shown in Table 29.1 or in more compact matrix notation as

$$\alpha X = y$$

Table 29.1 System of $(m-1)$ Equations Determining the $(m-1)$ Outputs X_j*

$$\alpha_{11}X_1 \quad + \alpha_{12}X_2 \quad + \cdots + \alpha_{1(m-1)}X_{m-1} \quad = x_{1m} \quad + x_{1(m+1)}$$

$$\alpha_{21}X_1 \quad + \alpha_{22}X_2 \quad + \cdots + \alpha_{2(m-1)}X_{m-1} \quad = x_{2m} \quad + x_{2(m+1)}$$

$$\cdots\cdots\cdots\cdots\cdots\cdots\cdots\cdots\cdots\cdots\cdots\cdots\cdots\cdots\cdots\cdots\cdots\cdots$$

$$\alpha_{(m-1)1}X_1 + \alpha_{(m-1)2}X_2 + \cdots + \alpha_{(m-1)(m-1)}X_{m-1} = x_{(m-1)m} + x_{(m-1)(m+1)}$$

* Where $\alpha_{gh} = -a_{gh}$ and $\alpha_{gg} = 1 - a_{gg}$.

where α is the $(m-1)(m-1)$ square matrix whose nondiagonal elements are α_{gh} and whose diagonal elements are α_{gg}, both defined under Table 29.1. The nondiagonal elements α_{gh} are nonpositive, for a_{gh} is nonnegative[1] for any g and h. The diagonal elements α_{gg} are positive, for a mere fraction of additional output of the gth industry will be withheld as an input by that industry.

Output X is a column vector of the $m-1$ variables X_j, and y is a column vector of the positive parameters $x_{jm} + x_{j(m+1)}$.

Let us now assume the square matrix α to be of rank $m-1$; then a unique solution for outputs X_j exists.

Having solved for outputs, we may solve for employment and income. Equation (2) determines employment. Employment multiplied by the money wage rate w is the money wage bill. If we insert Eqs. (1) and (2) into (5), and then insert (5) and (6) into (4), the result will reveal the profits bill.

At this point it will be useful to take a closer look at the special case of a two-industry Leontief model. We shall solve such a compact model both algebraically and graphically.

29.6 A COMPACT MODEL

Consider the special case of $m + 1 = 4$. Here, Sectors 1 and 2 are industries, Sector 3 is labor households, and Sector 4 is entrepreneur households. Further simplifying, let net output X_j by definition exclude x_{jj},

---

[1] An input-output coefficient may be zero. If $a_{gh} = 0$, it means that industry h does not use industry g's output for an input. Indeed, in the Bureau of Labor Statistics input-output coefficient matrix for the year 1947, in which $m - 1 = 45$, no less than 633 out of the 2025 coefficients were zero, (see Evans-Hoffenberg [1, p. 142, Table 5]). And in the input-output table for Israel, in which $m - 1 = 42$, prepared from data compiled by Michael Bruno of the Bank of Israel, no less than 789 out of the 1764 coefficients were zero (see Leontief [5, pp. 54–57]).

hence $a_{jj} = 0$. The system of Eqs. (1) through (6) in Section 29.4 then looks as follows:

(1a) $x_{12} = a_{12}X_2$ $x_{21} = a_{21}X_1$

(2a) $x_{31} = a_{31}X_1$ $x_{32} = a_{32}X_2$

(3a) $x_{41} = Z_1$ $x_{42} = Z_2$

(4a) $Z_1 = P_1(x_{12} + x_{13} + x_{14}) - C_1$ $Z_2 = P_2(x_{21} + x_{23} + x_{24}) - C_2$

(5a) $C_1 = P_2x_{21} + wx_{31}$ $C_2 = P_1x_{12} + wx_{32}$

(6a) $X_1 = x_{12} + y_1$ $X_2 = x_{21} + y_2$

where y_1 and y_2 are shorthand for the autonomous demands, called "the final bill of goods":

$$y_1 = x_{13} + x_{14} \qquad y_2 = x_{23} + x_{24}$$

29.7 ALGEBRAIC SOLUTION FOR OUTPUTS IN THE COMPACT MODEL

Using Eq. (1a) and the final bill of goods upon Eq. (6a) suffices to find the solutions for output.

(7)
$$X_1 = \frac{y_1 + a_{12}y_2}{1 - a_{12}a_{21}} \qquad X_2 = \frac{y_2 + a_{21}y_1}{1 - a_{12}a_{21}}$$

Are the solutions (7) positive and unique? Regarding the numerators, assume the final bill of goods y_1 and y_2 to be positive, and assume the coefficients a_{12} and a_{21} to be nonnegative. With respect to the denominators, the product $a_{12}a_{21}$ has the following economic meaning. Raise the output of the first commodity by one physical unit. This would require a_{21} additional units of the second commodity. That, in turn, would require $a_{12}a_{21}$ additional units of the first commodity. Now if to produce one physical unit of the first commodity would take that whole unit or more, there could be nothing left for the final bill of goods. For anything to be left, $a_{12}a_{21} < 1$. This is the Hawkins-Simon [2] condition. If the Hawkins-Simon condition is satisfied, the denominators of (7) will be positive, and the solutions (7) will be positive and unique.

29.8 GRAPHICAL SOLUTION FOR OUTPUTS IN THE COMPACT MODEL

Graphs alone can be treacherous. However, as a supplement to an already established algebraic solution they often add life to it. Using simple vector analysis, let us restate graphically the output solutions (7) for a two-industry Leontief model.

A vector a in two dimensions represents the ordered pair of elements (a_1, a_2). Another vector b represents the ordered pair of elements (b_1, b_2). Vectors may be added by adding the corresponding elements. So the sum s of our two vectors a and b is

$$s = a + b = (a_1 + b_1, a_2 + b_2)$$

Graphically we may think of the ordered pairs (a_1, a_2) and (b_1, b_2) as the Cartesian coordinates of the points a and b, respectively. And we may think of our vectors a and b as line vectors, which are straight-line segments from the origin to the points a and b. The direction of the straight-line segments is indicated by an arrowhead, as was done in Figs. 29.1 through 29.3. Graphically, the sum s of the two vectors a and b is found as the fourth vertex of a parallelogram having the origin and the points a and b as the other vertices, also shown in Figs. 29.1 through 29.3.

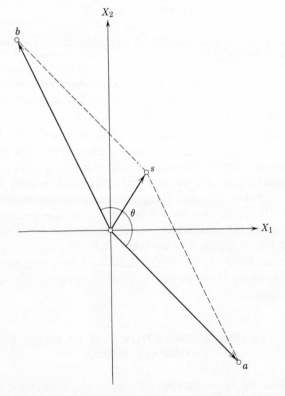

Figure 29.1

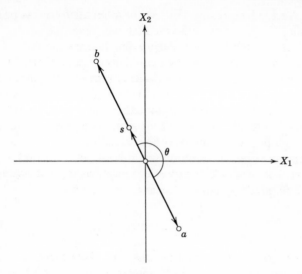

Figure 29.2

Let us now apply the vector idea to our Leontief model. In a Leontief world, no commodity is an output per se or an input per se. All commodities are at the same time outputs in some industries and inputs in others. So let the coordinates X_1 and X_2 in Figs. 29.1 through 29.3 be flows of commodities. A positive flow is output, a negative one is input. We may now let our vectors a and b mean levels of Leontief processes of production. Vector a represents the level of a Leontief process producing the first commodity and absorbing

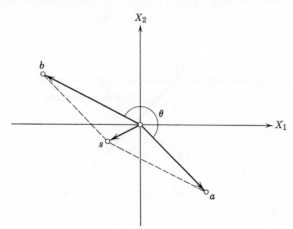

Figure 29.3

the second. Vector b represents the level of a Leontief process producing the second commodity and absorbing the first.

In Figs. 29.1 through 29.3 why did we always draw the vectors a and b in the second and fourth quadrants? We could not draw any in the first quadrant, for a vector here would mean a process level with two outputs and no inputs at all, and in practice we never get something for nothing. We should not draw any vectors in the third quadrant either, for a vector here would mean a process level with two inputs and no outputs at all, and such a process level—although possible—would be uninteresting.

The parameters needed for an output solution of a two-industry Leontief economy are first, technology expressed simply as a_{12} and a_{21}, and second, the final bill of goods y_1 and y_2. Assume, for example,

$$a_{12} = \tfrac{1}{2} \qquad a_{21} = 1$$
$$y_1 = 2 \qquad y_2 = 3$$

Let us start from scratch in Fig. 29.4 and show these parameters. The final bill of goods is easy. It must appear as the point $(2, 3)$ in the first

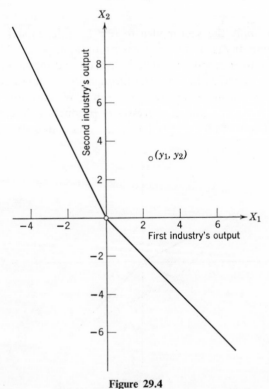

Figure 29.4

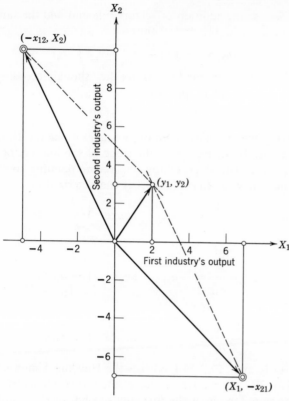

Figure 29.5

quadrant. As regards the Leontief processes of production, they must appear as the heavy straight lines in the second and fourth quadrants, having the slopes -2 and -1, respectively. As yet the lines do not have any end points with arrows pointing to them. Indeed, the end points are the variables for which we must solve. At which levels must the two Leontief processes of production be operated in order to satisfy, first, each other's need for input and, second, the final bill of goods?

Figure 29.5 gives the answer. Through the point (y_1, y_2) draw two broken lines parallel to the heavy straight lines. The broken lines will intersect the heavy ones in the two points identified by double circles, and those points represent the solution to the two-industry Leontief model. Why? Because we have now established the parallelogram of which the fourth vertex is at the same time the final bill of goods and the sum of the levels of the two Leontief processes. The other vertices are the origin and the required levels of the two Leontief processes. To establish the connection between our geometry and our algebra, we use the addition-of-vectors rule and find the sum of the two vectors identified by double circles; thus

$$(y_1, y_2) = (X_1 - x_{12}, -x_{21} + X_2)$$

which is nothing else than our Eq. (6). As they should according to (7), the double circles indicate the output solutions

$$X_1 = 7 \qquad X_2 = 10$$

Before leaving the graphical solution, let us examine the Hawkins-Simon condition graphically. In Fig. 29.5, the slope of the line vector pointing to $(X_1, -x_{21})$ is $-a_{21}$. The slope of the line vector pointing to $(-x_{12}, X_2)$ is $-1/a_{12}$. We may now say that Fig. 29.1 is characterized by

$$-\frac{1}{a_{12}} < -a_{21} \qquad \text{hence} \quad 1 > a_{12}a_{21}$$

Figure 29.2 is characterized by

$$-\frac{1}{a_{12}} = -a_{21} \qquad \text{hence} \quad 1 = a_{12}a_{21}$$

and Fig. 29.3 is characterized by

$$-\frac{1}{a_{12}} > -a_{21} \qquad \text{hence} \quad 1 < a_{12}a_{21}$$

In other words, only Fig. 29.1 satisfies the Hawkins-Simon condition. As a result, in Fig. 29.1 alternative lengths of the line segments ending at a and b will put the sum s in either the first, the second, or the fourth quadrant.

Figures 29.2 and 29.3, in contrast, do not satisfy the Hawkins-Simon condition. As a result, in Fig. 29.2 alternative lengths of the line segments ending at a and b will put the sum s in either the origin, the second, or the fourth quadrant, but never in the first. In Fig. 29.3 alternative lengths of the line segments ending at a and b will put the sum s in either the second, the third, or the fourth quadrant, but again never in the first.

Thus neither Fig. 29.2 nor Fig. 29.3 could put the sum s in the first quadrant and thus make it coincide with a positive final bill of goods for both commodities. Still another way of putting it is to say that what is wrong with Figs. 29.2 and 29.3 is that the angle θ is too large. Only if $\theta < 180°$, as it is in Fig. 29.1, can a positive final bill of goods be satisfied.

29.9 STABILITY OF OUTPUT EQUILIBRIUM

Are the output equilibria (7) stable ones? The Hawkins-Simon condition can help us answer that question, too. Let us disturb equilibrium by expanding arbitrarily the output X_1 of the first commodity by one physical unit beyond the value determined by (7). As we saw, this expansion would require a_{21} additional units of the second commodity. That, in turn, would require $a_{12}a_{21}$ additional units of the first commodity. Hence when output is increased by one unit, demand is increased by $a_{12}a_{21}$ units.

First, assume that the Hawkins-Simon condition is satisfied; then

$$a_{12}a_{21} < 1$$

In that case additional demand falls short of additional output; hence inventory accumulation will result and output will be induced to move back in the direction of its equilibrium value (7). Equilibrium, then, is stable.

Second, assume that the Hawkins-Simon condition is not satisfied; then

$$a_{12}a_{21} \geq 1$$

If, first, $a_{12}a_{21} > 1$, then inventory depletion will result and output would be induced to move farther away from equilibrium; hence the latter is unstable. If, second, $a_{12}a_{21} = 1$, then no inventory change would occur and output could come to rest at the new level. At least it would not be induced to move back to equilibrium, hence, it is not stable.

29.10   OUTPUT MULTIPLIERS

The sensitivity of equilibrium output to changes in the final bill of goods y_1 and y_2 is expressed by the following partial derivatives:

(8)
$$\frac{\partial X_1}{\partial y_1} = \frac{1}{1 - a_{12}a_{21}}$$

(9)
$$\frac{\partial X_1}{\partial y_2} = \frac{a_{12}}{1 - a_{12}a_{21}}$$

(10)
$$\frac{\partial X_2}{\partial y_1} = \frac{a_{21}}{1 - a_{12}a_{21}}$$

(11)
$$\frac{\partial X_2}{\partial y_2} = \frac{1}{1 - a_{12}a_{21}}$$

Technological progress may be thought of as a reduction in an input coefficient a_{ij}, which means that the jth industry has now organized its production or distribution process more efficiently so as to need less input from industry i to maintain the same output. The sensitivity of outputs to such technological progress is expressed by the following partial derivatives or multipliers:

$$(12) \qquad \frac{\partial X_1}{\partial a_{12}} = \frac{X_2}{1 - a_{12}a_{21}}$$

$$(13) \qquad \frac{\partial X_1}{\partial a_{21}} = \frac{a_{12}X_1}{1 - a_{12}a_{21}}$$

$$(14) \qquad \frac{\partial X_2}{\partial a_{12}} = \frac{a_{21}X_2}{1 - a_{12}a_{21}}$$

$$(15) \qquad \frac{\partial X_2}{\partial a_{21}} = \frac{X_1}{1 - a_{12}a_{21}}$$

Since we have assumed all input coefficients a_{ij} to be nonnegative and $a_{12}a_{21}$ to be less than one and therefore have found X_1 and X_2 to be positive, derivatives (8), (11), (12), and (15) will be positive, and derivatives (9), (10), (13), and (14) will be nonnegative.

29.11 SOLUTIONS FOR DISTRIBUTIVE SHARES IN COMPACT MODEL

By solving for the wage bill and the profits bill, we obtain

$$(16) \qquad w(x_{31} + x_{32})$$

and

$$(17) \qquad Z_1 = X_1(P_1 - P_2a_{21} - wa_{31}) \qquad Z_2 = X_2(P_2 - P_1a_{12} - wa_{32})$$

respectively.

29.12 SOLUTIONS FOR PRICES IN THE COMPACT MODEL

In a Leontief model there are no economies of scale; therefore assume all industries to be purely competitive. Also, in the long run let freedom of entry reduce all positive profits to zero, and let freedom of exit raise all negative profits to zero:

$$(18) \qquad Z_1 = Z_2 = 0$$

Hence, in Eqs. (17), either outputs X_1 and X_2 must be zero, which under our assumptions was found to be impossible, or the profit margins must be zero.

$$(19) \qquad P_1 - P_2a_{21} - wa_{31} = 0 \qquad P_2 - P_1a_{12} - wa_{32} = 0$$

Clearly the two equations (19) do not suffice to determine the three absolute prices P_1, P_2, and w. However, we may use any of the three, say the money wage rate w, as a *numeraire*. By dividing (19) by w,

(20) $$\frac{P_1}{w} = \frac{a_{21}a_{32} + a_{31}}{1 - a_{12}a_{21}} \qquad \frac{P_2}{w} = \frac{a_{12}a_{31} + a_{32}}{1 - a_{12}a_{21}}$$

Are the relative-price solutions (20) positive and unique? Let it take labor to produce both commodities; neither a_{31} nor a_{32} is zero. Let the Hawkins-Simon condition be satisfied: $a_{12}a_{21} < 1$. Then (20) will be positive and unique.

Notice that for a fixed technology, the absolute prices P_1 and P_2 are in proportion to the money wage rate w. Consequently, the real wage rate, that is, the reciprocals of (20), remains unaffected by changes in the money wage rate. The same thing can be said in yet another way. If the money wage rate rises by a certain percentage, (20) shows all commodity prices to rise by that same percentage. One sometimes hears the statement that the prices of labor-intensive commodities would rise by a higher percentage than would the prices of less labor-intensive commodities. No such thing, then, is possible in the static open Leontief model.

REFERENCES

[1] Evans, W. D., and M. Hoffenberg, "The Interindustry Relations Study for 1947," *Rev. Econ. Stat.*, **34**, 97–142 (May 1952).
[2] Hawkins, D., and H. A. Simon, "Some Conditions of Macroeconomic Stability," *Econometrica*, **17**, 245–248 (July–October 1949).
[3] Leontief, W., *The Structure of American Economy, 1919–1929*, Cambridge, Massachusetts, 1941; enlarged edition New York, 1951.
[4] Leontief, W., "Static and Dynamic Theory," in *Studies in the Structure of the American Economy*, edited by Leontief, New York, 1953.
[5] Leontief, W., *Input-Output Economics*, New York, 1966.
[6] Walras, L., *Eléments d'économie politique pure*, Lausanne, 1874. (Translated by W. Jaffe as *Elements of Pure Economics*, Homewood Illinois, 1954.)

CHAPTER 30

The Static Closed Leontief Model*

The [income-expenditure] function is approximately described by a straight line, not usually homogeneous; i.e., there is an intercept. The assumption of proportionality does not appear to hold for many of the consumption sectors of the economy.

GILBOY [1]

30.1 INTRODUCTION

The static open Leontief model does determine the wage bill and the profits bill but makes no use of them. Labor and entrepreneur consumption demands are parameters. The temptation to make consumption a function of income is almost irresistible, and we shall yield to it—not, however, in the conventional way of adopting homogeneous demand equations for all commodities. Empirically such equations are implausible, and mathematically they lead us nowhere. Instead we shall adopt nonhomogeneous demand equations. Thus the wage bill and the profits bill are no longer open ends of the model, in this sense we are now closing it.

30.2 NOTATION

For the static closed Leontief model the following notation will be assigned:

Variables

C_j = cost of jth industry defined as its money expenditure on input. $j = 1, \ldots, m - 1$.

x_{ij} = output of sector i absorbed by sector j, $i = 1, \ldots, m; j = 1, \ldots,$ $m - 1$ as in open model. In addition, $i = 1, \ldots, m - 1; j = m,$ $m + 1$

* Chapter 29 is a prerequisite for Chapter 30.

310

X_j = output of jth industry. $j = 1, \ldots, m - 1$
Z_j = profits of jth industry. $j = 1, \ldots, m - 1$

Parameters

a_{ij} = output of sector i absorbed per unit of output by sector j. $i = 1, \ldots, m; j = 1, \ldots, m - 1$

a_{jm} = marginal propensity of labor households to consume. $j = 1, \ldots, m - 1$

$a_{j(m+1)}$ = marginal propensity of entrepreneur households to consume. $j = 1, \ldots, m - 1$

A_{jm} = autonomous labor household consumption. $j = 1, \ldots, m - 1$

$A_{j(m+1)}$ = autonomous entrepreneur household consumption. $j = 1, \ldots, m - 1$

P_j = price of output of jth industry. $j = 1, \ldots, m - 1$

w = money wage rate

30.3 EQUATIONS*

Equations (1) through (6) of the open model are all retained unaltered, but two new equations are added. The first says that labor household consumption is now a function of labor's money income:

$$(21) \qquad x_{jm} = A_{jm} + a_{jm}w\sum_{k=1}^{m-1} x_{mk} \qquad (j = 1, \ldots, m - 1)$$

where A_{jm} is autonomous labor household consumption of the jth commodity, a_{jm} is labor's marginal propensity to consume it, and $w\sum_{k=1}^{m-1} x_{mk}$ is the wage bill. Of such equations we have $m - 1$.

The second new equation says that entrepreneur household consumption is now a function of the money income of entrepreneurs:

$$(22) \qquad x_{j(m+1)} = A_{j(m+1)} + a_{j(m+1)}\sum_{k=1}^{m-1} Z_k \qquad (j = 1, \ldots, m - 1)$$

where $A_{j(m+1)}$ is autonomous entrepreneur household consumption of the jth commodity, $a_{j(m+1)}$ is entrepreneur households' marginal propensity to consume it, and the summation $\sum_{k=1}^{m-1} Z_k$ is the profits bill. Of such equations we have $m - 1$.

* Equations (1) to (20) appear in Chapter 29.

Household consumption x_{jm} and $x_{j(m+1)}$ have been removed from the list of parameters and made variables. Thus, to the open model, we have added $2(m-1)$ new equations and $2(m-1)$ new variables.

30.4   SOLUTION

By using Eq. (1) and our new equations (21) and (22) upon Eq. (6), we may write (6) as the system shown in Table 30.1 or in more compact matrix notation as
$$\alpha X = A$$
where α is the $(m-1)(m-1)$ square matrix whose nondiagonal elements are α_{gh} and whose diagonal elements are α_{gg}, both defined under Table 30.1.

Nondiagonal elements α_{gh} are nonpositive, for a_{ij} is nonnegative[1] for any i and j, the wage rate is positive, and all profit margins are nonnegative.

Diagonal elements α_{gg} are positive. To see this we must look at the individual terms of α_{gg}. If output X_g rises by one physical unit, the gth industry will withhold a_{gg} physical units used as an input by that very same gth industry. Surely a_{gg} must be a very small fraction. Furthermore, labor income will rise by wa_{mg} dollars, and labor's consumption demand for the gth commodity will rise by $wa_{gm}a_{mg}$ physical units of that commodity, surely also a very small fraction. Finally profits will rise by $P_g - \sum\limits_{i=1}^{m-1} (P_i a_{ig}) - wa_{mg}$

Table 30.1   System of $(m-1)$ Equations Determining the $(m-1)$ Outputs X_j*

$\alpha_{11}X_1 \quad + \alpha_{12}X_2 \quad + \cdots + \alpha_{1(m-1)}X_{m-1} \quad = A_{1m} \quad + A_{1(m+1)}$

$\alpha_{21}X_1 \quad + \alpha_{22}X_2 \quad + \cdots + \alpha_{2(m-1)}X_{m-1} \quad = A_{2m} \quad + A_{2(m+1)}$

$\cdots\cdots\cdots\cdots\cdots\cdots\cdots\cdots\cdots\cdots\cdots\cdots\cdots\cdots\cdots\cdots\cdots\cdots$

$\alpha_{(m-1)1}X_1 + \alpha_{(m-1)2}X_2 + \cdots + \alpha_{(m-1)(m-1)}X_{m-1} = A_{(m-1)m} + A_{(m-1)(m+1)}$

* Where $\alpha_{gh} = -a_{gh} - wa_{gm}a_{mh} - a_{g(m+1)}\left[P_h - \sum\limits_{i=1}^{m-1} (P_i a_{ih}) - wa_{mh} \right]$

$\alpha_{gg} = 1 - a_{gg} - wa_{gm}a_{mg} - a_{g(m+1)}\left[P_g - \sum\limits_{i=1}^{m-1} (P_i a_{ig}) - wa_{mg} \right]$

[1] As in the open model, an input-output coefficient may be zero. In addition, in the closed model a marginal propensity to consume may be zero. In Gilboy's Table 1 [1] for a 20-industry model none was; but household marginal propensity to spend aggregate disposable income on the output of the Iron and Steel, Nonferrous Metals industry was merely 0.0001, and on the output of the Metalworking Machinery industry merely 0.0002; those two were the lowest among the 20 industries.

dollars, and entrepreneur households' consumption demand for the gth commodity will rise by

$$a_{g(m+1)}\left[P_g - \sum_{i=1}^{m-1}(P_i a_{ig}) - w a_{mg}\right]$$

physical units of that commodity, surely also a very small fraction. The sum of these three very small fractions is assumed to be less than one, hence α_{gg} is positive.

Output X is a column vector of the $m - 1$ variables X_j, and A is a column vector of the nonzero parameters $A_{jm} + A_{j(m+1)}$. We can now see why homogeneous demand equations for all commodities will lead us mathematically nowhere. All parameters $A_{jm} + A_{j(m+1)}$ would be zero. Hence if the determinant formed from the $(m-1)(m-1)$ square matrix α were not zero, the system would have only the trivial solution $X_j = 0$ $(j = 1, \ldots, m-1)$, and if the determinant formed from α were zero, the system would have infinitely many solutions.

The square matrix α is assumed to be of rank $m - 1$; hence a unique solution for outputs X_j exists.

Having solved for outputs, we may again solve for employment and incomes, as we did in the open model.

30.5 A COMPACT MODEL

Again consider the special case of $m + 1 = 4$. Again, Sectors 1 and 2 are industries, Sector 3 is labor households, and Sector 4 is entrepreneur households. Again let net output X_j exclude x_{jj}; hence $a_{jj} = 0$. Equations (1a) through (6a) remain as in the open model (Chapter 29), but our two new equations are

(21a) $x_{13} = A_{13} + a_{13}w(x_{31} + x_{32})$ $x_{23} = A_{23} + a_{23}w(x_{31} + x_{32})$

(22a) $x_{14} = A_{14} + a_{14}(Z_1 + Z_2)$ $x_{24} = A_{24} + a_{24}(Z_1 + Z_2)$

30.6 SOLUTIONS FOR OUTPUTS IN THE COMPACT MODEL

By using Eqs. (1a), (21a), and (22a) on Eq. (6a) we obtain

(23)
$$X_1 = \frac{\alpha_{22}(A_{13} + A_{14}) - \alpha_{12}(A_{23} + A_{24})}{\alpha_{11}\alpha_{22} - \alpha_{12}\alpha_{21}}$$

$$X_2 = \frac{\alpha_{11}(A_{23} + A_{24}) - \alpha_{21}(A_{13} + A_{14})}{\alpha_{11}\alpha_{22} - \alpha_{12}\alpha_{21}}$$

where:

$$\alpha_{11} = 1 - wa_{13}a_{31} - a_{14}(P_1 - P_2a_{21} - wa_{31})$$

$$\alpha_{12} = -a_{12} - wa_{13}a_{32} - a_{14}(P_2 - P_1a_{12} - wa_{32})$$

$$\alpha_{21} = -a_{21} - wa_{23}a_{31} - a_{24}(P_1 - P_2a_{21} - wa_{31})$$

$$\alpha_{22} = 1 - wa_{23}a_{32} - a_{24}(P_2 - P_1a_{12} - wa_{32})$$

As regards the numerators of (23), the intercepts A_{13}, A_{14}, A_{23}, and A_{24} are positive for goods whose income elasticity is less than one, zero for goods whose income elasticity equals one, and negative for goods whose income elasticity is greater than one.[2] From macroeconomic empirical consumption functions we know that the aggregate intercept $A_{13} + A_{14} + A_{23} + A_{24}$ is positive; assume that this is also true of the weighted sums of A's appearing in the numerators of (23). We have already seen that the nondiagonal elements α_{12} and α_{21} are nonpositive; hence all the weights are nonnegative. Assume furthermore that $\alpha_{11}\alpha_{22} - \alpha_{12}\alpha_{21}$ is positive; then X_1 and X_2 as determined by (23) are positive.

30.7   STABILITY OF OUTPUT EQUILIBRIUM

Let us disturb equilibrium by expanding arbitrarily the output X_1 of the first commodity by one physical unit beyond the value determined by (23). The parameter α_{11} is clearly one *minus* the number of additional physical units of the first commodity demanded per additional physical unit of that commodity by the labor and entrepreneur households employed by the first industry itself. Or in short, one *minus* the direct demand effect.

The expansion of the output X_1 will necessitate a primary expansion of *minus* α_{21} of the output X_2 of the second industry. The parameter α_{21} is clearly *minus* the number of additional physical units of the second commodity demanded by the first industry and its labor and entrepreneur households.

But the expansion by *minus* α_{21} of the output X_2 of the second industry is merely the primary one. It has the secondary effect upon demand and output of that industry of *minus* $\alpha_{21}(1 - \alpha_{22})$. The reader will recall that the parameter α_{22} is one *minus* the number of additional physical units of the second commodity demanded per additional physical unit of that commodity by labor and entrepreneur households of the second industry itself. The secondary expansion, in turn, will have the tertiary effect upon demand and

[2] In Gilboy's Table 1 [1] for a 20-industry model, the Agriculture, Fisheries, Food, Tobacco industry showed an autonomous aggregate consumption demand of 3.8 billion dollars, and the Textiles, Apparel, Leather, Miscellaneous industry 3.5 billion dollars; those two were the highest among the 20 industries. At the opposite end of the scale, the Eating and Drinking Places industry showed an autonomous aggregate consumption demand of −3.0 billion dollars, and the Motor Vehicles and Rubber Products industry −1.3 billion dollars; those were the lowest among the 20 industries.

output of the second industry of *minus* $\alpha_{21}(1 - \alpha_{22})^2$, etc. After n rounds, the sum of the n effects upon output of the second industry will be *minus* $\alpha_{21}[1 + (1 - \alpha_{22}) + (1 - \alpha_{22})^2 + \cdots + (1 - \alpha_{22})^n]$. We have already seen that $1 - \alpha_{22}$ is positive and less than one; hence for n approaching infinity the cited sum approaches *minus* α_{21}/α_{22}.

Thus the output X_2 of the second commodity comes to rest at *minus* α_{21}/α_{22} beyond the value determined by (23). This expansion releases an indirect effect upon demand for the first commodity. The number of additional physical units of the first commodity demanded by the second industry and its labor and entrepreneur households when *minus* α_{21}/α_{22} additional physical units of the second commodity is to be produced is clearly $\alpha_{12}\alpha_{21}/\alpha_{22}$.

As we saw, α_{11} was one *minus* the direct demand effect upon the first industry; hence α_{11} represents what is left of the original additional physical unit to satisfy indirect demand. Therefore, if $\alpha_{12}\alpha_{21}/\alpha_{22}$ were greater than α_{11}, inventory depletion would result, and output would be induced to move farther away from equilibrium. If $\alpha_{12}\alpha_{21}/\alpha_{22}$ were equal to α_{11}, no inventory change would occur, and output could come to rest at the new level. If $\alpha_{12}\alpha_{21}/\alpha_{22}$ is less than α_{11}, inventory accumulation will result, and output will be induced to move back in the direction of equilibrium as defined by (23). Hence our requirement that $\alpha_{11}\alpha_{22} - \alpha_{12}\alpha_{21}$ be positive, implying that $\alpha_{12}\alpha_{21}/\alpha_{22}$ be less than α_{11} is also necessary for equilibrium to be stable.

30.8 OUTPUT MULTIPLIERS

The concept of autonomous household consumption A_{jm} and $A_{j(m+1)}$ may again be generalized into autonomous demand y_j by households, government, and foreign countries. Therefore in (23) write y_1 and y_2 for $A_{13} + A_{14}$ and $A_{23} + A_{24}$, respectively. The sensitivity of outputs to the final bill of goods y_1 and y_2 is expressed by the following partial derivatives or multipliers.

$$(24) \qquad \frac{\partial X_1}{\partial y_1} = \frac{\alpha_{22}}{\alpha_{11}\alpha_{22} - \alpha_{12}\alpha_{21}}$$

$$(25) \qquad \frac{\partial X_1}{\partial y_2} = -\frac{\alpha_{12}}{\alpha_{11}\alpha_{22} - \alpha_{12}\alpha_{21}}$$

$$(26) \qquad \frac{\partial X_2}{\partial y_1} = -\frac{\alpha_{21}}{\alpha_{11}\alpha_{22} - \alpha_{12}\alpha_{21}}$$

$$(27) \qquad \frac{\partial X_2}{\partial y_2} = \frac{\alpha_{11}}{\alpha_{11}\alpha_{22} - \alpha_{12}\alpha_{21}}$$

Under the assumptions already made that α_{11} and α_{22} are positive, that $\alpha_{11}\alpha_{22} - \alpha_{12}\alpha_{21}$ is positive, and that α_{12} and α_{21} are nonpositive, we can see that (24) and (27) are positive and that (25) and (26) are nonnegative.

The sensitivity of outputs to technological progress is expressed by the following partial derivatives or multipliers:

$$(28) \qquad \frac{\partial X_1}{\partial a_{12}} = \frac{\alpha_{12} P_1 a_{24} + \alpha_{22}(1 - P_1 a_{14})}{\alpha_{11}\alpha_{22} - \alpha_{12}\alpha_{21}} X_2$$

$$(29) \qquad \frac{\partial X_1}{\partial a_{21}} = -\frac{\alpha_{22} P_2 a_{14} + \alpha_{12}(1 - P_2 a_{24})}{\alpha_{11}\alpha_{22} - \alpha_{12}\alpha_{21}} X_1$$

$$(30) \qquad \frac{\partial X_2}{\partial a_{12}} = -\frac{\alpha_{11} P_1 a_{24} + \alpha_{21}(1 - P_1 a_{14})}{\alpha_{11}\alpha_{22} - \alpha_{12}\alpha_{21}} X_2$$

$$(31) \qquad \frac{\partial X_2}{\partial a_{21}} = \frac{\alpha_{21} P_2 a_{14} + \alpha_{11}(1 - P_2 a_{24})}{\alpha_{11}\alpha_{22} - \alpha_{12}\alpha_{21}} X_1$$

Here, $1 - P_1 a_{14}$ and $1 - P_2 a_{24}$ are one *minus* entrepreneur households' marginal propensity to spend money on first and second commodity, respectively. These two differences may safely be assumed to be positive. However, since α_{11} and α_{22} are positive and α_{12} and α_{21} are nonpositive, each of the four derivatives (28) through (31) will consist of the sum of either a negative *plus* a nonnegative term or a positive *plus* a nonpositive term, and nothing *a priori* can be said about its sign.

This is as it should be. The unrealistic certainty with which we could predict the output effect of technological progress in the open model is now gone. There, technological progress reduced interindustry demand, but household demand was unaffected. In the closed model, however, household demand has an induced part. Hence when a_{ij} is reduced, industry j needs less of industry i's output per unit of its own output, consequently its profit margin increases, and entrepreneur household demand increases. Which of the two tendencies, the upward one in household demand or the downward one in interindustry demand, is the stronger we cannot say *a priori*.

30.9 SOLUTIONS FOR PRICES AND DISTRIBUTIVE SHARES IN THE COMPACT MODEL

The solutions for the distributive shares may be written exactly as Eqs. (16) and (17) in the open model with X_1 and X_2 now standing for our new solutions (23), of course. The price solutions may be written exactly as Eqs. (20) in the open model. Once again profits can be zero only if the profit margins are zero.

REFERENCE

[1] Gilboy, E., "Elasticity, Consumption, and Economic Growth," *Am. Econ. Rev.*, **46**, 124 (May 1956).

CHAPTER 31

The Dynamic Open Leontief Model*

These input coefficients [in the open static system] do not reflect ... the stock requirements of the economy; they do not and cannot explain the magnitude of those input flows which serve directly to satisfy the capital needs of all its various sectors.

LEONTIEF [1]

31.1 INTRODUCTION

In the static Leontief models all inputs were in direct proportion to output. Although this is often true of inputs on current account like raw materials, fuels, electric power, lubricants, etc., it is patently not true of inputs on capital account like the construction of durable plant and equipment. One way of handling the second type of inputs, and that was the way they were actually handled in the static Leontief models, would be to treat them as part of the final bill of goods. However, the latter is a parameter, that is, something left unexplained within the model. It would be much better to explain the demand for *all* input, whether on current account or on capital account, within the model. The dynamic Leontief [1] model does this, thus enabling us to determine the time paths, rather than the mere levels, of outputs.

31.2 NOTATION

For a dynamic open Leontief model the following notation will be assigned.

* Chapter 29 is a prerequisite for Chapter 31.

Variables

I_{ij} = net investment in output of sector i by sector j. $i, j = 1, \ldots, m - 1$

S_{ij} = capital stock of output of sector i held by sector j. $i, j = 1, \ldots,$ $m - 1$

x_{ij} = output of sector i absorbed by sector j on current account. $i, j = 1,$ $\ldots, m - 1$

X_j = output of jth industry. $j = 1, \ldots, m - 1$

Parameters

a_{ij} = output of sector i absorbed on current account per unit of output by sector j. $i, j = 1, \ldots, m - 1$

b_{ij} = capital stock of output of sector i held per unit of output by sector j. $i, j = 1, \ldots, m - 1$

y_j = final bill of goods produced by industry j. $j = 1, \ldots, m - 1$

Let t be the time coordinate dating all variables. A flow variable marked (t) refers to period t, a stock variable marked (t) refers to time t. Let period t be the period beginning at time t, ending at time $t + 1$. Thus $S_{ij}(t)$ indicates capital stock at the beginning of period t.

31.3   EQUATIONS

Let us begin with the definitional equation that net investment is the net increase of capital stock.

$$(1) \qquad I_{ij}(t) = S_{ij}(t + 1) - S_{ij}(t) \qquad (i, j = 1, \ldots, m - 1)$$

Of such equations we have $(m - 1)^2$. Next assume that capital stock of output of sector i held by sector j is in proportion to the latter's output:

$$(2) \qquad S_{ij}(t) = b_{ij}X_j(t) \qquad (i, j = 1, \ldots, m - 1)$$

Of such equations we have $(m - 1)^2$. Now if Eq. (2) holds for any t, it also holds for $t + 1$; thus

$$S_{ij}(t + 1) = b_{ij}X_j(t + 1) \qquad (i, j = 1, \ldots, m - 1)$$

Deduct (2) from this, use (1), and obtain the investment function

$$I_{ij}(t) = b_{ij}[X_j(t + 1) - X_j(t)] \qquad (i, j = 1, \ldots, m - 1)$$

On current account, the interindustry transactions are the same as those of the static open model:

$$(3) \qquad x_{ij}(t) = a_{ij}X_j(t) \qquad (i, j = 1, \ldots, m - 1)$$

Of such equations we have $(m - 1)^2$. The reader will notice the contrast between our investment function, which says that inputs on capital account are in proportion to the *increase* of output and Eq. (3) stating that inputs on current account are in proportion to output *itself*.

In order that inventory neither accumulates nor is depleted, output must equal demand:

$$(4) \qquad X_j(t) = \sum_{i=1}^{m-1} x_{ji}(t) + \sum_{i=1}^{m-1} I_{ji}(t) + y_j(t) \qquad (j = 1, \ldots, m-1)$$

Of such equations we have $m - 1$. Hence we have a total of $3(m-1)^2 + m - 1$ equations. As regards variables, there are $(m-1)^2$ interindustry transactions on capital account $I_{ij}(t)$, $(m-1)^2$ capital stocks $S_{ij}(t)$, $(m-1)^2$ interindustry transactions on current account $x_{ij}(t)$, and $m - 1$ outputs $X_j(t)$, that is, the same number as the number of equations.

31.4   A COMPACT MODEL

Consider the special case of $m - 1 = 2$. Sectors 1 and 2 are industries, and households are not studied explicitly. Further simplifying, let net output X_j by definition exclude I_{jj} and x_{jj}; hence $a_{jj} = b_{jj} = 0$. Our system of equations (1) through (4) then looks as follows:

(1a) $I_{12}(t) = S_{12}(t+1) - S_{12}(t)$ $I_{21}(t) = S_{21}(t+1) - S_{21}(t)$

(2a) $S_{12}(t) = b_{12}X_2(t)$ $S_{21}(t) = b_{21}X_1(t)$

(3a) $x_{12}(t) = a_{12}X_2(t)$ $x_{21}(t) = a_{21}X_1(t)$

(4a) $X_1(t) = x_{12}(t) + I_{12}(t) + y_1(t)$ $X_2(t) = x_{21}(t) + I_{21}(t) + y_2(t)$

31.5   SOLUTIONS FOR TIME PATHS OF OUTPUT IN THE COMPACT MODEL

By solving our eight-equation, eight-variable compact model, we obtain the following system of two simultaneous first-order difference equations, each in the two variables X_1 and X_2:

$$(5) \qquad \begin{aligned} b_{21}X_1(t+1) + (a_{21} - b_{21})X_1(t) - X_2(t) + y_2(t) = 0 \\ b_{12}X_2(t+1) + (a_{12} - b_{12})X_2(t) - X_1(t) + y_1(t) = 0 \end{aligned}$$

This system may be further reduced to two separate second-order difference equations, each in only one variable:

$$AX_1(t+2) + BX_1(t+1) + CX_1(t)$$
$$+ b_{12}y_2(t+1) + (a_{12} - b_{12})y_2(t) + y_1(t) = 0$$
$$AX_2(t+2) + BX_2(t+1) + CX_2(t)$$
$$+ b_{21}y_1(t+1) + (a_{21} - b_{21})y_1(t) + y_2(t) = 0$$

where

$$A = b_{12}b_{21}$$
$$B = b_{12}(a_{21} - b_{21}) + b_{21}(a_{12} - b_{12})$$
$$C = (a_{12} - b_{12})(a_{21} - b_{21}) - 1$$

The reader will notice that in the process of removing one variable from each difference equation its order increased by one. As a result, if the final bills of goods y_1 and y_2 were known for the periods t and $t + 1$, each of our difference equations will now determine an output in period $t + 2$ from knowledge of what that output was in periods t and $t + 1$.

REFERENCE

[1] Leontief, W., "Static and Dynamic Theory," in *Studies in the Structure of the American Economy*, edited by Leontief, New York, 1953.

CHAPTER 32

The von Neumann Model

32.1 INTRODUCTION

Several years before the appearance of static and dynamic Leontief models, von Neumann [2] had built a disaggregated growth model with explicit optimization in it. His solution weeds out all but the most profitable process or processes. His solution also tells us which goods will be free and which economic.[1]

Like Cassel, Harrod-Domar, Leontief, Tinbergen, and Solow, von Neumann confines himself to equilibrium growth. Unlike Tinbergen and Solow he ignores technological progress.

32.2 NOTATION

The following notation will be assigned.

Variables

C = aggregate cost
g_j = proportionate rate of growth of level of jth process
i = market rate of interest
K = sum of money lent by capitalists
P_i = price of ith commodity
R = aggregate revenue
X_j = level of jth process

Parameters

a_{ij} = input of ith commodity per unit of jth process level
k_{ij} = output of ith commodity per unit of jth process level

[1] This chapter owes much to Dorfman, Samuelson, and Solow [1].

32.3 PROCESSES, THEIR LEVEL, AND THEIR RATE OF GROWTH

A von Neumann process may have several inputs and several outputs, and its unit level may be arbitrarily defined as the unit of any one input or any one output per unit of time.

Let there be s commodities and n processes. Operated at unit level, the jth process converts $a_{1j}, \ldots, a_{sj}$ units of the s commodities absorbed as inputs into $k_{1j}, \ldots, k_{sj}$ units of the s commodities supplied as output. The coefficients a_{ij} and k_{ij} are nonnegative parameters. The level of the jth process is the pure number X_j by which unit level should be multiplied to get actual inputs and outputs. Each of them is X_j times larger than it was at unit level.

The proportionate rate of growth of the level of a process is defined as

(1) $$X_j(t + 1) = [1 + g_j(t)]X_j(t)$$

The processes of a von Neumann model may rashly be thought of as industries, but in at least four respects they are different from Leontief industries.

First, in Leontief models joint production was impossible, for each industry produced only one good. In the von Neumann model, any process using more than one input and producing more than one output represents joint demand as well as joint production.

Second, in Leontief models each industry producing one good knew of only one way of doing so. In the von Neumann model, there is substitution in the sense that the same output may occur in several different processes.

Third, in Leontief models all goods except one, that is, labor, were reproducible. In the von Neumann model all goods are reproducible. Labor is simply the output of one or more processes whose inputs are consumers' goods. Hence labor, too, may be produced in more than one way—by being fed alternative menus.

Fourth, in Leontief models in any industry inputs and outputs were simultaneous. In the von Neumann model all processes have a period of production of one time unit. Inputs absorbed at time t become outputs supplied at time $t + 1$. This is not as restrictive as it may seem; in fact, the von Neumann model handles circulating and fixed capital with equal ease. As regards circulating capital, if consumable wine has a period of production of two years, define two distinct processes and products as follows. Each process uses an intermediate product for an input, that is, zero-year old and one-year old wine, respectively. The first process supplies one-year old wine for an output, the second supplies consumable two-year old wine. As regards fixed capital, if the useful life of machines is two years, define another two distinct processes and products as follows. Processes absorbing zero-year old machines for an input will automatically, among other things, supply one-year old machines for an output. Processes absorbing one-year old machines for an input will automatically supply scrappable machines for an output.

Since a process absorbs its inputs at time t but supplies its outputs at time $t + 1$, should the time coordinate of its level X_j be t or $t + 1$? Arbitrarily, let it be $t + 1$.

32.4 EXCESS SUPPLIES MUST BE NONNEGATIVE

Let the levels of the n processes at time $t + 1$ be $X_j(t + 1)$, where $j = 1, \ldots, n$. The inputs required at time t as a result of these levels are $a_{ij}X_j(t + 1)$, where $i = 1, \ldots, s; j = 1, \ldots, n$.

Let the levels of the n processes at time t be $X_j(t)$, where $j = 1, \ldots, n$. The outputs supplied at time t as a result of these levels are $k_{ij}X_j(t)$, where $i = 1, \ldots, s, j = 1, \ldots, n$.

For any commodity the excess supply in period t must be nonnegative; hence for the ith commodity, the sum of all inputs of it required by all processes must be smaller than or equal to the sum of all outputs of it supplied by all processes.

$$(2) \quad a_{i1}X_1(t + 1) + \cdots + a_{in}X_n(t + 1) \leq k_{i1}X_1(t) + \cdots + k_{in}X_n(t)$$

where $i = 1, \ldots, s$. If for the ith commodity the "less than" sign of (2) should hold, that commodity at time t is a free good, hence should have zero price: $P_i(t) = 0$. Let us rule out the uninteresting case in which all commodities are free goods and assume that at least one is not, that is, that in the system (2) at least one equality sign holds.

32.5 PROFITS MUST BE NONPOSITIVE

At time $t + 1$ let a particular process, say the jth process, be operated at the level unity. The inputs required at time t at unit level are a_{ij}, $i = 1, \ldots, s$. Such inputs are purchased at the prices $P_i(t)$, $i = 1, \ldots, s$. Hence the input costs at unit level are $a_{ij}P_i(t)$, and their sum is

$$a_{1j}P_1(t) + \cdots + a_{sj}P_s(t)$$

The outputs supplied at time $t + 1$ at this level are k_{ij}, $i = 1, \ldots, s$. Such outputs are sold at the prices $P_i(t + 1)$, $i = 1, \ldots, s$. Hence the revenues at unit level are $k_{ij}P_i(t + 1)$, and their sum is

$$k_{1j}P_1(t + 1) + \cdots + k_{sj}P_s(t + 1)$$

Under pure competition and freedom of entry, profits must be nonpositive; hence, for the jth process, the sum of all input cost at time t with interest added to it must be greater than or equal to the sum of all revenue at time $t + 1$.

(3) $[1 + i(t)][a_{1j}P_1(t) + \cdots + a_{sj}P_s(t)]$
$$\geq k_{1j}P_1(t + 1) + \cdots + k_{sj}P_s(t + 1)$$

where $j = 1, \ldots, n$. If for the jth process the "greater than" sign of (3) should hold, that process at time $t + 1$ is a money-losing one; hence should be operated at zero level: $X_j(t + 1) = 0$. Let us rule out the uninteresting case in which all processes are money-losing ones and assume that at least one is not, that is, that in the system (3) at least one equality sign holds.

32.6   EQUILIBRIUM CONDITIONS

Von Neumann defined equilibrium in much the same way Cassel had done. First, the proportionate rate of growth of all process levels is the same and is constant over time.

(4) $g_1(t) = \cdots = g_n(t)$

(5) $g_j(t + 1) = g_j(t)$ $(j = 1, \ldots, n)$

Second, the market rate of interest and all prices remain constant.

(6) $i(t + 1) = i(t)$

(7) $P_i(t + 1) = P_i(t)$ $(i = 1, \ldots, s)$

32.7   GROWTH PATTERNS OF COMMODITIES

In inequality (2) use (1) to express all $X_j(t + 1)$ on the left-hand side in terms of $X_j(t)$. Use (4) to strip $g_j(t)$ of all its subscripts and (5) to strip it of its time coordinate:

(2a) $(1 + g)[a_{i1}X_1(t) + \cdots + a_{in}X_n(t)] \leq k_{i1}X_1(t) + \cdots + k_{in}X_n(t)$

where $i = 1, \ldots, s$. The system (2a) expresses the growth pattern of commodities. If the "less than" sign of (2a) should hold, the economy more than reproduces what it absorbed one period earlier of the ith commodity raised by the growth rate g; hence the ith commodity is growing at a higher rate than g. If the equality sign of (2a) should hold, the economy exactly reproduces what it absorbed one period earlier of the ith commodity raised by the growth rate g; hence the ith commodity is growing at exactly the rate

g—no more, no less. Now we have assumed that at least one equality sign holds; hence the equilibrium rate of growth g must be the rate of growth of the slowest-growing commodity or commodities. Commodities growing faster than that become free goods.

32.8 PROFITABILITY PATTERNS OF PROCESSES

In inequality (3) use (6) and (7) to strip $i(t)$ and $P_i(t)$ of their time coordinates:

$$(3a) \qquad (1 + i)(a_{1j}P_1 + \cdots + a_{sj}P_s) \geq k_{1j}P_1 + \cdots + k_{sj}P_s$$

where $j = 1, \ldots, n$. The system (3a) expresses the profitability pattern of processes. If the "greater than" sign of (3a) should hold, the entire revenue of a process falls short of its entire cost one period earlier with interest added to it at the rate i; hence the jth process has an internal rate of return less than i. If the equality sign of (3a) should hold, the entire revenue of the process exactly covers its entire cost one period earlier with interest added to it at the rate i; hence the jth process has an internal rate of return exactly equal to i—no more, no less. Now we have assumed that at least one equality sign holds; hence the equilibrium rate of interest must be the internal rate of return of the most profitable process or processes. Processes less profitable than that will remain unused.

32.9 RATE OF GROWTH EQUALS RATE OF INTEREST

Take another look at inequality (2a) valid for the ith commodity. Multiply it by the price P_i of that commodity, getting

$$(2b) \qquad \begin{aligned} (1 + g)[a_{i1}P_iX_1(t) + \cdots + a_{in}P_iX_n(t)] \\ \leq k_{i1}P_iX_1(t) + \cdots + k_{in}P_iX_n(t) \end{aligned}$$

There are s such inequalities, one for each commodity. However, recall that if for the ith commodity the "less than" sign holds, the ith commodity is a free good, that is, $P_i = 0$; hence our multiplying by P_i must have had the effect of killing all "less than" signs. Now add the s inequalities (2b), ignoring the "less than" sign, use the following definitions of aggregate cost, paid out at time $t - 1$, and aggregate revenue, received at time t:

$$(8) \qquad C(t - 1) = \sum_{i=1}^{s} \sum_{j=1}^{n} [a_{ij}P_iX_j(t)]$$

$$(9) \qquad R(t) = \sum_{i=1}^{s} \sum_{j=1}^{n} [k_{ij}P_iX_j(t)]$$

and obtain

(2c) $(1 + g)C(t - 1) = R(t)$

Now take another look at inequality (3a) valid for the jth process. Multiply it by the level of that process at time t, $X_j(t)$, getting

(3b) $(1 + i)[a_{1j}P_1X_j(t) + \cdots + a_{sj}P_sX_j(t)]$

$$\geq k_{1j}P_1X_j(t) + \cdots + k_{sj}P_sX_j(t)$$

There are n such inequalities, one for each process. However, recall that if for the jth process the "greater than" sign holds, the jth process is a money-losing one, that is, $X_j(t) = 0$; hence our multiplying by $X_j(t)$ must have had the effect of killing all "greater than" signs. Now add the n inequalities (3b), ignoring the "greater than" signs, use the definitions (8) and (9), and obtain

(3c) $(1 + i)C(t - 1) = R(t)$

Finally, combine (2c) and (3c) and see that

(10) $g = i$

We conclude that if an equilibrium exists, the rate of growth of all process levels equals the rate of interest. The equilibrium rate of growth of all process levels equals the rate of growth of the slowest-growing commodity or commodities. Commodities growing faster than that become free goods. The equilibrium rate of interest equals the internal rate of return of the most profitable process or processes. Processes less profitable than that will remain unused.

Using nonelementary mathematics, von Neumann proved that an equilibrium existed.

32.10   THE CAPITALISTS

Nothing keeps us from interpreting the von Neumann model as having real live capitalists in it, lending money to the process operators: At time $t - 1$ let capitalists lend the process operators, that is, labor households and entrepreneurs, the sum of money

(11) $K(t - 1) = C(t - 1)$

thus financing all input needs of the processes beginning at time $t - 1$ and to be completed at time t. Now ex post, what the process operators as a whole are purchasing, the process operators as a whole are selling, for the economy is a closed one, hence

(12) $C(t - 1) = R(t - 1)$

The proceeds from the sale (12) are promptly used to pay off old debt incurred in financing the processes begun at time $t - 2$ and just now at time $t - 1$ being completed.

The capitalists will charge the rate of interest i; hence at time t the sum of money owed them will be

$$(13) \qquad K(t) = (1 + i)C(t - 1)$$

However, process operators have been careful and have used nothing but the most profitable process or processes; hence at constant prices the value of their output at time t will have grown to $R(t)$ as defined by (3c). Combine (3c) and (13) and see that $K(t) = R(t)$. Consequently, at time t process operators can pay off their debt, provided the sale of their output at constant prices can be financed. It can, provided at time t the capitalists lend the process operators the sum of money

$$(11) \qquad K(t) = C(t)$$

thus financing all input needs of the processes beginning at time t and to be completed at time $t + 1$. Again ex post, what the process operators as a whole are purchasing, the process operators as a whole are selling, for the economy is still a closed one; hence

$$(12) \qquad C(t) = R(t)$$

Again the proceeds from the sale (12) are promptly used to pay off old debt incurred in financing the processes begun at time $t - 1$ and just now at the time t being completed.

We might continue in this way. New debt forever pays off old debt with interest, and the aggregate debt is a rising one, rising at the rate of growth $g = i$. What makes it all possible is the willingness of the capitalists to save their entire interest earnings. Thus only labor consumes in the von Neumann model. Entrepreneurs do not consume anything, because their income *qua* entrepreneurs is zero; pure competition and freedom of entry guarantee that. Capitalists do have an income, but their propensity to consume it is zero.

REFERENCES

[1] Dorfman, R., P. A. Samuelson, and R. Solow, *Linear Programming and Economic Analysis*, New York, Toronto, and London, 1958, pp. 381–388.

[2] von Neumann, J. ,"Über ein ökonomisches Gleichungssystem und eine Verallgemeinerung des Brouwerschen Fixpunktsatzes," in *Ergebnisse eines mathematischen Kolloquiums*, 8, Leipzig and Vienna, 1937, pp. 73–83. Translated as "A Model of General Economic Equilibrium," *Rev. Econ. Stud.*, **13**, 1–9 (1945–1946).

Part Five

Aggregate Equilibrium Levels

CHAPTER 33

The Aggregate Consumption Function*

33.1 INTRODUCTION

The aggregate consumption function is sometimes treated as if it were purely empirical. We would much rather derive it from individual savings functions, for example, those found in Chapter 6. We shall use the equations, equation numbers, and notation of Chapter 6.

33.2 NOTATION

In a macroeconomic model the following notation will be assigned.

Variables

C = country's output consumed
C_k = quantity consumed by kth household
S_k = money saving by kth household
W_k = money wage income of kth household
X = net national output
Y = net national money income
Y_k = money income of kth household

Parameters

A, B = parameters of a constant-elasticity-of-substitution utility function
α, β = parameters of a Cobb-Douglas utility function
c = propensity to consume
g_P = proportionate rate of change of price of output
g_W = proportionate rate of change of money wage income

* Chapter 6 is a prerequisite for Chapter 33.

331

i = rate of interest

P = price of country's output

Q = an agglomeration of parameters defined by Eqs. (12) and (16)

ρ = an exponent in a constant-elasticity-of-substitution function

33.3 THE INDIVIDUAL SUPPLY-OF-SAVING FUNCTION

In Chapter 6 we offered an optimization model of a household assumed to plan for two periods only. At the time of planning, that is, the beginning of Period 1, the household derived utility from consumption in Periods 1 and 2 only. If the unit period is thought of as short, then the household is a short-sighted one. However, the unit period may be thought of as long enough for the two periods to cover a household's saving for retirement *plus* dissaving during retirement. For the individual household, call it the kth household, Chapter 6 derived two alternative savings supply functions, (12) and (16); (12) is based upon a Cobb-Douglas utility function and (16) on a constant-elasticity-of-substitution utility function:

(12, 16) $$S_k(1) = QW_k(1)$$

where

(12) $$Q = 1 - \frac{\alpha}{\alpha + \beta} \frac{2 + g_W + i}{1 + i}$$

(16) $$Q = 1 - \frac{2 + g_W + i}{1 + i + (1 + g_P)\left(\dfrac{B}{A}\dfrac{1 + i}{1 + g_P}\right)^{1/(1+\rho)}}$$

In (12) and (16) let us make sure that the household will have positive saving in Period 1; therefore let us assume that

(12a) $$i > \frac{\alpha}{\beta}(1 + g_W) - 1$$

(16a) $$i > \frac{A}{B}(1 + g_P)^{-\rho}(1 + g_W)^{1+\rho} - 1$$

In both (12) and (16) individual household saving was seen to be in direct proportion to individual household money income in the same period. The proportionality factor Q contained such things as the proportionate rate of change of money wage income and the price of output, the rate of interest, and the parameters of the underlying individual utility functions. Now we consider aggregation.

33.4 AGGREGATION*

Let the economy consist of s households, all having the same utility function and the same proportionate rate of change of money wage income—but not necessarily the same money wage income. They are all facing the same proportionate rate of change of price of output and the same rate of interest. Consequently, according to (12) or (16) they will all have the same individual propensity to save money wage income.

Now if all the s households were in the same phase as the kth household, there would be alternation between saving and dissaving over time: There would be saving in Periods 1, 3, 5, ... and dissaving in Periods 2, 4, 6, ... To ensure an even flow of aggregate saving, let us divide the s households into two groups $1, \dots, i$ and $j, \dots, s$, such that in any period each group has half the aggregate money wage income:

$$(20) \qquad \sum_{k=1}^{i} W_k(t) = \sum_{k=j}^{s} W_k(t) = \frac{1}{2} \sum_{k=1}^{s} W_k(t) \qquad (t = 1, \dots)$$

and such that in any period one group consists exclusively of savers and the other of dissavers. Any saver behaves as did the household examined in Chapter 6 in Period 1. Any dissaver behaves as did that household in Period 2. For example, in Periods 1, 3, 5, ... let the first group $1, \dots, i$ be savers and the second $j, \dots, s$ be dissavers. Then in Periods 2, 4, 6, ... the first group are dissavers and the second savers.

33.5 PERIOD 1

In Period 1 households $1, \dots, i$ are savers, and we write the sum total of all their saving by aggregating (12) or (16):

$$(21) \qquad \sum_{k=1}^{i} S_k(1) = Q \sum_{k=1}^{i} W_k(1)$$

Because Q is the same for all households, aggregate saving depends upon aggregate money wage income, not upon its distribution.

33.6 PERIOD 2

According to (8), the individual household saved for the sake of future consumption only and would conclude Period 2 without any assets:

$$(8) \qquad S_k(2) = -S_k(1) \qquad (k = 1, \dots, i)$$

* Equations (1) to (19) appear in Chapter 6.

Thus in Period 2 households $1, \ldots, i$ are dissavers, and we write the sum total of all their dissaving by aggregating (8) and using (21) upon it:

$$(8a) \qquad \sum_{k=1}^{i} S_k(2) = -Q \sum_{k=1}^{i} W_k(1)$$

In contrast, in Period 2 households $j, \ldots, s$ are savers. In (21) replace "(1)" throughout by "(2)" and replace $1, \ldots, i$ by $j, \ldots, s$. Then the sum total of all their saving may be written:

$$(21a) \qquad \sum_{k=j}^{s} S_k(2) = Q \sum_{k=j}^{s} W_k(2)$$

Now as far as the economy as a whole is concerned, will not the saving by the savers and the dissaving by the dissavers simply cancel out? Generally, No, and the clue is our assumption (5) that within each period, the household expects to be receiving the money wage income $W_k(t)$ that is changing at the proportionate rate g_W defined as

$$(5) \qquad W_k(2) = (1 + g_W) W_k(1) \qquad (k = 1, \ldots, s)$$

To see if the saving by the savers and the dissaving by the dissavers will cancel out, insert (20) into the right-hand sides of (8a) and (21a), add them together, use (5) and find

$$(22) \qquad \sum_{k=1}^{i} S_k(2) + \sum_{k=j}^{s} S_k(2) = \sum_{k=1}^{s} S_k(2) = \frac{Q}{2} \frac{g_W}{1 + g_W} \sum_{k=1}^{s} W_k(2)$$

According to (12a) and (16a) Q was not zero; therefore (22) can be zero only if $g_W = 0$, that is, if money wage income is stationary. Then and only then will the saving by the savers and the dissaving by the dissavers cancel out.

33.7 AGGREGATE SAVING AS A FUNCTION OF AGGREGATE MONEY INCOME

Equation (22) expresses aggregate saving as a function of aggregate money *wage* income, not of all aggregate money income, as we would wish. That can be taken care of as follows. First, examine the households $1, \ldots, i$. In Period 2 they were dissavers, and from (7) we know that each of them entered Period 2 with assets equal to its saving during Period 1 and therefore had an overall income of

$$(7) \qquad Y_k(2) = W_k(2) + i S_k(1) \qquad (k = 1, \ldots, i)$$

We aggregate (7) over households $1, \ldots, i$, use (21) and then (5), and obtain the relationship between money income and money *wage* income for this group:

$$(23) \qquad \sum_{k=1}^{i} Y_k(2) = \left(1 + \frac{iQ}{1 + g_W} \right) \sum_{k=1}^{i} W_k(2)$$

Next examine the households $j, \ldots, s$. In Period 2 they were savers, each of them entering Period 2 without assets, hence having nothing but wage income. In (6) replace "(1)" by "(2)", aggregate over households $j, \ldots, s$, and obtain

$$(24) \qquad \sum_{k=j}^{s} Y_k(2) = \sum_{k=j}^{s} W_k(2)$$

Then add (23) and (24) and get the relationship between money income and money *wage* income for both groups combined:

$$(25) \qquad \sum_{k=1}^{i} Y_k(2) + \sum_{k=j}^{s} Y_k(2) = \sum_{k=1}^{s} Y_k(2) = \left(1 + \frac{Q}{2} \frac{i}{1 + g_W}\right) \sum_{k=1}^{s} W_k(2)$$

Finally insert (25) into (22) and get the aggregate saving function:

$$(26) \qquad \sum_{k=1}^{s} S_k(2) = (1 - c) \sum_{k=1}^{s} Y_k(2)$$

where

$$1 - c = \frac{g_W Q}{2(1 + g_W) + iQ}$$

There is a well-known hypothesis of saving, well summarized by Farrell [2], the *rate-of-growth hypothesis*, which states that the fraction of aggregate income saved is in proportion to the rate of growth of aggregate income. Is that what (26) states? Not quite, for with neither (12) nor (16) inserted for Q will $1 - c$ be in proportion to g_W. To be sure, g_W was the rate of growth of money *wage* income. Will that also be the rate of growth of all money income? Yes, it will, for, according to (25), for a given g_W, i, and Q, all money income is in proportion to money wage income, hence must be growing at the same rate g_W. For given g_W, i, and Q, $1 - c$ is also given, and (26) would tell us that aggregate saving would be a constant fraction of aggregate income. Has this been true historically? We shall try to answer that question in the appendices to Chapters 45 and 48.

33.8   AN AGGREGATE CONSUMPTION FUNCTION

Even (26) may not be quite what we want. Equation (26) is a saving function, and we may want a consumption function. That, too, can be achieved. Use (3) in its aggregate form, insert (26) into it, and get the aggregate consumption function

$$(27) \qquad \sum_{k=1}^{s} C_k(2) = c \frac{\displaystyle\sum_{k=1}^{s} Y_k(2)}{P(2)}$$

Let us polish (27) a bit. With each group of households accounting for one-half of aggregate money wage income and with the two groups being always in opposite phases of saving and dissaving, we are bound to get even flows of aggregate saving, consumption, and money income. Consequently, in (27) we may replace "(2)" by "(t)." Furthermore, we may drop the summation sign and the subscript k, which have served us so well. Finally, we may define net national money income as the price of output *times* net national output: $Y(t) = P(t)X(t)$. All this permits us to write (27) in its most compact form

$$(28) \qquad\qquad C(t) = cX(t)$$

where

$$c = \frac{2(1 + g_W) + (i - g_W)Q}{2(1 + g_W) + iQ}$$

Here is an aggregate consumption function stating that aggregate consumption in real terms is in proportion to aggregate income in real terms; hence c is both the average and the marginal propensity to consume. If money wage income (and with it aggregate money income) were stationary, that is, $g_W = 0$, (28) shows that c is equal to one. However, if money wage income (and with it aggregate money income) were growing, that is, $g_W > 0$, (28) shows that c is less than one.

Besides the growth rate g_W, (28) contains the rate of interest and all the parameters of the underlying individual utility functions. In consequence it can only be used in growth models with caution. However, it can safely be used in models of steady growth displaying a time trend neither in (1) labor's share, (2) the rate of interest, nor (3) consumer tastes, and that is precisely where we are going to use it.

But we are not going to use it in Keynesian models. Such models are best understood as dealing with the short run, and for reasons well summarized in the survey literature [1, 2, 3], the short-run, that is, the cyclical, consumption function is nonhomogeneous with a positive constant term; hence it has a marginal propensity to consume that is lower than the average one.

REFERENCES

[1] Ando, A., and F. Modigliani, "The 'Life Cycle' Hypothesis of Saving: Aggregate Implications and Tests," *Am. Econ. Rev.*, **53**, 55–84, especially 76–82 (March 1963).
[2] Farrell, M. J., "The New Theories of the Consumption Function," *Econ. Jour.*, **69**, 678–696, especially 682–687 (December 1959).
[3] Ferber, R., "Research on Household Behavior," *Am. Econ. Rev.*, **52**, 19–63, especially 20–32 (March 1962).

CHAPTER 34

A Truncated Keynesian Model*

34.1 INTRODUCTION

Compared to general-equilibrium models the Keynesian model is dramatically simple. Heavy aggregation reduces the number of its variables so drastically that simple algebra or geometry, or even verbal reasoning, can handle them. The ease of handling the Keynesian model was one important reason for its swift acceptance. Another was the practical importance of the questions to which it offered an answer: Mass unemployment, wartime inflation, the limits of monetary policy, and the threat of long-run stagnation.

Let us examine the Keynesian model in two steps. First, we shall set forth a truncated version and later its complete version. The truncated version has in it, first, firms producing net national output X out of which they invest I, and second, households earning the net national money income Y out of which they consume C. Perhaps the truncated version is best understood as our one-country general-equilibrium model as set forth in Chapter 25 but modified in three respects.

First, Keynesians ignore the composition of national output and think of it as composed of unspecified universal goods capable of being consumed as well as invested.

Second, Keynesians ignore inputs and input restrictions; therefore output is determined by aggregate demand alone. Output thus determined may absorb less than available inputs and leave the rest idle. It may fortuitously absorb exactly the available inputs. Or it may tend to absorb more than that with inflation resulting.

Third, Keynesians take the first step away from the stationary economy by assuming that households save and firms invest. However, it is only a first step. Capital stock—supposedly augmented by net investment—is ignored,

* Chapters 25 and 33 are prerequisites for Chapter 34.

and the solution of a Keynesian model gives us the equilibrium level of output, not a time path of output.

34.2 NOTATION

In our truncated Keynesian model the following notation will be assigned.

Variables

C = country's output consumed
X = net national output
Y = net national money income

Parameters

A = autonomous consumption
c = marginal propensity to consume
I = autonomous net investment
P = price of country's output
$\bar{X}$ = net national output using up all available input

The variables C and X and the parameters I and $\bar{X}$ are measured in physical units of output. Each unit carries the fixed price tag P.

34.3 CONSUMPTION

In this model, may we apply the result, Eq. (28), of Chapter 33? As we have already mentioned, (28) is ill suited for explaining the short run, and Keynesian models are best understood as dealing with the short run other-wise, how could they treat net investment as positive, yet ignore capital stock? And how could they be concerned with the equilibrium level of output rather than the time path of output?

For reasons well summarized in the survey literature [1, 2, 3], the short-run (that is, cyclical) consumption function is

(1) $$C = A + cX$$

where $A > 0$, and $0 < c < 1$. As we shall see in Eq. (7), X may also be written as net national real income Y/P.

34.4 EQUILIBRIUM

Equilibrium requires the sum of consumption and investment demand to equal output, or inventory would accumulate or be depleted:

(2) $$X = C + I$$

34.5 SOLUTION

Insert (1) into (2) and solve for net national output

(3)
$$X = \frac{A + I}{1 - c}$$

where

$$X \le \bar{X}$$

or, expressed in words: The output solution (3) is assumed to be a feasible one, that is, one requiring quantities of the (unspecified) inputs which are less than or equal to those available. The upper bound $\bar{X}$ is the net national output which would use up all available input. Under this assumption output (3) is determined by demand alone and equals the sum of autonomous consumption and net investment divided by the marginal propensity to save.

Let us take a closer look at the possible patterns of the solution (3). In a diagram measure output X on the horizontal axis and aggregate demand $C + I$ on the vertical one. The equilibrium condition that the two be equal will then appear as the familiar 45° line, always shown as a broken line in our diagrams. Add I on both sides of (1) and arrive at a second relationship between $C + I$ and X, that is, $C + I = A + I + cX$. This relationship is shown as a solid line in our diagrams. At equilibrium, net national output must satisfy both relationships. Consequently, output must be the abscissa to the point of intersection between the broken and the solid line, if any.

In Fig. 34.1, $A + I > 0$ and $c = 1$. The broken and the solid lines are parallel. No point of intersection, hence no equilibrium output, exists.

In Fig. 34.2, $A + I > 0$ and $c > 1$. The two lines will certainly intersect, but equilibrium output will be negative.

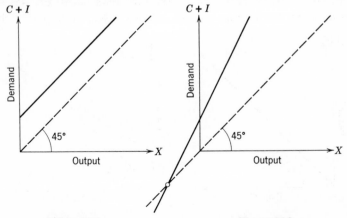

Figure 34.1   Figure 34.2

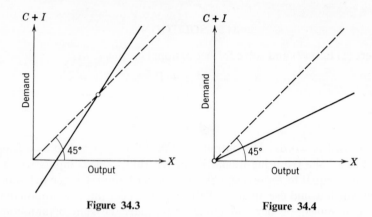

Figure 34.3   Figure 34.4

In Fig. 34.3, $A + I < 0$ and $c > 1$. The lines will intersect in the first quadrant, and equilibrium output will be positive.

In Fig. 34.4, $A + I = 0$ and $c < 1$. The lines will intersect in the point of origin (as they would have done if $c > 1$), and equilibrium output is zero.

In Fig. 34.5, $A + I = 0$ and $c = 1$. The lines will coincide; hence any output will satisfy both relationships, and equilibrium output is not unique.

Simple as it is, then, the Keynesian truncated model is still rich enough to permit such unpleasant outcomes as output being not positive or not unique. Fortunately, in the real world $A + I > 0$ and $c < 1$. In that case, as shown in Fig. 34.6, output will be positive and unique. But so it was in Fig. 34.3; then why should Fig. 34.6 be superior to Fig. 34.3? The equilibrium in Fig. 34.6 is superior, because it is stable. To see this, note that in Fig. 34.6 the aggregate demand curve, the solid line, runs above the 45° line for outputs less than equilibrium output, but below the 45° line for outputs in

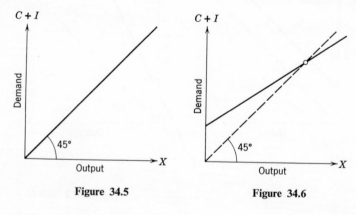

Figure 34.5   Figure 34.6

excess of equilibrium output. Consequently, when output is less than equilibrium output, aggregate demand exceeds output, and inventory must fall, which induces firms to increase their output. And when output is in excess of equilibrium output, aggregate demand falls short of output, and inventory must accumulate, which induces firms to decrease their output. Therefore, in Fig. 34.6, if output deviates from equilibrium, the deviation releases forces pulling output back to equilibrium. In Fig. 34.3, by contrast, the deviation releases forces pulling output even farther away from equilibrium. The equilibrium in Fig. 34.3, then, is inferior because it is unstable.

34.6 NUMERICAL EXERCISE

Let us choose the following set of numerical values for our parameters:

$$A = 30$$
$$c = \tfrac{3}{4}$$
$$I = 21$$

This, by the way, is the numerical example underlying Fig. 1 of the Introduction to this book. For these three values Eq. (3) will give us the solution

$$X = 204$$

Let us vary each of the three values in turn and watch the effect upon X. The results are shown in Fig. 34.7 through 34.9. The figures use double-logarithmic scales to permit the elasticities of output with respect to autonomous consumption A, the marginal propensity to consume c, and autonomous net investment I to appear visibly as the steepness of the curves. The elasticity with respect to I is seen to be moderate, somewhat higher with respect to A, and very high indeed, with respect to c.

34.7 DERIVING THE ELASTICITIES

More generally, the three elasticities may be derived directly from the solution (3):

(4)
$$\frac{\partial X}{\partial A} \frac{A}{X} = \frac{A}{A + I}$$

(5)
$$\frac{\partial X}{\partial c} \frac{c}{X} = \frac{c}{1 - c}$$

(6)
$$\frac{\partial X}{\partial I} \frac{I}{X} = \frac{I}{A + I}$$

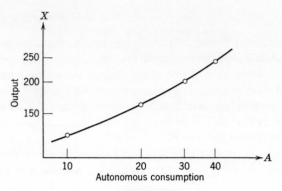

Figure 34.7

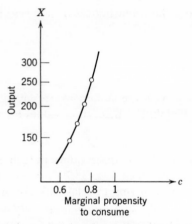

Figure 34.8

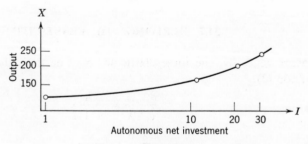

Figure 34.9

342

Under the realistic assumptions that $A > 0$, $0 < c < 1$, and $I > 0$, all three elasticities are positive. Thus equilibrium output will rise if autonomous consumption rises, if the marginal propensity to consume rises, or if autonomous net investment rises. Moreover, both (4) and (6) are less than one; thus equilibrium output always rises in less than proportion to A and I. Under the additional realistic assumption that $c > \frac{1}{2}$, (5) is greater than one; hence equilibrium output always rises in more than proportion to c.

34.8   NET NATIONAL MONEY INCOME

Net national money income is defined as the money value of net national output:

$$(7) \qquad\qquad Y = PX$$

Hence, given the solution (3), we also have a solution for net national money income Y. However, since the consumption function (1) had no money illusion in it, we never really need net national money income Y in our truncated Keynesian model. As for the price of output, P does not appear in (3); hence it has no effect upon equilibrium net national output. This will be very different in the complete Keynesian model.

34.9   CONCLUSION

Assuming that the sum of autonomous consumption and net investment $A + I$ is positive and that the marginal propensity to consume c is less than one, we have found that equilibrium net national output is positive and unique. We have also found that it rises if autonomous consumption rises, if the marginal propensity to consume rises, or if autonomous net investment rises.

For these simple results we have paid a fourfold price. First, the Keynesian model is aggregative: No attempt is made to examine the composition of net national output. Second, the model is static: It determines an equilibrium level, not an equilibrium time path. Third, the model is an equilibrium model: Only in equilibrium will aggregate demand and aggregate output have to be equal. Fourth, the equilibrium is a short-run flow equilibrium: On long-run stock equilibrium of inventory, not to speak of capital stock, the model is silent.

REFERENCES

[1] Ando, A., and F. Modigliani, "The 'Life Cycle' Hypothesis of Saving: Aggregate Implications and Tests," *Am. Econ. Rev.*, **53**, 55–84, especially 76–82 (March 1963).
[2] Farrell, M. J., "The New Theories of the Consumption Function," *Econ. Jour.*, **69**, 678–696, especially 682–684 (December 1959).
[3] Ferber, R., "Research on Household Behavior," *Am. Econ. Rev.*, **52**, 19–63, especially 20–32 (March 1962).

CHAPTER 35

The Complete Keynesian Model*

35.1 INTRODUCTION

Like the truncated Keynesian model the complete Keynesian model [10] contains, first, firms producing the net national output X out of which they invest I, second, households earning the net national money income Y out of which they consume C. However, in addition to this real sphere, the complete Keynesian model has a money sphere in which, third, asset owners may hold their assets either in the form of bonds or in the form of money H. Money demanded for asset-holding H plus money demanded for transactions T must add up to the total money supply M supplied by fourth, the monetary authorities.

The truncated Keynesian model was a linear and very simple model of equilibrium output. The complete Keynesian model is a nonlinear and not quite so simple model of both equilibrium output and equilibrium rate of interest. Perhaps because it is nonlinear and contains more variables than the truncated one does, the complete Keynesian model is rarely solved algebraically. Usually a multistage graphical solution is suggested [4, 7]. The purpose of this chapter is, first, to offer an unabashed algebraic solution, second, to show (in Section 35.7) how two important stumbling blocks to easy money result from the nonlinearities of the complete Keynesian model.

35.2 NOTATION

In our complete Keynesian model the following notation will be assigned.

Variables

$C =$ country's output consumed
$I =$ net investment

* Chapter 34 is a prerequisite for Chapter 35.

i = rate of interest
H = demand for money for asset-holding purposes
T = demand for money for transactions purposes
X = net national output
Y = net national money income

Parameters

A = autonomous consumption
c = marginal propensity to consume
j = a parameter of the investment ellipse
k = a parameter of the investment ellipse
l = the reciprocal of the velocity of transaction money T
M = money supply
m = a parameter of the liquidity-preference hyperbola
n = a parameter of the liquidity-preference hyperbola
P = price of country's output

The variables C, I, and X are measured in physical units of output. These units carry the price tag P. The variables H, T, and Y and the parameter M are measured in monetary units. The variable i is a pure number per unit of time.

35.3   THE REAL-SPHERE BEHAVIOR EQUATIONS

The consumption function is the same as that of the truncated model:

$$(1) \qquad\qquad C = A + cX$$

However, net investment is no longer a parameter but a variable depending upon the rate of interest. Depending how? Hansen [5] has summarized much of the debate in the statement that the investment curve "is fairly elastic with respect to the rate of interest at *high* interest rate levels, and is fairly inelastic within a rather wide range of interest rates at the *lower* levels." An ellipse-shaped curve represented by the equation

$$(2) \qquad\qquad I = \sqrt{j - ki^2}$$

would have the property described by Hansen. In (2) j is a positive parameter whose square root measures the maximum volume of investment possible, that is, that which would result from a zero rate of interest. It is assumed that $i < \sqrt{j/k}$, for otherwise I would be either zero or a complex number. An ellipse can be thought of as a stretched circle, and the parameter k determines the extent of the stretching. We are ignoring the part of the ellipse lying outside the first quadrant.

35.4 THE MONEY-SPHERE BEHAVIOR EQUATIONS

Neither firms nor households can fully synchronize income and outlay; hence they need transaction money. What do they want to transact? We ignore both intermediate goods transacted among firms and old paintings, used cars, used houses, etc., and say that $Y = PX$, the money value of net national output, is all that must be transacted. Follow tradition and make the transaction demand for money a linear and homogeneous function of the money value of output:

$$(3) \qquad\qquad T = lPX$$

where l is a positive parameter representing the reciprocal of the velocity of circulation of transaction money.

Keynesian asset holders may hold their assets in only two forms, bonds or money. Define the interest rate as the effective bond yield. If the interest rate is high, it is because bond prices are low; hence they may be expected to rise, and asset owners will prefer to hold bonds. If the interest rate is low, it is because bond prices are high; hence they may be expected to fall, and asset owners will prefer to hold money. From all this we should expect the demand for money for asset-holding purposes to be a downward-sloping function of the interest rate. The reason it is not L-shaped is that at a given price of bonds, all asset owners do not have the same expectations of future bond prices. Only at extremely low bond prices will every asset owner expect them to rise, and only at extremely high bond prices will every asset owner expect them to fall. Therefore, at the former extreme all assets will be held in bond form; at the latter extreme all assets will be held in money form. As we shall see presently, econometric estimates of the liquidity-preference function suggest a hyperbolic form; hence let us adopt the form

$$(4) \qquad\qquad H = \frac{m}{i - n}$$

where m is a positive parameter depending upon the total mass of assets and where it is assumed that $n < i$; for otherwise H would be meaningless or negative. The asymptotes of the hyperbola (4) are the i-axis and the line parallel to the H-axis at a distance n from the H-axis. We are ignoring the parts of the hyperbola lying outside the first quadrant.

35.5 TWO EQUILIBRIUM CONDITIONS

In both the goods and the money spheres demand must equal supply. First, in the goods sphere equilibrium requires that output equal demand:

$$(5) \qquad\qquad X = C + I$$

Second, in the money sphere the sum of the demand for money for transaction and for asset-holding purposes must equal the money supply. If it did not, one of two things would be true. Either asset owners would want to hold more money than is available and in their attempts to get it they would be selling bonds, thereby depressing bond prices, raising the interest rate, and making money less attractive to hold. Or conversely, asset owners would want to hold less money than is available and in their attempts to get rid of it they would be buying bonds, thereby raising bond prices, depressing the interest rate, and making money more attractive to hold. Consequently, in equilibrium

$$(6) \qquad\qquad M = H + T$$

35.6 SOLUTION

Now let us solve our six equations in six variables for output X, obtaining the following fourth-degree equation in X alone:

$$(7) \qquad\qquad \alpha_1 X^4 + \alpha_2 X^3 + \alpha_3 X^2 + \alpha_4 X + \alpha_5 = 0$$

where

$$\alpha_1 = (1 - c)^2 l^2 P^2$$

$$\alpha_2 = -(1 - c)2lP[AlP + (1 - c)M]$$

$$\alpha_3 = (1 - c)M[4AlP + (1 - c)M] + l^2 P^2(A^2 - j + kn^2)$$

$$\alpha_4 = -2M[AM(1 - c) + (A^2 - j)lP] - 2klnP(m + nM)$$

$$\alpha_5 = (A^2 - j)M^2 + k(m + nM)^2$$

Quite a solution! To illustrate it, let us select the following set of values of our parameters:

$A = 30$	$k = 10{,}000$	$m = 1.16$
$c = 0.75$	$l = 0.50$	$n = 0.02$
$j = 457$	$M = 160$	$P = 1$

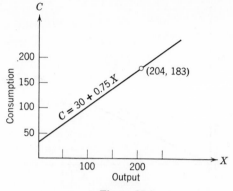

Figure 35.1

For these values our behavior equations will appear as shown in Figs. 35.1 through 35.4, and Eq. (7) now is:

(7a) $0.015625X^4 - 13.75X^3 + 4111.75X^2 - 455,752X + 11,530,900 = 0$

Of the four roots of the polynomial (7a) only one lies within the domain prescribed for our Eqs. (2) and (4), that is, the domain in which $n < i < \sqrt{j/k}$. That root is $X = 204$. Putting it back into Eqs. (1) through (6) gives us the real, positive, and unique solutions of the whole system:

$C = 183$ $i = 0.04$ $T = 102$

$I = 21$ $H = 58$ $X = 204$

For each behavior function in Figs. 35.1 through 35.4, a small circle indicates one pair of those six solution values.

As we did in the truncated Keynesian model, we shall assume the solution for output to be a feasible one, that is, that output requires quantities of the

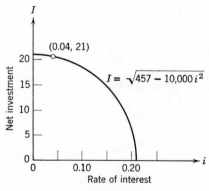

Figure 35.2

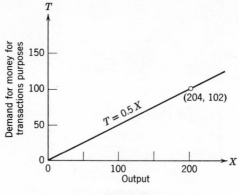

Figure 35.3

(unspecified) inputs which are less than or equal to those available. Under this assumption, output is determined by aggregate demand alone.

Now let us vary each of the parameters A, c, j, l, M, m, and n in turn and watch the effects upon X. To each parameter we have attached three alternative values different from the first value used while keeping the values of all other parameters equal to the corresponding first value used. Consequently, we obtain four different observations of (7) for each parameter, or 22 different versions of (7). The resulting solutions are shown on double-logarithmic scales in Figs. 35.5 through 35.11.

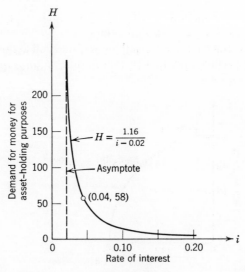

Figure 35.4

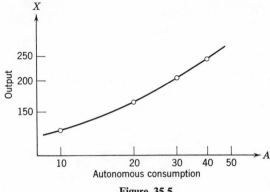

Figure 35.5

35.7 FISCAL AND MONETARY POLICY

The policy implications of Fig. 35.5 through 35.11 are clear: Within the domains studied, the parameter to whose changes output is most sensitive is the marginal propensity to consume c. No other curve is as steep as the $X-c$ curve in Fig. 35.6. But how could public policy affect c? We remember that c is the marginal propensity to consume net national product. This propensity can be raised by reducing the marginal personal income tax rate (not explicitly included in the model), provided the propensity to consume disposable income stays put. Such a tax reduction will raise the disposable income paid out of a given net national product.

As regards monetary policy, output is seen to be sensitive to changes in the money supply M only in the left-hand side of the $X-M$ curve in Fig. 35.9, that is, when the economy is starved for money. This was true after 1952 in the United States, and monetary policy seemed potent enough. However,

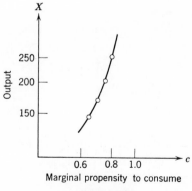

Figure 35.6

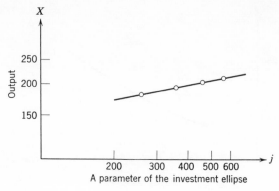

Figure 35.7

twenty years earlier the economy had not been starved for money, and monetary policy seemed impotent. After 1952 monetary policy was supposed to, and actually did, check inflation. After 1932 monetary policy was supposed to, but did not quite, initiate an expansion. This experience is sometimes summarized by saying that monetary policy can contract an economy but cannot expand one. Such a statement implies irreversibility, but we do not need irreversibility to explain 1952 and 1932. The X–M curve in Fig. 35.9 has no irreversibility; all we need is its curvature. As Samuelson [16] has put it:

"In buoyant times when interest rates are already high and credit already tight, monetary policy is quite potent enough to *both* expand and contract the system from its previous situation; in slack times when interest rates are near the floor and the system is swimming in liquidity, monetary policy is quite impotent with respect to contraction *and* expansion of the system from its previous level."

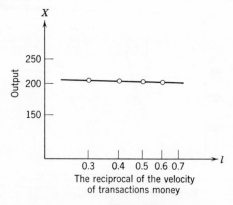

Figure 35.8

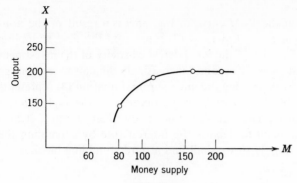

Figure 35.9

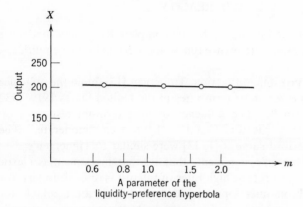

Figure 35.10

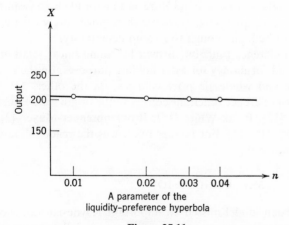

Figure 35.11

353

The peculiar shape of the $X-M$ curve in Fig. 35.9 is a result of the nonlinearities of Eqs. (2) and (4). Equation (2) represents the first stumbling block to easy money: Because of the low interest elasticity of the investment function at low interest rates, it becomes increasingly difficult to encourage additional investment by depressing the interest rate. Equation (4) represents the second stumbling block to easy money: Because of the high interest elasticity of the liquidity-preference function at low interest rates, it also becomes increasingly difficult to depress the interest rate by expanding the money supply. (In Section 35.10 we shall find a third stumbling block in an open economy.)

35.8 CONFRONTATION OF BEHAVIOR EQUATIONS WITH REALITY

The new behavior equations added by the complete Keynesian model are the investment and liquidity-preference functions. What is known empirically about their shapes?

With regard to the investment function, Tinbergen [17] found the influence of discount rates and other short-term rates in the United States 1919–1932 to have been "very small." The influence of long term-interest rates on investment in durable goods was found to have been "moderate." The findings of the two Oxford surveys [1, 13] were similar to Tinbergen's.

The first half of Hansen's statement, that is, that investment is elastic with respect to the interest rate at high rates of interest is difficult to test, for in mature capitalist economies for which data and tools are available for testing, the rate of interest has never been very high. But on *a priori* grounds the statement sounds plausible. Henderson [6] and others have pointed to uncertainty of demand and cost in a distant future as a factor likely to swamp the interest rate in long-range planning. However there must surely exist an interest rate which would be high enough to swamp uncertainty.

As for the liquidity-preference function, Brown [3] found linear relationships between the demand for money for asset-holding purposes, on the one hand, and interest rate and wholesale price changes, on the other. More Keynesian-like liquidity-preference functions convex to the origin were found by Tobin [18], Latané [12], Polak-White [15], Bronfenbrenner-Mayer [2], and Scandinavian writers [11, 14]. For further references the reader should consult the survey literature [9].

35.9 CONCLUSION

The truncated Keynesian model missed an important Keynesian achievement, the successful integration of the theory of money and the theory of goods output.

To begin with, we now have a threefold symmetry between the money sphere and the goods sphere: First, in both spheres there was the equilibrium condition that demand and supply be equal. Equality between demand and supply in the goods market defined the equilibrium level of output, and equality between demand and supply in the money market defined the equilibrium level of the rate of interest. Second, in both spheres demand was composed of two parts, one depending upon the level of output (the consumption function and the transaction-money function) and another depending upon the rate of interest (the investment function and the liquidity-preference function). Third, the symmetry between the two spheres was complete in that the two functions whose independent variable was the level of output were both linear, whereas the two functions whose independent variable was the rate of interest were both nonlinear.

One important asymmetry between the two spheres was pointed out by Hicks [8]. Within a given period we may choose price as a parameter and let quantity transacted be the variable to be explained, and this was what Keynes did in his goods sphere. The resulting equilibrium would be a flow equilibrium ensuring absence of inventory accumulation or depletion, but it would not necessarily be a stock equilibrium: The actual inventory co-efficient could differ from the desired one, not to mention that the actual capital coefficient could differ from the desired one.

However, we could choose instead quantity transacted as a parameter and let price be the variable to be explained, and this was what Keynes did in his money sphere. Here, the stock of bonds would at any moment of time be given, and the price of bonds would be determined by the willingness of the asset owners to hold bonds rather than money. Such a stock equilibrium would ignore the flow of additions to, and the flow of subtractions from, the stock of bonds. Such flows could be ignored only by using a period of time so short that it would approximate a point in time. Thus, according to Hicks, Keynes boiled down the whole economy into two markets only: the first a quantity market ignoring stocks, and the second a price market ignoring flows, both markets being linked together by the rate of interest.

35.10 EASY MONEY: AN OPEN-ECONOMY RESERVATION

The complete Keynesian model as now described was a model of a closed economy. Until caught in the Keynesian liquidity trap, a closed-economy central bank could expand net national output by open-market operations: Its purchase of bonds would raise the price of such bonds and put cash into the hands of the country's bondholders.

In an open economy there may be an additional stumbling block to easy money. Assume the existence of foreign bondholders. At long-run fixed exchange rates, these foreign bondholders will represent a practically infinitely price-elastic supply of foreign bonds whenever the domestic price of bonds rises ever so slightly above the foreign price of similar bonds. At that point further purchase of bonds by the domestic central bank will encounter a ceiling to the price of bonds. Encountering that ceiling, the bank cannot increase the price of bonds any further and can put no further cash into the hands of the country's own bondholders. Instead, it will put cash (ultimately gold) into the hands of foreign bondholders.

United States monetary experience in the early 1960's illustrates the helplessness of an open-economy central bank trying to keep domestic interest rates low by purchasing bonds in the open market. Eventually, the government came to its help and raised the ceiling by announcing in 1963 and enacting in 1964 the interest-equalization tax on foreign bonds acquired by United States residents. Thereafter, to the price-elastic supply curve of foreign bonds would have to be added the amount of the tax on acquisition.

REFERENCES

[1] Andrews, P. W. S., "A Further Inquiry into the Effects of Rates of Interest," *Oxford Economic Papers*, **3**, 32–73 (March 1940). (Reprinted in *Oxford Studies in the Price Mechanism*, edited by T. Wilson and P. W. S. Andrews, Oxford, 1951, pp. 51–67.)

[2] Bronfenbrenner, M., and T. Mayer, "Liquidity Functions in the American Economy," *Econometrica*, **28**, 810–834 (October 1960).

[3] Brown, A. J., "Interest, Prices, and the Demand Schedule for Idle Money," *Oxford Economic Papers*, **2**, 46–69 (May 1939). (Reprinted in *Oxford Studies in the Price Mechanism*, edited by T. Wilson and P. W. S. Andrews, Oxford, 1951, pp. 31–51.)

[4] Hansen, A. H., *Business Cycles and National Income* (New York, 1951, p. 133).

[5] Hansen, A. H., *Monetary Theory and Fiscal Policy*, New York, 1949.

[6] Henderson, H. D., "The Significance of the Rate of Interest," *Oxford Economic Papers*, **1**, 1–13 (October 1938). (Reprinted in *Oxford Studies in the Price Mechanism*, edited by T. Wilson and P. W. S. Andrews, Oxford, 1951, pp. 16–27.)

[7] Hicks, J. R., "Mr. Keynes and the 'Classics', a suggested Interpretation," *Econometrica*, **5**, 147–159 (April 1937). (Reprinted in *Readings in the Theory of Income Distribution*, edited by B. F. Haley and W. Fellner, Philadelphia, 1946, pp. 461–476.)

[8] Hicks, J. R., "Methods of Dynamic Analysis," in *25 Essays in Honour of Erik Lindahl, 21 November 1956*, Stockholm, 1956, pp. 139–151. (Further elaborated in Hicks, J. R., *Capital and Growth*, Oxford, 1965.)

[9] Johnson, H. G., "Monetary Theory and Policy," *Am. Econ. Rev.*, **52**, especially 345–357 (June 1962).

[10] Keynes, J. M., *The General Theory of Employment, Interest, and Money*, London, 1936.

[11] Kragh, B., *Prisbildningen på kreditmarknaden*, Uppsala, Sweden, 1951.

[12] Latané, H. A., "Cash Balances and the Interest Rate—A Pragmatic Approach," *Rev. Econ. Stat.*, **36**, 456–460 (November 1954).

[13] Meade, J. E., and P. W. S. Andrews, "Summary of Replies to Questions on Effects of Interest Rates," *Oxford Economic Papers*, **1**, 14–31 (October 1938). (Reprinted in

Oxford Studies in the Price Mechanism, edited by T. Wilson and P. W. S. Andrews, Oxford, 1951, pp. 27–30.)

[14] Philip, K., "A Statistical Measurement of the Liquidity Preference of Private Banks," *Rev. Econ. Stud.*, 1949–1950, 71–77.

[15] Polak, J. J., and W. H. White, "The Effect of Income Expansion on the Quantity of Money," *International Monetary Fund Staff Papers*, **4**, 398–433 (August 1955).

[16] Samuelson, P. A., "Reflections on Central Banking," *Nat. Banking Rev.*, **1**, 15–28 (September 1963).

[17] Tinbergen, J., *Business Cycles in the United States of America*, Geneva, 1939, p. 184.

[18] Tobin, J., "Liquidity Preference and Monetary Policy," *Rev. Econ. Stat.*, **29**, 124–131 (May 1947).

CHAPTER 36

A Keynesian Two-Country Model*

36.1 INTRODUCTION

A Keynesian two-country model is, perhaps, best understood as the two-country general-equilibrium model that was described in Chapter 26, but modified in three respects.

First, Keynesians simplify things by ignoring the composition of national output; therefore they think of Country 1's national output as composed of unspecified Country 1 Goods and of Country 2's national output as composed of unspecified Country 2 Goods. Think of Country 1 Goods and Country 2 Goods as substitutes but not perfect ones (much like the complete-specialization case) but also think of them as universal goods capable of being consumed, invested, or exported. For simplicity we shall assume that consumers in both countries demand their country's own goods as well as imported ones, but that firms invest in their own country's goods only.

Second, as we have already seen in the closed-economy Keynesian model, Keynesians ignore inputs and input restrictions. Third, assume that households save and firms invest.

36.2 NOTATION

In our two-country Keynesian model the following notation will be assigned.

Variables

C_{ji} = ith country's output consumed in jth country

* Chapters 26 and 34 are prerequisites for Chapter 36.

E = exchange rate, in number of monetary units of Country 1 equivalent to one monetary unit of Country 2

P_i = price of ith country's output expressed in ith country's monetary unit

U_{ik} = utility to kth person in ith country, resulting from his consumption

X_i = ith country's net national output

Y_i = ith country's net national money income

Parameters

A_i = elasticity of utility with respect to first country's output consumed in ith country

B_i = elasticity of utility with respect to second country's output consumed in ith country

c_i = propensity to consume in ith country

I_i = autonomous net investment of ith country in its own products

N_i = multiplicative factor in the utility functions in ith country

The variables C_{ji} and X_i and the parameter I_i are measured in physical units of output of the ith country. These units carry the price tag P_i expressed in the ith country's monetary unit. Subscripts $i = j = 1$, 2 refer to the two countries.

To illuminate alternative economic policies we shall switch variables and parameters around somewhat: In Section 36.9, E and P_i are both parameters; in Sections 36.10 and 36.11, E is a parameter, but the ratio P_1/P_2 is a variable; and in Sections 36.12 and 36.13, P_i is a parameter, but E is a variable.

36.3   UTILITY FUNCTIONS

Within each country let all persons have the same utility function, and let it be of Cobb-Douglas form. However, the utility functions may differ between countries. The utility functions of the kth person in the first and second country are, respectively:

$$U_{1k} = N_1 C_{11k}{}^{A_1} C_{12k}{}^{B_1}$$

$$U_{2k} = N_2 C_{21k}{}^{A_2} C_{22k}{}^{B_2}$$

where A_i and B_i are parameters lying between zero and one, and where N_i is a positive multiplicative factor dependent upon the units of measurement. It is unnecessary to assume that $A_1 \gtrless A_2$, that $B_2 \gtrless B_1$, or that $A_i + B_i = 1$, $i = 1, 2$.

36.4 BUDGET CONSTRAINTS

Let X_{ik} be the kth person's contribution to the ith country's net national output; thus his money income is $Y_{ik} = P_i X_{ik}$. Now let all persons in the ith country spend the same fraction c_i of their money income on consumption of their country's own products as well as imported ones. Then the budget constraints of the kth person in each of the two countries are

$$c_1 P_1 X_{1k} = P_1 C_{11k} + E P_2 C_{12k}$$

$$c_2 P_2 X_{2k} = \frac{P_1}{E} C_{21k} + P_2 C_{22k}$$

where c_i is a parameter lying between zero and one, $i = 1, 2$. Note that in the first country, C_{12k} is import carrying the price tag P_2. For a resident in that country, the price P_2 must be multiplied by the exchange rate E in order to be expressed in the monetary units he uses. In the second country, C_{21k} is import carrying the price tag P_1. For a resident in the second country, the price P_1 must be divided by the exchange rate E in order to be expressed in the monetary units he uses.

36.5 UTILITY MAXIMIZATION

By applying the standard method of maximizing the kth persons' utility, subject to his budget constraint, we find the following four demand functions of the kth person in the first and second countries, respectively:

$$C_{11k} = \frac{c_1 A_1}{A_1 + B_1} X_{1k} \qquad C_{12k} = \frac{c_1 B_1}{A_1 + B_1} \frac{P_1}{E P_2} X_{1k}$$

$$C_{21k} = \frac{c_2 A_2}{A_2 + B_2} \frac{E P_2}{P_1} X_{2k} \qquad C_{22k} = \frac{c_2 B_2}{A_2 + B_2} X_{2k}$$

36.6 AGGREGATION

As Keynesians we must aggregate, and our assumptions, that within each country all persons have the same utility function and the same propensity to consume, make the task an easy one. Let the ith country have s_i persons; if we add the s_i demand functions for each good in each country, we find the four national aggregate demand functions in the first and second countries:

$$\sum_{k=1}^{s_1} C_{11k} = \frac{c_1 A_1}{A_1 + B_1} \sum_{k=1}^{s_1} X_{1k} \qquad \sum_{k=1}^{s_1} C_{12k} = \frac{c_1 B_1}{A_1 + B_1} \frac{P_1}{EP_2} \sum_{k=1}^{s_1} X_{1k}$$

$$\sum_{k=1}^{s_2} C_{21k} = \frac{c_2 A_2}{A_2 + B_2} \frac{EP_2}{P_1} \sum_{k=1}^{s_2} X_{2k} \qquad \sum_{k=1}^{s_2} C_{22k} = \frac{c_2 B_2}{A_2 + B_2} \sum_{k=1}^{s_2} X_{2k}$$

or simply

(1)
$$C_{11} = \frac{c_1 A_1}{A_1 + B_1} X_1$$

(2)
$$C_{12} = \frac{c_1 B_1}{A_1 + B_1} \frac{P_1}{EP_2} X_1$$

(3)
$$C_{21} = \frac{c_2 A_2}{A_2 + B_2} \frac{EP_2}{P_1} X_2$$

(4)
$$C_{22} = \frac{c_2 B_2}{A_2 + B_2} X_2$$

Equations (1) and (4) are demand for domestic products. Here all prices have disappeared, for the output which generates income carries the same price tag as do the products demanded; hence that price tag does not matter. Equations (2) and (3), by contrast, are demand for imported products. Here the output which generates income carries one country's price tag, whereas the products demanded carry the other country's price tag. Consequently, the relative price tags as well as the exchange rate do matter, hence enter Eqs. (2) and (3) as they should.

Thus from our individual utility and spending functions we have derived aggregate consumption functions (1) and (4) whose income elasticity is *plus* one and whose cross-elasticity with respect to the price of import and the exchange rate is zero. We have also derived the aggregate import functions (2) and (3) whose income elasticity is *plus* one and whose direct price elasticity is *minus* one.

36.7 DOMESTIC EQUILIBRIUM

Domestic equilibrium requires the sum of consumption, investment, and export demand for national output to equal national output; otherwise, inventory would either accumulate or be depleted:

(5)
$$X_1 = C_{11} + I_1 + C_{21}$$

(6)
$$X_2 = C_{22} + I_2 + C_{12}$$

36.8 INTERNATIONAL EQUILIBRIUM

International equilibrium requires the balance of payment, when measured in any country's monetary unit, say the first, to equal zero:

$$(7) \qquad P_1 C_{21} - E P_2 C_{12} = 0$$

or first country's export *minus* its import equals zero. Since each country's export is the other country's import, it follows from (7) that second country's import *minus* its export also equals zero.

36.9 IGNORING THE INTERNATIONAL EQUILIBRIUM REQUIREMENT

Few voters are concerned with international equilibrium, and many politicians distrust the price mechanism. Like these politicians, but for a very different reason, the theorist may recoil from a system such as Eqs. (1) through (7). His reason is this: If either the exchange rate E or the price ratio P_1/P_2 is a variable, the system is a nonlinear one. To avoid this, the theorist might eliminate Eq. (7) and consider E and P_1/P_2 parameters. That would give him a neat linear system of six equations in the six variables C_{11}, C_{12}, C_{21}, C_{22}, X_1, and X_2. Its solutions for the two national outputs would be

$$(8) \qquad X_1 = \frac{I_1 + I_2 \dfrac{c_2 A_2}{A_2 + (1 - c_2)B_2} \dfrac{EP_2}{P_1}}{1 - \dfrac{c_1}{A_1 + B_1}\left[A_1 + \dfrac{c_2 A_2 B_1}{A_2 + (1 - c_2)B_2}\right]}$$

$$(9) \qquad X_2 = \frac{I_2 + I_1 \dfrac{c_1 B_1}{(1 - c_1)A_1 + B_1} \dfrac{P_1}{EP_2}}{1 - \dfrac{c_2}{A_2 + B_2}\left[B_2 + \dfrac{c_1 A_2 B_1}{(1 - c_1)A_1 + B_1}\right]}$$

Solutions (8) and (9) are complicated to say the least. Equilibrium output in each country depends upon all the parameters of *both* countries. In this sense the two countries are highly dependent upon each other. Solutions (8) and (9) are examples of the pure "absorption" approach to international trade theory. Matters will be greatly simplified, and the mutual dependence of the two countries greatly reduced, if the price mechanism is allowed to function, that is, if the "absorption" approach marries the "elasticity" approach.

The price mechanism, however, has two distinct parts: First, there is the internal price mechanism consisting of price-level adjustments. Second, there is the external price mechanism consisting of exchange-rate adjustments. We shall examine each part in turn.

36.10   THE INTERNAL PRICE MECHANISM

The system studied in Section 36.9 will only balance international trade fortuitously, because the balancing Eq. (7) was eliminated from it. Now we restore Eq. (7), and assuming that the relative price level of a country may be controlled by monetary policy, we make the price ratio P_1/P_2 a variable. The exchange rate E is still considered a parameter. As a result, we now have a system of seven equations in the seven variables C_{11}, C_{12}, C_{21}, C_{22}, P_1/P_2, X_1, and X_2. However as we saw, the system is a nonlinear one, for Eqs. (2), (3), and (7) now contain products of variables. As we shall now see, however, the nonlinearities will disappear in the process of solving the system.

Use (5), (7), (1), and (2) in that order and find the first country's national output

$$(10) \qquad X_1 = \frac{I_1}{1 - c_1}$$

Use (6), (7), (4), and (3) in that order and find the second country's national output

$$(11) \qquad X_2 = \frac{I_2}{1 - c_2}$$

The propensities to consume c_i were assumed to lie between zero and one, $i = 1, 2$. If we assume that the autonomous investment I_i is positive, the national outputs as determined by (10) and (11) must be positive.

The solutions (10) and (11) are as simple as (8) and (9) were complicated. In fact, (10) and (11) look exactly like the standard Keynesian output solution for the one-country case, ignoring autonomous consumption. Thus, under flexible relative prices, equilibrium national output in each country is seen to depend upon the parameters of that country alone, not upon those of the other country. In this sense the two countries are now highly independent of each other—highly but not fully independent, as we shall see in Section 36.14.

How precisely equilibrium national output depends upon the national parameters is shown by the four multipliers:

(12) $$\frac{\partial X_1}{\partial c_1} = \frac{X_1}{1 - c_1}$$

(13) $$\frac{\partial X_2}{\partial c_2} = \frac{X_2}{1 - c_2}$$

(14) $$\frac{\partial X_1}{\partial I_1} = \frac{X_1}{I_1}$$

(15) $$\frac{\partial X_2}{\partial I_2} = \frac{X_2}{I_2}$$

Under the two assumptions made about c_i and I_i, all four multipliers are positive: If a country's propensity to consume c_i or its autonomous investment I_i rises, its equilibrium output will rise—trade remaining balanced by flexible prices.

But *how* high should the flexible price ratio P_1/P_2 be in equilibrium? Use (7), (2), and (3) in that order, insert (10) and (11), and find

(16) $$\frac{P_1}{P_2} = \frac{c_2}{c_1} \frac{1 - c_1}{1 - c_2} \frac{A_2}{B_1} \frac{A_1 + B_1 I_2}{A_2 + B_2 I_1} E$$

To the assumptions already made add the assumption that the exchange rate E is positive. Then the equilibrium flexible price ratio P_1/P_2 as determined by (16) must be positive. The economic interpretation is easy: The equilibrium price ratio P_1/P_2 is lower the higher is the first country's propensity to consume, the more intensively the people of the first country desire the products of the second, the higher is the first country's autonomous investment, and the lower is the exchange rate.

Furthermore, the equilibrium price ratio P_1/P_2 is lower, the lower is the second country's propensity to consume, the less intensively the people of the second country desire the products of the first, and the lower is the second country's autonomous investment.

36.11 RICARDO ON THE INTERNAL PRICE MECHANISM

Through which particular mechanism do price levels adjust? Through the flows of gold from deficit countries to surplus countries so aptly described by Ricardo [8] a century and a half ago. In his *Principles*, Ricardo described a country much like the Federal Republic of Germany around 1960 which "excels in manufactures, so as to occasion an influx of money towards it." In such a country, Ricardo went on to say, one of two things must happen, that is, either "bills may continue to be negotiated at par," or "the current of money is forcibly stopped." In the first case:

"... the prices of corn and labour will be relatively higher in that country than in any other .... Under the circumstances supposed, such a difference of prices is the natural order of things, and the exchange [rate] can only be at par when a sufficient quantity of money is introduced into the country excelling in manufactures, so as to raise the price of its corn and labour."

Raise it how far? Until (16) is satisfied.

36.12   THE EXTERNAL PRICE MECHANISM

But suppose that either relative price levels do not respond to monetary policy or no such policy is undertaken. Hence we again consider P_1/P_2 a parameter, as we did in Section 36.9. However, we turn the exchange rate E loose as a variable and otherwise change nothing. Thus we still have a system of seven equations in seven variables, but this time the latter are C_{11}, C_{12}, C_{21}, C_{22}, X_1, X_2, and E. Solving it for the two national outputs we once again find Eqs. (10) and (11). Consequently, the two countries are equally independent of each other, whether the internal or the external price mechanism is functioning.

But *how* high should the flexible exchange rate E be in equilibrium? Our seven equations are the same as before; hence simply rearrange (16) and obtain

(17)
$$E = \frac{c_1}{c_2} \frac{1 - c_2}{1 - c_1} \frac{B_1}{A_2} \frac{A_2 + B_2}{A_1 + B_1} \frac{I_1}{I_2} \frac{P_1}{P_2}$$

To the assumptions already made add the assumption that the price levels P_i are both positive. Then the exchange rate as determined by (17) must be positive. The economic interpretation of (17) is easy: The equilibrium exchange rate E is higher, the higher is the first country's propensity to consume, the more intensively the people of the first country desire the products of the second, the higher are the first country's autonomous investment and its relative price level.

Furthermore, the equilibrium exchange rate E is higher, the lower is the second country's propensity to consume, the less intensively the people of the second country desire the products of the first, and the lower are the second country's autonomous investment and its relative price level.

36.13   RICARDO ON THE EXTERNAL PRICE MECHANISM

The functioning of the external price mechanism will occur in Ricardo's [8] second alternative, that is, where "the current of money is forcibly stopped." Ricardo describes his second alternative as follows:

"If foreign countries should prohibit the exportation of money, and could successfully enforce obedience to such a law, they might indeed prevent the rise in the prices of the corn and labour of the manufacturing country; for such rise can only take place after the influx of the precious metals, supposing paper money not to be used; but they could not prevent the exchange [rate] from being very unfavourable to them. If England were the manufacturing country, and it were possible to prevent the importation of money, the exchange [rate] with France, Holland, and Spain might be 5, 10, or 20 per cent. against those countries."

How far would the exchange rate rise against France, Holland, and Spain? Until (17) is satisfied.

36.14   COUNTRIES STILL NOT FULLY INDEPENDENT

Although independent as far as their equilibrium national outputs are concerned, why are the two countries not fully independent? Let Country 1 wish to expand its output and employment, and let it raise its autonomous investment I_1 to that effect. If it chooses to rely on the internal price mechanism, Eq. (16) shows that it must somehow reduce the price ratio P_1/P_2 in proportion to the increase in autonomous investment I_1. The reduced price ratio means that Country 1's real income will expand less than its output. For real income is the physical quantity of goods which Country 1 could buy for its output, and one physical unit of Country 1's goods now buys fewer physical units of Country 2's goods, because the relative price of Country 1's goods is lower at an unaltered exchange rate.

If, however, Country 1 chooses to rely on the external price mechanism, Eq. (17) shows that the exchange rate E must rise in proportion to the increase in autonomous investment I_1. The same penalty will still have to be paid: One physical unit of Country 1's goods now buys fewer physical units of Country 2's goods, for the exchange rate is up at unaltered relative prices.

Consequently, the two countries may be independent as far as their physical outputs are concerned, but they are still dependent, via (16) or (17), as far as their real incomes are concerned.

36.15   INFLATION AND VARIABLE EXCHANGE RATES

Should a country rely on the internal or the external price mechanism? In Haberler's [1] judgment, "the imposition of financial and wage discipline is, after all, the most important advantage that can be claimed for the system of stable exchange rates." Do fixed exchange rates really offer better protection against inflation than variable ones do?

As for inflation originating outside a country's borders, the answer is easy: That country could protect itself from inflation simply by an appreciation of its currency. In contrast, under fixed exchange rates the rising prices of its imports and the rising profitability of its exports would release strong upward wage and price pressures.

But what about inflation originating inside a country's borders? Surely the extent of a money wage increase depends upon two things: labor's incentive to push for it and management's will to resist it.

Under fixed exchange rates labor has more incentive to push for a money wage increase than under variable exchange rates. Under fixed exchange rates domestic money wage increases leave import prices unchanged, whereas under variable exchange rates import prices measured in domestic monetary units would have risen along with the domestic money wage rate. Consequently, under fixed exchange rates labor's real wage rate is up, at least *vis-a-vis* imported goods, whereas under variable exchange rates the real wage rate is up much less if at all. This difference is particularly striking in countries like Great Britain in whose import food looms so large.

On the other side of the fence, management also has more incentive to resist a money wage increase under fixed than under variable exchange rates. Under fixed exchange rates exporters cannot easily shift domestic wage cost increases onto their foreign customers, hence will vigorously resist such increases. Under variable exchange rates export prices measured in domestic monetary units would have risen along with the domestic money wage rate and exporters could have lived with it.

On balance, then, what are we to conclude about inflation originating inside a country's borders? Under fixed exchange rates we have a strong incentive strongly resisted, whereas under variable exchange rates we have a weak incentive weakly resisted. Which of the two cases results in more "wage discipline" we cannot say on *a priori* grounds. It remains true, of course, that inflation originating outside a country's borders is best kept away by variable exchange rates.

36.16   CONCLUSION

This Chapter replaces a Keynesian two-country model which has suspended its price mechanism by a Keynesian two-country model which relies on the price mechanism for balanced trade. As a result, the equilibrium level of each country's output, but not that of its real income, now depends upon that country's own parameters alone.

The price paid for such a clear-cut result was a number of highly simplifying assumptions. First, there was the assumption of utility functions of Cobb-Douglas form, common to all persons within a country. Second, there was the assumption that all persons within a country spend the same fraction of their money income on consumption. From all this we derived aggregate consumption functions whose income elasticity was *plus* one and whose cross-elasticity with respect to the price of import and the exchange rate was zero. We also derived aggregate import functions whose income elasticity was *plus* one and whose direct price elasticity was *minus* one. The income-elasticity results seem empirically plausible (see Appendix I). However, little is known about the empirical soundness of the price-elasticity and the cross-elasticity results (see Appendix II).

APPENDIX I   EMPIRICAL   INCOME   ELASTICITIES

For the prewar United Kingdom and the United States, Neisser-Modigliani [5, p. 80] found the income elasticities of import to be very close to unity indeed. In the United Kingdom the elasticity was 1.15, 1.05, and 1.09 in 1928, 1932, and 1935, respectively. In the United States it was 0.99, 0.91, and 0.94 for the same years, respectively. However, Germany had considerably higher income elasticities. Polak [7] found prewar marginal propensities to import for a large number of countries. Taking advantage of the fact that the income elasticity of import equals the marginal divided by the average propensity to import, Harberger [2] calculated income elasticities from Polak's data and found them to be 0.95 and 1.00 for prewar United Kingdom and United States, respectively. However, income elasticities of import for the Netherlands, Canada, Australia, New Zealand, South Africa, and Sweden were found to be between 1.30 and 1.65.

APPENDIX II   EMPIRICAL   PRICE   ELASTICITIES

As regards price elasticities of import, Neisser-Modigliani [5, p. 288] failed to find reliable ones for United Kingdom and United States raw materials and food import. But reliable price elasticities for United Kingdom, United States, and Swedish import of manufactured goods were found to be between −1.00 and −1.67. Attributing to price movements whatever part of the late 1930's to mid-1950's change in import demand not explained by Polak's income elasticities, Harberger [2] calculated price elasticities of United Kingdom and United States demand for import equal to −0.56 and −0.95, respectively. Price elasticities of the import of other countries varied from −2.12 to 0.23. Weighing this and other evidence, Harberger judged that in the relatively short run the elasticity of import demand for a typical country lies in or numerically above the range −0.5 to −1.0, whereas the elasticity of demand for its export is probably near or numerically above −2. Two findings, both significant at the 0.99 level, were numerically slightly above Harberger's range: Krause [4] found the price elasticity of United States import of manufactured products not close to the raw-material stage to be −1.2 in the short run and −1.8 in the long run, and van Rijckeghem [9] found the price elasticity of Belgian import of food, raw materials, and investment goods to be −2.28, −0.76, and −1.69, respectively.

Errors in the measurement of the price variable could bias least-squares estimates of import price elasticities toward zero, as shown by Orcutt [6]. Errors in the measurement of the quantity variable could bias them toward *minus* one, as shown by Kemp [3].

REFERENCES

[1] Haberler, G., "Integration and Growth of the World Economy in Historical Perspective," *Am. Econ. Rev.*, **54**, 20 (March 1964).

[2] Harberger, A. C., "Some Evidence on the International Price Mechanism," *Jour. Pol. Econ.*, **65**, 509 (December 1957).

[3] Kemp, M. C., "Errors of Measurement and Bias in Estimates of Import Demand Parameters," *Econ. Record*, **38**, 369–372 (September 1962).

[4] Krause, L. B., "United States Imports 1947–1958," *Econometrica*, **30**, 221–238 (April 1962).

[5] Neisser, H., and F. Modigliani, *National Incomes and International Trade*, Urbana, Illinois, 1953.

[6] Orcutt, G. H., "Measurement of Price Elasticities in International Trade," *Rev. Econ. Stat.*, **32**, 117–132 (May 1950).

[7] Polak, J. J., *An International Economic System*, Chigago, 1953.

[8] *The Works and Correspondence of David Ricardo*, I, edited by P. Sraffa, New York, 1951, pp. 146–147.

[9] van Rijckeghem, W., "De prijselasticiteit van de Belgische invoer," *Cahiers Economique de Bruxelles*, **16**, 563–572 (October 1962).

CHAPTER 37

A Keynesian Model of Fiscal Policy*

37.1 INTRODUCTION

In the United States, government purchases of goods and services account for roughly one-fifth of the gross national product. In Western European nations [4] the same fraction varies between one-tenth and one-fifth. (Neither fraction includes purchases by government-owned business enterprises.)

Such a massive component of aggregate demand, and the massive taxes necessary to finance it, must have a significant effect upon national output formation. That effect was first studied by pre-Keynesians like Lindahl [5] and Myrdal [6]. Lindahl was probably the first economist to consider systematic variations in the fiscal budget balance an instrument for macroeconomic public policy. The analysis gathered momentum in the hands of the Keynesians [1, 2, 3, 9] rather than in those of Keynes himself. Keynes hinted at fiscal policy, but in his model proper, even in its complete form, there is no room for government, and taxes do not rear their ugly heads.

The time has come to bring in government and taxation explicitly. To maintain simplicity let us once again throw out the monetary sphere and consider a closed economy.

37.2 NOTATION

The following notation will be assigned.

Variables

C = country's output consumed

R = tax revenue

* Chapter 34 is a prerequisite for Chapter 37.

s = fiscal surplus
X = net national output
Y = net national money income
y = disposable national money income

Parameters

A = autonomous consumption
B = autonomous tax revenue
c = marginal propensity to consume
G = autonomous government demand for country's output
I = autonomous net investment
P = price of country's output
t = marginal tax rate

The variables C and X and the parameters G and I are measured in physical units of output. These units carry the positive price tag P. The variables R, s, and y are measured in monetary units.

37.3   INCOME CONCEPTS

Define net national money income as the money value of net national output:

(1) $$Y = PX$$

Define disposable national money income as net national money income *minus* tax revenue:

(2) $$y = Y - R$$

37.4   CONSUMPTION

In our Keynesian models consumption was a linear function of net national real income which, as long as taxes were nonexistent, was fully disposable. Now that we are introducing taxes we must make consumption a linear function of disposable national real income instead:

(3) $$C = A + c\frac{y}{P}$$

Assume autonomous consumption A to be positive and the marginal propensity to consume disposable real income c to lie between zero and one.

37.5 TAX BEHAVIOR

In Western tradition, as developed from the Magna Carta and the American Revolution, taxes are collected according to statute, and statutes define tax base and tax rate. Typical tax bases are the money value of income, assets, or final sales to consumers. As a good first approximation let statute be summarized in the statement that tax revenue is a linear function of net national money income:

$$(4) \qquad\qquad R = B + tY$$

If the constant term B is negative, the tax system is a progressive one, if B equals zero, it is a proportional one, and if B is positive, it is a regressive one. Assume B to be nonpositive, that is, assume the tax system to be either progressive or proportional. Assume the marginal tax rate t to lie between zero and one.

37.6 THE FISCAL SURPLUS

Define the fiscal surplus as tax revenue *minus* the money value of government demand for country's output:

$$(5) \qquad\qquad s = R - PG$$

Government demand for the country's output G is assumed to be autonomous and positive.

37.7 EQUILIBRIUM

Equilibrium requires the sum of consumption, investment, and government demand for output to equal output, or inventory would accumulate or be depleted:

$$(6) \qquad\qquad X = C + I + G$$

Net investment is assumed to be autonomous and positive.

37.8 THREE ALTERNATIVE PRIORITY PATTERNS

Before trying to solve our system (1) through (6), let us remind the reader of a few mathematical facts of life.

A solution for a variable means an equation having only that variable on one side and nothing but parameters on the other side. Once such a solution has been found, we may study the result of manipulating any parameter by taking the partial derivative of the variable with respect to the parameter (such a derivative is often called a multiplier). That this can be legitimately done follows from the definition of a parameter as a magnitude to be fixed at will, and manipulated at will, by the investigator using information coming from outside the model. No such thing can be done with a variable. Variables are solved for within the model, and the solution must be respected: They can have their solution value only and cannot be manipulated at will by the investigator. From this arises the importance of knowing which magnitudes are variables and which are parameters in a model.

Now which are which in our present model? There are three fiscal-policy magnitudes: Government demand G, fiscal surplus s, and tax rate t. Clearly, they cannot all three be parameters at the same time, or government could decide to buy all it desired at zero or low tax rates, yet run a fiscal surplus. A choice will have to be made: The government can fix two of the three magnitudes as parameters and let the economy determine the third as a variable. Which two? Since $\binom{3}{2} = 3$, there are three different ways in which two elements can be selected from three. This gives us three alternative priority patterns: Either the government fixes government demand G and the tax rate t and lets the economy determine what the fiscal surplus s will be. Or the government fixes government demand G and fiscal surplus s and lets the economy determine the necessary tax rate t. Or, finally, the government fixes fiscal surplus s and tax rate t and lets the economy determine how much the government can afford to buy. These three priority patterns will now be examined in turn.

I.   VARIABLE FISCAL SURPLUS

37.9   FIRST SOLUTION FOR OUTPUT

Under the first priority pattern government fixes government demand G and the tax rate t and lets the economy determine what the fiscal surplus s will be. The notation as given in Section 37.2 applies to this pattern. To solve for output insert (1) through (4) into (6):

$$(7) \qquad X = \frac{A + G + I - cB/P}{1 - c(1 - t)}$$

As always in Keynesian models our first output solution (7) is assumed to be feasible: Output requires quantities of the (unspecified) inputs which are less than or equal to those available. Under this assumption, output depends upon aggregate demand alone. Under the assumptions made about our parameters A, B, c, G, I, P, and t, our solution (7) will always be positive and unique.

Let us examine the sensitivity of our output solution (7) to manipulations of the fiscal parameters of the first priority pattern, that is, G and t:

$$(8) \qquad \frac{\partial X}{\partial G} = \frac{1}{1 - c(1 - t)}$$

$$(9) \qquad \frac{\partial X}{\partial t} = - \frac{c}{1 - c(1 - t)} X$$

where X stands for the output solution (7) above. Under the assumptions made, the derivative (8) is always positive: Raising autonomous government demand will raise output. The derivative (9) is always negative: Reducing the marginal tax rate t will raise output.

37.10   SOLUTION FOR FISCAL SURPLUS

Use (1), (4), and (5) to express the fiscal surplus

$$(10) \qquad s = B + tPX - PG$$

where X stands for the output solution (7) above. Let us examine the sensitivity of our fiscal-surplus solution (10) to manipulations of the same two fiscal parameters G and t.

Under the assumptions made about our parameters A, B, c, G, I, P, and t, our solution (10) will always be unique. However, nothing can be said about its sign: A sufficiently high government demand G will make the surplus s nonpositive. To see this, take the derivative

$$(11) \qquad \frac{\partial s}{\partial G} = - \frac{(1 - c)(1 - t)}{1 - c(1 - t)} P$$

Under the assumptions made, this derivative is always negative. Since no upper bound was imposed upon government demand G, the fiscal surplus s may be lowered to any depth by running a sufficiently high government demand. However, since government demand G was assumed to be positive, the fiscal surplus cannot be raised to any height by running a sufficiently low government demand.

To see how the fiscal surplus depends upon the tax rate, take the derivative

$$(12) \qquad \frac{\partial s}{\partial t} = \frac{1 - c}{1 - c(1 - t)} PX$$

where X stands for the output solution (7) above. Under the assumptions made, the derivative (12) is always positive: Reducing the marginal tax rate t will reduce the fiscal surplus s. Notice that as a result our assumptions leave no room for the illusion that reducing the marginal tax rate t will expand the tax base Y enough to raise the product of the two, tY, and thus raise the fiscal surplus s.

37.11 GRAPHICAL ILLUSTRATION OF THE VARIABLE-FISCAL-SURPLUS CASE

Graphs alone can be treacherous. But as a supplement to an already established algebraic solution they may add life to it. Let us see if we can expand the 45° diagram used in the truncated Keynesian model in order to illuminate the delicate mechanism of income and output formation in the variable-fiscal-surplus case.

No graphical solution can be anything but a numerical example visually illustrated, so let us start by selecting the following set of values for our parameters:

$$\begin{array}{ll} A = 19 & I = 40 \\ B = -20 & P = 2 \\ c = 0.9 & t = 0.2 \\ G = 100 \end{array}$$

For these values our system will give us the following positive and unique solutions for our variables:

$$\begin{array}{ll} C = 460 & X = 600 \\ R = 220 & Y = 1200 \\ s = 20 & y = 980 \end{array}$$

We are now ready to attempt a graphical solution. In Fig. 37.1 we have consolidated four two-dimensional diagrams. The reader is invited to begin with the upper right part of Fig. 37.1. Here is the most familiar of our four functions, that is, the consumption function (3), $C = A + cy/P$. This function has the intercept A on the consumption axis and as now seen has the slope c.

Now turn Fig. 37.1 90° clockwise and look at the equilibrium condition (6) $X = C + I + G$. This function has the intercept $I + G$ on the net-national-output axis and as now seen has the slope one.

For the second time turn Fig. 37.1 90° clockwise (the book now stands on its head) and look at disposable national money income as a function of net

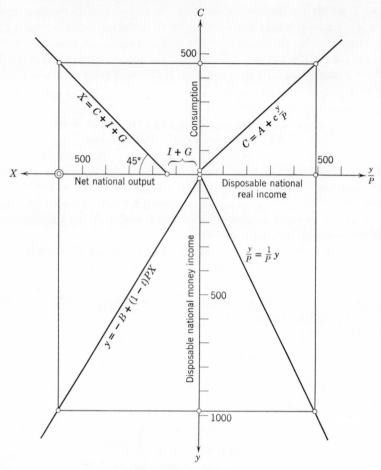

Figure 37.1

national output. This function is derived by inserting (1) and (4) into (2), getting $y = -B + (1 - t)PX$. This function has the intercept $-B$ on the disposable-national-money-income axis and as now seen has the slope $(1 - t)P$.

For the third and last time turn Fig. 37.1 90° clockwise and look at disposable national real income as a function of disposable national money income $y/P = (1/P)y$. This function has the intercept zero on the disposable-national-real-income axis and as now seen has the slope $1/P$. If we would now turn Fig. 37.1 a fourth time we would be back where we started, that is, at the consumption function.

Now let us follow Fig. 37.1 counterclockwise all the way around, starting at the double circle indicating equilibrium net national output. In all its delicacy, equilibrium means that net national output is exactly large enough to generate a disposable national money income which, at given prices, represents a disposable national real income exactly large enough to generate a consumption demand which, when added to autonomous investment and government demand, will exactly exhaust that net national output. At the parameter values selected such a net national output is 600, indicated by the double circle, and it cannot be anything else.

To see that it cannot, the reader should try any net national output less than 600 and follow Fig. 37.1 counterclockwise all the way around. He will find that such an output, everything taken into account, would generate an aggregate demand greater than itself (but less than 600) and thus would deplete inventory. If he tries any net national output greater than 600, he will find that such an output would generate an aggregate demand less than itself (but greater than 600) and thus would accumulate inventory.

For a graphical illustration of our multipliers (8) and (9) the reader may manipulate the vitals of Fig. 37.1 as follows. Produce an increase in autonomous government demand G by a parallel shift to the left of the 45° line. The equilibrium output is now in excess of 600, as the positive multiplier (8) told us it would be. Produce a marginal-tax-rate reduction by swinging the function $y = -B + (1 - t)PX$ around its hinge $-B$, moving it closer to the y-axis. (More disposable national money income now results from a given net national output.) The equilibrium output once again is in excess of 600, as the negative multiplier (9) told us it would be. But now it is time to examine our second priority pattern.

II. VARIABLE TAX RATE

37.12 NOTATION

Under the second priority pattern, government fixes government demand G and fiscal surplus s and lets the economy determine the necessary tax rate t. To deal with this case we need neither new concepts nor new equations. All we need to do is to reshuffle our variables and parameters as follows:

Variables: C, R, t, X, Y, y.

Parameters: A, B, c, G, I, P, s.

Now that the marginal tax rate t assumes the status of a variable, we must lift the restriction imposed upon it previously, that is, that it lie between zero and one. Upon our new parameter, the fiscal surplus s, no restrictions are to be imposed: It may be negative, zero, or positive.

37.13   SECOND SOLUTION FOR OUTPUT

Some variables and parameters may have been interchanged, but we still have the same six equations as before. To solve for output insert (1) through (5) into (6):

$$(13) \qquad X = \frac{A + I - cs/P}{1 - c} + G$$

As always in Keynesian models our second output solution (13) is assumed to be feasible. Under the assumptions made about our parameters A, B, c, G, I, P, and s, it will always be unique. However, as we shall soon see, nothing can be said about its sign.

Let us examine the sensitivity of our output solution (13) to manipulations of the fiscal parameters of the second priority pattern, that is, G and s. Equation (13) shows output X to depend upon government demand G in a particularly simple way: Take the derivative

$$(14) \qquad \frac{\partial X}{\partial G} = 1$$

Under the assumptions made about our parameters, nothing can be said about the sign of our second output solution (13): sufficiently high fiscal surplus s will make output X nonpositive. To see this take the derivative

$$(15) \qquad \frac{\partial X}{\partial s} = - \frac{c}{(1 - c)P}$$

Under the assumptions made about our parameters, this derivative is always negative. Since no restrictions were imposed upon the fiscal surplus s, output may be lowered to any depth by running a sufficiently high surplus and raised to any height by running a sufficiently low surplus. But remember the usual assumption that output was feasible. When that assumption becomes untenable, inflation will result from lowering the fiscal surplus any further.

37.14   SOLUTION FOR MARGINAL TAX RATE

Which value of the marginal tax rate t is necessary to keep the fiscal surplus s constant? Insert (1) and (4) into (5)

$$(16) \qquad t = \frac{PG + s - B}{PX}$$

where X stands for the output solution (13). If according to (13) $X = 0$, the solution (16) becomes meaningless. Otherwise the solution will be unique.

Let us examine its sensitivity to manipulations of the same two fiscal parameters G and s. Take the derivative

(17)
$$\frac{\partial t}{\partial G} = \frac{1 - t}{X}$$

where X stands for the output solution (13) above. If according to (13) $X = 0$, the derivative (17) becomes meaningless. Otherwise it will be unique. Under the second priority pattern, now under examination, the marginal tax rate t is a variable for which the solution is (16) and upon which no restrictions are being imposed. If according to (16) t happens to be less than one, the derivative (17) must have the same sign as output X; hence if according to (13) X happens to be positive, the derivative (17) is also positive. In such a "normal" case, raising government demand under a constant fiscal surplus will raise the marginal tax rate.

Under the assumptions made about our parameters A, B, c, G, I, P, and s, nothing can be said about the sign of the solution (16). A sufficiently low fiscal surplus s will make the tax rate t nonpositive. To see this, take the derivative

(18)
$$\frac{\partial t}{\partial s} = \frac{(A + G + I)P - cB}{(1 - c)(PX)^2}$$

where again X stands for the output solution (13) above. If according to (13) $X = 0$, the derivative (18) becomes meaningless. But notice that in (18) X only occurs squared; hence for all nonzero values of X, under the assumptions made, (18) is always positive.

37.15 GRAPHICAL ILLUSTRATION OF THE VARIABLE-TAX-RATE CASE

To illustrate our second priority pattern graphically, let us select the following set of values for our parameters:

$$
\begin{array}{ll}
A = \ \ 19 & I = 40 \\
B = -20 & P = \ \ 2 \\
c = \ \ \ \ 0.9 & s = 20 \\
G = \ \ 100 &
\end{array}
$$

For these values our system will give us the following positive and unique solutions for our variables:

$$
\begin{array}{ll}
C = 460 & X = \ \ 600 \\
R = 220 & Y = 1200 \\
t = \ \ \ \ 0.2 & y = \ \ \ 980
\end{array}
$$

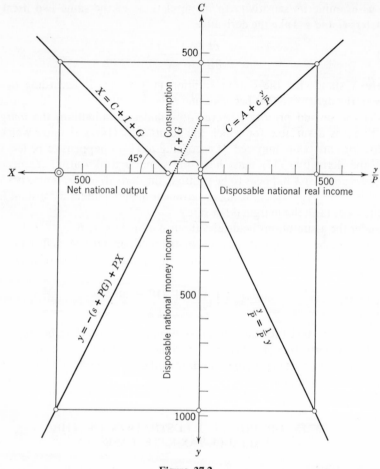

Figure 37.2

In our diagrams all intercepts and slopes must be parameters, and in Fig. 37.1 they were. However, under the second priority pattern the tax rate t is a variable; therefore the lower left part of Fig. 37.1 must be modified. Insert (1) and (5) into (2) and get the disposable national money income function $y = -(s + PG) + PX$, shown in Fig. 37.2. This function has the intercept $-(s + PG)$ and the slope P, both parameters under the second priority pattern.

Output, indicated by the double circle, is the same in Figs. 37.1 and 37.2, but the underlying mechanism of output determination is not the same.

37.16   THE BALANCED BUDGET

The balanced budget is a special case of the case just examined, that is, the case in which the fiscal surplus assumes the value zero. Haavelmo [2] found the balanced-budget multiplier to be one: An expansion of a balanced budget by one dollar would expand output by one dollar. As Nörregaard Rasmussen [7] has pointed out, the balanced-budget multiplier of one had already been discovered by Gelting [1], who, however, had credited Ricardo [8] with the discovery, for toward the end of his famous Chapter XXXI ("On Machinery") Ricardo had said:

"If I were not called upon for a tax of £500 during the war, and which is expended on men in the situations of soldiers and sailors, I might probably expend that portion of my income on furniture, clothes, books, &c. &c., and whether it was expended in the one way or in the other, there would be the same quantity of labour employed in production; for the food and clothing of the soldier and sailor would require the same amount of industry to produce it as the more luxurious commodities; but in the case of the war, there would be the additional demand for men as soldiers and sailors; and, consequently, a war which is supported out of the revenue, and not from the capital of a country, is favourable to the increase of population.

"At the termination of the war, when part of my revenue reverts to me, and is employed as before in the purchase of wine, furniture, or other luxuries, the population which it before supported, and which the war called into existence, will become redundant, and by its effect on the rest of the population, and its competition with it for employment, will sink the value of wages, and very materially deteriorate the condition of the labouring classes."

In the special case of a balanced budget, our second solution for output becomes

$$(13a) \qquad X = \frac{A + I}{1 - c} + G$$

and the derivative (14) still holds, indeed was first discovered for that special case and labeled *the balanced-budget multiplier*. Our marginal-tax-rate solution now becomes

$$(16a) \qquad t = \frac{PG - B}{PX}$$

where X now stands for the output solution (13a). The derivative (17) still holds for the special case of a balanced budget as long as we remember that X stands for (13a) and t stands for (16a).

III.   VARIABLE GOVERNMENT DEMAND

37.17   NOTATION

Under the third priority pattern, government fixes fiscal surplus s and tax rate t and lets the economy determine how much the government can afford to buy. To handle this case, again we need neither new concepts nor new equations. All we need is yet another reshuffling of variables and parameters as follows:

Variables: C, G, R, X, Y, y.

Parameters: A, B, c, I, P, s, t.

Now that government demand G assumes the status of a variable, we must lift the restriction imposed upon it previously, that is, that it be positive. The fiscal surplus s remains a parameter with no restrictions imposed upon it: It may still be negative, zero, or positive. The marginal tax rate t is now being restored to its original status of a parameter, and with it the original restriction upon it that it lie between zero and one.

37.18   THIRD SOLUTION FOR OUTPUT

Once again some variables and parameters may have been interchanged, but we still have the same old six equations. To solve for output insert (1) through (5) into (6):

$$(19) \qquad X = \frac{A + I + \dfrac{(1 - c)B - s}{P}}{(1 - c)(1 - t)}$$

As always in Keynesian models our third output solution (19) is assumed to be feasible. Under the assumptions made about our parameters A, B, c, I, P, s, and t, it will always be unique. However, nothing can be said about its sign: A sufficiently high fiscal surplus s will make output X nonpositive. To see this take the derivative

$$(20) \qquad \frac{\partial X}{\partial s} = - \frac{1}{(1 - c)(1 - t)P}$$

Under the assumptions made about our parameters, this derivative is always negative. Since no restrictions were imposed upon the fiscal surplus s, output may again be lowered to any depth by running a sufficiently high surplus and raised to any height by running a sufficiently low surplus. But again we should remember the assumption that output was feasible. When that assumption becomes untenable, inflation will result from lowering the fiscal surplus any further.

To see how output depends upon tax rate take the derivative

$$(21) \qquad \frac{\partial X}{\partial t} = \frac{X}{1 - t}$$

where X stands for the output solution (19) above. Under the third priority pattern, now under examination, the marginal tax rate t is a parameter assumed to lie between zero and one. Consequently, the derivative (21) must have the same sign as output X; hence, if according to (19) X happens to be positive, the derivative (21) will be positive: The higher the tax rate, the higher the output. Is this surprising? Not when we remember that to keep the fiscal surplus s constant, government demand G must always increase by the same amount as tax revenue. Now taxation amounts to taking income away from households, whose marginal propensity to spend it falls short of one, and transferring to government, whose marginal propensity to spend it must equal one in order to keep the fiscal surplus s constant. Hence we are not at all surprised that the higher the tax rate, the higher the output.

37.19 SOLUTION FOR GOVERNMENT DEMAND

How much can government afford to buy, given the fiscal surplus s and the marginal tax rate t? Insert (1) and (4) into (5):

$$(22) \qquad G = \frac{B - s}{P} + tX$$

where X stands for the output solution (19) above. Let us examine the sensitivity of our government-demand solution (22) to manipulations of the same two fiscal parameters s and t.

Under the assumptions made about our parameters A, B, c, I, P, s, and t, our solution (22) will always be unique. But nothing can be said about its sign: A sufficiently high fiscal surplus s will make government demand G nonpositive. To see this, take the derivative

$$(23) \qquad \frac{\partial G}{\partial s} = - \frac{1 - c(1 - t)}{(1 - c)(1 - t)P}$$

Under the assumptions made, this derivative is always negative. Since no restrictions were imposed upon the fiscal surplus s, government demand G may be lowered to any depth by insisting on a sufficiently high fiscal surplus and raised to any height by permitting a sufficiently low surplus. Once again we should remember the assumption that output was feasible. When that assumption becomes untenable, inflation will result from lowering the fiscal surplus any further. In such a situation the government will be sure of spending more money, PG. But government can be sure of getting a larger physical quantity G only at the expense of consumption C or net investment I, necessitating rationing of households and firms.

To see how government purchases depend upon the tax rate, take the derivative

(24)
$$\frac{\partial G}{\partial t} = \frac{X}{1-t}$$

where again X stands for the output solution (19) above. Like (21), and for the same reason, the derivative (24) must have the same sign as output X. Hence, if according to (19) X happens to be positive, the derivative (24) will be positive: The higher the tax rate, the more the government can afford to buy. Is this surprising? Not when we remember that to keep the fiscal surplus s constant, government demand G must always increase by the same amount as tax revenue, and we just saw that the higher the tax rate, the higher the output, hence also the higher the tax revenue.

37.20 GRAPHICAL ILLUSTRATION OF THE VARIABLE-GOVERNMENT-DEMAND CASE

To illustrate our third priority pattern graphically, let us select the following set of values for our parameters:

$$
\begin{array}{ll}
A = 19 & P = 2 \\
B = -20 & s = 20 \\
c = 0.9 & t = 0.2 \\
I = 40 &
\end{array}
$$

For these values our system will give us the following positive and unique solutions for our variables:

$$
\begin{array}{ll}
C = 460 & X = 600 \\
G = 100 & Y = 1200 \\
R = 220 & y = 980
\end{array}
$$

In our diagrams all intercepts and slopes must be parameters, and in Figs. 37.1 and 37.2 they were. However, under the third priority pattern, government demand G is a variable, so the upper left part of Fig. 37.1 must be modified. Insert (4) and (5) into (6) and express the equilibrium condition

$$X = \frac{I + (B - s)/P}{1-t} + \frac{C}{1-t}$$

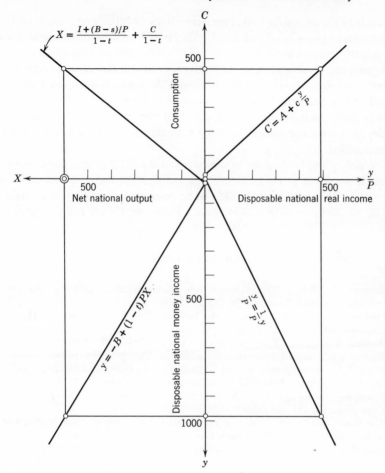

Figure 37.3

shown in Fig. 37.3. This function has the intercept $[I + (B - s)/P]/(1 - t)$ and the slope $1/(1 - t)$, both parameters under the third priority pattern.

Output, indicated by the double circle, is the same in Figs. 37.1, 37.2, and 37.3. However, there are three different underlying mechanisms of output determination.

37.21   CONCLUSION

For each of our three priority patterns we have found two solutions, one for output and one for whichever fiscal-policy magnitude was a variable under the priority pattern examined. Under each of the three priority patterns, for each of the two solutions, two derivatives (multipliers) have been found with respect to whichever two fiscal-policy magnitudes were parameters under the priority pattern examined.

Among the resulting twelve derivatives, none was found to be zero; consequently, no fiscal surplus, no government demand, and no tax rate can be raised or lowered without affecting net national output (or, if the economy is already fully employed, without affecting the inflationary pressure). The reader may convince himself that for realistic values of the parameters used all multipliers are quite powerful.

The policy implication is, of course, that no fiscal-policy decision should be made on fiscal grounds alone. For example, reducing government debt by running a fiscal surplus should not be done *solely* for the sake of reducing it. The effects upon output of running a fiscal surplus are too powerful to be ignored.

REFERENCES

[1] Gelting, J., "Nogle bemaerkninger om financieringen af offentlig virksomhed," *Nationalökonomisk Tidsskrift*, **79**, 293–299 (1941).

[2] Haavelmo, T., "Multiplier Effects of a Balanced Budget," *Econometrica*, **13**, 311–318 (October 1945).

[3] Hansen, A. H., *Fiscal Policy and Business Cycles*, New York, 1941.

[4] Johansen, L., *Public Economics*, Amsterdam and Chicago, 1965, p. 158.

[5] Lindahl, E., *Penningpolitikens medel*, Lund, Sweden, 1929, especially pp. 62–67.

[6] Myrdal, G., *Finanspolitikens ekonomiska verkningar*, Stockholm, 1934.

[7] Nörregaard Rasmussen, P., "A Note on the History of the Balanced-Budget Multiplier, *Econ. Jour.*, **68**, 154–156 (March 1958).

[8] *The Works and Correspondence of David Ricardo, I*, edited by Piero Sraffa, with the collaboration of Maurice H. Dobb, New York, 1951, pp. 393–394.

[9] Samuelson, P., "The Simple Mathematics of Income Determination," *Income, Employment and Public Policy, Essays in Honor of Alvin H. Hansen*, New York, 1948, 133–155.

CHAPTER 38

Labor and Capital in a Keynesian Model

38.1 INTRODUCTION

In this chapter let us take a closer look at output and the distributive shares as affected by wage, price, and tax policies in a modern corporate[1] economy. Our model, to be presented mathematically, may be summarized as follows. Private employment is a function of output. Corporate income tax is a function of net profits. Dividends are a function of net profits after tax, and so is investment. Personal income taxes of entrepreneurs and labor are functions of personal income. Consumption by entrepreneurs and labor are functions of disposable income. Export, government purchases, interest paid by government, and government employment are parameters. Such a model, if still Keynesian, clearly will have to be quite a bit more differentiated than the Keynesian models used in previous chapters. In fact, it will have to have five sectors in it, among which twelve transactions will have to be considered. A rational notation for such a model is Leontief-like rather than Keynesian. Therefore let the five sectors be designated by f for firms, g for government, e for entrepreneur households, l for labor households, and F for foreign countries. Let the twelve transactions be x_{ij} as shown in Table 38.1, in which subscript i stands for the sector of origin and subscript j stands for the sector of destination.

Individual goods and services are produced by firms and households and transacted through a market. This category includes x_{ef}, x_{eg}, x_{fe}, x_{ff}, x_{fF}, x_{fg}, x_{fl}, x_{lf}, and x_{lg}. All of them are straightforward except three: All intra-sector transactions are ignored except x_{ff}, which is defined as gross private

---

[1] Although in the United States since World War II gross business saving has been two to three times larger than personal saving, econometricians have paid far less attention to business than to personal saving. Honorable exceptions include Brittain [2], Darling [4], and Lintner [7].

387

Table 38.1 Transactions

	Firms	Government	Entrepreneur households	Labor households	Foreign countries
Firms	x_{ff}	x_{fg}	x_{fe}	x_{fl}	x_{fF}
Government	x_{gf}	—	x_{ge}	x_{gl}	—
Entrepreneur households	x_{ef}	x_{eg}	—	—	—
Labor households	x_{lf}	x_{lg}	—	—	—
Foreign countries	—	—	—	—	—

domestic real investment. Transactions x_{ef} and x_{eg} are purchases of entrepreneurial services by firms and government as measured by the dollar flow of dividends and interest, respectively, in the opposite direction.

Collective goods and services are produced by government and are not transacted to their specific beneficiaries through a market. They are to be measured by the dollar flow of tax payments in the opposite direction. In this category we find x_{ge}, x_{gf}, and x_{gl}.

Let real depreciation D/P, price P, the money wage rate w, money interest paid by government x_{eg}, export x_{fF}, government purchases of goods x_{fg}, and government purchases of labor services x_{lg}, be current-situation parameters.

An alphabetical list of variables and parameters follows.

Variables

X = output of goods produced by firms, in physical number of goods per unit of time

x_{ef} = money dividends paid by firms, in dollars per unit of time

x_{fe} = consumption of domestic goods by entrepreneur households, in physical number of goods per unit of time

x_{ff} = gross private domestic real investment, in physical number of goods per unit of time

x_{fl} = consumption of domestic goods by labor households, in physical number of goods per unit of time

x_{ge} = money personal income tax payment by entrepreneur households, in dollars per unit of time

x_{gf} = money corporate income tax payment by firms, in dollars per unit of time

x_{gl} = money personal income tax payment by labor households, in dollars per unit of time

x_{lf} = labor purchases by firms, in physical number of man hours per unit of time

y_e = disposable money income of entrepreneur households, in dollars per unit of time

y_l = disposable money income of labor households, in dollars per unit of time

Z = net money profits earned by firms, in dollars per unit of time

Parameters

A_{ef} = autonomous dividends, in physical number of goods per unit of time

a_{ef} = marginal dividend rate, in physical number of goods per unit of net real profits after tax, a pure number

A_{fe} = autonomous consumption of domestic goods by entrepreneur households, in physical number of goods per unit of time

a_{fe} = marginal propensity to consume domestic goods out of real disposable entrepreneur income, a pure number

A_{ff} = autonomous gross private domestic real investment, in physical number of goods per unit of time

a_{ff} = marginal inducement to invest domestic goods out of net real profits after tax, a pure number

A_{fl} = autonomous consumption of domestic goods by labor households, in physical number of goods per unit of time

a_{fl} = marginal propensity to consume domestic goods out of real disposable labor income, a pure number

A_{ge} = autonomous money personal income tax payment by entrepreneur households, in dollars per unit of time

a_{ge} = marginal money personal income tax rate of entrepreneur households, a pure number

A_{gf} = autonomous money corporate income tax payment by firms, in dollars per unit of time

a_{gf} = marginal money corporate income tax rate of firms, a pure number

A_{gl} = autonomous money personal income tax payment by labor households, in dollars per unit of time

a_{gl} = marginal money personal income tax rate of labor households, a pure number

A_{lf} = overhead labor, in physical number of man hours per unit of time

a_{lf} = marginal labor input-output coefficient, in physical number of man hours per physical unit of goods

D/P = real capital consumption allowances (depreciation), in real terms per unit of time

P = price of output, in dollars per physical unit of goods

w = the money wage rate, in dollars per man hour

x_{eg} = money interest paid by government, in dollars per unit of time

x_{fF} = export of goods by firms, in physical number of goods per unit of time

x_{fg} = government purchases of goods from firms, in physical number of goods per unit of time

x_{lg} = government purchases of services from labor households, in number of man hours per unit of time

38.2   EQUATIONS

To solve our system we shall need the following ten equations. First, labor purchases by firms, in man hours per unit of time x_{lf}, are a linear function of the domestic business gross product:

$$(1) \qquad x_{lf} = A_{lf} + a_{lf}X$$

where A_{lf} and a_{lf} are structure parameters.

Let all firms be corporations financed by stock issue and retained earnings alone. Their net money profits, in dollars per unit of time Z, are defined as the money value of the domestic business gross product *minus* the money value of purchases of labor *minus* the money value of capital consumption allowances:

$$(2) \qquad Z = PX - wx_{lf} - D$$

where P is the price of output, w the money wage rate, and D money capital consumption allowances. Price P, money wage rate w, and real capital consumption allowances D/P are current-situation parameters.

All firms being corporations, let money corporate income tax payment by firms, in dollars per unit of time x_{gf}, be a linear function of net money profits:

$$(3) \qquad x_{gf} = A_{gf} + a_{gf}Z$$

Let no resident own firms abroad, and let no nonresident own domestic firms. Then define real dividends as money dividends, in dollars per unit of time x_{ef}, divided by the price of output P. Real dividends are a linear function of net real profits after tax:

$$(4) \qquad \frac{x_{ef}}{P} = A_{ef} + a_{ef}\frac{Z - x_{gf}}{P}$$

where A_{ef} and a_{ef} are structure parameters.

Gross private domestic real investment, in number of physical goods per unit of time x_{ff}, is a linear function of net real profits after tax:

$$(5) \qquad x_{ff} = A_{ff} + a_{ff} \frac{Z - x_{gf}}{P}$$

where A_{ff} and a_{ff} are structure parameters.[2]

Money personal income tax payment by entrepreneur and labor households, respectively, in dollars per unit of time x_{ge} and x_{gl}, are linear functions of the respective money personal incomes:

$$(6) \qquad x_{ge} = A_{ge} + a_{ge}(x_{ef} + x_{eg})$$

$$(7) \qquad x_{gl} = A_{gl} + a_{gl}w(x_{lf} + x_{lg})$$

where A_{ge}, a_{ge}, A_{gl}, and a_{gl} are structure parameters.

Consumption of domestic goods by entrepreneurs and labor households, respectively, in number of physical goods per unit of time x_{fe} and x_{fl}, are linear functions of the respective real disposable incomes:

$$(8) \qquad x_{fe} = A_{fe} + a_{fe} \frac{x_{ef} + x_{eg} - x_{ge}}{P}$$

$$(9) \qquad x_{fl} = A_{fl} + a_{fl} \frac{w(x_{lf} + x_{lg}) - x_{gl}}{P}$$

where A_{fe}, a_{fe}, A_{fl}, and a_{fl} are structure parameters.

Finally, the equilibrium condition that if inventory is neither to accumulate nor to be depleted, output must equal aggregate demand:

$$(10) \qquad X = x_{fe} + x_{ff} + x_{fF} + x_{fg} + x_{fl}$$

38.3   SOLUTION

Solving our system of ten equations for the domestic business gross

---

[2] There is good econometric evidence for such an investment function. Klein-Goldberger [6] used capital stock, business liquid assets, and lagged profits to explain investment. But the coefficients of the first two variables were not significantly different from zero at the 5 per cent level. Moreover, as regards the lagging, Christ [3] found the current rather than the lagged value of the Klein-Goldberger profit variable to serve better in explaining investment.

Three interpretations of the investment-profit correlation are possible. First, the closer firms are to capacity (and with it the need for expansion), the higher their profits. Second, in the United States, almost three-fourths of corporate gross investment is self-financed. Third, even if investment were autonomous it would expand output via the multiplier and with it profits.

product, we get

(i) $\quad X = \dfrac{\alpha_{ff} + A_{fe} + A_{fl} + x_{fF} + x_{fg}}{m} + \dfrac{\dfrac{a_{fe}}{P}[(1 - a_{ge})(P\alpha_{ef} + x_{eg}) - A_{ge}]}{m}$

$\quad\quad + \dfrac{\dfrac{a_{fl}}{P}[(1 - a_{gl})(A_{lf} + x_{lg})w - A_{gl}]}{m}$

where

$$\alpha_{ef} = A_{ef} - a_{ef}\frac{(1 - a_{gf})(wA_{lf} + D) + A_{gf}}{P}$$

$$\alpha_{ff} = A_{ff} - a_{ff}\frac{(1 - a_{gf})(wA_{lf} + D) + A_{gf}}{P}$$

$$m = 1 - \frac{P - wa_{lf}}{P}(1 - a_{gf})[a_{ff} + a_{ef}a_{fe}(1 - a_{ge})] - \frac{w}{P}a_{fl}a_{lf}(1 - a_{gl})$$

Next solve for the disposable real income of the entrepreneur households:

(ii) $\quad \dfrac{y_e}{P} = \dfrac{x_{ef} + x_{eg} - x_{ge}}{P}$

$$= (1 - a_{ge})\left[\alpha_{ef} + a_{ef}(1 - a_{gf})\frac{P - wa_{lf}}{P}X + \frac{x_{eg}}{P}\right] - \frac{A_{ge}}{P}$$

Finally, solve for the disposable real income of labor households:

(iii) $\quad \dfrac{y_l}{P} = \dfrac{w(x_{lf} + x_{lg}) - x_{gl}}{P} = \dfrac{w}{P}(1 - a_{gl})(A_{lf} + x_{lg} + a_{lf}X) - \dfrac{A_{gl}}{P}$

The responsiveness of the solutions (i), (ii), and (iii) to variations of the wage, price, and tax parameters will now be examined.

38.4   WAGE POLICY

The derivatives of the domestic business gross product and of the distributive shares with respect to the wage rate w are

(iv) $\quad \dfrac{\partial X}{\partial w} = x_{lf}\dfrac{a_{fl}(1 - a_{gl}) - (1 - a_{gf})[a_{ff} + a_{ef}a_{fe}(1 - a_{ge})]}{mP}$

$\quad\quad + x_{lg}\dfrac{a_{fl}(1 - a_{gl})}{mP}$

(v) $\quad \dfrac{\partial \dfrac{y_e}{P}}{\partial w} = a_{ef}(1 - a_{ge})(1 - a_{gf})\left(\dfrac{P - wa_{lf}}{P}\dfrac{\partial X}{\partial w} - \dfrac{x_{lf}}{P}\right)$

(vi) $\quad \dfrac{\partial \dfrac{y_l}{P}}{\partial w} = (1 - a_{gl})\left(a_{lf}\dfrac{w}{P}\dfrac{\partial X}{\partial w} + \dfrac{x_{lf} + x_{lg}}{P}\right)$

A priori nothing can be said about the sign of derivative (iv), hence nothing about the signs of derivatives (v) and (vi) either. This is not surprising. At unchanged price of output let the money wage rate rise. The money profit margin will fall. Since the price of output is unchanged, the real profit margin will fall as well. Investment depends upon the amount of real profits. Hence at unchanged level of national output but falling real profit margin, investment will be discouraged.

Real dividend payments depend upon the amount of real profits. Hence at unchanged level of national output but falling real profit margin, real dividend payments will fall. Thus the part of real entrepreneurial income which originates in business will fall. The part which originates in government interest payments will remain unaffected. Consumption depends upon real income; hence consumption by entrepreneur households will fall.

On the other hand, if at unchanged price of output the money wage rate rises, then at unchanged private and public employment the real wage bill would rise. (At unchanged money transfer payments *minus* social security contributions the real value of the nonwage part of labor's income would remain unchanged.) Since consumption depends upon real income, labor's consumption would rise.

But will national output actually remain unchanged? It is not likely to, for it depends upon national demand, and we have just seen that investment demand and entrepreneur household consumption both tend to fall, whereas labor household consumption tends to rise. Without knowing the relative strength of those opposing forces we cannot say whether national output will fall or rise.

38.5   PRICE POLICY

Recalling that not D but D/P is a parameter, we find the derivatives of the domestic business gross product and of the distributive shares with respect to the price P of goods to be

(vii)
$$\frac{\partial X}{\partial P} = \frac{A_{fe} + A_{ff} + A_{fl} + x_{fF} + x_{fg} + a_{fe}(1 - a_{ge})A_{ef}}{mP}$$
$$+ \frac{(1 - a_{gf})[a_{ff} + a_{ef}a_{fe}(1 - a_{ge})](X - D/P) - X}{mP}$$

(viii)
$$\frac{\partial \frac{y_e}{P}}{\partial P} = a_{ef}(1 - a_{ge})\left[(1 - a_{gf})\left(\frac{P - wa_{lf}}{P}\frac{\partial X}{\partial P} + \frac{wx_{lf}}{P^2}\right) + \frac{A_{gf}}{P^2}\right]$$
$$+ \frac{A_{ge} - (1 - a_{ge})x_{eg}}{P^2}$$

(ix)
$$\frac{\partial \frac{y_l}{P}}{\partial P} = \frac{w}{P}(1 - a_{gl})\left(a_{lf}\frac{\partial X}{\partial P} - \frac{x_{lf} + x_{lg}}{P}\right) + \frac{A_{gl}}{P^2}$$

A priori nothing can be said about the sign of derivative (vii), hence nothing about the signs of derivatives (viii) and (ix) either. Again, this is not surprising. At unchanged money wage rate let the price of output rise. The money profit margin will rise. Since it rises by the *same* dollar amount as price does but is itself *less* than price, its rise is more than proportional to price. Hence the real profit margin will rise as well. Investment depends upon the amount of real profits. Thus at unchanged level of national output but rising real profit margin, investment will be encouraged.

Real dividend payments depend upon the amount of real profits. Hence at unchanged level of national output but rising real profit margin, real dividend payments will rise. Thus the part of real entrepreneurial income which originates in business will rise. At unchanged money government interest payments but rising price of output, the part of real entrepreneurial income which originates in government interest payments will fall. Thus the active capitalists benefit but the passive ones suffer from the rising price of output. Consequently, even at an unchanged level of national output we cannot say whether real entrepreneurial income as a whole will rise or fall. Nor can we say whether consumption, which depends upon real income, will rise or fall.

As for labor, if at unchanged money wage rate the price of output rises, then at unchanged private and public employment the real wage bill would fall. (At unchanged money transfer payments *minus* social security contributions the real value of the nonwage part of labor's income would also fall.) Since consumption depends upon real income, labor's consumption would fall.

Again we must ask if national output will really remain unchanged, for it depends upon national demand, and we have seen that investment demand tends to rise, whereas labor's consumption demand tends to fall with entrepreneurial consumption demand uncertain. Again, without knowing the relative strength of the opposing forces we cannot say whether national output will fall or rise.

38.6 CORPORATE INCOME TAX POLICY

The derivatives of the domestic business gross product and of the distributive shares with respect to the marginal corporate income tax rate a_{gf} are

(x)
$$\frac{\partial X}{\partial a_{gf}} = -\frac{a_{ff} + a_{ef}a_{fe}(1 - a_{ge})}{mP} Z$$

(xi)
$$\frac{\partial \frac{y_e}{P}}{\partial a_{gf}} = a_{ef}(1 - a_{ge})\left[(1 - a_{gf})\frac{P - wa_{lf}}{P}\frac{\partial X}{\partial a_{gf}} - \frac{Z}{P}\right]$$

(xii)
$$\frac{\partial \frac{y_l}{P}}{\partial a_{gf}} = \frac{w}{P}a_{lf}(1 - a_{gl})\frac{\partial X}{\partial a_{gf}}$$

Although we failed to say anything *a priori* about the signs of our wage and price policy derivatives, we are rather sure of the signs of our tax derivatives. We may realistically assume the following:

1. All marginal propensities to spend, that is, on dividends a_{ef}, on investment a_{ff}, on consumption a_{fe} and a_{fl}, and on labor inputs a_{lf}, are positive and normally less than one.
2. All marginal tax rates, that is, on corporate income a_{gf} and on personal income a_{ge} and a_{gl}, are positive and less than one.
3. The dividends bill $x_{ef} + x_{eg}$ and the wage bill $x_{lf} + x_{lg}$ are both positive.
4. The real gross profit margin $(P - wa_{lf})/P$ is positive and less than one.
5. The amount of net profits is positive.

Corporate and household savings leakages as well as all tax leakages thus being positive, the denominator m of (i) is positive—it had better be or the solution (i) could turn negative.

Under those assumptions all corporate income tax derivatives (x) through (xii) are negative: By encouraging spending, reduced corporate income tax rates would raise output and real income of entrepreneurs and labor alike.

38.7 PERSONAL INCOME TAX POLICY

The derivatives of the domestic business gross product and of the distributive shares with respect to the marginal personal entrepreneur income tax rate a_{ge} are

(xiii)
$$\frac{\partial X}{\partial a_{ge}} = -\frac{a_{fe}(x_{ef} + x_{eg})}{mP}$$

(xiv)
$$\frac{\partial \frac{y_e}{P}}{\partial a_{ge}} = a_{ef}(1 - a_{ge})(1 - a_{gf})\frac{P - wa_{lf}}{P}\frac{\partial X}{\partial a_{ge}} - \frac{x_{ef} + x_{eg}}{P}$$

(xv)
$$\frac{\partial \frac{y_l}{P}}{\partial a_{ge}} = \frac{w}{P}a_{lf}(1 - a_{gl})\frac{\partial X}{\partial a_{ge}}$$

The derivatives with respect to the marginal personal labor income tax rate a_{gl} are

(xvi)
$$\frac{\partial X}{\partial a_{gl}} = -\frac{wa_{fl}(x_{lf} + x_{lg})}{mP}$$

(xvii)
$$\frac{\partial \frac{y_e}{P}}{\partial a_{gl}} = a_{ef}(1 - a_{ge})(1 - a_{gf})\frac{P - wa_{lf}}{P}\frac{\partial X}{\partial a_{gl}}$$

(xviii)
$$\frac{\partial \frac{y_l}{P}}{\partial a_{gl}} = \frac{w}{P}\left[a_{lf}(1 - a_{gl})\frac{\partial X}{\partial a_{gl}} - (x_{lf} + x_{lg})\right]$$

Under the assumptions 1 through 5 above, all personal income tax derivatives (xiii) through (xviii) are negative: By encouraging spending, reduced personal income tax rates would raise output and real income of entrepreneurs and labor alike.

38.8 EMPIRICAL ORDERS OF MAGNITUDE OF PARAMETERS

For evaluation of our fifteen derivatives we would need empirical values for all our parameters. The United States Department of Commerce, however, distinguishes neither between entrepreneur and labor personal income tax payments, nor between entrepreneur and labor consumption, nor between domestic and imported components of consumption and investment. Moreover, United States corporations account for two-thirds of the total value of United States private output rather than for all of it. How do we treat the remaining one-third? Should Proprietors' Income be considered entrepreneur income or labor income?

Using unsophisticated statistical techniques, the author [1] estimated the parameters of our behavior equations (1) and (3) through (9) for the United

Table 38.2 Structure Parameters Adopted

$A_{ef} = 13$	$a_{ge} = 0.17$
$a_{ef} = 0.73$	$A_{gf} = -5.5$
$A_{fe} + A_{fl} = 8.5$	$a_{gf} = 0.24$
$a_{fe} = 0.77$	$A_{gl} = -6.1$
$A_{ff} = -18$	$a_{gl} = 0.13$
$a_{ff} = 0.84$	$A_{lf} = -15$
$a_{fl} = 0.88$	$a_{lf} = 0.57$
$A_{ge} = -3.0$	

Table 38.3 Current Situation Parameters Adopted for 1960

$D/P = 77.82$	$x_{fF} = 24.91$
$P = 1.123$	$x_{fg} = 46.25$
$w = 1.123$	$x_{lg} = 49.57^a$
$x_{eg} = 7.77$	$x_{lg} = 42.14^b$

[a] In our solutions (i) through (iii) x_{lg} includes transfer payments to persons *minus* total contributions for social insurance. It also does this in the derivative (ix), for a price increase will reduce the real value of such transfer payments.

[b] In the derivatives (iv), (vi), (xvi), and (xviii) x_{lg} does not include transfer payments to persons *minus* total contributions for social insurance, assumed unaffected by changes in the wage rate w or the marginal personal labor income tax rate a_{gl}.

States economy 1929–1960, modified them, and adopted the parameter values shown in Tables 38.2 and 38.3 for insertion into our fifteen derivatives.

38.9 CONCLUSIONS

For maximum usefulness our derivatives should be turned into elasticities. The elasticity of a variable X with respect to a parameter a is

$$\frac{\partial X}{\partial a} \frac{a}{X}$$

Because it is a pure number, the elasticity permits comparisons among the efficacies of alternative parameters. Table 38.4 shows the fifteen elasticities of our three variables X, y_e/P, and y_l/P with respect to each of our five wage, price, and tax parameters.

As regards wage policy, a one per cent wage increase *ceteris paribus* leads to a 0.26 per cent decrease in output and a 1.64 per cent decrease in real entrepreneur income. However, labor benefits from a 0.73 per cent increase in real labor income. There is a category of macroeconomic income distribution models referred to as "widow's cruse models" [5]. In such models investment never depends upon profits and entrepreneurs always have a lower propensity to consume than has labor. Consequently, wage increases always raise effective demand, output, and employment. By contrast, our model allows for investment-reducing effects of a wage increase reducing

Table 38.4   Wage, Price, and Tax Elasticities of Output and Distributive Shares

With respect to	Elasticity of domestic business gross product, X	Elasticity of disposable real income of entrepreneur households, y_e/P	Elasticity of disposable real income of labor households, y_l/P
Money wage rate w	−0.26	−1.64	0.73
Price P^a	−0.19	0.98	−1.16
Corporate tax rate a_{gf}	−0.61	−0.88	−0.51
Entrepreneur tax rate a_{ge}	−0.20	−0.42	−0.17
Labor tax rate a_{gl}	−0.54	−0.59	−0.59

^{a} Prices of exports assumed to remain unaltered.

profits. The model shows that as far as output is concerned, the consumption-encouraging effects are more than offset by the investment-discouraging effects.

As regards price policy, a one per cent price increase *ceteris paribus* leads to a 0.19 per cent decrease in output and a 1.16 per cent decrease in real labor income. However, entrepreneurs benefit from a 0.98 per cent increase in real entrepreneur income.

Is it not strange that the consumption-discouraging effects of a price increase are not more than offset by the investment-encouraging effects? In short, why does not a price increase work like a wage increase in reverse? The main reason why it does not is that all tax functions have a negative constant term, hence are progressive: Money tax payment rises in more than proportion to money tax base. Therefore a price increase cannot wholly undo the damage done by a wage increase: The net effect of both of them is a more severe tax bite. In widow's cruse models, no taxes rear their ugly heads. Another reason why a price increase does not work like a wage increase in reverse is that a wage increase is assumed not to raise money transfer payments to persons, while a price increase will reduce their value. In widow's cruse models money transfer payments to persons do not appear.

The elasticities so far considered illuminate the effects of what is often referred to as cost-push inflation. Prices and wages have been known to rise even in years with considerable unemployment and idle capacity—like the year 1960, to which our current-situation parameters refer. For such a year, our elasticities hint that output suffers but labor benefits from a wage increase and that output suffers but entrepreneurs benefit from a price increase. A very different kind of inflation, referred to as demand-pull inflation, is examined in Chapters 39 and 40.

As regards tax policies, the elasticities with respect to a_{ge}, a_{gf}, and a_{gl} are all negative, as we expected them to be. In all cases a one per cent tax rate increase will reduce output or real income by less than one per cent. As regards the relative efficacy of alternative taxes, the corporate income tax rate is seen to affect output more powerfully than do personal income tax rates. However, it is only fair to conclude by emphasizing the sensitivity of elasticities to parameter estimates and by repeating that the estimates rest upon unsophisticated statistical techniques.

REFERENCES

[1] Brems, H., "Wage, Price, and Tax Elasticities of Output and Distributive Shares," *Jour. Am. Stat. Ass.*, **57**, 607–621 (September 1962).
[2] Brittain, J. A., *Corporate Dividend Policy*, Washington, D.C., 1966.
[3] Christ, C. F., "Aggregate Econometric Models," *Am. Econ. Rev.*, **46**, 385–408 (June 1956).
[4] Darling, P. G., "The Influence of Expectations and Liquidity on Dividend Policy, *Jour. Pol. Econ.*, **65**, 209–224 (June 1957).
[5] Kaldor, N., "Alternative Theories of Distribution," *Rev. Econ. Stud.*, 1955–56, **23**, 83–100.
[6] Klein, L. R., and A. S. Goldberger, *An Econometric Model of the United States* 1929–1952, Amsterdam, 1955.
[7] Lintner, J., "Distribution of Incomes of Corporations Among Dividends, Retained Earnings and Taxes," *Am. Econ. Rev.*, **46**, 97–113 (May 1956).

Part Six

Aggregate Equilibrium Time Paths

CHAPTER 39

The Wicksellian Model of Inflation*

39.1 INTRODUCTION

Modern dynamic aggregate analysis dates back to the Wicksellian [1] cumulative process of inflation or deflation. A simple distinction between the rate of interest in banks and the internal rate of return in firms enabled Wicksell to integrate general equilibrium theory, which determines relative prices, with monetary theory, which determines absolute prices. Wicksell could show that if the two rates are equal, a constant price level will result. If they differ, a cumulative process of either rising or falling prices will be unleashed.

39.2 NOTATION

The following notation will be assigned.

Variables

i = the borrowing and lending rate of interest in banks, called "the money rate"
K = available money capital

Parameter

ι = the internal rate of return in firms, called "the real rate"

39.3 THE MODEL

Wicksell's point of departure was a Böhm-Bawerk general-equilibrium model determining the *relative* equilibrium prices of labor, land, and

* Chapter 27 is a prerequisite for Chapter 39.

consumers' goods and with them the internal rate of return. In Chapter 27 we simplified such a model by assuming land to be a free good, and we found the equilibrium internal rate of return to be

$$(4) \qquad \iota = \frac{2\alpha}{\tau(1 - \alpha) - \alpha}$$

where α was a parameter of the production function and τ was the equilibrium period of production. Wicksell assumed capital stock in equilibrium to be just sufficient to permit a one-year period of production; hence he could freeze the latter at $\tau = 1$ and treat the internal rate of return ι as a parameter.

Concerning *absolute* prices the Böhm-Bawerk model could say nothing. To do better, Wicksell separated entrepreneurs and capitalists. Between them he put a bank capable of creating drawing rights upon itself—and sometimes willing to do so. To bridge their one-year gap between input and output, entrepreneurs must borrow from the bank. Capitalists keep their money capital in the form of bank deposits. For an instant, capitalists have a part-time job retailing. At the end of each year they buy the year's output of consumers' goods. Immediately at the beginning of the next year they sell some of it to laborers and landlords and keep the rest for their own consumption. Laborers and landlords stock up for the entire year, relieving the capitalist-retailers of any inventory burden. Entrepreneurs and capitalist-retailers alike expect current prices to prevail in the future.

39.4   EQUILIBRIUM: FIRST   YEAR

At the beginning of the first year, let the entrepreneurs borrow the sum K from the banks and immediately spend it hiring labor and land services, initiating their one-year period of production. Receiving the sum K, laborers and landlords immediately spend it on the consumers' goods produced during last year. The consumers' goods are sold by the capitalist-retailers who deposit the proceeds K in the banks at the rate of interest i. At the end of the first year the value of the capitalists' deposit, then, will be $(1 + i)K$.

When, at the beginning of the first year, the entrepreneurs borrowed the sum K from the banks, they also borrowed at the rate of interest i. At the end of the first year the value of their debt, then, will be $(1 + i)K$.

The internal rate of return in firms embarking upon the one-year period of production is ι. Hence the value of output of consumers' goods at the end of the first year is $(1 + \iota)$ times the value of input purchased at the beginning of the first year, or $(1 + \iota)K$.

Wicksell defined monetary equilibrium as the equality between the money rate and the real rate:

$$i = \iota$$

Since at the end of the first year the value of the capitalists' deposit and the value of the entrepreneurs' debt both equal $(1 + i)K$, and since in monetary equilibrium this, in turn, equals the value of output at the end of the year $(1 + \iota)K$, the capitalist-retailers will be willing and able to buy the output offered them by the entrepreneurs at a value enabling the latter to pay their debts to the banks in full.

39.5   EQUILIBRIUM: SECOND   YEAR

At the beginning of the second year, entrepreneurs again borrow the sum K from the banks, spend it on labor and land services, and embark on another one-year period of production. Laborers and landlords again spend the sum K on consumers' goods.

The capitalist-retailers are spending the first year's income at the beginning of the second year. The first year's income of the capitalist-retailers was iK, which in monetary equilibrium equals ιK. The entrepreneurs, too, are spending the first year's income at the beginning of the second year. During the first year the entrepreneurs earned the real rate but had to pay the money rate on their circulating capital. Since in equilibrium the two rates are equal, no income is left for the entrepreneurs *qua* entrepreneurs. This is as it should be: In a purely competitive economy with freedom of entry, anticipated net profits are zero; and in equilibrium, realized profits equal anticipated profits.

Everybody's propensity to consume being equal to one, at the beginning of the second year aggregate consumption demand by laborers, landlords, capitalists, and entrepreneurs combined is $(1 + \iota)K$. This enables the capitalist-retailers to sell at the beginning of the second year the output of the first year at the value they paid for it at the close of the first year. Harmony prevails, and as long as the money rate and the real rate remain equal, harmony and equilibrium will repeat themselves year after year.

39.6   DISEQUILIBRIUM: FIRST   YEAR

Let the banking system interrupt such an equilibrium by reducing the money rate by one percentage point:

$$i = \iota - 0.01$$

As a result, at the beginning of the first year it must look to the entrepreneurs as if they could make a one percentage point net profits over and above the interest charge: At the prices existing up to this time the interest charge is down by one percentage point. However, anticipated positive net profits are incompatible with a purely competitive economy with freedom of entry. The anticipated positive net profits will be washed away by competitive bidding by entrepreneurs in the input markets, raising *input* prices without affecting total employment. Once input prices have been driven up by one per cent, anticipated net profits have been driven back to zero; and for the time being no further price increases will occur.

To finance constant output and employment at one per cent higher input prices, at the beginning of the first year entrepreneurs had to borrow $1.01K$ rather than K from the banks. Receiving the sum $1.01K$, laborers and landlords in turn spend it on consumers' goods. But last year's physical output and the part of it retained by the capitalists for their own consumption is still the same; so a higher aggregate consumption demand is now chasing a constant physical quantity of consumers' goods. Prices of *consumers' goods* must rise by one per cent.

The consumers' goods are sold by the capitalist-retailers who deposit the proceeds $1.01K$ in the banks at the rate of interest $i = \iota - 0.01$. To the capitalists the increment of $0.01K$ due to a one per cent increase of consumers goods prices is not considered consumable income: The capitalists have no money illusion. At the end of the first year, then, the value of the capitalists' deposit will be $(1 + \iota - 0.01)1.01K$.

When, at the beginning of the first year, the entrepreneurs borrowed the sum $1.01K$ from the banks, they borrowed it at the rate of interest $i = \iota - 0.01$; hence at the end of the first year the value of their debt to the banks will be $(1 + \iota - 0.01)1.01K$.

Since inputs absorbed at the beginning of the year are physically the same, the output of consumers' goods supplied at the end of the year is also physically the same. But the capitalist-retailers always expect current prices to prevail in the future. Hence they will expect to sell in the second year the output of consumers' goods produced during the first year at the new one per cent higher price. At the end of the first year they will therefore engage in competitive bidding in the output market, and the price of output will be one per cent higher than the entrepreneurs had anticipated at the time they embarked upon the first year's one-year period of production. To be sure, the capitalists themselves do not own enough money capital to buy the same physical quantity of consumers' goods at a one per cent higher price. That would require the sum $(1 + \iota)1.01K$, for the real rate is ι. They own merely $(1 + \iota - 0.01)1.01K$, for the money rate is now merely $\iota - 0.01$. But the capitalists, too, may borrow in the banks. So at the end of the first year they will borrow the trifle $0.0101K$ and buy the year's full output at a price one per cent higher than last year.

39.7 DISEQUILIBRIUM: SECOND YEAR

At the beginning of the second year the entrepreneurs have adjusted their expectations upward according to their recent experience. Like the capitalist-retailers they always expect current prices to prevail in the future. Hence they now expect a one per cent higher price of output than they did one year ago.

It seems to the entrepreneurs, although this time for a different reason, that there is again going to be a one percentage point net profits over and above the interest charge. Last year the reason was the reduced money rate. This year the reason is the raised price expectation. But whatever the reason anticipated positive net profits are still incompatible with a purely competitive economy with freedom of entry. Once again, then, the anticipated positive net profits will be washed away by competitive bidding by entrepreneurs in the input markets. Input prices will rise by *another* one per cent, and at the beginning of the second year the entrepreneurs will need and borrow the sum 1.01^2K rather than $1.01K$ from the banks and spend it on labor and land services. Laborers and landlords will spend 1.01^2K rather than $1.01K$ on consumers' goods.

The capitalist-retailers are spending the first year's income at the beginning of the second year. The first year's income of the capitalists is down. True, at the beginning of the first year the bank deposit by capitalists was up by one per cent. But then the money rate was down by one percentage point. Thus on a one per cent larger deposit equal to $1.01K$ they made a one percentage point lower interest rate equal to $i = \iota - 0.01$; hence interest earnings are down at $(\iota - 0.01)1.01K$. The entrepreneurs, too, are spending the first year's income at the beginning of the second year, and for the first time they had a realized but not anticipated positive income. Whereas their output turned out to be worth $(1 + \iota)1.01K$, because the real rate was still ι, they had to repay the banks merely $(1 + \iota - 0.01)1.01K$, because the money rate was merely $\iota - 0.01$. The difference equaling $0.0101K$ they could pocket as a realized net profit over and above interest charges.

Recalling that everybody's propensity to consume equals one, add together the consumption demand of laborers and landlords equal to 1.01^2K, of capitalists equal to $(\iota - 0.01)1.01K$, and of entrepreneurs equal to $0.0101K$, and get the sum $(1.01 + \iota)1.01K$. Once again a higher aggregate consumption demand is chasing a constant physical quantity of consumers' goods, and once again prices of consumers' goods must rise by one per cent. This enables the capitalist-retailers to sell at the beginning of the second year the output of the first year at the value $(1.01 + \iota)1.01K$ exceeding the value $(1 + \iota)1.01K$ they paid for it at the close of the first year. To the capitalists this excess of

$0.0101K$, caused by another one per cent increase of the price of consumers' goods, is not considered consumable income. The excess $0.0101K$ is the trifle they borrowed from the banks, and they will now repay it.

In this way the prices of consumers' goods will keep rising at the rate of one per cent per year until such time that the equality of the money rate and the real rate is restored. When that happens the price level will freeze at whatever new level it happens to have reached.

In similar fashion Wicksell showed that if instead of being reduced, the money rate had been raised so as to exceed the real rate, the prices of consumers' goods would have kept falling until such time that the equality of the money rate and the real rate had been restored.

39.8 CONCLUSION

Wicksell's analysis broke new ground in two respects. First, his distinction between the money rate and the real rate enabled him to bridge the gap between general-equilibrium theory, which determines relative prices, and monetary theory, which determines absolute prices.

Second, Wicksell's emphasis on the timing of events and his careful dating of his variables made his model a pioneering effort in economic dynamics. Whereas economic statics determine the equilibrium level of a variable, economic dynamics determine the equilibrium time path of a variable.

Two important economic phenomena are time paths, hence can be analyzed successfully only within the framework of economic dynamics. The first phenomenon is inflation, and here Wicksell gave us a good start. In Chapter 40 we apply his method of carefully dating all variables to a Keynesian model of inflation. The second phenomenon is growth, to be examined in Chapters 42 through 48.

REFERENCE

[1] Wicksell, K., *Geldzins und Güterpreise*, Jena, 1898. (Translated as *Interest and Prices*, London, 1936.)

CHAPTER 40

Keynesian Models of Inflation*

40.1 INTRODUCTION

Keynes' *General Theory* [1] was written during the Great Depression and determined output by aggregate demand alone. But Keynes' use of aggregates is a powerful tool lending itself to the analysis of inflation as well, as he demonstrated in *How to Pay for the War* [2]. Even the truncated Keynesian model, duly dynamized, has enough power for such a purpose, as we shall now see.

40.2 NOTATION

Applying the truncated Keynesian model to inflation requires a slight addition to, but no change in, the notation used in Chapter 34. It does require an important reshuffling of variables and parameters as follows.

Variables

C = country's output consumed
g_P = proportionate rate of growth of price of country's output
P = price of country's output
X = net national output
Y = net national money income

Parameters

A = autonomous consumption
c = marginal propensity to consume
I = autonomous net investment
$\bar{X}$ = net national output using up all available input

* Chapters 34 and 35 are prerequisites for Chapter 40.

The variables C and X and the parameters I and $\bar{X}$ are measured in physical units of output. Each unit carries the variable price tag P.

40.3 THE STATIC TRUNCATED MODEL

Let us first try to apply the familiar static truncated Keynesian model to the phenomenon of inflation. Let us touch neither its consumption function (1), its equilibrium condition (2), nor its definition of net national money income (7).[1] However, let us tamper, seemingly ever so slightly, with its output solution (3), replacing $X \leq \bar{X}$ by

$$X > \bar{X}$$

The moment we do this we find ourselves in deep trouble. In Fig. 40.1 the shaded vertical line through $\bar{X}$ divides our two-dimensional space into three subsets: First, points on the line itself in which $X = \bar{X}$, second, points to

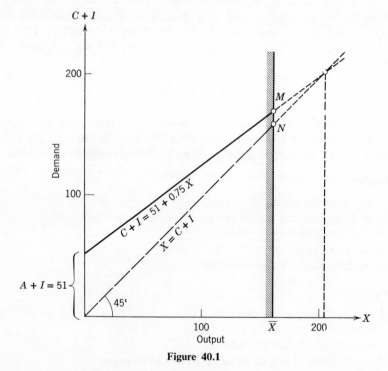

Figure 40.1

[1] Equations (1) through (7) are contained in Chapter 34.

the left of it in which $X < \bar{X}$, and third, points to the right of it in which $X > \bar{X}$. The first two subsets include all feasible solutions, hitherto assumed to prevail. The last subset includes all the nonfeasible ones, now to be examined. Our trouble stems from the fact that the only output compatible with equilibrium is no longer feasible: Figure 40.1 shows the solid aggregate demand line and the broken 45° line to intersect to the right of the shaded vertical line.

Output cannot be pushed beyond $\bar{X}$, but here aggregate demand is in excess of output, consequently the economy will find itself with an inventory depletion MN in Fig. 40.1. After inventory had been run down, and perhaps before that, we would have the situation of "too much money chasing too few goods", and in the absence of price control the price P of goods would start rising.

But price rise is inflation, is it not? Hence have we not explained inflation? We really have not. The trouble is that although the price rise is a necessary consequence of the gap between demand and output, there is nothing in the price rise which tends to eliminate that gap. The consumption function (1) of the truncated Keynesian model has no money illusion in it, and autonomous investment has been defined in terms of physical unit of output; hence consumption and autonomous investment alike are insensitive to the price P. No price rise will curtail demand then. But are not firms and households at least going to run out of money? Not in the truncated Keynesian model,

Table 40.1   The Twelve OECD Countries 1950–1960

Country	Unemployment proportion of labor force	G.N.P. Proportionate price index increase
Switzerland	0.002	0.126
France	0.013	0.861
Sweden	0.017	0.596
Netherlands	0.019	0.383
Norway	0.020	0.494
United Kingdom	0.025	0.479
Germany	0.041	0.373
Denmark	0.043	0.380
Canada	0.044	0.361
United States	0.045	0.279
Belgium	0.054	0.264
Italy	0.079	0.277

for its Eq. (7) says that any price rise will automatically produce a proportionate rise in net national money income. Being incapable of eliminating its own source and meeting no bounds, the price rise must be instant and boundless.

However, neither the Central European hyperinflations of the early twenties nor the Latin American ones of the fifties were instant and boundless, not to mention the mild Western European inflations of the fifties: Using Maddison [3], Table 40.1 shows price increase and unemployment for the twelve OECD countries 1950–1960. Five of them, that is, France, the Netherlands, Norway, Sweden, and Switzerland, had an average unemployment proportion of 2 per cent or less for the whole decade, and rarely have highly developed economies been closer to sustained full employment than that. Yet their G.N.P. price indices showed rather moderate proportionate increases.

In passing we may notice the close relationship between inflation and unemployment. Plot the data from Table 40.1 as shown in Fig. 40.2 and see how tempting it would be to ignore Switzerland and fit a modified Phillips [5, 6] curve to the remaining eleven points, "modified" in the sense that it would use price increases rather than wage increases and cross-section rather than time-series data. We shall return to Switzerland in Section 40.7.

Real-world inflation being quite moderate rather than instant and boundless, we must ask *how* moderate and why, and this the static truncated Keynesian model cannot tell us. We must borrow a leaf from Wicksell's book and try to dynamize that model.

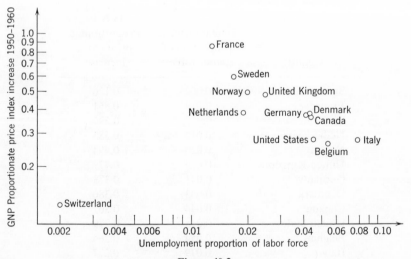

Figure 40.2

40.4   THE DYNAMIC TRUNCATED MODEL

Let a magnitude dated (t) refer to period t. Which magnitudes should be dated? First and foremost all variables, but in addition we shall also be dating two parameters, I and $\bar{X}$, for unlike such structural parameters as A and c, autonomous investment I may change from one period to the next, and so may capacity $\bar{X}$, for example, because of labor migration or the completion of new plant.

In our static truncated Keynesian model in Chapter 34 the consumption function (1) was $C = A + cX$. But since according to (7), $Y = PX$, we could also have written it $C = A + cY/P$. Written in this form it may be dated, and let all its variables refer to the same period. Hence consumption in any one period is assumed to be a function of the real income of that period:

$$(1a) \qquad C(t) = A + c\,\frac{Y(t)}{P(t)}$$

Equilibrium in any one period requires the sum of consumption and investment demand in that period to equal the output of that period, or inventory would accumulate or be depleted:

$$(2a) \qquad X(t) = C(t) + I(t)$$

So far, no intertemporal relationships have been introduced. Within Eqs. (1a) and (2a) all variables refer to the same period; thus our dating still has not made the model dynamic. Our last chance of dynamizing the truncated Keynesian model comes in Eq. (7) of Chapter 34. Remembering that the model is a short-run model, hence should have a short unit period, let us dynamize Eq. (7) by saying that the money value of *this* period's net national output becomes the net national money income of the *next* period:

$$(7a) \qquad Y(t + 1) = P(t)X(t)$$

Equation (7a) introduces an intertemporal relationship, for it contains variables referring to different periods. As long as at least one equation of a system does that, the system is dynamic. How did we dynamize it? Not by introducing the income-expenditure lag, which Metzler [4] found to be unimportant, but by introducing the output-income lag, which he found to be important, especially for income in the form of dividends.

Introducing the output-income lag in the form of Eq. (7a) has far-reaching consequences. No longer can a price rise within a period automatically produce a proportionate rise in the net national money income within the same period; it can only produce such a rise in the next period. In other words, once period t is over, $Y(t + 1)$ has become frozen. Consequently, a rise of $P(t + 1)$ may now make people run out of money, make them curtail demand, and thus eliminate the gap between demand and output. As a result, for any period t equilibrium output may now be a feasible one:

(8) $X(t) = \bar{X}(t)$

If so—and it still remains to be seen if the system has a solution—the price rise would no longer be instant and boundless but slow and manageable. To see explicitly *how* slow, we should define the proportionate rate of growth $g_P(t)$ of price from period t to period $t + 1$:

(9) $P(t + 1) = [1 + g_P(t)]P(t)$

40.5 SOLUTION

The time has come to see if the system (1a), (2a), (7a), (8), and (9) has a solution determining the time path of price P. Write (1a), (2a), and (8) for period $t + 1$, and insert (1a) and (8) into (2a):

(10) $\bar{X}(t + 1) - [A + I(t + 1)] = c\,\dfrac{Y(t + 1)}{P(t + 1)}$

Although it is not a solution, (10) permits us to see the mechanism at work determining the price $P(t + 1)$. On the left-hand side of (10) we have for period $t + 1$ capacity output *minus* all autonomous demand, that is, the capacity available for satisfying induced demand. On the right-hand side we have induced demand itself, $cY(t + 1)/P(t + 1)$. Now, according to (7a), net national money income $Y(t + 1)$ is determined solely by what took place in period t; hence it is unaffected by what is going to take place in period $t + 1$. Once period t is over, $Y(t + 1)$ has become frozen. The role of the variable price $P(t + 1)$ now becomes visible: Regardless of how high $Y(t + 1)$ has become, induced demand $cY(t + 1)/P(t + 1)$ can always be pared down to match capacity available for satisfying it, simply by letting price $P(t + 1)$ rise enough. The assumption is, of course, that such capacity exists in the first place, that is, that the left-hand side of (10) is positive.

To arrive at our solution, insert (7a), (8), and (9) into (10):

(11) $1 + g_P(t) = \dfrac{c\,\bar{X}(t)}{\bar{X}(t + 1) - [A + I(t + 1)]}$

Only parameters appear on the right-hand side of (11); hence (11) is the solution we have been looking for. Our original truncated Keynesian model assumed that $0 < c < 1$. Add two more assumptions, that is, that for period t, capacity output $\bar{X}(t)$ is positive, and that for period $t + 1$, capacity output

$\bar{X}(t + 1)$ exceeds the sum of the autonomous demand of that period. It follows that our solution (11) is positive and unique.

40.6 NUMERICAL EXERCISE

Let us choose the following set of numerical values of our parameters:

$$A = 30$$
$$c = \tfrac{3}{4}$$
$$I(t + 1) = 21$$
$$\bar{X}(t) = \bar{X}(t + 1) = 160$$

This is the numerical example underlying Fig. 40.1. For these five values Eq. (11) will give us the solution

$$g_P(t) = \tfrac{11}{109}$$

In other words, from period t to period $t + 1$ prices will rise by approximately 10 per cent.

40.7 CONCLUSIONS

Our system has the positive and unique solution (11); hence (8), which is part of the system, may hold. The price rise is no longer instant and boundless; its speed as determined by (11) depends upon all the parameters of the system. To see precisely how, let us find the five elasticities:

(12) $$\frac{\partial[1 + g_P(t)]}{\partial c}\frac{c}{1 + g_P(t)} = \frac{\partial[1 + g_P(t)]}{\partial \bar{X}(t)}\frac{\bar{X}(t)}{1 + g_P(t)}$$

(13) $$= 1$$

(14) $$\frac{\partial[1 + g_P(t)]}{\partial \bar{X}(t + 1)}\frac{\bar{X}(t + 1)}{1 + g_P(t)} = -\frac{\bar{X}(t + 1)}{\bar{X}(t + 1) - [A + I(t + 1)]}$$

(15) $$\frac{\partial[1 + g_P(t)]}{\partial A}\frac{A}{1 + g_P(t)} = \frac{A}{\bar{X}(t + 1) - [A + I(t + 1)]}$$

(16) $$\frac{\partial[1 + g_P(t)]}{\partial I(t + 1)}\frac{I(t + 1)}{1 + g_P(t)} = \frac{I(t + 1)}{\bar{X}(t + 1) - [A + I(t + 1)]}$$

The elasticities (12), (13), (15), and (16) are positive. Consequently, inflation is accelerated by a higher propensity to consume, for the higher the propensity to consume, the more induced demand is generated to chase the output of period $t + 1$. Inflation is also accelerated by higher capacity output $\bar{X}(t)$, for the higher the capacity output in period t, the more induced demand is generated to chase the output of period $t + 1$. Finally, inflation is accelerated by higher autonomous demands A and $I(t + 1)$, leaving less of the available capacity output for satisfying induced demand.

The elasticity (14) is negative. Consequently, inflation is slowed down by a higher capacity output $\bar{X}(t + 1)$, leaving more of the available capacity for satisfying induced demand. A rising capacity output is what explains the remarkable slowness of the Swiss price increase in the fifties, which we noticed in Fig. 40.2: Switzerland had by far the lowest unemployment proportion but also by far the lowest price increase. However, notice that Italy, Switzerland's neighbor, had the highest unemployment proportion. The main reason for the slowness of the Swiss price increase must have been the highly elastic supply of Italian labor flowing into Switzerland so rapidly that by 1960 foreign labor constituted a third of the Swiss labor force.

40.8   THE COMPLETE KEYNESIAN MODEL

With as few assumptions as those underlying our dynamic truncated Keynesian model we managed to explain inflation without bringing up the subject of the money supply. In the hope of an even better explanation, let us now consider the complete Keynesian model with its emphasis on the money supply. Like the truncated Keynesian model, the complete model assumes a closed economy.

Originally we assumed the solution for output in the complete Keynesian model, Eq. (7), to be a feasible one. With that assumption dropped to make room for inflation, everything develops at first just as described in the truncated model: Output cannot keep up with demand, inventory is being depleted, and prices must rise. However, now comes the difference between the truncated and the complete Keynesian model. At higher prices the same physical consumption and net investment would require more transactions money T [see Eqs. (3) and (5) of the complete Keynesian model in Chapter 35].

At this point everything is up to the monetary authorities. Suppose for the time being that they refuse to expand the money supply M. Then additional transactions money T must come out of asset-holding money H [see Eq. (6), Chapter 35]. But only a higher rate of interest will persuade asset holders to part with money. According to Eq. (2) of the complete Keynesian model, such a higher rate of interest will reduce physical net investment, and as a result equilibrium output may now have become feasible. By restricting the money supply M, the monetary authorities can always stop inflation. The guarantee that they can lies in the steepness of the left-hand side of the X-M curve in Fig. 35.9.

40.9 TIGHT MONEY: AN OPEN-ECONOMY RESERVATION

The complete Keynesian model has shown how a determined closed-economy central bank can always stop inflation. Its instrument is open-market operations: Its sale of bonds will depress the price of such bonds and absorb cash held by the country's capitalists and private banks.

In an open economy, however, there may be a stumbling block to tight money. Assume the existence of foreign capitalists. At long-run fixed exchange rates those foreign capitalists will represent a practically infinitely price-elastic demand for the country's bonds whenever the domestic price of bonds falls ever so slightly below the foreign price of similar bonds. At that point, further sale of bonds by the domestic central bank will encounter a floor to the price of bonds. Encountering that floor the central bank cannot depress the price of bonds any further and can absorb no cash held by the country's own capitalists and private banks. Instead it will attract cash (ultimately gold) held by foreign capitalists and banks.

West German monetary experience in the 1960's illustrates the helplessness of an open-economy central bank trying to raise domestic interest rates by selling bonds in the open market. Eventually, the government came to its help and lowered the floor by announcing in 1964 a bill taxing away 25 per cent of the interest payments on bonds issued in West Germany but owned by nonresidents of that country.

40.10 EASY MONEY

Returning now to the complete Keynesian model of a closed economy, what if the monetary authorities had willingly expanded the money supply M to meet the increased demand for transactions money T? Then no curtailment of asset-holding money H, no increase in the rate of interest, and no reduction of physical net investment would have been called for, and equilibrium output would not have come any closer to feasibility.

Thus we would have been back at the truncated Keynesian model: Inflation would have gone on at the speed determined by our solution (11) of this chapter. If the money supply is not being used for a brake, it may as well be left out of the model, and that is exactly what the truncated Keynesian model does.

REFERENCES

[1] Keynes, J. M., *The General Theory of Employment, Interest, and Money*, London and New York, 1936.

[2] Keynes, J. M., *How to Pay for the War*, London and New York, 1940.

[3] Maddison, A., *Economic Growth in the West*, New York, 1964, pp. 44–45.

[4] Metzler, L. A., "Three Lags in the Circular Flow of Income," in *Income Employment and Public Policy, Essays in Honor of Alvin H. Hansen*, New York, 1948, pp. 11–32.

[5] Phillips, A. W., "The Relation between Unemployment and the Rate of Change of Money Wage Rates in the United Kingdom, 1861–1957," *Economica*, **25**, 283–299 (November 1958).

[6] Samuelson, P. A., and R. M. Solow, "Analytical Aspects of Anti-Inflation Policy," *Am. Econ. Rev.*, **50**, 177–194 (May 1960).

CHAPTER 41

Suppressed Inflation

41.1 INTRODUCTION

A wartime economy suppressing its inflation by direct price, wage, and dividend controls invites gap analysis. A Keynesian model ignores the markets for inputs; hence it can analyze merely the output gap and price control. A Swedish model [3, 4] distinguishes between input and output markets, hence can find an input gap as well as an output gap and analyze wage and dividend controls as well as price control. Above all, it can show us the asymmetry between wage and dividend controls, on the one hand, and price control on the other: Laxity of wage and dividend controls widens the gaps, whereas laxity of price controls narrows the gaps.

A Swedish model also distinguishes between *ex ante* and *ex post*, which is always illuminating but becomes vital in the analysis of wartime suppressed inflation.

41.2 NOTATION

In our Swedish gap model, the following notation will be assigned.

Variables

v_{ij} = sale by sector i to sector j
x_{ij} = purchase by sector j from sector i
X = gross national output
$\bar{X}$ = gross national output using up all available input

Parameters

a_{fh} = household propensity to consume personal real income
a_{hf} = input absorbed per unit of output

p = price of inputs

P = price of output

$*x_{ff}$ = gross real investment expected by firms, including military output

$\bar{x}_{hf}$ = available inputs

41.3 GENERAL CASE: EQUILIBRIUM IN A BUYER'S MARKET

Ignore for the moment our wartime economy and think of a buyer's market. In such a market *ex ante* purchases are planned by the purchasers and *ex ante* sales are expected by the sellers. At frozen prices of input and output let all plans and expectations be single-valued. Let the asterisk *, and later the small circle °, denote *ex ante* magnitudes, and let their absence denote *ex post* magnitudes. Apply the distinction between *ex ante* and *ex post* to a static closed Leontief-like model with only two sectors, that is, firms and households. Let planned purchases of inputs by firms be in proportion to planned output:

(1) $$*x_{hf} = a_{hf} * X$$

where $a_{hf} > 0$. Let planned purchases of output by households be in proportion to expected personal real income:

(2) $$*x_{fh} = a_{fh} \frac{p}{P} *v_{hf}$$

where $0 < a_{fh} < 1$. In a buyer's market, for firms and households alike, purchase plans may materialize:

(3) $$*x_{hf} = x_{hf}$$

(4) $$*x_{fh} = x_{fh}$$

And production plans may also materialize:

(5) $$*X = X$$

Looked at *ex post*, any sector's realized purchases from another sector constitutes the latter's realized sales to the former:

(6) $$x_{hf} = v_{hf}$$

(7) $$x_{fh} = v_{fh}$$

As an equilibrium condition, any sector's expected sales to another sector must equal its realized sales:

(8) $$*v_{hf} = v_{hf}$$

(9) $$*v_{fh} = v_{fh}$$

Finally, let firms plan their output so as to equal expected sales:

(10) $$*X = *x_{ff} + *v_{fh}$$

These ten equations suffice to determine our ten variables, that is, two planned purchases $*x_{ij}$, two realized ones x_{ij}, two expected sales $*v_{ij}$, two realized ones v_{ij}, planned output $*X$, and realized output X. Subscripts ij equal hf or fh. Solve for equilibrium output and input:

(11) $$*X = \frac{*x_{ff}}{1 - a_{fh}a_{hf}p/P}$$

(12) $$*x_{hf} = \frac{a_{hf}*x_{ff}}{1 - a_{fh}a_{hf}p/P}$$

We assumed $0 < a_{fh} < 1$. Assume $*x_{ff} > 0$. In the denominators, the term $a_{fh}a_{hf}p/P$ is interpreted as follows. The factor $a_{hf}p/P$ is the personal income paid out per dollar's worth of gross output and must be less than one, because of both capital consumption allowances and corporate withholdings of profits. Consequently, $0 < a_{fh}a_{hf}p/P < 1$, and our solutions (11) and (12) are positive and unique.

41.4   DEFINITIONS OF FULL GAPS

The levels of output and input determined by our solutions (11) and (12) are equilibrium levels in the sense that plans are carried out and expectations come true. However, they need not be full-employment solutions. They may be, but for all we know they may also leave some input unused, or they may be nonfeasible, requiring more input than is available. Here is where our gaps should be defined. Let all available input be $\bar{x}_{hf}$, where $\bar{x}_{hf} > 0$. Since the input coefficient a_{hf} is a positive parameter, by using up all available input firms could produce the positive output:

(13) $$\bar{X} = \frac{\bar{x}_{hf}}{a_{hf}}$$

The full output gap may now be defined as

(14) $$*X - \bar{X}$$

And the full input gap may be defined as

(15) $$*x_{hf} - \bar{x}_{hf}$$

Since in our simple two-sector model there is only one input x_{hf}, the full output gap and the full input gap are either both negative, both zero, or both positive. If they are negative, they are called deflationary gaps; hence we are having buyer's markets, and equilibrium is feasible. In this case the minuend of the gaps (14) and (15) is materializing.

If the gaps are zero, equilibrium is still feasible, and the minuend and subtrahend of the gaps (14) and (15) are both materializing, for they are equal.

If the gaps are positive, they are called inflationary gaps; then we are having seller's markets and equilibrium is nonfeasible. In this case the subtrahend of the gaps (14) and (15) is materializing, and we shall now turn our attention to it.

41.5 DEFINITION OF PARTIAL INFLATIONARY GAPS

While serving the purpose of comparing an imaginary buyer's market with the existing seller's market, the positive gaps (14) and (15) do not measure the pressure on wage, dividend, and price controls. For no demand for output is bred by the nonexisting income of the lacking labor force; demand can be bred only by the income earned by the actual labor force. Let us therefore allow for the fact that in a seller's market, household money income is not going to be p^*v_{hf} but $p\bar{x}_{hf}$; consequently planned purchases of output by households is not going to be (2) but

$$(16) \qquad °x_{fh} = a_{fh} \frac{p}{P} \bar{x}_{hf}$$

Consequently, the demand faced by the firms, and pressing against the price controls, is

$$(17) \qquad °X = {}^*x_{ff} + °x_{fh}$$

Therefore the partial output gap, faced by the firms and measuring the pressure against the price controls, is

$$(18) \qquad °X - \bar{X}$$

Insert (13), (16), and (17) into (18), and express the partial output gap in terms of parameters alone:

$$(19) \qquad °X - \bar{X} = {}^*x_{ff} + \left(a_{fh} \frac{p}{P} - \frac{1}{a_{hf}} \right) \bar{x}_{hf}$$

Furthermore, if firms could sell, not $^*X$ as defined by (10), but $°X$ as defined by (17), their planned purchases of inputs are not going to be (1) but

$$(20) \qquad °x_{hf} = a_{hf} °X$$

Hence the partial input gap, faced by the households and measuring the pressure against the wage and dividend controls, is

(21) $$°x_{hf} - \bar{x}_{hf}$$

Insert (16), (17), and (20) into (21), and express the partial input gap in terms of parameters alone:

(22) $$°x_{hf} - \bar{x}_{hf} = a_{hf}{}^* x_{ff} + \left(a_{fh}a_{hf}\frac{p}{P} - 1\right)\bar{x}_{hf}$$

41.6 SENSITIVITY OF GAPS TO PRICE, WAGE, AND DIVIDEND CONTROLS

Let us find the sensitivity of the partial output and input gaps (19) and (22) to the controlled prices p and P. First, the derivatives of the gaps with respect to the price of input p:

(23) $$\frac{\partial(°X - \bar{X})}{\partial p} = \frac{a_{fh}\bar{x}_{hf}}{P}$$

(24) $$\frac{\partial(°x_{hf} - \bar{x}_{hf})}{\partial p} = \frac{a_{fh}a_{hf}\bar{x}_{hf}}{P}$$

Then the derivatives with respect to the price of output P:

(25) $$\frac{\partial(°X - \bar{X})}{\partial P} = - \frac{a_{fh}p\bar{x}_{hf}}{P^2}$$

(26) $$\frac{\partial(°x_{hf} - \bar{x}_{hf})}{\partial P} = - \frac{a_{fh}a_{hf}p\bar{x}_{hf}}{P^2}$$

We have already assumed that $0 < a_{fh} < 1$, $a_{hf} > 0$, and that $\bar{x}_{hf} > 0$. Consequently, at positive price p of input and price P of output, the derivatives (23) and (24) are positive; hence lax wage and dividend controls, permitting the price p of input to rise, will widen the gaps. Under the same assumptions, the derivatives (25) and (26) are negative; hence lax price controls, permitting the price P of output to rise, will narrow the gaps. This important asymmetry between the two kinds of controls can be seen only from a model distinguishing between an input market and an output market. Unlike a Keynesian model, that is precisely what a Swedish model does.

What if input price controls and output price controls alike are lax, permitting p and P to rise in proportion, so that the ratio between them p/P remains unchanged? Neither the solution (19) of the partial output gap nor the solution (22) of the partial input gap contains the prices p and P in any other form than the ratio between them p/P. Hence (19) and (22) will remain unchanged as long as the latter ratio does. Laxity of all controls does not affect the gaps.

41.7 USE OF GAPS

The sizes of the partial gaps (19) and (22) measure the pressure on output and input price controls, respectively. Consequently, estimation of their sizes is important when considering the introduction of a rationing system. The more law-abiding and honest the population is, the more politically alert and vocal it is, and the more honest and efficient the administration is, the sooner a given size of gaps will lead to rationing. Why rationing? Rationing of output will prevent scarce consumers' goods from going mostly to those who have enough spare time for queuing up for hours, nights, and days—that is, those who contribute the least to the war effort. Rationing of input will prevent scarce inputs from going mostly to those industries which produce the least essential goods, lampshades for example, for such industries may not have been found important enough to qualify for price controls; hence they are likely to operate under fat profit margins permitting all sorts of fringe benefits being offered to labor. Even when qualifying for price controls, such industries are likely to consist of a large number of small proprietors, much more difficult to supervise than large corporations. It is an important purpose of central labor allocation to starve such industries of labor.

But how does one estimate the size of gaps? It follows from their nature that estimates cannot be checked against experience, for experience consists of *ex post* magnitudes, and between the latter there can be no gaps.[1] "What Petterson has purchased, Anderson must have sold," as Ohlin used to say.

However, inflationary gaps display symptoms, and symptoms may be measured. Good symptom statistics are such things as number of employment applications per 100 vacancies, number of building permits granted per 100 applications, number of bankruptcies per annum, and number of protested notes per annum.

41.8 THE THEORY OF GROWTH

Inflation was the proportionate rate of growth of a country's prices. Let us now turn our attention to a different proportionate rate of growth—that of a country's net national output. We shall begin with Harrod-Domar models, which assume no supply limitations to exist other than a fixed

---

[1] Unlike the Warburton [5] gap, but like the Friedman [2] and Ensley–Goode [1] gap, the Swedish gaps are—in the words of Friedman—"never of the past or the present; [they are] always in the future."

capital coefficient. Later, we shall introduce labor supply, substitution between labor and capital, and embodied as well as disembodied technological progress.

REFERENCES

[1] Ensley, G. W., and R. Goode, "Mr. Warburton on the Inflationary Gap," *Am. Econ. Rev.*, **33**, 897–99 (December 1943).

[2] Friedman, Milton, "Discussion of the Inflationary Gap," *Am. Econ. Rev.*, **32**, 314–20 (June 1942).

[3] Hansen, B., *A Study in the Theory of Inflation*, London, 1951.

[4] Lundberg, E., *Konjunkturer och ekonomisk politik*, Stockholm, 1953. (Translated by J. Potter as *Business Cycles and Economic Policy*, London, 1957.)

[5] Warburton, C., "Measuring the Inflationary Gap," *Am. Econ. Rev.*, **33**, 365–69 (June 1943); and "Who Makes the Inflationary Gap," *ibid.*, **33**, 607–12 (September 1943).

CHAPTER 42

The One-Country Harrod-Domar
Model of Growth*

42.1 INTRODUCTION

The net flow of water into a reservoir can be assumed to leave the level
of water in the reservoir unaffected only if an ultrashort period of time is
considered. The Keynesian model did exactly that. In the Keynesian model,
the level of water in the reservoir is represented by capital stock, and the net
flow of water into the reservoir is represented by net investment. Hence the
paradox that the Keynesian model treats net investment as positive, yet
evidently considers capital stock a constant. Had a unit period of finite
length been considered, a positive net investment would have expanded
capital stock and with it output. A growth path of output could have been
traced rather than the level of output.

Actually, this had been done long before Harrod [6], Domar [4], or even
Keynes: Cassel [3] had a growth equation identical with Harrod's equation
$GC = s.$[1] The Cassel-Harrod-Domar model is much more than a minor

---

* Chapters 33 and 34 are prerequisites for Chapter 42.
[1] Cassel's [3] notation was

Capital stock	C
Annual income	I
Percentage rate of growth per annum	p
Propensity to save	$1/s$
Equation	$\dfrac{I}{s} = \dfrac{p}{100} C$

Cassel estimated the reciprocal of the capital coefficient I/C to be 0.15, the propensity
to save $1/s$ to be 0.20, giving him a percentage rate of growth per annum $p = 3$, which
he considered normal for pre-World War I Europe.

modification of a Keynesian model. Technically, it substitutes difference or differential equations with respect to time for equations whose variables carry no reference to time at all. Economically, it seems to restore thriftiness to the place of honor it held before Keynes.

42.2 NOTATION

In a dynamic macroeconomic model the following notation will be assigned.

Variables

C = country's output consumed
g = proportionate rate of growth of the country's net national output
I = net investment
S = capital stock
X = net national output

Parameters

b = Harrod-Domar capital coefficient
c = propensity to consume

The stock variable S is measured in physical units of output. The flow variables C, I, and X are measured in physical units of output per unit of time.

Let t be the time coordinate dating variables: A flow variable marked (t) refers to period t, a stock variable marked (t) refers to time t. Let period t be the period beginning at time t, ending at time $t + 1$.

42.3 THE MODEL

First, define the proportionate rate of growth of output:

(1) $$X(t + 1) = [1 + g(t)]X(t)$$

Second, define net investment as the net increase of capital stock:

(2) $$I(t) = S(t + 1) - S(t)$$

Harrod's [6] notation was

Capital coefficient	C
Proportionate rate of growth	G
Propensity to save	s
Equation	$GC = s$

Third, let required capital stock be in proportion to output, the factor of proportionality being the Harrod-Domar capital coefficient b:

(3) $$S(t) = bX(t)$$

Fourth, apply the aggregate consumption function (28) derived in Chapter 33:

(4) $$C(t) = cX(t)$$

Fifth, equilibrium requires the sum of consumption and investment demand for output to equal output, or inventory would accumulate or be depleted:

(5) $$X(t) = C(t) + I(t)$$

Equations (1) through (5) constitute the Harrod-Domar model and are assumed to hold for any t. When solved for $X(t + 1)$, the system (2) through (5) gives us the simplest form of a first-order difference equation, that is, a linearly homogeneous one:

(6) $$X(t + 1) + AX(t) = 0$$

where

$$A = - \frac{1 - c + b}{b}$$

42.4 SOLUTION FOR THE PROPORTIONATE RATE OF GROWTH OF OUTPUT

If we are merely interested in the proportionate rate of growth of output, we now have all we need. Combine (1) and (6):

(7) $$g(t) = \frac{1 - c}{b}$$

Here is the famous Harrod-Domar result that the proportionate rate of growth of output equals the propensity to save $1 - c$ divided by the capital coefficient b. Notice the absence of any time coordinate on the right-hand side of (7); hence the proportionate rate of growth has no time trend in it. Thus the constancy of the rate is a result, not an assumption.

Now a contradiction starts to emerge between static Keynesian reasoning and dynamic Harrod-Domar reasoning: In a truncated Keynesian model, a lower propensity to save could not hurt investment, for the latter was a parameter; saving was a bad thing, and the less of it the better for an under-employed economy. By contrast, a lower propensity to save can hurt Harrod-Domar investment, for the latter is no parameter but a variable permitting growth; hence a lower propensity to save reduces the rate of growth; saving is a good thing and the less of it the worse for a growing economy. To this contradiction we shall return.

42.5 RECURSIVE SOLUTION FOR THE GROWTH PATH OF OUTPUT

The proportionate rate of growth of output is only part of the story. In addition, we may wish to know the exact location of the entire growth path of output. Here, Eq. (6) is not enough; to set the system in motion we need a point of departure, that is, an initial condition:

$$(8) \qquad\qquad X(0) = B$$

Now the system can move: Putting $X(0)$ as determined by (8) into Eq. (6) gives us $X(1)$. Putting $X(1)$ right back into (6) gives us $X(2)$, etc. In this way we could calculate our way ahead to any desired future period. Such a solution is always possible; it is called a recursive one. But is there no easier way?

42.6 ANALYTICAL SOLUTION FOR THE GROWTH PATH OF OUTPUT

As a bold guess let us try

$$(9) \qquad\qquad X(t) = x^t$$

Insert (9) into (6):

$$x^{t+1} + Ax^t = 0$$

Divide by x^t and use (6):

$$(10) \qquad\qquad x = -A = \frac{1 - c + b}{b}$$

To convince ourselves that $X(t) = (-A)^t$ does satisfy (6), insert it into the latter and factor out $(-A)^t$:

$$(-A)^t[(-A) + A] = 0$$

Since the expression in the brackets is always zero, we have the identity $0 = 0$. So our bold guess worked well as far as the original difference equation (6) is concerned. But it does not work as far as the initial condition (8) is concerned. In (9) set $t = 0$ and get $X(0) = 1$. However, (8) stated that $X(0) = B$; hence our guess generally does not work. Let us repair the damage by introducing the following theorem: If $X(t) = x^t$ satisfies (6), so does

$$(11) \qquad\qquad X(t) = mx^t$$

where m is an arbitrary constant. As a proof, insert (11) into (6):

$$m(x^{t+1} + Ax^t) = 0$$

This must be true regardless of the value of m, for $X(t) = x^t$ satisfies (6); hence it makes the expression in parentheses on the left-hand side zero. Now apply our theorem and in (11) set $t = 0$:

(12) $X(0) = m$

Since m was an arbitrary constant, nothing keeps us from setting it equal to B, thereby arriving at a solution:

(13) $X(t) = B(-A)^t$

which satisfies the original difference equation (6) as well as the initial condition (8). Now as we know from (6), behind A we find our old friends the propensity to consume c and the capital coefficient b. Hence from a knowledge of those two behavior parameters and of the initial condition B, (13) permits us to calculate $X(t)$ for any future or past t without having to calculate it for any other t.

42.7 INTERPRETATION OF SOLUTION

Our solution (13) permits the time path of output $X(t)$ to display seven alternative patterns:

If $-A < -1$, $X(t)$ explodes and fluctuates. For t equal to even numbers, $X(t)$ will have the same sign as B. For t equal to odd numbers, $X(t)$ will have the opposite sign.

If $-A = -1$, $X(t)$ fluctuates but will neither explode nor vanish. For t equal to even numbers, $X(t) = B$. For t equal to odd numbers, $X(t) = -B$.

If $-1 < -A < 0$, $X(t)$ vanishes and fluctuates. For t equal to even numbers $X(t)$ will have the same sign as B. For t equal to odd numbers $X(t)$ will have the opposite sign.

If $-A = 0$, $X(t) = 0$.

If $0 < -A < 1$, $X(t)$ vanishes and always has the same sign as B.

If $-A = 1$, $X(t) = B$.

If $-A > 1$, $X(t)$ explodes upward if B is positive, downward if B is negative.

Now where does $-A$ lie? As we recall from (6),

$$-A = \frac{1 - c + b}{b}$$

The capital coefficient b must be nonnegative, for if it were negative, Eq. (3) would give us a negative capital stock for a positive output, and a negative capital stock is meaningless.

Furthermore, the propensity to consume c must be around one. If $c < 1$, then $-A > 1$, and the economy will be a growing one. If $c = 1$, then $-A = 1$, and the economy will be a stationary one. If $c > 1$, then $-A < 1$, and the economy will be a decaying one.

Thus the Harrod-Domar model is a model of decay or of the stationary state no less than it is a model of growth. Economies of the Middle Ages may have been stationary. And for brief periods more recently, open economies may have displayed decay, like that of Ireland under the mass emigration following the failure of the potato crop in the 1840's, or like that of the German Democratic Republic at the height of the Soviet exploitation of it before 1953.

42.8 THE DIMENSION OF THE CAPITAL COEFFICIENT

We should like to illustrate the Harrod-Domar growth equilibrium graphically, but before doing that we must clear up the matter of the dimension of the capital coefficient b. Write Eq. (3):

$$(3) \qquad b = \frac{S(t)}{X(t)}$$

Now we said that the stock variable $S(t)$ was measured in physical units of output, and that the flow variable $X(t)$ was measured in physical units of output per unit of time. Consequently, the dimension of the capital coefficient b is number of units of time. By way of illustration, let the time unit be one year and the capital stock be, say, five years' output. Choosing a different time unit should not change the underlying technological relationship between capital stock and output. So if the unit of time were not a year but a decade, the capital coefficient would be one-half decade for capital stock still to be equal to five years' output. And if the unit of time had been two years, the capital coefficient would be $2\frac{1}{2}$ two-year periods for capital stock still to be equal to five years' output. Had the unit of time been a quarter, the capital coefficient would be 20 quarters. And now we are ready for our graphical illustration.

42.9 GRAPHICAL ILLUSTRATION

To illustrate the Harrod-Domar growth equilibrium, let us select a two-year period for our unit of time. Let us then select the following values of our parameters:

$$b = 2\tfrac{1}{2} \text{ two-year periods}$$
$$c = \tfrac{4}{5}$$

For these two values, Eq. (7) gives us the solution for the proportionate rate of growth:

$$g(t) = \tfrac{2}{25}$$

per two-year period, compounded once per two-year period. This would correspond to slightly under 4 per cent per annum, compounded annually.

In Fig. 42.1, let us begin with the second quadrant, representing Eq. (1) and showing future output $X(t + 1)$ as a function of current output $X(t)$. The heavy line has the slope $1 + g(t)$. The thin 45° line serves the purpose of transferring current output $X(t)$ to the $X(t + 1)$-axis.

Now turn Fig. 42.1 90° clockwise and look at the third quadrant, representing Eq. (3) and showing required future capital stock $S(t + 1)$ as a function of future output $X(t + 1)$. The line has the slope b. Since Eq. (3) holds for any t, current capital stock $S(t)$ is just what is required for current output $X(t)$ as transferred to the $X(t + 1)$-axis. Hence the distance between the two points on the $S(t + 1)$-axis measures the required increase in capital stock from period t to period $t + 1$.

According to Eq. (2), that increase is nothing but the net investment which must be completed within period t. Turning Fig. 42.1 90° clockwise a second time, we see in the fourth quadrant the 45° line representing Eq. (2).

Having thus established required net investment, we may combine it with the consumption function, Eq. (4), and draw the standard Keynesian aggregate-demand diagram shown in the first quadrant. Because the equilibrium condition, Eq. (5) holds, the double-circle output we chose at the outset has generated exactly an investment and consumption demand exhausting it.

If the reader tries any other output and follows Fig. 42.1 counterclockwise all the way around, he will find that smaller outputs generate inventory accumulation and larger outputs inventory depletion. Thus the diagram hints that the Harrod-Domar equilibrium is an unstable one. Is this just because we have selected our time unit to be as short as 2 years, giving us a capital coefficient as high as $2\tfrac{1}{2}$, or is it generally true?

42.10   THE INSTABILITY OF THE HARROD-DOMAR EQUILIBRIUM

Without giving up their long-term expectation of a growth rate $g(t)$ as determined by (7), let firms in a bout of temporary optimism or pessimism

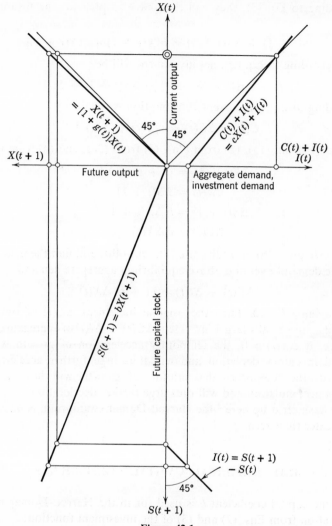

$X(t)$

Current output

$= [1 + g(t)]X(t)$

$\dfrac{X(t+1)}{}$

45°   45°

$C(t) + I(t)$
$= cX(t) + I(t)$

$X(t + 1)$

$C(t) + I(t)$
$I(t)$

Future output

Aggregate demand,
investment demand

$S(t + 1) = bX(t + 1)$

Future capital stock

$I(t) = S(t + 1)$
$- S(t)$

45°

$S(t + 1)$

Figure 42.1.

in period t be producing at a rate of growth from period $t - 1$ to period t slightly different from $g(t)$ thus determined. Let their output in period t be not $X(t)$ but $X(t) + \Delta X(t)$, where $\Delta X(t) \gtrless 0$. If $\Delta X(t) > 0$, the capital coefficient b must permit some excess capacity as a normal phenomenon. Still expecting the proportionate rate of growth $g(t)$ from period t to period $t + 1$, firms will, according to Eq. (1), plan for the future output:

(1a) $X(t + 1) + \Delta X(t + 1) = [1 + g(t)][X(t) + \Delta X(t)]$

According to Eq. (3), they will then have to plan for the future capital stock:

(3a) $S(t + 1) + \Delta S(t + 1) = b[X(t + 1) + \Delta X(t + 1)]$

And according to Eq. (2), net investment will be

(2a) $I(t) + \Delta I(t) = S(t + 1) + \Delta S(t + 1) - S(t)$

According to Eq. (4), current consumption will be

(4a) $C(t) + \Delta C(t) = c[X(t) + \Delta X(t)]$

Deduct (1) from (1a), (2) from (2a), (3) from (3a), and (4) from (4a):

(1b) $\Delta X(t + 1) = [1 + g(t)]\,\Delta X(t)$

(2b) $\Delta I(t) = \Delta S(t + 1)$

(3b) $\Delta S(t + 1) = b\,\Delta X(t + 1)$

(4b) $\Delta C(t) = c\,\Delta X(t)$

Insert (1b) and (3b) into (2b), use (7), add (4b), and find the increment of aggregate demand over and above equilibrium aggregate demand:

(14) $\Delta C(t) + \Delta I(t) = (1 + b)\,\Delta X(t)$

Now assume $b > 0$. Then the original increment $\Delta X(t)$ of output has generated a numerically larger increment $\Delta C(t) + \Delta I(t)$ of aggregate demand. Therefore, if $\Delta X(t) > 0$, the temporary acceleration of growth will have generated inventory depletion and will thus urge further acceleration. If $\Delta X(t) < 0$, the temporary deceleration of growth will have generated inventory accumulation and will thus urge further deceleration.

As we have set it up here,[2] the Harrod-Domar equilibrium is unstable for any b greater than zero.

42.11   EMPIRICAL CAPITAL COEFFICIENTS

What the capital coefficient b is used for in the Harrod-Domar model is the derivation from Eqs. (2) and (3) of the investment function:

(3c) $I(t) = b[X(t + 1) - X(t)]$

From this it follows that the capital coefficient that the Harrod-Domar model requires is the incremental one showing the ratio between required

---

[2] In an alternative formulation of the Harrod-Domar model (see Brems [2]), a very long unit period will permit the equilibrium to be stable. The trick required is twofold: Let capital stock of period t refer to the *end* of period t, and distinguish between a short-run consumption function with a constant term in it and a long-run consumption function without such a term.

net investment and incremental output. But this, in turn, means that we should be looking for data on undepreciated rather than depreciated capital stock. Leontief is quoted by Domar [5] as saying that ". . . recent information indicates that the undepreciated [capital] coefficients correspond much more closely to the incremental [capital] coefficients than do the depreciated ones. Use of the depreciated coefficients implies that capital stocks decrease in efficiency in exact relation to the depreciation charge. Most available evidence indicates that this is not a reliable assumption. Use of the undepreciated coefficients implies that capital stocks have a constant efficiency from the time of purchase until the time they are fully written off. . . ." Similarly Barna [1] states: ". . . For important classes of assets efficiency does not decline [with age] at all. For this reason the relationship between replacement cost new and output . . . is more relevant in forecasting incremental requirements of capital."

Thus the numerator of our capital coefficient must be undepreciated capital stock. What do we want in the denominator? It follows from Eqs. (2) and (5) that investment and output are both net. Thus the denominator must be net domestic product. The best statistical counterpart to the capital coefficient b thus defined in the Harrod-Domar model is the net domestic capital formation to incremental net domestic product ratio estimated by Kuznets [7], 23:

1869/78–1884/93	2.6
1884/93–1909/18	3.6
1914/23–1934/43	3.0
1939/48–1948/57	2.0

REFERENCES

[1] Barna, T., "On Measuring Capital," in The Theory of Capital, edited by F. A. Lutz and D. C. Hague, London, 1961, p. 80.

[2] Brems, H., "Stability and Growth," Ec. Jour., 65, 615–625 (December 1955).

[3] Cassel, G., Theoretische Sozialökonomie, Erlangen and Leipzig, 1923, pp. 51–52, (Translated by J. McCabe as The Theory of Social Economy, New York, 1924, pp. 62–63.)

[4] Domar, E. D., "Capital Expansion, Rate of Growth, and Employment," Econometrica, 14, 137–147 (April 1946).

[5] Domar, E. D., "The Capital-Output Ratio in the United States: Its Variation and Stability," in The Theory of Capital, London, 1961, pp. 98–99, 101, edited by F. A. Lutz and D. C. Hague.

[6] Harrod, R. F., Towards a Dynamic Economics, London, 1948, p. 77.

[7] Kuznets, S., "Quantitative Aspects of the Economic Growth of Nations: VI. Long Term Trends in Capital Formation Proportions," Econ. Development and Cultural Change, 9, 23 (July 1961).

CHAPTER 43

The Differential Equations of the
Harrod-Domar Model*

43.1 NO RECURSIVE SOLUTION

Underlying the difference-equations approach to dynamics is the notion of a unit period of finite length. Underlying the differential-equations approach is the notion of the length of the unit period approaching zero. Equation (2) of Chapter 42 contained the term $S(t + 1) - S(t)$. How can this equation be translated into a differential equation? Let the length of the unit period be Δt; then write this term as

$$\frac{S(t + \Delta t) - S(t)}{\Delta t}$$

Let the length of the unit period Δt approach zero and get

$$\frac{dS}{dt}$$

Hence, corresponding to the term $S(t + 1) - S(t)$ in difference equations we have the form dS/dt in differential equations. Now express the difference equations (2) through (5) of Chapter 42 in terms of differential equations:

Difference equations:	Differential equations:
(2) $I(t) = S(t + 1) - S(t)$	$I = dS/dt$
(3) $S(t) = bX(t)$	$S = bX$
(4) $C(t) = cX(t)$	$C = cX$
(5) $X(t) = C(t) + I(t)$	$X = C + I$

* Chapter 42 is a prerequisite for Chapter 43.

Why are the variables of differential equations not dated? The answer is that differential equations make no statements about values of a variable at different times, merely statements about the value of a variable at an instant of time *plus* its tendency to change at that same instant. Solving our system (2) through (5) in the differential-equation form gives us

(6)
$$\frac{dX}{dt} + AX = 0$$

where

$$A = -\frac{1-c}{b}$$

Like the system from which it was derived, Eq. (6) is a statement about the value of a variable X at an instant of time *plus* its tendency to change dX/dt at that same instant. Being in that sense a march on the spot, Eq. (6) permits no recursive solution. Hence, even more than for difference equations, we need a formula for differential equations permitting us to find the value of our variable X at any time.

Let the initial condition be the following, and here we do need dating:

(7)
$$X(0) = B$$

43.2 ANALYTICAL SOLUTION

As a bold guess, try

(8)
$$X = e^{xt}$$

where e is Euler's number, the base of natural logarithms. As we know, e has the remarkable quality that

(9)
$$\frac{d(e^{xt})}{dt} = xe^{xt}$$

Insert (8) into (6) and make good use of the quality (9):

$$xe^{xt} + Ae^{xt} = 0$$

Since e^{xt} is not zero, we may divide it away:

(10)
$$x = -A = \frac{1-c}{b}$$

However, (8) does not satisfy the initial condition (7), giving us $X(0) = 1$. But the reader may prove the theorem that if $X = e^{xt}$ satisfies (6) so does

(11)
$$X = me^{xt}$$

where m is an arbitrary constant. In (11) set $t = 0$:

(12) $X(0) = m$

Since m was an arbitrary constant, nothing keeps us from setting it equal to B, thereby arriving at a solution

(13) $X = Be^{(-A)t}$

which satisfies the original differential equation (6) as well as the initial condition (7).

43.3 INTERPRETATION OF SOLUTION

Our solution (13) permits the time path of output X to display three alternative patterns:

If $-A < 0$, X vanishes smoothly and always has the same sign as B.
If $-A = 0$, $X = B$.
If $-A > 0$, X explodes smoothly, upward if B is positive, downward if B is negative.

43.4 COMPARISON OF DIFFERENTIAL WITH DIFFERENCE EQUATIONS

For all the similarity in appearance and in technique of solution, the dissimilarities between differential and difference equations should not be overlooked. The following three such dissimilarities are important to us.

First and foremost, differential and difference equations looking very much alike may not have the same economic content. For example, Eq. (6) of our Harrod-Domar model looked very much the same in its two versions:

(6) $X(t + 1) + AX(t) = 0 \qquad \dfrac{dX}{dt} + AX = 0$

but the coefficient A had the two different meanings

$$A = -\frac{1 - c + b}{b} \qquad A = -\frac{1 - c}{b}$$

Digging deeper, go back to the underlying behavior assumptions, combine Eqs. (2) and (3) and form the two alternative investment functions

(3a) $I(t) = b[X(t + 1) - X(t)]$

(3b) $I = b\dfrac{dX}{dt}$

We have said that underlying a difference equation like (3a) is the concept of a unit period of finite length. Thus, according to (3a), investment is a decision taking place at discrete instants of time and involving advance planning: Investment planned at the beginning of period t for the entire period t allows for output as planned for the entire period $t + 1$.

By contrast, we have said that underlying a differential equation like (3b) is the notion of the length of the unit period approaching zero. Thus according to (3b) investment is a decision taking place continually at every instant of time and involving no advance planning at all. At any instant investment I is geared to the instantaneous rate of change of output dX/dt. Needless to say, to the economist (3a) has much more realism than (3b).

A second dissimilarity is that difference equations do permit but differential equations do not permit recursive solutions. This fact assumes majestic importance in the case of nonlinear systems, not encountered in the Harrod-Domar model but encountered in more complicated economic models. Written in the form of difference equations, such systems may be solved recursively on electronic digital computers. However, if they will ultimately have to be written in that form, they may as well be written thus from the outset.

A third dissimilarity is that difference equations may generate more alternative time paths than do the corresponding differential equations. For example, Eq. (13) of our Harrod-Domar model written in difference-equation form generated seven alternative patterns of the time path of output. Written in differential-equation form it generated only three alternative patterns.

CHAPTER 44

A Two-Country Harrod-Domar Model of Growth*

44.1 INTRODUCTION

The exchange rate is no less important in dynamic models than in static ones; yet almost all international growth models ignore it and with it the substitution between imported and domestically produced goods.

To be sure, once admitted as a variable the exchange rate threatens to destroy the linearity of the system of difference equations. The purpose of this chapter is to admit it under assumptions preserving linearity.

For simplicity we shall assume, as we did in the two-country Keynesian model, that consumers in both countries demand their country's own products as well as imported ones, but that firms invest in their own country's products only.

44.2 NOTATION

In a two-country dynamic macroeconomic model, the following notation will be assigned.

Variables

C_{ji} = ith country's output consumed in jth country
E = exchange rate, in number of monetary units of Country 1 equivalent to one monetary unit of Country 2
G = proportionate rate of growth of the exchange rate
g_{Xi} = proportionate rate of growth of ith country's net national output
I_i = net investment of ith country in its own products

---

* Chapters 36 and 42 are prerequisites for Chapter 44.

P_i = price of ith country's output expressed in ith country's monetary unit

S_i = ith country's capital stock

U_{ik} = utility to kth person in ith country, resulting from his consumption

X_i = ith country's net national output

Y_i = ith country's net national money income

Parameters

A_i = elasticity of utility with respect to first country's output consumed in ith country

B_i = elasticity of utility with respect to second country's output consumed in ith country

b_i = ith country's Harrod-Domar capital coefficient

c_i = propensity to consume in ith country

g_{Pi} = proportionate rate of growth of ith country's price of output

N_i = multiplicative factor in the utility functions in ith country

The stock variable S_i is measured in physical units of output of the ith country. The flow variables C_{ji}, I_i, and X_i are measured in physical units of output of the ith country per unit of time. Such units carry the price tag P_i expressed in the ith country's monetary unit. Subscripts $i = j = 1, 2$ refer to the two countries.

Let t be the time-coordinate dating variables: A flow variable marked (t) refers to period t, a stock variable marked (t) refers to time t. Let period t be the period beginning at time t, ending at time $t + 1$.

44.3 DEFINITIONS OF GROWTH RATES

First define three growth rates: two variable ones and one parameter.

(1) $$E(t + 1) = [1 + G(t)]E(t)$$

(2, 3) $$P_i(t + 1) = (1 + g_{Pi})P_i(t)$$

(4, 5) $$X_i(t + 1) = [1 + g_{Xi}(t)]X_i(t)$$

44.4 DEFINITION OF NET INVESTMENT

Net investment is defined as the net increase of capital stock:

(6, 7) $$I_i(t) = S_i(t + 1) - S_i(t)$$

44.5 PRODUCTION FUNCTIONS

Required capital stock is in proportion to output, the factor of proportionality being the Harrod-Domar capital coefficient. On other input requirements, the model is silent:

$$(8, 9) \qquad\qquad S_i(t) = b_i X_i(t)$$

44.6 UTILITY FUNCTIONS

Within each country let all persons have the same utility function, and let the utility function be of Cobb-Douglas form. However, the utility functions may differ between countries. The utility functions of the kth person in the first and second country are, respectively

$$U_{1k}(t) = N_1 [C_{11k}(t)]^{A_1} [C_{12k}(t)]^{B_1}$$

$$U_{2k}(t) = N_2 [C_{21k}(t)]^{A_2} [C_{22k}(t)]^{B_2}$$

where A_i and B_i are parameters lying between zero and one, and where N_i is a positive multiplicative factor dependent upon the units of measurement. It is unnecessary to assume that $A_1 \gtrless A_2$, that $B_2 \gtrless B_1$, or that $A_i + B_i = 1$, $i = 1, 2$.

44.7 BUDGET CONSTRAINTS

Let $X_{ik}(t)$ be the kth person's contribution to the ith country's net national output; hence his money income is $Y_{ik}(t) = P_i(t)X_{ik}(t)$. Let all persons in the ith country spend the same fraction c_i of their money income on consumption of their country's own products as well as imported ones. Then the budget constraints of the kth person in the two countries are

$$c_1 P_1(t) X_{1k}(t) = P_1(t) C_{11k}(t) + E(t) P_2(t) C_{12k}(t)$$

$$c_2 P_2(t) X_{2k}(t) = \frac{P_1(t)}{E(t)} C_{21k}(t) + P_2(t) C_{22k}(t)$$

44.8 UTILITY MAXIMIZATION

Just as we did in our Keynesian two-country model, let us apply our standard method of maximizing the kth person's utility subject to his budget constraint and find the four individual demand functions of the kth person in the two countries. Let the ith country have s_i persons, add the s_i demand functions for each good in each country, and find the four national aggregate demand functions:

$$(10) \qquad C_{11}(t) = \frac{c_1 A_1}{A_1 + B_1} X_1(t)$$

$$(11) \qquad C_{12}(t) = \frac{c_1 B_1}{A_1 + B_1} \frac{P_1(t)}{E(t)P_2(t)} X_1(t)$$

$$(12) \qquad C_{21}(t) = \frac{c_2 A_2}{A_2 + B_2} \frac{E(t)P_2(t)}{P_1(t)} X_2(t)$$

$$(13) \qquad C_{22}(t) = \frac{c_2 B_2}{A_2 + B_2} X_2(t)$$

44.9   DOMESTIC EQUILIBRIUM

Domestic equilibrium requires the sum of consumption, investment, and export demand for national output to equal national output; otherwise, inventory would either accumulate or be depleted:

$$(14) \qquad X_1(t) = C_{11}(t) + I_1(t) + C_{21}(t)$$
$$(15) \qquad X_2(t) = C_{22}(t) + I_2(t) + C_{12}(t)$$

44.10   INTERNATIONAL EQUILIBRIUM

International equilibrium requires the balance of payment, when measured in the monetary unit of any country, say the first, to equal zero:

$$(16) \qquad P_1(t)C_{21}(t) - E(t)P_2(t)C_{12}(t) = 0$$

or first country's export *minus* its import equals zero. Since each country's export is the other country's import, it follows from (16) that second country's import *minus* its export also equals zero.

44.11   PARAMETRIC EXCHANGE RATE

At first one might recoil from such a nonlinear system. For comfort, let us eliminate one equation and one variable from it: Let the exchange rate

$E(t)$ be a parameter and ignore (16). This would give us a neat linear system of difference equations that reduces easily to the following two linear second-order difference equations, each in one variable only:

(17, 18) $$DX_i(t + 2) + FX_i(t + 1) + HX_i(t) = 0$$

where

$$D = b_1 b_2$$

$$F = -\left[b_1\left(b_2 + 1 - \frac{c_2 B_2}{A_2 + B_2} \right) + b_2\left(b_1 + 1 - \frac{c_1 A_1}{A_1 + B_1} \right) \right]$$

$$H = \left(b_1 + 1 - \frac{c_1 A_1}{A_1 + B_1} \right)\left(b_2 + 1 - \frac{c_2 B_2}{A_2 + B_2} \right) - \frac{c_1 B_1}{A_1 + B_1} \frac{c_2 A_2}{A_2 + B_2}$$

Thus Eqs. (17) and (18) have identical coefficients D, F, and H; hence they must have identical pairs of roots. As we know, the numerically larger root will ultimately dominate the numerically smaller one; consequently, the two countries will ultimately have identical proportionate rates of growth.

Would they not have identical proportionate rates of growth even in isolation? Set the elasticities of utility with respect to imported goods A_2 and B_1 equal to zero to produce isolation, then (17) and (18) still seem to have identical coefficients: However, two of the operations required to find (17) and (18) are division by A_2 and B_1; hence (17) and (18) cannot hold for $A_2 = B_1 = 0$. Anyway, we have ruled out isolation by our assumption that A_i and B_i are parameters lying between zero and one.

44.12   VARIABLE EXCHANGE RATE

Except fortuitously, the system studied in Section 44.11 will not balance international trade, for Eq. (16) was eliminated from it. Therefore let the exchange rate $E(t)$ be a variable again and restore Eq. (16). Clearly this full system is a nonlinear one, for Eqs. (11), (12), and (16) contain products of, or ratios between, variables. The nonlinearities, however, will disappear: Use (10), (6), (8), (16), and (11) in that order upon (14) for Country 1, proceed similarly for Country 2, and reduce our system to two linear first-order difference equations, each in only one variable:

(19, 20) $$X_i(t + 1) - \frac{1 - c_i + b_i}{b_i} X_i(t) = 0$$

Hence, turning the exchange rate loose as a variable has rewarded us with first-order solutions rather than second-order ones. As we saw in Chapter 42, first-order difference equations such as (19) and (20) are satisfied by

$$(21, 22) \qquad\qquad X_i(t) = m_i x_i{}^t$$

where m_i was an arbitrary constant depending upon the initial conditions, not specified in our present model and where

$$(23, 24) \qquad\qquad x_i = \frac{1 - c_i + b_i}{b_i}$$

The parameter c_i has been assumed to lie between zero and one; hence the economy will be growing at a constant proportionate rate. To find this rate, combine (4) and (5) with (19) and (20):

$$(25, 26) \qquad\qquad g_{Xi}(t) = \frac{1 - c_i}{b_i}$$

Notice the absence of any time coordinate on the right-hand side: (25) and (26) have no time trend in them. Thus the constancy of the proportionate rate of growth of outputs is a result, not an assumption.

Throughout this chapter we are assuming that the propensity to save $1 - c_i$ as well as the capital coefficient b_i are positive; hence the rates of growth of outputs determined by (25) and (26) are positive.

Notice further that the proportionate rate of growth of a country's output now depends upon the parameters of that country alone, not upon those of the other country. In this sense the two countries are now highly independent of each other. Highly, but not fully independent, as we shall see in Section 44.13. In each of the two solutions (25) and (26) two national parameters c_i and b_i are present. To see how precisely the rates of growth depend upon those two parameters, take the partial derivatives:

$$(27, 28) \qquad\qquad \frac{\partial g_{Xi}(t)}{\partial c_i} = -\frac{1}{b_i}$$

$$(29, 30) \qquad\qquad \frac{\partial g_{Xi}(t)}{\partial b_i} = -\frac{g_{Xi}(t)}{b_i}$$

Under the assumptions made, both derivatives are negative: If a country's propensity to spend c_i or its capital coefficient b_i rises, its rate of growth will fall.

44.13 THE TIME PATH OF THE EXCHANGE RATE

Use (11), (12), and (16) to express the exchange rate $E(t)$ in terms of c_i, A_i, B_i, $P_i(t)$, and $X_i(t)$. Rewrite the expression for period $t + 1$, divide the resulting expression by the original one, then use (1) through (5), and get

$$(31) \qquad 1 + G(t) = \frac{1 + g_{P1}}{1 + g_{P2}} \frac{1 + g_{X1}(t)}{1 + g_{X2}(t)}$$

The form (31) permits us to see that the two countries are not fully independent of each other. Let Country 1's output be growing more rapidly than that of Country 2: $g_{X1}(t)$ exceeds $g_{X2}(t)$. If the price levels of the two countries were growing at identical rates, $g_{P1} = g_{P2}$, then (31) shows $G(t)$ to be positive: The exchange rate would be rising. Thus Country 1 would be paying a penalty for enjoying more rapid growth than Country 2, that is, that Country 1's real income would be growing less rapidly than its output. One physical unit of Country 1's goods buys fewer physical units of Country 2's goods, for the exchange rate is rising with stationary relative prices.

Conversely, if the exchange rate were to remain stationary, $G(t) = 0$, Country 1's price level would have to rise less rapidly than that of Country 2: g_{P1} would have to be less than g_{P2}. Still, the penalty would have to be paid. Now one physical unit of Country 1's goods would buy fewer physical units of Country 2's goods, because the relative price of Country 2's goods is rising at a stationary exchange rate.

Thus, whereas the countries are independent as far as the growth rate of output is concerned, they are dependent, via (31), as far as the growth rate of real income is concerned.

To express the growth rate of the exchange rate in terms of parameters only, insert (25) and (26) into (31) and obtain:

$$(32) \qquad 1 + G(t) = \frac{b_2}{b_1} \frac{1 + g_{P1}}{1 + g_{P2}} \frac{1 - c_1 + b_1}{1 - c_2 + b_2}$$

Notice the absence of any time coordinate on the right-hand side: (32) has no time trend in it. Thus the constancy of the proportionate rate of growth of the exchange rate is a result, not an assumption.

In addition to the two assumptions already made, make the assumption that in each country the growth factor $1 + g_{Pi}$ of that country's price level is positive; this means that once it is positive, a country's price level will never become negative. Then (32) shows the growth factor $1 + G(t)$ to be positive: The growth *rate* $G(t)$ itself may be positive, zero, or negative, but will never be *minus* one or less. In (32) all six parameters b_i, c_i, and g_{Pi} are present. To see how precisely the equilibrium proportionate rate of growth $G(t)$ of the exchange rate depends upon those six parameters, take the partial derivatives:

(33)
$$\frac{\partial G(t)}{\partial c_1} = -\frac{1 + G(t)}{1 - c_1 + b_1}$$

(34)
$$\frac{\partial G(t)}{\partial b_1} = -\frac{1 + G(t)}{1 - c_1 + b_1} g_{X1}(t)$$

(35)
$$\frac{\partial G(t)}{\partial g_{P1}} = \frac{1 + G(t)}{1 + g_{P1}}$$

(36)
$$\frac{\partial G(t)}{\partial c_2} = \frac{1 + G(t)}{1 - c_2 + b_2}$$

(37)
$$\frac{\partial G(t)}{\partial b_2} = \frac{1 + G(t)}{1 - c_2 + b_2} g_{X2}(t)$$

(38)
$$\frac{\partial G(t)}{\partial g_{P2}} = -\frac{1 + G(t)}{1 + g_{P2}}$$

Under the three assumptions already made, (35), (36), and (37) will be positive: The equilibrium proportionate rate of growth of the exchange rate will *rise* if the rate of growth of Country 1's price level rises, if Country 2's propensity to spend rises, and if Country 2's capital coefficient rises.

The derivatives (33), (34), and (38) will be negative. The equilibrium proportionate rate of growth of the exchange rate will *fall* if Country 1's propensity to spend rises, if Country 1's capital coefficient rises, and if the rate of growth of Country 2's price level rises.

44.14   CONCLUSION

In this chapter we have replaced a two-country Harrod-Domar model of growth having a parametric exchange rate by a similar model having a variable exchange rate. As a result, the equilibrium rate of growth of a country's output, but not that of its real income, was found to depend upon that country's own parameters only. In this sense, the variable exchange rate made the countries less dependent upon each other.

As for the equilibrium proportionate rate of growth of the exchange rate itself, it was found to depend upon the parameters of both countries. Anything, such as an increase of the propensity to spend or an increase of the capital coefficient in Country 1, which would reduce the growth rate of that country's output, would reduce the growth rate of the exchange rate. Anything, such as an increase of the propensity to spend or an increase of the capital coefficient in Country 2, which would reduce the growth rate of that country's output, would raise the growth rate of the exchange rate.

A stark contradiction between static Keynesian reasoning and dynamic Harrod-Domar reasoning about the exchange rate thus exists. In the Keynesian model, a higher propensity to spend implies a lower propensity to save, but the lower propensity to save cannot possibly hurt Keynesian investment, for the latter is a parameter. Consequently, the lower propensity to save cannot possibly reduce aggregate demand and with it the demand for import; quite the contrary. In the Harrod-Domar model, however, investment is no parameter; it is a variable which must absorb the impact of a lower propensity to save. Net investment is what makes the Harrod-Domar economy grow, there being no other supply limitations. Hence the lower propensity to save reduces the growth rate of output. This retardation eases the pressure on the trade balance and makes the exchange rate rise less rapidly, makes it switch from rising to falling, or makes it fall more rapidly than it otherwise would have been doing.

Finally, an increase in the rate of growth of prices in Country 1 would raise the growth rate of the exchange rate, whereas an increase in the rate of growth of prices in Country 2 would reduce it. This is nothing but a straightforward formulation of the purchasing power parity theory of the exchange rate.

The most general policy conclusion one can draw from our solution for the exchange rate (32) is this: For long periods of time, sovereign nations are unlikely to be able *as well as* willing to maintain the equality

$$b_2(1 + g_{P1})(1 - c_1 + b_1) = b_1(1 + g_{P2})(1 - c_2 + b_2),$$

which would be required for $G(t) = 0$, that is, required for the exchange rate to remain stationary. Rather than trying to freeze the structure of exchange rates we should, then, try to facilitate their adjustment from time to time.

The price to be paid for the clear-cut results of the two-country Harrod-Domar model were some highly simplifying assumptions, above all the assumption of no supply limitations other than the fixed Harrod-Domar capital coefficient in each country. As we shall see presently, much would have been different had we used a Cobb-Douglas production function, permitting capital-labor substitution, coupled with labor supply restrictions.

CHAPTER 45

Labor and Capital in a Cobb-Douglas Growth Model*

45.1 INTRODUCTION

On input requirements other than capital stock the Harrod-Domar model was silent, hence like a Keynesian model would permit employment that is less than full, full, or more than full. Halfway through World War II it occurred to Tinbergen [18] to put a Cobb-Douglas production function into a growth model with capital stock being the result of accumulated savings and with labor growing autonomously. Thus a full-employment growth model with input substitution was born, but because of the time and place of its birth, as well as its language, it had to be rediscovered by English-speaking theorists, above all by Solow [16].

The purposes of this chapter are, first, to restate in simple difference equations a purely competitive Cobb-Douglas model of growth; second, to find its implications for the distributive shares and for the marginal productivities of capital and labor; third, to find the sensitivities of such implications to changes in thriftiness and to the passage of time; fourth, to solve the Cobb-Douglas model for the Harrod-Domar capital coefficient; and fifth, to confront the two models with reality, however imperfectly known.

45.2 NOTATION

In a dynamic macroeconomic model the following notation will be assigned.

* Chapter 8 is a prerequisite for Chapter 45.

Variables

C = consumption
g_S = proportionate rate of growth of capital stock
g_X = proportionate rate of growth of net national output
I = net investment
ι = marginal internal rate of return on capital stock
L = labor force
M = multiplicative factor in the production function
P = price of output
S = capital stock
w = money wage rate
X = net national output

Parameters

α = elasticity of net national output with respect to labor force
β = elasticity of net national output with respect to capital stock
c = propensity to consume
g_L = proportionate rate of growth of labor force
g_M = proportionate rate of growth of multiplicative factor

The stock variable S is measured in physical units of output, the flow variables C, I, and X are measured in physical units of output per unit of time.

Let t be the time coordinate dating variables: A flow variable marked (t) refers to period t, a stock variable marked (t) refers to time t. Let period t be the period beginning at time t, ending at time $t + 1$.

45.3 THE MODEL

First define four proportionate rates of growth: two variable ones $g_S(t)$ and $g_X(t)$, and two parameters $g_L \geq 0$ and $g_M > 0$:

$$(1) \qquad L(t + 1) = (1 + g_L)L(t)$$

$$(2) \qquad M(t + 1) = (1 + g_M)M(t)$$

$$(3) \qquad S(t + 1) = [1 + g_S(t)]S(t)$$

$$(4) \qquad X(t + 1) = [1 + g_X(t)]X(t)$$

Net investment is defined as the net increase of capital stock:

$$(5) \qquad I(t) = S(t + 1) - S(t)$$

Let consumption be the fixed proportion c of output:

(6) $$C(t) = cX(t)$$

Let the aggregate production function be of Cobb-Douglas form

(7) $$X(t) = M(t)[L(t)]^{\alpha}[S(t)]^{\beta}$$

where $0 < \alpha < 1$, $\alpha + \beta = 1$, and $M(t) > 0$. The production function (7) is adopted with the restrictions $L(t) \geq 0$, $S(t) \geq 0$, and $X(t) \geq 0$. $M(t)$ is assumed to represent technological progress.

Equilibrium requires output to equal demand:

(8) $$X(t) = C(t) + I(t)$$

Because (3) and (4) are nonlinear, the entire system (1) through (8) is nonlinear. No analytical solution to such a system is known to mathematicians; hence we shall have to settle for approximations.

45.4 APPROXIMATE SOLUTION FOR GROWTH RATE OF OUTPUT

Express the production function (7) for periods $t + 1$ and t, divide the first expression by the second, use (1) through (4), and get

(9) $$1 + g_X(t) = (1 + g_M)(1 + g_L)^{\alpha}[1 + g_S(t)]^{\beta}$$

Express (9) for periods $t + 1$ and t, divide the first expression by the second, and get

(10) $$\frac{1 + g_X(t + 1)}{1 + g_X(t)} = \left[\frac{1 + g_S(t + 1)}{1 + g_S(t)}\right]^{\beta}$$

Now is the time to use the consumption function (6) and the equilibrium requirement (8) jointly with the definitions (3) and (5):

(11) $$g_S(t) = (1 - c)\frac{X(t)}{S(t)}$$

Express (11) for periods $t + 1$ and t, divide the first expression by the second, use (3) and (4), and obtain

(12) $$\frac{g_S(t + 1)}{g_S(t)} = \frac{1 + g_X(t)}{1 + g_S(t)}$$

Recalling that $\alpha + \beta = 1$, insert (9) into (12):

(13) $$\frac{g_S(t + 1)}{g_S(t)} = \left[\frac{Q}{1 + g_S(t)}\right]^{\alpha}$$

where

$$Q = (1 + g_M)^{1/\alpha}(1 + g_L)$$

Now three possibilities exist. The first one is that

$$1 + g_S(t) > Q$$

In this case, the expression in brackets on the right-hand side of (13) is less than one, and so is the αth power of it. Consequently,

(14) $$g_S(t + 1) < g_S(t)$$

The second possibility is that

(15) $$1 + g_S(t) = Q$$

In this case, the expression in brackets on the right-hand side of (13) equals one, and so does the αth power of it. Consequently,

(16) $$g_S(t + 1) = g_S(t)$$

The third possibility is that

$$1 + g_S(t) < Q$$

In this case, the expression in brackets on the right-hand side of (13) is greater than one, and so is the αth power of it. Consequently,

(17) $$g_S(t + 1) > g_S(t)$$

Thus as long as $1 + g_S(t)$ is greater than Q, (14) shows it to be falling. As long as it is equal to Q, (16) shows it to remain equal. And as long as it is less than Q, (17) shows it to be rising. It seems, then, as if $1 + g_S(t)$ converges towards Q. However, before we can be sure that it does, two things will have to be shown.

First, is it possible that $1 + g_S(t)$ kept alternating around Q being, say, above it in period t and below it in period $t + 1$? Let us prove that this cannot be. Hence, given $1 + g_S(t) > Q$, prove that $1 + g_S(t + 1) > Q$. Write (13) as

(13a) $$1 + g_S(t + 1) = 1 + \left[\frac{Q}{1 + g_S(t)}\right]^\alpha g_S(t)$$

Let us take advantage of the fact that if $0 < \alpha < 1$, then a number less than one raised to the power α is greater than that number:

$$\left[\frac{Q}{1 + g_S(t)}\right]^\alpha > \frac{Q}{1 + g_S(t)}$$

Hence on the right-hand side of (13a) we may remove the α, provided we replace the equality sign by a greater-than sign. Thus written, rearrange (13a):

$$1 + g_S(t + 1) > \frac{1 + g_S(t) + Q g_S(t)}{1 + g_S(t)}$$

It was given that $1 + g_S(t) > Q$; hence by replacing $1 + g_S(t)$ in the numerator on the right-hand side by Q we make that side even smaller, and the inequality sign holds *a fortiori*. After doing this, we may factor out $1 + g_S(t)$, divide it away, and arrive at what we wanted to prove.

Conversely, given $1 + g_S(t) < Q$, we could prove that $1 + g_S(t + 1) < Q$. Here we would take advantage of the fact that if $0 < \alpha < 1$, then a number greater than one raised to the power α is less than that number. The preceding reasoning could therefore be repeated with inequality signs reversed. Whether falling or rising, then, $1 + g_S(t)$ stays on the same side of Q. Consequently, it is monotonically falling or rising.

In the second place, even so, could $1 + g_S(t)$ be converging toward any value other than Q? Assume $g_S(t) > 0$ and write (13) as

(13b)
$$g_S(t + 1) - g_S(t) = \left\{ \left[\frac{Q}{1 + g_S(t)} \right]^{\alpha} - 1 \right\} g_S(t)$$

Now if $1 + g_S(t)$ were to converge toward anything other than Q, then by letting enough time elapse it would be possible for the absolute difference on the left hand-side of (13b) to become and remain less than any arbitrarily assignable positive constant ε, however small, without the same being possible for the right-hand side of (13b).

Finally, we are able to conclude that if at some time $1 + g_S(t)$ equals Q, it will remain equal to Q, and that if it does not equal Q, it will converge toward Q. We shall therefore consider (15) a good approximation; hence let us write it out fully as

(15)
$$1 + g_S(t) = (1 + g_M)^{1/\alpha}(1 + g_L)$$

Insert (16), which was a result of (15), into (10):

$$g_X(t + 1) = g_X(t)$$

Hence the proportionate rate of growth of output, too, will become approximately stationary. At what value? Inserting (15) into (9),

(18)
$$1 + g_X(t) = (1 + g_M)^{1/\alpha}(1 + g_L)$$

In summing up: Either from the beginning output and capital stock are growing at the same proportionate rates defined by (15) and (18), or, if they are not, (15) and (18) will ultimately become good approximations. However, "ultimately" may be a very long time, indeed; thus logical grounds alone are not enough to inspire confidence in (15) and (18). Could history be a supplement to logic? If neither the proportionate rate of growth of net output, $g_X(t)$, nor the capital coefficient $S(t)/X(t)$ have displayed any pronounced historical trend, we would have more confidence in (15) and (18). We shall return to history in the Appendix.

One last observation: In (15) and (18) we notice that the proportionate rates of growth do not depend upon the propensity to save: $1 - c$ is absent from (15) and (18). This shows how sensitive economic dogma is to slight changes in behavior assumptions. Keynes had removed the saver from the pedestal erected by the neoclassicists. By showing that in their models the proportionate rate of growth of output would be in direct proportion to the propensity to save, Harrod and Domar had put the saver back on his pedestal. Now, by applying a Cobb-Douglas production function to the theory of growth, we once again remove him: As far as the proportionate rate of growth of output is concerned, the saver is neither beneficial nor harmful, he is simply neutral.

However, if the proportionate rate of growth of output is not affected, then something else in our system should be affected by the propensity to save. Let us see if it could be the distributive shares.

45.5 DISTRIBUTIVE SHARES

Recalling that output is defined as *net* output $X(t)$, the marginal internal rate of return $\iota(t)$ is

$$(19) \qquad \iota(t) = \frac{\partial X(t)}{\partial S(t)} = \beta \frac{X(t)}{S(t)}$$

The model implies full employment at all times and assumes pure competition in labor and goods markets. Pure competition will establish a real wage rate which always clears the labor market by equaling the physical marginal productivity of labor:

$$(20) \qquad \frac{w(t)}{P(t)} = \frac{\partial X(t)}{\partial L(t)} = \alpha \frac{X(t)}{L(t)}$$

From (19) and (20) get the real profits bill and the real wage bill:

$$(19) \qquad \iota(t)S(t) = \beta X(t)$$

$$(20) \qquad \frac{w(t)}{P(t)} L(t) = \alpha X(t)$$

The relative distributive shares of capital and labor are, than, β and α, respectively. The propensity to save is again conspicuous by its absence: Therefore we have not yet found anything in the model which *is* affected by the propensity to save. Let us now try the marginal internal rate of return and the real wage rate.

45.6 THE MARGINAL INTERNAL RATE OF RETURN AND THE REAL WAGE RATE

Use (3), (5), (6), (8), (15), and (18) upon (19) to solve for the marginal internal rate of return:

$$(21) \qquad \iota(t) = \frac{\beta}{1 - c} [(1 + g_M)^{1/\alpha}(1 + g_L) - 1]$$

which has no time trend in it. Finally here is something which is affected by the propensity to save $1 - c$. The marginal internal rate of return is in inverse proportion to the propensity to save $1 - c$.

Use (7), (19), (20), (21) upon (20) to solve for the real wage rate:

$$(22) \qquad \frac{w(t)}{P(t)} = \alpha[M(t)]^{1/\alpha}\left[\frac{(1 + g_M)^{1/\alpha}(1 + g_L) - 1}{1 - c}\right]^{-\beta/\alpha}$$

Unlike the marginal internal *rate* of return, but like the marginal internal *amount* of return, the real wage rate has a time trend it, apparent in the factor $[M(t)]^{1/\alpha}$ in (22). Like the marginal internal rate of return, the real wage rate is affected by the propensity to save $1 - c$: Recall that α and β are both positive; hence the exponent $-\beta/\alpha$ in (22) is a negative one. Consequently, if $\alpha < \beta$, the real wage is more than proportional to the propensity to save; if $\alpha = \beta$, the real wage rate is in direct proportion to the propensity to save; and if $\alpha > \beta$ the real wage rate is less than proportional to the propensity to save. Nevertheless, in all three cases, Wicksell's [20] famous statement applies to a Cobb-Douglas world: "The capitalist saver is thus, fundamentally, the friend of labour . . . ."

Now if an increase in thriftiness raises the real wage rate, and if employment is always full, then the real wage *bill* must also be raised. Labor's share remaining α, however, the relative wage bill remains unaffected. Consequently, at any given time, a high-saving economy moving along its equilibrium path will have a larger real output than a low-saving one also moving along its equilibrium path.

Figure 45.1 illustrates this. Plot output $X(t)$ on a vertical logarithmic scale and time t on a horizontal nonlogarithmic scale. A family of upward-sloping parallel straight lines, three of which are shown, represent alternative time

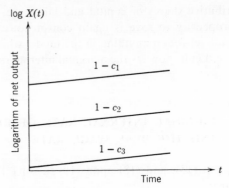

Figure 45.1. Condition: $1 - c_1 > 1 - c_2 > 1 - c_3$.

paths of $X(t)$, each straight line corresponding to a specific degree of thriftiness: The higher the degree, the higher the output $X(t)$ for a given t.

45.7   THE   CAPITAL   COEFFICIENT

Solving the Cobb-Douglas model for the capital coefficient is illuminating —and very simple. Use (19) and (21) to find

$$(23) \qquad \frac{S(t)}{X(t)} = \frac{1 - c}{(1 + g_M)^{1/\alpha}(1 + g_L) - 1}$$

which has no time trend in it. Thus the Cobb-Douglas model displays the same constancy of the capital coefficient as did the Harrod-Domar model, but for different reasons. In the Harrod-Domar model the constancy was supposedly a matter of constant technology. In the Cobb-Douglas model, technology progresses at the constant proportionate rate g_M, and the capital coefficient as expressed by (23) will stay constant only as long as the propensity to save $1 - c$ does.

APPENDIX   EMPIRICAL   MEASUREMENTS

1. Behavior Equations

One might confront first, the behavior equations and second, the solutions, of the Cobb-Douglas model of growth with empirical measurements. Let us begin with the behavior equations.

2. The Propensity to Save

In our first behavior equation, the consumption function (6), the propensity to save $1 - c$ is a parameter. Has it really remained stationary over the long pull? For the United States Goldsmith [6] gave an affirmative answer, but later findings are less conclusive. Kuznets [10, 249] found the following net national savings to net national product ratios:

1869–1888	0.13
1889–1908	0.14
1909–1928	0.12
1929–1938	0.03
1946–1955	0.10
1950–1959	0.10

Using Kuznets data on consumption and net national product, Klein [7] found an upward trend between 1900 and 1953 in the propensity to consume c of $\frac{1}{8}$ of one per cent semiannually. Residually determined, the propensity to save $1 - c$ of households, firms, and government must then display a downward trend.

3. The Production Function

As for our second behavior equation, the Cobb-Douglas aggregate production function (7), numerous attempts have been made to estimate its parameters α, β, and g_M. Earlier attempts, summarized by Seton [15, 6], usually used a cross-section approach and hence could not include $M(t)$. Our Table 48.1 summarizes some postwar attempts of which most include $M(t)$. Why include $M(t)$? Assuming its absence Mendershausen [11] and Phelps Brown [14] have shown that the elasticity β of output with respect to capital stock can lie between zero and unity only if the proportionate rates

Table 48.1 Empirical Estimates of a Cobb-Douglas Production Function

Author	Country	Period	Labor exponent	Capital exponent	Proportionate annual rate of growth g_M
Aukrust [1]	Norway	1900–1955	0.76	0.20	0.018
Aukrust [2]	Norway	1900–1955	0.58	0.30	0.015
Klein [7]	U.S.A.	1900–1953	0.84[a]	0.16	0.011
Niitamo [12]	Finland	1925–1952	0.74	0.26	0.012
Seton [15]	U.S.S.R.	1928–1934	0.72	0.35	0.008
Seton [15]	U.S.S.R.	1950–1955	0.24	0.46	0.050
Solow [17]	U.S.A.	1909–1949	—	0.35	0.015
Valavanis [19]	U.S.A.	1869–1948	0.25	0.70	—
Valavanis [19]	U.S.A.	1869–1948	0.54[a]	0.25[a]	0.008

[a] Factor's share of national income.

of growth of output and capital stock differ. However, if they differ, the capital coefficient must have a time trend in it. The inclusion of $M(t)$ makes an elasticity β between zero and unity compatible with a stationary capital coefficient.

4. The Solutions: The Approximation (18)

Turning now to the solutions of the Cobb-Douglas model, we may ask if the growth rate of output, $g_X(t)$, has remained stationary, as our approximation (18) would have it. The output of the Cobb-Douglas model is net output, and Kuznets [9, p. 23] has estimated the proportionate rate of growth of United States net national product:

1869/78–1884/93	0.054
1884/93–1909/18	0.035
1914/23–1934/43	0.020
1939/48–1948/57	0.043

5. The Distributive Shares

In Section 45.5, we reached the conclusion that the distributive shares of capital and labor were β and α, respectively, thus ruling out any time trend in them. Have they really remained stationary? Klein [7] found labor's share to be the only one of his Great Ratios which did not have a time trend in it. Kuznets [10, p. 173] found the proportionate share of income from assets to have remained stationary in the United States from the turn of the century to the end of World War II. After World War II the share declined (as it did in Belgium, Norway, Japan, Australia, and New Zealand). Kravis [8] questioned the constancy of the distributive shares in the United States. For Britain, Phelps Brown and Weber [13] found that over each span, 1870–1913 and 1924–1938 wage and salary earnings remained much the same proportion of national income.

6. The Rate of Return

In Section 45.6, we reached the conclusion that the marginal internal rate of return had no time trend in it but was in inverse proportion to the propensity to save. Klein [7] found a statistically significant downward trend in the interest rate, that is, 0.6 per cent semiannually. Goode and Birnbaum [5] found an even more pronounced downward trend. Such findings are inconsistent with a Cobb-Douglas growth model with a constant let alone a declining propensity to save. For Britain Phelps Brown and Weber [13] found that over each span 1870–1913 and 1924–1938 the rate of return on capital of all kinds, defined as the ratio between yield and replacement cost, remained almost stationary. This would be consistent with a Cobb-Douglas model with constant propensity to save.

7. The Capital Coefficient

In Section 45.7, we reached the conclusion that the capital coefficient had no time trend in it and was in proportion to the propensity to save. Just as we did in the Harrod-Domar model in Chapter 42, we want undepreciated capital stock in the numerator of our capital coefficient. It follows from Eqs. (5) and (8) of the Cobb-Douglas model that investment and output are both net; thus in the denominator of the capital coefficient we again want net domestic product. The best statistical counterpart to the capital coefficient $S(t)/X(t)$ thus defined is the net domestic capital formation to incremental net domestic product ratio estimated by Kuznets [9, p. 23] for the United States and reproduced at the end of Chapter 42. Fabricant [4] found the United States capital coefficient to be falling by 0.5 per cent per annum during 1889–1919 and by 1.3 per cent per annum during 1919–1957. Klein, too, found a significant downward trend, that is, $\frac{1}{3}$ of one per cent semiannually. Kuznets' [9, p. 25] word of caution should be borne in mind, however: "When a ratio can double or more, as it did in Australia and the United Kingdom, or drop to half, as it did in Canada, from one two-decade period to the next, it is not a stable statistic or coefficient in an economy; and any trend observed in it cannot be treated as a dominant and irreversible pattern." Taken at their face values, Fabricant's and Klein's findings would be consistent with a Cobb-Douglas growth model with a declining propensity to save.

REFERENCES

[1] Aukrust, O., "Investment and Economic Growth," *Productivity Measurement Review*, February 1959, 35–53.

[2] Aukrust, O., private communication to author, reporting on revised estimates leaving out excess-capacity years.

[3] Cobb, C. W., and P. H. Douglas, "A Theory of Production," *Am. Econ. Rev.*, **18**, 139–165 (Supplement 1928).

[4] Fabricant, S., *Basic Facts on Productivity Change*, New York, 1958.

[5] Goode, R., and E. A. Birnbaum, "The Relation Between Long-Term and Short-Term Interest Rates in the United States," *International Monetary Fund Staff Papers*, **7**, 224–243 (1959).

[6] Goldsmith, R. W., *A Study of Savings in the United States*, I, III, Princeton, 1955 and 1956.

[7] Klein, L. R., and R. F. Kosobud, "Some Econometrics of Growth: Great Ratios of Economics," *Quart. Jour. Econ.*, **75**, 173–198 (May 1961).

[8] Kravis, I. B., "Relative Income Shares in Fact and Theory," *Am. Econ. Rev.*, **49**, 917–949 (December 1959).

[9] Kuznets, S., "Quantitative Aspects of the Economic Growth of Nations: VI. Long-Term Trends in Capital Formation Proportions," *Econ. Development and Cultural Change*, **9**, 3–124 (July 1961).

[10] Kuznets, S., *Modern Economic Growth: Rate, Structure, and Spread*, New Haven and London, 1966.

[11] Mendershausen, H., "On the Significance of Professor Douglas' Production Function" *Econometrica*, **6**, 143–153 (April 1938), with correction in the October 1939 issue, **7**, 362.

[12] Niitamo, O., "The Development of Production in Finnish Industry 1925–1952," *Productivity Measurement Review*, November 1958, 30–41.

[13] Phelps Brown, E. H., and B. Weber, "Accumulation, Productivity and Distribution in the British Economy, 1870–1938," *Econ. Jour.*, **63**, 263–288 (June 1953).

[14] Phelps Brown, E. H., "The Meaning of the Fitted Cobb-Douglas Function," *Quart. Jour. Econ.*, **71**, 546–560 (November 1957).

[15] Seton, F., "Production Functions in Soviet Industry," *Am. Econ. Rev.*, **49**, 1–14 (Supplement 1959).

[16] Solow, R. M., "A Contribution to the Theory of Economic Growth," *Quart. Jour. Econ.*, **70**, 76–77 (February 1956).

[17] Solow, R. M., "Technical Change and the Aggregate Production Function," *Rev. Econ. Stat.*, **39**, 312–330 (August 1957).

[18] Tinbergen, J., "Zur Theorie der langfristigen Wirtschaftsentwicklung," *Weltwirtschaftliches Archiv*, **55**, 511–549 (May 1942).

[19] Valavanis-Vail, S., "An Econometric Model of Growth U.S.A. 1869–1953," *Am. Econ. Rev.*, **45**, 208–221 (Supplement 1955).

[20] Wicksell, K., *Lectures on Political Economy I*, London, 1934, p. 164.

CHAPTER 46

The Differential Equations of the Cobb-Douglas Model*

46.1 THE MODEL

Let us restate the Cobb-Douglas model of growth in terms of differential equations, with each carrying the same number as the corresponding difference equation did in Chapter 45. First, the definitions of the growth rates are

$$(1) \qquad g_L = \frac{dL}{dt}\frac{1}{L}$$

$$(2) \qquad g_M = \frac{dM}{dt}\frac{1}{M}$$

$$(3) \qquad g_S = \frac{dS}{dt}\frac{1}{S}$$

$$(4) \qquad g_X = \frac{dX}{dt}\frac{1}{X}$$

Of these, (1) and (2) are parameters, (3) and (4) are variables. Next, the definition of net investment:

$$(5) \qquad I = \frac{dS}{dt}$$

The consumption function:

$$(6) \qquad C = cX$$

---

* Chapter 45 is a prerequisite for Chapter 46.

the Cobb-Douglas production function:

(7) $$X = ML^\alpha S^\beta$$

and, finally, the equilibrium condition:

(8) $$X = C + I$$

46.2 SOLUTION FOR GROWTH RATE OF OUTPUT

Take the derivative of (7) with respect to time:

(7a) $$\frac{dX}{dt} = \frac{\partial X}{\partial M}\frac{dM}{dt} + \frac{\partial X}{\partial L}\frac{dL}{dt} + \frac{\partial X}{\partial S}\frac{dS}{dt}$$

Use (7), carry out the derivations, divide through by X, use (1) through (4), and find

(9) $$g_X = g_M + \alpha g_L + \beta g_S$$

Recalling that g_L and g_M are parameters, differentiate (9) with respect to time and find

(10) $$\frac{dg_X}{dt} = \beta\frac{dg_S}{dt}$$

From the consumption function (6) and the equilibrium requirement (8) jointly with the definitions (3) and (5) we get

(11) $$g_S = (1 - c)\frac{X}{S}$$

Using (3) and (4), we differentiate (11) with respect to time and obtain

(12) $$\frac{dg_S}{dt} = g_S(g_X - g_S)$$

Insert (9) into (12), recall that $\alpha + \beta = 1$, and express the proportionate rate of growth *of* the proportionate rate of growth of capital stock:

(13) $$\frac{dg_S}{dt}\frac{1}{g_S} = \alpha\left(\frac{g_M}{\alpha} + g_L - g_S\right)$$

Now there are three possibilities. The first one is that

$$g_S > \frac{g_M}{\alpha} + g_L$$

In this case, the expression in parentheses on the right-hand side of (13) becomes negative, as well as that expression multiplied by α, hence

(14) $$\frac{dg_S}{dt}\frac{1}{g_S} < 0$$

The second possibility is

(15)
$$g_S = \frac{g_M}{\alpha} + g_L$$

In this instance, the expression in parentheses on the right-hand side of (13) becomes zero, as well as that expression multiplied by α, hence

(16)
$$\frac{dg_S}{dt} \frac{1}{g_S} = 0$$

The third possibility is

$$g_S < \frac{g_M}{\alpha} + g_L$$

In this case, the expression in parentheses on the right-hand side of (13) becomes positive, as well as that parenthesis multiplied by α, hence

(17)
$$\frac{dg_S}{dt} \frac{1}{g_S} > 0$$

Therefore, as long as g_S is greater than the value (15), (14) shows it to be falling. As long as it is equal to that value, (16) shows it to remain equal. And as long as it is less than that value, (17) shows it to be rising.

Now differential equations trace a continuous time path, consequently g_S cannot alternate around the value (15). For to get from a value higher than (15) to one lower than (15) it would have to pass through the value (15); but if it did, (16) would keep it there.

However, could not g_S converge toward anything other than the value (15)? If it did, then by letting enough time elapse it would be possible for the left-hand side of (13) to become and remain less than any arbitrarily assignable positive constant ε, however small, without the same being possible for the right-hand side.

We conclude that if at some time g_S equals $g_M/\alpha + g_L$, it will remain equal to it, and that if it does not equal that quantity, it will converge toward it.

Insert (16), which was a result of (15), into (10):

$$\frac{dg_X}{dt} = 0$$

So the proportionate rate of growth of output, too, will become approximately stationary. Stationary at what value? Insert (15) into (9):

(18)
$$g_X = \frac{g_M}{\alpha} + g_L$$

Thus either from the beginning, output and capital stock are growing at the same proportionate rate defined by (15) and (18) or if they are not, (15) and (18) will ultimately become good approximations.

CHAPTER 47

A Two-Country Cobb-Douglas Model*

47.1 INTRODUCTION

International growth models almost always use the Leontief-Harrod-Domar assumption of no supply limitations other than a fixed capital coefficient [1, 2, 4]. However, the Harrod-Domar model is merely one variety of growth model, and the purpose of this chapter is to admit into a two-country growth model an alternative variety, the Cobb-Douglas model.

Again, the exchange rate will be admitted under assumptions preserving linearity. Moreover, as we did in our Keynesian and Harrod-Domar two-country models, we shall assume that consumers in both countries demand their country's own products as well as imported ones, but that firms invest in their own country's products only.

47.2 NOTATION

In a two-country dynamic macroeconomic model the following notation will be assigned.

Variables

$C_{ji} = i$th country's output consumed in jth country

$E = $ exchange rate, in number of monetary units of Country 1 equivalent to one monetary unit of Country 2

$G = $ proportionate rate of growth of the exchange rate

$g_{Si} = $ proportionate rate of growth of ith country's capital stock

$g_{Xi} = $ proportionate rate of growth of ith country's net national output

---

* Chapters 36 and 45 are prerequisites for Chapter 47.

I_i = net investment of ith country in its own products
L_i = ith country's labor force
M_i = a multiplicative factor in ith country's production function
P_i = price of ith country's output expressed in ith country's monetary unit
S_i = ith country's capital stock
U_{ik} = utility to kth person in ith country, resulting from his consumption
X_i = ith country's net national output
Y_i = ith country's net national money income

Parameters

A_i = elasticity of utility with respect to first country's output consumed in ith country

α_i = elasticity of ith country's net national output with respect to labor force

B_i = elasticity of utility with respect to second country's output consumed in ith country

β_i = elasticity of ith country's net national output with respect to capital stock

c_i = propensity to consume in ith country

g_{Li} = proportionate rate of growth of ith country's labor force

g_{Mi} = proportionate rate of growth of ith country's multiplicative factor

g_{Pi} = proportionate rate of growth of ith country's price of output

The stock variable S_i is measured in physical units of output of the ith country. The flow variables C_{ji}, I_i, and X_i are measured in physical units of output of the ith country per unit of time. These units carry the price tag P_i expressed in the ith country's monetary unit. Subscripts $i = j = 1$, 2 refer to the two countries.

Let t be the time coordinate dating variables: A flow variable marked (t) refers to period t, a stock variable marked (t) refers to time t. Let period t be the period beginning at time t, ending at time $t + 1$.

47.3 DEFINITIONS OF GROWTH RATES

First, we define six growth rates; three variable ones and three parameters.

(1)	$E(t + 1) = [1 + G(t)]E(t)$
(2, 3)	$L_i(t + 1) = (1 + g_{Li})L_i(t)$
(4, 5)	$M_i(t + 1) = (1 + g_{Mi})M_i(t)$
(6, 7)	$P_i(t + 1) = (1 + g_{Pi})P_i(t)$
(8, 9)	$S_i(t + 1) = [1 + g_{Si}(t)]S_i(t)$
(10, 11)	$X_i(t + 1) = [1 + g_{Xi}(t)]X_i(t)$

47.4 DEFINITION OF NET INVESTMENT

Net investment is defined as the net increase of capital stock:

(12, 13) $$I_i(t) = S_i(t + 1) - S_i(t)$$

47.5 PRODUCTION FUNCTIONS

Let each country's aggregate production function be linearly homogeneous and of Cobb-Douglas form

(14, 15) $$X_i(t) = M_i(t)[L_i(t)]^{\alpha_i}[S_i(t)]^{\beta_i}$$

where α_i and β_i are parameters lying between zero and one, where $\alpha_i + \beta_i = 1$, and where $M_i(t)$ is a positive multiplicative factor whose growth represents technological progress.

47.6 UTILITY MAXIMIZATION

Just as we did in our Keynesian and Harrod-Domar two-country models, apply our standard method of maximizing the kth person's utility subject to his budget constraint and find the four individual demand functions of the kth person in the two countries. Let the ith country have s_i persons, add the s_i demand functions for each good in each country, and find the four national aggregate demand functions:

(16) $$C_{11}(t) = \frac{c_1 A_1}{A_1 + B_1} X_1(t)$$

(17) $$C_{12}(t) = \frac{c_1 B_1}{A_1 + B_1} \frac{P_1(t)}{E(t)P_2(t)} X_1(t)$$

(18) $$C_{21}(t) = \frac{c_2 A_2}{A_2 + B_2} \frac{E(t)P_2(t)}{P_1(t)} X_2(t)$$

(19) $$C_{22}(t) = \frac{c_2 B_2}{A_2 + B_2} X_2(t)$$

47.7 DOMESTIC EQUILIBRIUM

Domestic equilibrium requires the sum of consumption, investment, and export demand for national output to equal national output; otherwise inventory would either accumulate or be depleted:

(20) $X_1(t) = C_{11}(t) + I_1(t) + C_{21}(t)$

(21) $X_2(t) = C_{22}(t) + I_2(t) + C_{12}(t)$

47.8 INTERNATIONAL EQUILIBRIUM

International equilibrium requires the balance of payment, when measured in the monetary unit of any country, say the first, to equal zero:

(22) $P_1(t)C_{21}(t) - E(t)P_2(t)C_{12}(t) = 0$

or the first country's export *minus* its import equals zero. Since each country's export is the other country's import, it follows from (22) that the second country's import *minus* its export also equals zero.

47.9 SOLUTIONS FOR GROWTH RATES OF OUTPUT

The reader will recall the proof in Section 45.4 that either from the very beginning, output and capital stock are growing at the same proportionate rate or, if they are not, they eventually will. Will this proof survive the internationalization of the model? After all, the proof was not merely a manipulation of the Cobb-Douglas production function, it utilized the consumption function and the domestic equilibrium condition that output equals demand. Both the consumption function and the domestic equilibrium condition are now more complicated. Hence, will the proof survive?

To see if it will, take the production function (14) for the first country, express it for periods $t + 1$ and t, divide the first expression by the second, use (2), (4), (8), and (10) upon it, and get

(23) $1 + g_{X1}(t) = (1 + g_{M1})(1 + g_{L1})^{\alpha_1}[1 + g_{S1}(t)]^{\beta_1}$

Express (23) for periods $t + 1$ and t, divide the first expression by the second, and obtain

(24) $\dfrac{1 + g_{X1}(t + 1)}{1 + g_{X1}(t)} = \left[\dfrac{1 + g_{S1}(t + 1)}{1 + g_{S1}(t)}\right]^{\beta_1}$

We are now approaching the perilous point at which our new consumption functions and our new domestic equilibrium condition must enter: From the domestic equilibrium condition (20), the international equilibrium condition (22), the consumption functions (16) and (17), the investment definition (12), and the growth definition (8), in that order, find

$$(25) \qquad\qquad g_{S1}(t) = (1 - c_1) \frac{X_1(t)}{S_1(t)}$$

Except for the country subscript, (23) is the same as (9) and (25) is the same as (11) in Chapter 45. Therefore everything may now proceed exactly as it did in that chapter. Thus our one-country proof did survive the internationalization of the model. In either country, either from the very beginning, output and capital are growing at the same proportionate rate or, if they are not, they eventually will. That rate is

$$(26) \qquad\qquad 1 + g_{Si}(t) = (1 + g_{Mi})^{1/\alpha_i}(1 + g_{Li})$$
$$(27) \qquad\qquad 1 + g_{Xi}(t) = (1 + g_{Mi})^{1/\alpha_i}(1 + g_{Li})$$

Notice again the absence of any time coordinate on the right-hand side: (26) and (27) have no time trend in them.

Throughout the last three chapters we are assuming each country to have some technological progress; hence g_{Mi} is positive. We are assuming no country's labor force to be declining; hence g_{Li} is nonnegative. We are also assuming $0 < \alpha_i < 1$. Under these three assumptions, the right-hand side of (26) and (27) will exceed one, that is, the equilibrium proportionate rates of growth of each country's output will be positive.

The proportionate rate of growth of a country's output depends upon the parameters of that country alone, not upon those of the other country. In that sense the two countries are highly independent of each other. Highly, but not fully independent, as we shall see in Section 47.10. In each of the solutions (26) and (27), three national parameters are present: α_i, g_{Mi}, and g_{Li}. To see precisely how the rates of growth depend upon those three parameters, take the three partial derivatives of the logarithmic form of (27):

$$(28, 29) \qquad \frac{\partial \log [1 + g_{Xi}(t)]}{\partial \alpha_i} = - \frac{\log (1 + g_{Mi})}{\alpha_i^2}$$

$$(30, 31) \qquad \frac{\partial \log [1 + g_{Xi}(t)]}{\partial \log (1 + g_{Mi})} = \frac{1}{\alpha_i}$$

$$(32, 33) \qquad \frac{\partial \log [1 + g_{Xi}(t)]}{\partial \log (1 + g_{Li})} = 1$$

Derivatives (28) and (29) show the growth factor $1 + g_{Xi}(t)$ of a country's output to fall if the labor elasticity of its output rises. Derivatives (30) and (31) show the elasticity of the growth factor $1 + g_{Xi}(t)$ of output with respect to the growth factor $1 + g_{Mi}$ of the multiplicative factor to be $1/\alpha_i$, which is greater than one, because $0 < \alpha_i < 1$. Derivatives (32) and (33) show the elasticity of the growth factor $1 + g_{Xi}(t)$ of output with respect to the growth factor of labor force $1 + g_{Li}$ to be unity.

No other parameters are present in (26) and (27). Specifically, and unlike Harrod-Domar models, the Cobb-Douglas model does not permit the propensity to save $1 - c_i$ to affect the rate of growth of output.

47.10   THE TIME PATH OF THE EXCHANGE RATE

Use (17), (18), and (22) to express the exchange rate $E(t)$ in terms of c_i, A_i, B_i, $P_i(t)$, and $X_i(t)$. Rewrite the expression for period $t + 1$, divide the second expression by the first, and use (1), (6), (7), (10), and (11):

$$(34) \qquad 1 + G(t) = \frac{1 + g_{P1}}{1 + g_{P2}} \frac{1 + g_{X1}(t)}{1 + g_{X2}(t)}$$

The form (34) permits us to see, just as we saw for the Harrod-Domar model, that although the two countries are independent as far as the growth rates of their outputs are concerned, they are dependent, *via* (34), as far as the growth of their real incomes is concerned. If Country 1 enjoys more rapid growth of its output than does Country 2, one physical unit of Country 1's goods buys fewer and fewer physical units of Country 2's goods, either because the exchange rate is rising at stationary relative prices, or because the relative price of Country 2's goods is rising at a stationary exchange rate. Either way Country 1 is paying a penalty for enjoying more rapid growth.

To express the growth rate of the exchange rate in terms of parameters only, insert (26) and (27) into (34):

$$(35) \qquad 1 + G(t) = \frac{(1 + g_{M1})^{1/\alpha_1}}{(1 + g_{M2})^{1/\alpha_2}} \frac{1 + g_{L1}}{1 + g_{L2}} \frac{1 + g_{P1}}{1 + g_{P2}}$$

Notice the absence of any time coordinate on the right-hand side: (35) has no time trend in it.

In addition to the assumptions already made, make the assumption that the growth factor $1 + g_{Pi}$ of each country's price level is positive; this means that once it is positive, a country's price level will never become negative. Then (35) shows the growth factor $1 + G(t)$ to be positive. The growth *rate* $G(t)$ itself may be positive, zero, or negative, but it will never be *minus* one or less. In (35) all eight parameters α_i, g_{Mi}, g_{Li}, and g_{Pi} occur. How precisely the equilibrium proportionate rate of growth of the exchange rate depends upon those eight parameters is shown by taking the eight partial derivatives of the logarithmic form of (35):

$$(36) \qquad \frac{\partial \log [1 + G(t)]}{\partial \alpha_1} = - \frac{\log (1 + g_{M1})}{\alpha_1{}^2}$$

$$(37) \qquad \frac{\partial \log [1 + G(t)]}{\partial \log (1 + g_{M1})} = \frac{1}{\alpha_1}$$

$$(38) \qquad \frac{\partial \log [1 + G(t)]}{\partial \log (1 + g_{L1})} = 1$$

$$(39) \qquad \frac{\partial \log [1 + G(t)]}{\partial \log (1 + g_{P1})} = 1$$

$$(40) \qquad \frac{\partial \log [1 + G(t)]}{\partial \alpha_2} = \frac{\log (1 + g_{M2})}{\alpha_2{}^2}$$

$$(41) \qquad \frac{\partial \log [1 + G(t)]}{\partial \log (1 + g_{M2})} = - \frac{1}{\alpha_2}$$

$$(42) \qquad \frac{\partial \log [1 + G(t)]}{\partial \log (1 + g_{L2})} = -1$$

$$(43) \qquad \frac{\partial \log [1 + G(t)]}{\partial \log (1 + g_{P2})} = -1$$

What do all these derivatives show? Derivatives (36) and (40) show that the growth factor $1 + G(t)$ of the exchange rate falls if the labor elasticity α_1 of Country 1's output rises, but it rises if the labor elasticity α_2 of Country 2's output rises.

Derivatives (37) and (41) show the elasticity of the growth factor $1 + G(t)$ of the exchange rate with respect to the growth factors $1 + g_{M1}$ and $1 + g_{M2}$ of the two countries' multiplicative factors to be simply $1/\alpha_1$ and $-1/\alpha_2$, respectively.

Derivatives (38) and (42) show the elasticities of the growth factor $1 + G(t)$ of the exchange rate with respect to the growth factors $1 + g_{L1}$ and $1 + g_{L2}$ of the two countries' labor forces to be, even more simply, *plus* and *minus* one, respectively.

Finally, (39) and (43) show the elasticities of the growth factor $1 + G(t)$ of the exchange rate with respect to the growth factors $1 + g_{P1}$ and $1 + g_{P2}$ of the two countries' price levels to be *plus* and *minus* one, respectively.

No other parameters are present in (35). Again, unlike the Harrod-Domar model, the Cobb-Douglas model does not permit the rate of growth of the exchange rate to depend upon the propensities to save $1 - c_i$ in the two countries.

47.11 CONCLUSIONS

In this chapter, we have replaced a Harrod-Domar by a Cobb-Douglas international model of growth, and the results turned out to be remarkably different. Now the propensity to save no longer affects any equilibrium proportionate rate of growth, neither that of national output nor that of the exchange rate. Instead, the proportionate rates of growth are determined by the input elasticities of the Cobb-Douglas production function, by technological progress, and by the growth of the labor force.

As regards the equilibrium proportionate rate of growth of the exchange rate, our findings are contained in the partial logarithmic derivatives (36) through (43). Most of these findings are not surprising. For example, (39) and (43) are merely concise statements of a theory of the exchange rate dating back to the early post-World War I days, that is, the purchasing power parity theory.

Our findings (37) and (41), however, are at odds with widely held views. Around 1950 the European dollar shortage was widely explained by an alleged higher productivity growth factor in the United States than in Western Europe. To be sure, the actual existence of such a difference was questioned by MacDougall [3]. Undaunted, the explanation reappeared when the dollar shortage had turned into a dollar glut: Around 1960 the United States gold outflow was equally widely explained by an alleged higher productivity growth factor in Continental Western Europe.

In our model, however, if the growth factor $1 + g_{M1}$ of Country 1's multiplicative factor were raised by one per cent, our partial derivative (37) shows the growth factor $1 + G(t)$ to rise by $1/\alpha_1$ per cent; thus the exchange rate rises *against* the country accelerating its productivity growth. Therefore the widely held explanation, perhaps based upon Marshallian partial-equilibrium reasoning, does not stand up in a general-equilibrium growth model. It does not even stand up if the country's monetary policy were to keep the growth factor $1 + g_{P1}$ of its price level varying inversely with the growth factor $1 + g_{M1}$ of its productivity. True, this brings into the reasoning another parameter change, that of P_1, besides the productivity change. However, our model can handle that as well: The exchange rate will still rise against Country 1, for our partial derivative (39) shows the growth factor $1 + G(t)$ to fall by one per cent if the growth factor of the price level $1 + g_{P1}$ falls by one per cent. Nevertheless, this one per cent fall will not outweigh the $1/\alpha_1$ per cent rise in $1 + G(t)$, for $0 < \alpha_1 < 1$; hence $1/\alpha_1 > 1$. It would, then, take an even more restrictive monetary policy than the one mentioned to keep the exchange rate from rising against Country 1.

The most general conclusion one can draw from our solution (35) for the exchange rate is the following. For long periods of time, sovereign nations are unlikely to be able as well as willing to maintain the equality

$$(1 + g_{M1})^{1/\alpha_1}(1 + g_{L1})(1 + g_{P1}) = (1 + g_{M2})^{1/\alpha_2}(1 + g_{L2})(1 + g_{P2})$$

required for $G(t) = 0$, that is, required for the exchange rate to remain stationary. Nations may agree on the desirability of stationary exchange rates, but they are unlikely to be willing, let alone able, to control their price levels as required.

REFERENCES

[1] Brems, H., "The Foreign Trade Accelerator and the International Transmission of Growth," *Econometrica*, **24**, 223–238 (July 1956).
[2] Brown, M., and R. Jones, "Economic Growth and the Theory of International Income Flows," *Econometrica*, **30**, 88–97 (January 1962).
[3] MacDougall, G. D. A., "Does Productivity Rise Faster in the United States?" *Rev. Econ. Stat.*, **38**, 155–176 (May 1956).
[4] Johnson, H. G., "Equilibrium Growth in an International Economy," *Can. Jour. Econ. Pol. Sci.*, **19**, 478–500 (November 1953).

CHAPTER 48

The Equilibrium Rate of Interest in a
Vintage Model of Growth*

As technical progress is a diffused process offering more or less equal opportunities to different countries, it is necessary to explain why these opportunities were not seized in equal degree, and why the productivity gap between Europe and America was permitted to become so wide.

MADDISON [14, p. 89]

48.1 INTRODUCTION

In the Harrod-Domar growth model technological progress was absent. In the neoclassical Cobb-Douglas growth model technological progress was present in the form of a multiplicative factor, growing over time, in the production function. Technological progress was embodied in neither labor input nor capital stock.

Such an assumption of disembodied technological progress can be no more than a first approximation. Historically almost all technological progress has made its way into the economy in the form of new and different hardware.

However, it is not only new investment that consists of new and different hardware. Under steady technological progress, no retired producers' good will be replaced by another unit mechanically identical to it; it will be replaced by a new and different one. Thus retirement, replacement, and with them depreciation, move into prominence.

The traditional Harrod-Domar model and the traditional Cobb-Douglas model were constitutionally incapable of dealing with retirement, replacement, and depreciation, for they were net models defining saving, investment, and

* Chapter 17 is a prerequisite for Chapter 48.

473

national output as net saving, net investment, and net national output, respectively. Clearly, then, a gross model will have to be formulated, as was done by Johansen [9], Solow [16], Massell [15], and others.

However, it is not enough to make room for retirement, replacement, and depreciation by formulating a gross model. Retirement is a function of useful life, and useful life must be an important economic variable and should be treated as such.[1] Under steady technological progress there must be a right time to retire producers' goods. They should not be retired too soon, or the capital cost of acquiring them occurs too frequently. They should not be retired too late either, or they put their owner at a competitive disadvantage *vis-a-vis* firms, actual or potential, owning newer, more advanced, producers' goods. When exactly should they be retired? Intuition as well as our model of optimum replacement in Chapter 17, to be briefly summarized in Section 48.3, show that the higher the rate of interest the more urgent it becomes to save capital cost by lengthening the useful life of producers' goods.

If established, such a relationship between the rate of interest and optimum useful life implies that whether or not the *making* of technological progress is induced, the *adoption* of it surely is. Two economies facing the same technological progress will adopt it at different speeds if their interest rates differ: The capital-rich low-rate-of-interest economy will adopt it faster.

Such a result is realistic. It is well known that in industries of the underdeveloped economies the useful life of plant and equipment is much longer than in the corresponding industries of the developed economies, and observers from the developed economies are often struck by the antiquated equipment still in use [1].

Upon the microeconomic foundations laid in Chapter 17 we shall now set forth a simple vintage model of growth emphasizing useful life as a key variable whose optimum value depends upon the rate of interest and the rate of technological progress. Does our simple vintage model have substitution between labor and capital in it? Not quite as much as do the models of Johansen [9] and Massell [15], let alone that of Solow [16]. Our model considers technological progress autonomous and concentrates on the practically very important form of labor-capital substitution at the margin of replacement. Here there is substitution between the more automatic replacing unit and the less automatic replaced unit of producers' goods, each being operated by one man. At the margin of replacement, whose location is determined by the rate of interest and the rate of technological progress, the efficiency difference between the replacing and the replaced units may be very substantial. For example, let technological progress amount to a 3

---

[1] Eisner [5] and Domar [4] showed that in a growing economy with stationary prices depreciation allowances would exceed replacement requirements. Here, useful life was a parameter. Eisner [6] did consider useful life varying with technological progress but not with the rate of interest.

per cent efficiency increase per annum with continuous compounding, and let useful life of producers' goods be 26 years. Then the replacing unit has a 2.18 times higher efficiency than the replaced one.

48.2 NOTATION

Variables

B = money gross capital coefficient

C = consumption demand per annum

c = the consumption to net income ratio

D = depreciation per physical unit of producers' goods

f = labor's share of net income

h = gross investment to gross output ratio

i = rate of interest per annum

k = worth of a unit of producers' goods, determined as the sum of the discounted revenue *minus* operating labor cost over its remaining useful life

L = new jobs created by manning annual output of producers' goods

l = employment in building annual output of producers' goods

n = present net worth of a new unit of producers' goods

P = price of consumers' goods

p = price of a new unit of producers' goods

π = net income to gross output ratio, the "payout" ratio

S = output of producers' goods per annum

u = useful life of producers' goods

V = money interest bill per annum

W = money wage bill per annum

X = output of consumers' goods per annum

Y_{gross} = money gross output per annum

Y_{net} = money net income per annum

Parameters

a = minimum labor required to build one unit of producers' goods

b = physical capital coefficient

c_V = propensity to consume real interest income

c_W = propensity to consume real wage income

e = Euler's number, the base of natural logarithms

η = price elasticity of demand faced by firms in the consumers' goods industry

F = available labor force

g = proportionate rate of growth of labor force

μ = proportionate rate of technological progress

w = the money wage rate—the *numeraire*

Let t be the time coordinate dating variables: A flow variable marked (t) refers to the instantaneous rate of that variable as of time t. All flow variables are measured per annum. How can an instantaneous rate be measured per annum? It is possible to do this in much the same way as the speedometer of an automobile measures the instantaneous rate of speed in miles per *hour*.

Besides the time coordinate t we shall use the vintage coordinate v: Capital coefficients $b(v)$, new jobs $L(v)$ created by manning the annual output of producers' goods $S(v)$, as well as the resulting annual output of consumers' goods $X(v)$ all refer to a vintage v of durable producers' goods.

48.3 MICROECONOMICS

The present chapter is firmly based upon the microeconomics developed in Chapter 17. Let us therefore collect, in their original numbering the equations needed from that chapter. First, we defined a physical unit of producers' goods as the equipment operated by one man, hence:

(2) $$L(v) = S(v)$$

Second, we defined the physical capital coefficients:

(3) $$b(v) = \frac{S(v)}{X(v)}$$

Third, we defined technological progress as a steady reduction of the physical capital coefficient:

(4) $$b(t) = e^{\mu(t-v)}b(v) \qquad (v < t)$$

Fourth, we assumed price policy to be

(5) $$P(t) = e^{\mu(t-v)}P(v) \qquad (v < t)$$

Fifth, we defined net worth of a new unit of producers' good of vintage v, as seen at time v:

(8) $$n(v) = \frac{P(v)}{b(v)} \frac{1 - e^{(\mu-i)u}}{i - \mu} - w \frac{1 - e^{-iu}}{i} - p$$

Sixth, we determined the price of producers' goods:

(9) $$p = aw$$

Seventh, from (4) and (5) we found

(11) $$\frac{P(t)}{b(t)} = \frac{P(v)}{b(v)}$$

Eighth, we maximized the net worth of an endless series of generations of capital stock of constant capacity $S(0)$, $S(u)$, $S(2u)$, ... , as seen from time $t = 0$. The resulting solutions for optimum initial consumers' goods price

$P(0)$ and for optimum useful life of producers' goods u were

(18) $$P(0) = \frac{\eta}{1 + \eta} \frac{i - \mu}{i} \frac{1 - e^{-iu} + ai}{1 - e^{(\mu - i)u}} b(0)w$$

(19) $$ie^{-\mu u} - \mu e^{-iu} = (ai + 1)(i - \mu)$$

Table 48.1 and Fig. 48.1 illustrate (19).

Table 48.1   Useful Life u
as Computed from (19)

Developed economy	
$a = 8, \mu = -0.03$	
i	u
0.04	23.4
0.08	26.4
0.12	29.8
0.16	33.2
Underdeveloped economy	
$a = 4, \mu = -0.02$	
i	u
0.08	24.0
0.12	27.1
0.16	30.6

Finally, ninth, we inserted (19) into (18) and found

(20) $$P(0) = \frac{\eta}{1 + \eta} e^{-\mu u} b(0)w$$

We shall also find it useful to insert (9), (11), and (18) into (8) and express optimum net worth as

(8a) $$n(v) = -\frac{1}{1 + \eta} \frac{1 - e^{-iu} + ai}{i} w$$

48.4   PURE COMPETITION

We shall simplify our macroeconomics by confining ourselves to the special case of pure competition. Let the price elasticity η approach *minus* infinity and use the approximation

(26) $$\frac{\eta}{1 + \eta} = 1$$

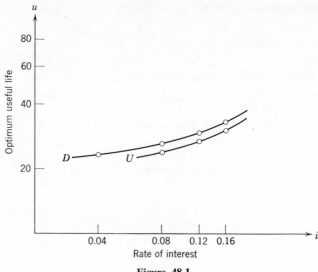

Figure 48.1

Deduct one on both sides of (26), insert into (8a), and find

(8b) $$n(v) = 0$$

The economic mechanism through which net worth $n(v)$ vanishes is the familiar one of price competition under freedom of entry. Over the optimized useful life of producers' goods the price $P(t)$ of their output will be such that full cost, including the cost of capital, is covered, no more, no less.

48.5 MACROECONOMICS

Let us now turn from microeconomics to macroeconomics. Let the economy consist of firms all of which are exactly like the one just described. Consequently, within any year the economy will produce only two goods, that is, consumers' goods and producers' goods. Consumers' goods do not change from year to year, but producers' goods do change, according to (4).

Furthermore, the economy includes households whose propensity to consume interest income is less than one and whose propensity to consume wage income is one.

Finally, the economy includes a money capital market in which firms may borrow and savers may lend funds at the rate of interest i per annum with continuous compounding. The government is ignored.

Let the labor force be growing at a constant proportionate rate per annum.

Define steady-state growth [8, p. 781], as the constancy of the proportionate rates of growth of all relevant variables. In our economy, then, could there be steady-state growth at full employment? If so, what would be the necessary rate of interest? What would be the real wage rate, and what would be labor's share? Needless to say, the existence of such a steady-state growth path would not guarantee that the economy would actually be following it.

As a first step toward answering our questions, let us study the capital structure of our model.

48.6 PHYSICAL CAPITAL STOCK AND ITS STRUCTURE

The entire physical capital stock in use at time t is a heterogeneous mass of objects, "a fossilized history of technology," as Maddison [14] calls it. Write the physical capital stock at time t as the following integral:

$$\int_{t-u}^{t} S(v)\, dv$$

While producers' goods of different vintages are not alike, the number of physical units of each vintage remains well defined: For any vintage v, Eq. (2) defined a physical unit of producers' goods as the equipment operated by one man. Thus measured, let the output of producers' goods per annum $S(t)$ grow at the proportionate rate g per annum with continuous compounding:

(27) $$S(t) = e^{g(t-v)}S(v)$$

where $v \leq t \leq v + u$ and $g > 0$.

Now insert (27) into the integral above and write it:

(28) $$\int_{t-u}^{t} S(v)\, dv = \int_{t-u}^{t} e^{-g(t-v)}S(t)\, dv = \frac{1 - e^{-gu}}{g} S(t)$$

Equation (28) expresses the entire physical capital stock in terms of the output of producers' goods of the latest vintage within it. From (28) we see that since $S(t)$ is growing at the proportionate rate g per annum, so is the entire physical capital stock.

48.7 FULL EMPLOYMENT AND ITS STRUCTURE

For any vintage v Equation (2) defined a physical unit of producers' goods as the equipment operated by one man. Consequently the expression (28) for physical capital stock also applies to the number of men employed by the consumers' goods industry and manning that stock:

$$(29) \qquad \int_{t-u}^{t} L(v) \, dv = \int_{t-u}^{t} S(v) \, dv = \frac{1 - e^{-gu}}{g} S(t)$$

At time t what is the employment in the producers' goods inductry? $S(t)$ represents the instantaneous rate of output per annum in the producers' goods industry at time t. The minimum building labor required to build one unit of producers' goods was a, so employment in the producers' goods industry is:

$$(30) \qquad l(t) = aS(t)$$

Now add (29) and (30) and let the total employment be equal to the available labor force:

$$(31) \qquad \left(a + \frac{1 - e^{-gu}}{g} \right) S(t) = F(t)$$

On the left-hand side of (31) the time coordinate t occurs only once, in $S(t)$. Consequently, total employment is growing at the proportionate rate g per annum. This is as it should be: The full-employment equation (31) requires producers goods output to be growing at the same proportionate rate as does the labor force.

48.8 OUTPUT OF PRODUCERS' GOODS

$S(t)$ represents the instantaneous rate of output per annum in the producers' goods industry at time t. To find its money value multiply it by p, use (9), and find

$$(32) \qquad pS(t) = awS(t)$$

Thus the money value of the output of producers' goods is in proportion to $S(t)$, hence must be growing at the proportionate rate g per annum.

48.9 OUTPUT OF CONSUMERS' GOODS

Use Eq. (3) to find the instantaneous rate of output of consumers' goods flowing from the entire physical capital stock existing at time t:

$$(33) \qquad \int_{t-u}^{t} X(v) \, dv = \int_{t-u}^{t} \frac{S(v)}{b(v)} \, dv$$

Insert (4) and (27) into (33):

(34)
$$\int_{t-u}^{t} X(v) \, dv = \int_{t-u}^{t} e^{-(g-\mu)(t-v)} \frac{S(t)}{b(t)} \, dv$$
$$= \frac{1 - e^{-(g-\mu)u}}{g - \mu} \frac{S(t)}{b(t)}$$

Output of consumers' goods as expressed by (34) is in proportion to the ratio between $S(t)$ and $b(t)$, hence must be growing at the same proportionate rate as does that ratio. To find that rate, use (4) and (27) and write:

(35)
$$\frac{S(t)}{b(t)} = e^{g-\mu} \frac{S(t-1)}{b(t-1)}$$

Therefore physical output of consumers' goods is growing at the proportionate rate per annum $g - \mu$. To find the money value of consumers' goods output multiply (34) by $P(t)$, use (11), (20), and (26), and write it as

(36)
$$P(t) \int_{t-u}^{t} X(v) \, dv = e^{-\mu u} \frac{1 - e^{-(g-\mu)u}}{g - \mu} w S(t)$$

The money value of consumers' goods output as expressed by (36) is in proportion to $S(t)$; hence it is growing at the proportionate rate per annum g. That the money value of consumers' goods output should be growing less rapidly than physical output of consumers' goods is, of course, due to the steady price decline of consumers' goods expressed by (5).

48.10 MONEY VALUE OF GROSS OUTPUT

Since producers' and consumers' goods are measured in different physical units we cannot add their physical outputs but merely the money values of their output. Add (32) and (36):

(37)
$$Y_{gross}(t) = \left[a + e^{-\mu u} \frac{1 - e^{-(g-\mu)u}}{g - \mu} \right] w S(t)$$

48.11 THE GROSS INVESTMENT TO GROSS OUTPUT RATIO

Divide (32) by (37) and find the gross investment to gross output ratio

(38)
$$h = \frac{pS(t)}{Y_{gross}(t)} = \frac{a}{a + e^{-\mu u} \dfrac{1 - e^{-(g-\mu)u}}{g - \mu}}$$

Table 48.2   Values of Parameters and Variables in a Developed Economy
$a = 8, g = 0.01, \mu = -0.03$

Value of	As computed from equation	Rate of interest i			
		0.04	0.08	0.12	0.16
h	(38)	0.207	0.181	0.158	0.138
π	(49)	0.809	0.830	0.857	0.874
f	(50)	0.923	0.851	0.777	0.716
c_V	(52)	0.762	0.907	0.920	0.950
c	(56)	0.981	0.987	0.982	0.986
B	(57)	4.32	4.20	4.07	3.90

The time coordinate t occurs nowhere in (38), hence the ratio of gross investment to gross output has no time trend in it. However, useful life does occur, and optimum useful life was found to be a function of the rate of interest i (see Table 48.1). When we allow for that relationship, Tables 48.2 and 48.3 and Fig. 48.2 show a low rate of interest i accompanying a high ratio h of gross investment to gross output—as we have always believed it would.

The ratio of consumers' goods output to gross output would, of course, be $1 - h$. Thus we have found the effect of the rate of interest upon the allocation of full-employment output between producers' and consumers' goods. We shall refer to this effect as the output effect of the rate of interest.

Table 48.3   Values of Parameters and Variables in an Underdeveloped Economy

$a = 4, g = 0.03, \mu = -0.02$

Value of	As computed from equation	Rate of interest i		
		0.08	0.12	0.16
h	(38)	0.150	0.136	0.122
π	(49)	0.883	0.898	0.913
f	(50)	0.899	0.851	0.800
c_V	(52)	0.637	0.738	0.813
c	(56)	0.962	0.963	0.963
B	(57)	2.57	2.51	2.43

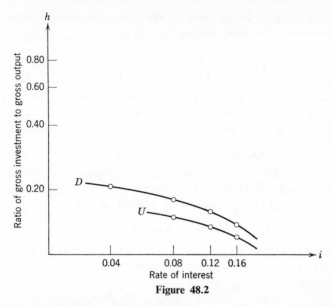

Figure 48.2

Let us now study the effect of the rate of interest upon net income and demand.

48.12   NET INCOME PER UNIT OF PRODUCERS' GOODS

The most important determinant of consumption demand is net income; hence we must now examine net income formation. Let us begin with the net income flowing from one physical unit of producers' goods of vintage v. At time t, where $v \le t \le v + u$, revenue per annum from such a unit is $P(t)/b(v)$. Use (5) to write it as

$$\frac{P(v)}{b(v)} e^{\mu(t-v)}$$

Let w be the money wage rate per annum. Since one physical unit of producers' goods is by definition operated by one man, operating labor cost per annum per physical unit of producers' goods is w. Revenue *minus* operating labor cost, then, is

$$\frac{P(v)}{b(v)} e^{\mu(t-v)} - w$$

At time τ, where $v \le \tau \le v + u$, the worth of revenue *minus* operating labor cost per small fraction dt of a year located at time t is

$$\left[\frac{P(v)}{b(v)} e^{\mu(t-v)} - w \right] e^{-i(t-\tau)} dt$$

At time τ the worth of the sum total of revenue *minus* operating labor cost over the entire remaining useful life of the unit is

$$(39) \qquad k(v, \tau) = \int_\tau^{v+u} \left[\frac{P(v)}{b(v)} e^{\mu(t-v)} - w \right] e^{-i(t-\tau)} \, dt$$

By using (39), we may define depreciation and net income. Depreciation on the unit of producers' goods of vintage v during the year from time τ to time $\tau + 1$ is defined as the deterioration of its worth during that year:

$$(40) \qquad D(v, \tau) = k(v, \tau) - k(v, \tau + 1)$$

Economists often fail to define income, but let us again follow Lindahl [13] who did not fail to do so. Define net income at time τ from the physical unit of producers' goods of vintage v as the interest on its worth.

$$(41) \qquad V(v, \tau) = ik(v, \tau)$$

To find that net income let us concentrate on $k(v, \tau)$. Use (11), (20), and (26) to express $P(v)/b(v)$ simply as $we^{-\mu u}$, insert this expression, multiply out, and write (39) as

$$(42) \qquad k(v, \tau) = w \left[e^{-\mu u} \int_\tau^{v+u} e^{\mu(t-v)-i(t-\tau)} \, dt - \int_\tau^{v+u} e^{-i(t-\tau)} \, dt \right]$$

$$= w \, \frac{ie^{-\mu(v+u-\tau)} - \mu e^{-i(v+u-\tau)} - (i - \mu)}{i(i - \mu)}$$

which is, we repeat, the worth of one physical unit of producers' goods of vintage v as seen at time τ.

48.13   THE AGGREGATE INTEREST BILL

Just as the interest bill on one unit of producers' goods was the interest on its worth, so the aggregate interest bill is the interest on the worth of the aggregate capital stock. To find that worth, proceed as follows.

The output of producers' goods per annum as of time v is $S(v)$. Therefore, the number of physical units of producers' goods of vintages from v to $v + dv$, where dv is a small fraction of a year located at time v, is $S(v) \, dv$. As seen at time τ, the worth of all of them is

$$k(v, \tau)S(v) \, dv$$

As seen at time τ, the worth of all producers' goods existing at that time, that is, of vintages from $\tau - u$ to τ, is

$$(43) \qquad \int_{\tau-u}^\tau k(v, \tau)S(v) \, dv$$

Now write (27) as:

(27) $$S(v) = e^{g(v-\tau)}S(\tau)$$

Insert (27) thus written and (42) into the integral (43) and find the integral:

(44)
$$\int_{\tau-u}^{\tau} k(v,\tau)S(v)\,dv = \frac{wS(\tau)}{i(i-\mu)}\int_{\tau-u}^{\tau} [ie^{-\mu(v+u-\tau)+g(v-\tau)}$$

$$- \mu e^{-i(v+u-\tau)+g(v-\tau)} - (i-\mu)e^{g(v-\tau)}]\,dv = \frac{w}{i}QS(\tau)$$

where

$$Q = \frac{ie^{-\mu u}}{(g-\mu)(i-\mu)} + \frac{\mu e^{-iu}}{(i-g)(i-\mu)} - \frac{i\mu e^{-gu}}{g(g-\mu)(i-g)} - \frac{1}{g}$$

Replacing τ by t, we may then say that at time t aggregate depreciated capital stock has the worth:

(44a) $$\frac{w}{i}QS(t)$$

Now net income from this stock is the interest on it; therefore multiply (44a) by i and get the aggregate interest bill in the economy:

(45) $$V(t) = wQS(t)$$

48.14   THE AGGREGATE WAGE BILL

At full employment the aggregate wage bill is

$$W(t) = wF(t)$$

Into this insert (31):

(46) $$W(t) = \left(a + \frac{1 - e^{-gu}}{g}\right)wS(t)$$

48.15   AGGREGATE NET INCOME

Aggregate net income is the sum of the aggregate interest and wage bills:

(47) $$Y_{net}(t) = V(t) + W(t)$$

Into (47) insert (45) and (46):

$$Y_{net}(t) = \left(Q + a + \frac{1 - e^{-gu}}{g}\right)wS(t)$$

Now Q is a rather unwieldy agglomeration of parameters, hence let us use (19) to express $\mu e^{-iu} = i e^{-\mu u} - (ai + 1)(i - \mu)$, insert that into Q and Q into $Y_{net}(t)$, rearrange, and write $Y_{net}(t)$ in the much simpler form

$$(48) \qquad Y_{net}(t) = \frac{ie^{-\mu u} + (g - \mu - i)e^{-gu} - (1 + ag)(g - \mu)}{(g - \mu)(i - g)} wS(t)$$

48.16 THE NET INCOME PAYOUT RATIO

Define[2] the net income payout ratio π as the ratio of net income to gross output. Express it by dividing (48) by (37):

$$(49) \qquad \pi = \frac{Y_{net}(t)}{Y_{gross}(t)} = \frac{\dfrac{ie^{-\mu u} + (g - \mu - i)e^{-gu} - (1 + ag)(g - \mu)}{(g - \mu)(i - g)}}{a + e^{-\mu u}\dfrac{1 - e^{-(g-\mu)u}}{g - \mu}}$$

The time coordinate t occurs nowhere in (49); hence the net income payout ratio has no time trend in it. But useful life does occur, and optimum useful life was found to be a function of the rate of interest (see Table 48.1). When

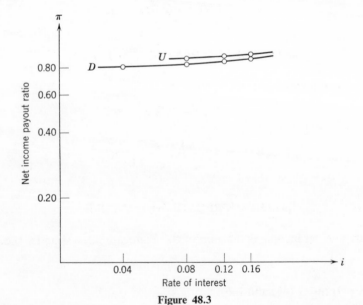

Figure 48.3

[2] Our national income payout ratio π must not be confused with the dividends to net profit ratio in corporations, often [2] referred to as a payout ratio, too.

we allow for that relationship, Tables 48.2 and 48.3 and Fig. 48.3 show a low rate of interest i accompanies a low net income payout ratio π.

Given the propensity to consume net income, the net income payout ratio π determines the consumption demand generated by a given gross output; consequently it is just as important as the propensity to consume and deserves far more attention than the Keynesians have paid to it. Without including the payout ratio as a variable, Keynes himself [10, pp. 98, 104], certainly saw its importance:

"We must not underestimate the importance of the fact ... that ... consumption is, *cet. par.*, a function of *net* income. ... It is important to emphasize the magnitude of the deduction which has to be made from the income of a society, which already possesses a large stock of capital, before we arrive at the net income which is ordinarily available for consumption. For if we overlook this, we may underestimate the heavy drag on the propensity to consume which exists even in conditions where the public is ready to consume a very large proportion of its net income."

48.17   LABOR'S SHARE

Now that we have found aggregate net income, let us find labor's share of it. Divide (46) by (48), let $wS(t)$ cancel out, and write labor's share as

$$(50) \qquad f = \frac{W(t)}{Y_{\text{net}}(t)} = \frac{a + \dfrac{1 - e^{-gu}}{g}}{\dfrac{ie^{-\mu u} + (g - \mu - i)e^{-gu} - (1 + ag)(g - \mu)}{(g - \mu)(i - g)}}$$

The time coordinate t occurs nowhere in (50); hence labor's share has no time trend in it. But useful life does occur, and optimum useful life was found to be a function of the rate of interest i (see Table 48.1). When we allow for that relationship, Tables 48.2 and 48.3 and Fig. 48.4 show a low rate of interest i accompanies a high labor's share f.

48.18   CONSUMPTION DEMAND

Let us take advantage of our model's distinction between interest income and wage income by letting the propensity to consume interest income be less than the propensity to consume wage income, as Lindahl [13, p. 174] and the Cambridge, England school [8, pp. 793–794] have insisted it should.

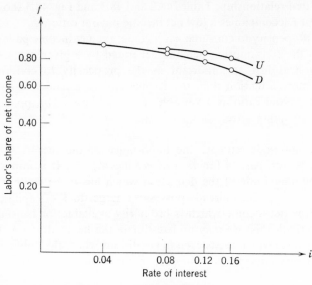

Figure 48.4

Let c_V and c_W be the propensities to consume real interest and real wage income, respectively, and set

$$0 < c_V < 1$$
$$c_W = 1$$

Consumption demand is, then

$$C(t) = c_V \frac{V(t)}{P(t)} + \frac{W(t)}{P(t)}$$

Into this insert (45) and (46):

(51) $$C(t) = \left(c_V Q + a + \frac{1 - e^{-gu}}{g} \right) w \frac{S(t)}{P(t)}$$

Consumption demand as expressed by (51) is in proportion to the ratio between $S(t)$ and $P(t)$; hence it must be growing at the same proportionate rate as does that ratio. To find that rate use (5) and (27) and write

$$\frac{S(t)}{P(t)} = e^{g-\mu} \frac{S(t-1)}{P(t-1)}$$

Thus, like the output of consumers' goods, the demand for them is growing at the proportionate rate per annum $g - \mu$.

48.19 LONG-RUN EQUILIBRIUM IN THE
CONSUMERS' GOODS MARKET

Since the physical output of and the demand for consumers' goods are growing at the same proportionate rate, sustained equality between them is possible. Write such an equality by equating (34) and (51). Multiply by $P(t)$ on both sides, insert (11), (20), and (26), then divide $wS(t)$ away, and solve for the propensity to consume real interest income:

$$(52) \quad c_V = \frac{P(t)C(t) - W(t)}{V(t)} = \frac{e^{-\mu u}\dfrac{1 - e^{-(g-\mu)u}}{g - \mu} - \left(a + \dfrac{1 - e^{-gu}}{g}\right)}{Q}$$

The time coordinate t occurs nowhere in (52); hence the equilibrium propensity to consume real interest income c_V has no time trend in it. But useful life u does occur, and optimum useful life was found to be a function of the rate of interest i (see Table 48.1). When we allow for that relationship, Tables 48.2 and 48.3 and Fig. 48.5 show a low rate of interest accompanies a low propensity to consume real interest income.

But the propensity c_V was a parameter, was it not? And what does it mean to solve for a parameter? We should, of course, have preferred to solve explicitly for the rate of interest i, a variable. However (52) and (19) combined

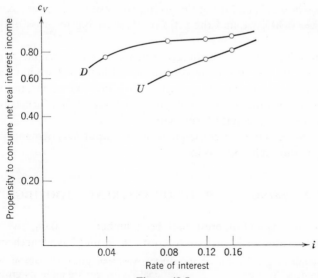

Figure 48.5

do not permit this. Equation (52) does, however, have a significant meaning, and let us now see what that meaning is.

48.20 THE LONG-RUN EQUILIBRIUM RATE OF INTEREST

Equation (52) is the clue to a determination of the long-run equilibrium rate of interest. Consider a case which, as demonstrated in the Appendix, may not be too far removed from that of a highly developed economy: $a = 8$, $c_V = 0.907$, $g = 0.01$, and $\mu = -0.03$.

To keep such an economy in a steady-state full-employment growth equilibrium would, we submit, require an interest rate $i = 0.08$. Let us now show why. According to Table 48.1, such an interest rate would induce firms to adopt a useful life of durable producers' goods $u = 26.4$ years. According to Table 48.2, the output effect of the interest rate $i = 0.08$ is a ratio of gross investment to gross output $h = 0.181$.

Next we study the demand effect. Using (49), (50), and (52), write the ratio of gross saving to gross output as

$$(53) \qquad \frac{Y_{gross}(t) - P(t)C(t)}{Y_{gross}(t)} = 1 - \frac{c_V V(t) + W(t)}{Y_{gross}(t)}$$

$$= 1 - \pi[c_V(1 - f) + f]$$

Now according to Table 48.2 an interest rate $i = 0.08$ would result in a net income payout ratio $\pi = 0.830$ and a labor's share of $f = 0.851$. Inserting these values into (53) and using the given propensity to consume real interest income $c_V = 0.907$, we find the ratio of gross saving to gross output to be 0.181.

Taken in conjunction with the given propensity to consume real interest income, then, the net income payout ratio and labor's share have generated exactly the gross saving needed to finance gross investment. Or, in the jargon[3] of the national income accountants, gross *domestic* capital formation exactly equals gross *national* capital formation.

Let us now examine the consequences for output and demand if the rate of interest is too high and too low.

48.21 LONG-RUN RATE OF INTEREST "TOO HIGH"

Suppose the rate of interest had been higher than 0.08, say $i = 0.16$. According to Table 48.1, such an interest rate would have lengthened useful

---

[3] By a country's gross domestic investment we mean gross investment within that country's borders. By a country's gross national investment we mean its gross domestic investment *plus* capital outflow *minus* capital inflow.

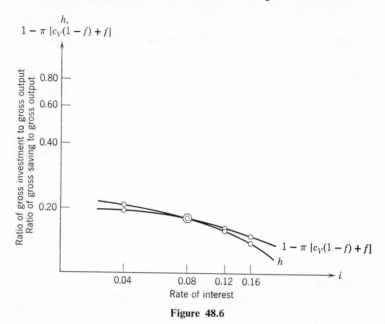

Figure 48.6

life from 26.4 to 33.2 years. According to Table 48.2, the output effect would have been a reduction of the ratio of gross investment to gross output from 0.181 to 0.138.

As for the demand effect, according to Table 48.2 the higher rate of interest $i = 0.16$ would result in a net income payout ratio $\pi = 0.874$ and a labor's share $f = 0.716$. Consequently, at the given propensity to consume real interest income $c_V = 0.907$ the ratio of gross saving to gross output would be

$$(54) \qquad 1 - \pi[c_V(1 - f) + f] = 0.149$$

Hence we have found the demand effect of the higher rate of interest to be weaker than the output effect: The economy is left with an excess of gross national saving over gross domestic investment as illustrated in Fig. 48.6. Indeed, as Table 48.2 shows, for balance at such a high rate of interest the propensity to consume real interest income c_V should have been not 0.907 but higher, that is, 0.950.

In an open economy, balance does not have to be restored for a considerable time. The excess of gross national saving over gross domestic investment can persist when it is manifesting itself in a net capital outflow. However, in the absence of such an outflow the excess supply of money capital would depress the rate of interest.

48.22   LONG-RUN RATE OF INTEREST "TOO LOW"

Suppose the rate of interest had been lower than 0.08, say $i = 0.04$. According to Table 48.1, such an interest rate would have shortened useful life from 26.4 to 23.4. According to Table 48.2, the output effect would have been a boost of the ratio of gross investment to gross output from 0.181 to 0.207.

As regards the demand effect, according to Table 48.2 the lower rate of interest $i = 0.04$ would result in a net income payout ratio $\pi = 0.809$ and a labor's share $f = 0.923$. Consequently, at the given propensity to consume real interest income $c_V = 0.907$ the ratio of gross saving to gross output would be

$$(55) \qquad 1 - \pi[c_V(1 - f) + f] = 0.197$$

Once more, we have found the demand effect to be weaker than the output effect: The economy is now left with an excess of gross domestic investment over gross national saving as illustrated in Fig. 48.6. Indeed, as Table 48.2 shows, for balance at such a low rate of interest the propensity to consume real interest income c_V should have been not 0.907 but considerably lower, that is, 0.762.

Again, in an open economy, balance does not have to be restored for considerable time. The excess of gross domestic investment over gross national saving can persist if equaled by a net foreign capital inflow. However, in the absence of such an inflow the excess demand for money capital would raise the rate of interest. We conclude that our equilibrium is stable.

48.23   GENERALIZATION

Similarly, we could have shown a stable equilibrium rate of interest to exist at $i = 0.12$ in an example which, as demonstrated in the Appendix, may not be too far removed from that of an underdeveloped economy: $a = 4$, $c_V = 0.738$, $g = 0.03$, and $\mu = -0.02$. However, let us generalize even further.

Without considering useful life a variable, let alone a function of the rate of interest, Eisner [5] and Domar [4] found depreciation allowances to exceed replacement requirements in a growing economy with stationary prices. Our model may be thought of as a generalization of their idea of a "depreciation drag." Defining a generalized drag as the excess of gross national saving over gross domestic investment, we have found a zero drag to exist at our equilibrium rate of interest, a positive drag to exist at a rate of interest higher than that, and a negative drag to exist at a rate of interest lower than that.

48.24   THE CONSUMPTION TO NET INCOME RATIO

Although the propensity to consume real interest income c_V and the propensity to consume real wage income $c_W = 1$ were parameters, the consumption to net income ratio c is a variable. Calculate it by dividing (36) by (48):

$$(56) \quad c = \frac{P(t) \displaystyle\int_{t-u}^{t} X(v)\, dv}{Y_{net}(t)} = \frac{e^{-\mu u} \dfrac{1 - e^{-(g-\mu)u}}{g - \mu}}{\dfrac{ie^{-\mu u} + (g - \mu - i)e^{-gu} - (1 + ag)(g - \mu)}{(g - \mu)(i - g)}}$$

The time coordinate t occurs nowhere in (56); hence the ratio of consumption to net income has no time trend in it. Useful life u does occur, and useful life was a function of the rate of interest. Allowing for that relationship, Tables 48.2 and 48.3 and Figure 48.7 nevertheless show no sensitivity of c to i within the range examined. This result may explain something that seemed a paradox to Kuznets.

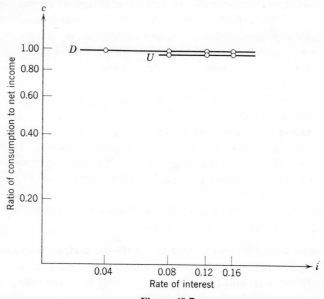

Figure 48.7

48.25 GROSS AND NET SAVING RATIOS UNDER STEADY-STATE GROWTH

At the realistic interest rates $i = 0.08$ in a developed economy and $i = 0.12$ in an underdeveloped economy, the gross and net saving ratios are as follows:

		Developed	Underdeveloped
Gross	$1 - \pi[c_V(1 - f) + f]$	0.181	0.136
Net	$1 - c$	0.013	0.037

Our first conclusion from our vintage model is that in the developed economy net saving is less significant relative to gross saving than in the underdeveloped economy. Let us now apply, somewhat rashly, this conclusion for steady-state equilibrium growth to the rough-and-tumble real world.

48.26 GROSS AND NET SAVING RATIOS UNDER UNSTEADY-STATE GROWTH

We may perhaps think of the economic history of industrialized economies as the slow switching from one steady-state equilibrium to another. Such a switch from a capital-short, high-rate-of-interest, steady-state growth equilibrium to a capital-abundant, low-rate-of-interest, steady-state growth equilibrium was gathering momentum in England 200 years ago, in the United States 150 years ago, somewhat later in Germany, and more recently in Japan and Sweden.

Our numerical solutions have shown that switching from a high to a low rate of interest *within* Table 48.2 or 48.3 does not affect c and hence does not affect the net saving ratio $1 - c$ at all. However, switching from the underdeveloped steady-state Table 48.3 to the developed steady-state Table 48.2 raises c and hence reduces the net saving ratio $1 - c$. In striking contrast, both switches will be accompanied by a marked rise in the gross saving ratio $1 - \pi[c_V(1 - f) + f]$.

Seen in this light, Kuznets' [12, p. 251] findings on the history of the net saving ratio do not surprise us. Kuznets found:

"In the United Kingdom and United States the *net* savings proportion declined significantly; in Norway it showed no definite trend over the period preceding World War II, and there is some question as to the existence of a rising trend in Australia. In the remaining four countries—Italy, Denmark,

Canada, and Japan—the net national savings proportion rose. But it is curious that in Italy before 1900, in Denmark before 1890, in Canada before 1910, and in Japan before 1906, the net national savings proportion was 5 per cent or less (in Canada actually negative in the first period), while per capita real income rose markedly in the preceding decades."

Kuznets pauses to ask:

"Why have the [net savings] ratios declined or failed to rise in some countries, and why were they so low in others—all in periods of rather vigorous growth and marked rise in real income per capita?"

Switching within our Table 48.2 or 48.3 or switching from Table 48.3 to Table 48.2 simulates such behavior superbly.

48.27   THE MONEY GROSS CAPITAL COEFFICIENT

Suppose a Kuznets wanted to measure the money gross capital coefficient in the economy represented by our model. Equation (28) defined physical capital stock at time t. Multiply it by the price of producers' goods $p = aw$ and find its undepreciated value. Divide the undepreciated value by the money value of gross output as expressed by (37) and find the money gross capital coefficient

$$(57) \qquad B = \frac{p \displaystyle\int_{t-u}^{t} S(v)\,dv}{Y_{\text{gross}}(t)} = \frac{a \dfrac{1 - e^{-gu}}{g}}{a + e^{-\mu u}\dfrac{1 - e^{-(g-\mu)u}}{g - \mu}}$$

Now the very essence of automation is the expansion of the output of one man and his machine or, what is the same thing, the reduction of the physical capital coefficient b. Indeed, we have defined technological progress as just that. Yet the time coordinate t occurs nowhere in (57); hence our second conclusion from our vintage model is that the money gross capital coefficient B has no time trend in it: The steady decline in the physical capital coefficient b as defined by (3) is completely hidden. Very realistically, the reason for the hiding lies in the steady rise in the relative price of producers' goods. The ratio between the prices of producers' and consumers' goods is $p/P(t)$. The price p of producers' goods is a parameter, but the price $P(t)$ of consumers' goods is a variable which is falling by $-\mu$ per annum; hence the ratio $p/P(t)$ is rising by $-\mu$ per annum. As demonstrated in the Appendix, a steady rise in the relative price of producers' goods is an established fact.

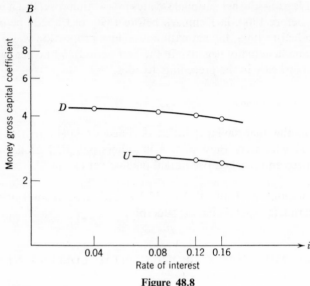

Figure 48.8

Although the time coordinate t occurred nowhere in (57), the useful life u does occur, and optimum useful life was a function of the rate of interest (see Table 48.1). When we allow for that relationship, Tables 48.2 and 48.3 and Fig. 48.8 show a low rate of interest i accompanies a high money gross capital coefficient B.

48.28   BENEFITS OF A LOW RATE OF INTEREST UNDER STEADY-STATE GROWTH

Section 48.9 showed the proportionate rate of growth per annum of physical output of consumers' goods to be $g - \mu$, that is, the sum of the rate of growth of the labor force and the rate of technological progress. No matter how promptly new technology is adopted, then, the physical output of consumers' goods is growing at exactly the same proportionate rate per annum $g - \mu$. To that rate the low rate of interest and the high rate of capital formation contribute nothing. But if this is so, why this race with technology? What is so wonderful about being developed? Does anybody in particular benefit from a low rate of interest inducing firms to adopt short useful lives of durable producers' goods in order to adopt new technology promptly, in order to be right at the fringe of known technology, thus maintaining a high rate of gross capital formation such as we have it in the developed economies?

The first thing to observe is that private firms engaged in such a race are in it because the low interest rate *plus* competition force them to be in it. However, it so happens that labor benefits from the race. To see how, let us use (20) with (11) and (26) inserted into it and write the real wage rate as

$$(58) \qquad \frac{w}{P(t)} = \frac{e^{\mu u}}{b(t)}$$

Equation (58) shows that the real wage rate has a time trend in it. The time coordinate t appears on the right-hand side. According to (4) technological progress reduces the physical capital coefficient $b(t)$ by $-\mu$ per annum; consequently, the real wage rate as expressed by (58) must be rising by $-\mu$ per annum.

But no matter how promptly new technology is adopted, then, the real wage rate is rising at exactly the same proportionate rate per annum $-\mu$. To that proportionate rate the low rate of interest and the high rate of capital formation contribute nothing either. They do, however, contribute to the level the real wage rate will have reached at a given time t. For a given t, (58) becomes higher the lower is useful life u; for as long as $\mu < 0$, $e^{\mu u}$ becomes higher the lower is u. Thus the lower the rate of interest, the higher is the level of the real wage rate.

But if according to (58) the real wage rate becomes the higher the lower the rate of interest, then since employment remains full, the real wage bill also is higher. And since labor's propensity to consume its real wage bill was assumed to be one, labor's consumption is the higher the lower the rate of interest. Our third conclusion from our vintage model is that after all, for labor at least, life in a highly developed economy has its attractions.

48.29 BENEFITS OF A LOW RATE OF INTEREST UNDER UNSTEADY-STATE GROWTH

We thought before of the economic history of industrialized economies as a slow switching from a capital-short, high-rate-of-interest, steady-state growth equilibrium to a capital-abundant low-rate-of-interest, steady-state growth equilibrium. In the process of such switching there will be an additional source of growth permitting the economy to grow for quite some time at a proportionate rate in excess of $g - \mu$. The more abundant capital and the falling rate of interest will reduce optimum useful life and with it the average age of producers' goods. Consequently, the gap between newest practice and average practice will be narrowing. That gap is no doubt wider in Europe than in the United States, as pointed out by the Englishman Maddison [14, p. 93]:

"The U.S. . . . is operating nearer to the fringe of known technology . . . In Europe there is a vast range of the economy working well below known best-practice technology. In some activities like steel making, motor car assembly or aircraft production European technology is nearer American . . . We are not suggesting that the whole U.S. economy is operating at a technical frontier. Even if technical progress dried up altogether, the United States would continue to show productivity gains for a long time as the worst sectors and firms caught up, but in Europe productivity would grow for several decades longer as the best firms would also have a great deal of leeway."

APPENDIX: EMPIRICAL MEASUREMENTS

1. Empirically Plausible Ranges of a, i, g, and μ.

For Tables 48.1, 48.2, and 48.3 we need empirically plausible ranges of a, i, g, and μ.

First, as for minimum building labor, in Chapter 17 Section 12 we found an empirically plausible value for a to be from 8 to 4 in developed and under-developed economies, respectively.

Second, as regards the rate of interest i, both Kuznets [12, p. 421] and Kravis [11, p. 938] have estimated the yield on assets counted at their depreciated value. In that sense, both were applying the same net income concept we defined in our Eq. (41), but in other respects their approaches differed. Kuznets estimated the yield on all income-yielding material assets, including land, outside the equity of individual noncorporate enterprise to be 6.1 and almost 13 per cent, respectively, in the developed and underdeveloped countries. Kravis divided the income of noncorporate enterprise between labor and property income in the same proportion as that prevailing outside the non-corporate enterprise sector, and using depreciation at reproduction cost rather than original cost, estimated the rate of return on reproducible assets alone in the United States:

1900–1909	0.088
1910–1919	0.095
1920–1929	0.087
1930–1939	0.056
1939–1948	0.092
1949–1957	0.089

For the period 1955–1961 Maddison [14, pp. 54–55] added per annum divident yield and capital gain, divided their sum by the rise in a cost of living index, and found real annual return on capital received by equity investors:

United Kingdom   0.121
United States   0.098

When all is said and done, let us adopt as a very rough approximation a rate of interest $i = 0.08$ and 0.12, respectively for developed and under-developed economies.

Finally, as regards the rate of technological progress μ, it follows from (2) and (3) that $1/b(v) = X(v)/L(v)$: The reciprocal of the physical capital coefficient equals average labor productivity in the consumers' goods industry. Ignoring the fact that labor productivity rises faster in the consumers' goods industry than in the producers' goods industry, let us look for labor productivity in the economy as a whole. For twelve developed economies Maddison [14, pp. 36–37], shows the average proportionate rates of growth per annum of total man hours worked and of output per man hour. The rate of growth of man hours worked is our g, that of output per man hour is our $-\mu$:

g	United Kingdom	United States	Average of 12 OECD countries
1870–1913	0.007	0.019	0.008
1913–1950	0.000	0.005	0.002
1950–1960	0.006	0.009	0.007
$-\mu$			
1870–1913	0.015	0.024	0.019
1913–1950	0.017	0.024	0.017
1950–1960	0.020	0.024	0.035

As a rounded-off approximation to the growth pattern of a developed economy in the postwar years let us assume, then: $g = 0.01$ and $\mu = -0.03$.

For the decade 1950–1960 the United Nations [17, p. 37] estimated the proportionate rate of growth of the gross national product of all under-developed countries to be 0.044. For a sample of 31 underdeveloped countries in the period 1957–1962 Chenery and Strout [3, p. 684] found a proportionate rate of growth of 0.046.

Kuznets [12, p. 440] estimated the proportionate rate of growth of population of the underdeveloped countries to be about 0.025. Assuming man hours per capita to have remained unchanged, we find output per man hour to be growing at 0.0205. As a rounded-off approximation to the growth pattern of an underdeveloped economy in the postwar years let us assume, then: $g = 0.03$ and $\mu = -0.02$.

So much for the empirically plausible ranges of a, i, g, and μ. Let us now scan the literature for empirical measurements of the ratios predicted, with or without success, by our vintage model of growth.

2. Gross Saving, Capital Consumption, and Net Saving Ratios

Kuznets [12, pp. 236–239 and 248–250, respectively] estimated the ratio of gross domestic capital formation to gross national product as well as the ratio of capital consumption to gross domestic capital formation. Multiplying these two ratios, we calculate the ratio of capital consumption to gross national product. Moreover, from the same tables, we reproduce Kuznets' ratio of gross national saving to gross national product as well as his ratio of net national saving to net product:

	Gross national saving to gross national product	Capital consumption to gross national product	Net national saving to net national product
United Kingdom			
1860–1879	0.125	0.019	0.109
1880–1899	0.123	0.018	0.110
1900–1914	0.140	0.017	0.132
1921–1929	0.091	0.038	0.058
1950–1958	0.162	0.082	0.087
United States			
1869–1888	0.197	0.081	0.131
1889–1908	0.219	0.101	0.139
1909–1928	0.204	0.108	0.115
1929–1938	0.127	0.110	0.025
1946–1955	0.182	0.115	0.098
1950–1959	0.184	0.094	0.098

The equilibrium ratio of gross national saving to gross national product in our model of a developed economy was

$$1 - \pi[c_V(1 - f) + f] = 0.181$$

This is practically the same as the empirically observed value for postwar United States.

The equilibrium payout ratio in our model of a developed economy was $\pi = 0.830$. Since our model has no government, hence no indirect taxes *less* subsidies in it, this is just another way of saying that our model's ratio of capital consumption to gross output was $1 - \pi = 0.170$. This is certainly not the same as the empirically observed value for postwar United States. The empirical values just reproduced are at most two-thirds of 0.170. An overshooting of at least one-third calls for explanation.

In our model, the price of a new physical unit of producers' goods was p. If set aside, depreciation allowances as defined by Eq. (40) would always maintain the asset in money terms $k(v, v) = p$, [see Eq. (8b)]. They would also maintain the asset in real terms in the sense that once the unit wears out at time $v + u$, the accumulated depreciation allowances would suffice to purchase a new physical unit priced p. However, it is the essence of technological progress that the new physical unit differs mechanically from the one it replaces: It is by definition still operated by one man but it has a lower capital coefficient b or, what is the same thing, a higher capacity. In contrast, due to the steady decline of the price P of its output, the new physical unit has the same net worth as the replaced unit had when new [see (8) and (11)]. In short, in a turbulent world of technological progress, depreciation as defined in our model comes as close as it can to "correct" depreciation maintaining the asset in real terms. Notice that because as determined by (9) the price p is stationary, our model cannot contain any difference between depreciation at original cost and depreciation at replacement cost.

In the real world, however, there can be a very considerable difference. The United States Department of Commerce price deflator for gross fixed capital formation rose more than two and one-half times from 1929 to 1959, yet the Department calculates depreciation at original cost rather than replacement cost, thus understating depreciation, overstating net income, and classifying as net saving what should have been classified as depreciation allowances.

Similarly, our model of an underdeveloped economy predicts the gross national savings ratio well but overshoots on the capital consumption allowances. For 31 underdeveloped countries in 1957–1962 Chenery and Strout [3, p. 684] estimated gross national saving to constitute 0.12 of gross national product. Our model of an underdeveloped economy offered the value 0.136.

3. Labor's Share

Dividing the income of noncorporate enterprise between labor and property income in the same proportion as that prevailing outside the noncorporate enterprise sector, and using depreciation at reproduction cost rather than original cost, Kravis [11, p. 930] estimated labor's share of national income in the United States to have been 0.837 in 1957. Our model of a developed economy offered the value 0.851.

For underdeveloped economies empirical estimates of similar sophistication are not available.

4. Money Gross Capital Coefficient

Two empirical questions arise here. First, is it true that the ratio $p/P(t)$ is rising over time? Gordon [7, p. 937] called attention to "a phenomenon which seems largely to have escaped the attention of all but a few economists. There has apparently been, for half a century or more, a secular tendency in the United States and some other countries for capital-goods prices to rise faster than those of consumers' goods." Gordon [7, p. 939] found capital goods in the United States to be about 50 per cent more expensive in terms of consumers' goods in 1959 than they were in 1929, and about 75 per cent more expensive than in the 1890's. From 1929 to 1959 this amounts to a proportionate increase of 0.013 per annum. This is merely about half the proportionate increase of $p/P(t)$ in our model, which is $-\mu = 0.03$. The reason for this discrepancy is, of course, that our model assumes producers' goods to be made from labor alone, hence not to benefit from technological progress at all. In the real world producers' goods are not made from labor alone, although according to Gordon [7, p. 948], "taken as a whole, the capital goods sector is more labor-intensive than that for consumers goods."

The second empirical question arising in connection with the money gross capital coefficient is whether that coefficient is higher in developed economies than in underdeveloped ones.

The numerator of B as defined by (57) was undepreciated reproducible capital stock. What we want in the denominator is clearly gross output. The best statistical counterpart to B as defined by (57) is the ratio of gross domestic capital formation to incremental gross output, estimated by Kuznets [12, pp. 252–256] or by Maddison [14, p. 77]:

	United Kingdom	United States
1900–1913	6.4	5.2
1913–1950	4.6	5.1
1950–1960	5.9	5.8

Chenery and Strout [3, p. 684] found a gross investment to incremental gross national product ratio of 3.52 for their 31 underdeveloped countries in 1957–1962.

Our model offered the values 4.20 and 2.51 for developed and underdeveloped economies, respectively. Both values undershoot somewhat.

REFERENCES

[1] Bhatt, V. V., "Capital Intensity of Industries, A Comparative Study of Certain Countries," *Bulletin of the Oxford University of Statistics*, **18,** 188 (May 1956).

[2] Brittain, J. A., *Corporate Dividend Policy*, Washington, D. C. 1966.

[3] Chenery, H. B., and A. M. Strout, "Foreign Assistance and Economic Development," *Am. Econ. Rev.*, **56,** 679–733 (September 1966).

[4] Domar, E. D., "Depreciation, Replacement, and Growth," *Econ. Jour.*, **63,** 1–32 (March 1953).

[5] Eisner, R., "Depreciation Allowances, Replacement Requirements, and Growth," *Am. Econ. Rev.*, **42,** 820–831 (December 1952).

[6] Eisner, R., "Technological Change, Obsolescence and Aggregate Demand," *Am. Econ. Rev.*, **46,** 92–105 (March 1956).

[7] Gordon, R. A., "Differential Changes in the Prices of Consumers' and Capital Goods," *Am. Econ. Rev.*, **51,** 937–957 (December 1961).

[8] Hahn, F. H., and R. C. O. Matthews, "The Theory of Economic Growth: A Survey," *Econ. Jour.*, **74,** 779–902 (December 1964).

[9] Johansen, L., "Substitution versus Fixed Production Coefficients in the Theory of Economic Growth: A Synthesis," *Econometrica*, **27,** 157–176 (April 1959).

[10] Keynes, J. M., *The General Theory of Employment, Interest, and Money*, London, 1936, pp. 98, 104.

[11] Kravis, I. B., "Relative Income Shares in Fact and Theory," *Am. Econ. Rev.*, **49,** 917–949 (December 1959).

[12] Kuznets, S., *Modern Economic Growth: Rate, Structure, and Spread*, New Haven and London, 1966.

[13] Lindahl, E., *Studies in the Theory of Money and Capital*, London, 1939, pp. 99–101, 143–146.

[14] Maddison, A., *Economic Growth in the West*, New York, 1964.

[15] Massell, B. F., "Investment, Innovation, and Growth," *Econometrica.* **30,** 239–252 (April 1962).

[16] Solow, R. M., "Investment and Technical Progress," in *Mathematical Models in the Social Sciences*, edited by K. J. Arrow et al., Stanford, 1960.

[17] United Nations, *World Economic Survey 1963*, Part I, New York, 1964.

INDEX